t h eeeeee eeeeee eeeeee eeeeee eeeeee eeeeee eeeeee eeeeee

eeeeee eeeeee t e llllll lllll lllll llllll eeeeeeeeeeeeeeeeeeeeeeeeeeeeeeeeeeeeeeeeeeeee

eeeeeeeeeeeeee p h o

nnnnnnnnnnnnnnnnnnnnnnnnnnnnnnnnnnnnn e b

0 *0*

AVITAL RONELL

THE TELEPHONE BOOK

Technology — Schizophrenia — Electric Speech —

University of Nebraska Press: Lincoln & London

Manufactured in the United States of America. The paper in this book meets the minimum requirements of American National Standard for Information Sciences – Permanence of Paper for Printed Library Materials, ANSI Z39.48-1984. Library of Congress Cataloging-in-Publication Data Ronell, Avital. The telephone book. Bibliography: p. Includes index. 1. Oral communication – Philosophy. 2. Oral communication – Psychological aspects. 3. Technology – Psychological aspects. 4. Telephone. I. Title. P95.R65 1989 191 88-27960 ISBN 0-8032-3876-2 Publication of this book was assisted by a grant from The Andrew W. Mellon Foundation. Second Printing

To my brother, Tom Ronell

Directory Assistance

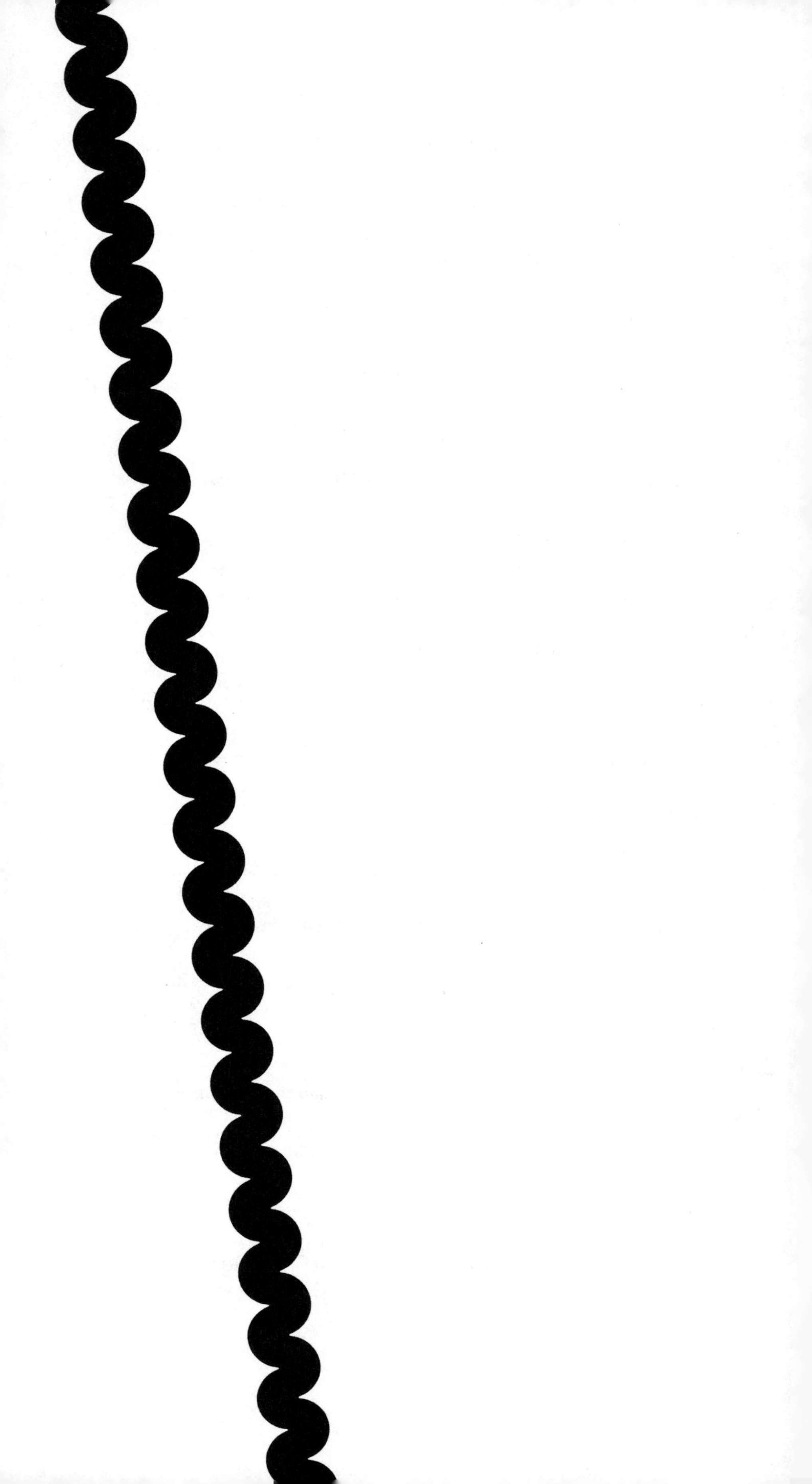

A User's Manual

Warning: *The Telephone Book* is going to resist you. Dealing with a logic and topos of the switchboard, it engages the destabilization of the addressee. Your mission, should you choose to accept it, is to learn how to read with your ears. In addition to listening for the telephone, you are being asked to tune your ears to noise frequencies, to anticoding, to the inflated reserves of random indeterminateness—in a word, you are expected to stay open to the static and interference that will occupy these lines. We have attempted to install a switchboard which, vibrating a continuous current of electricity, also replicates the effects of scrambling. At first you may find the way the book runs to be disturbing, but we have had to break up its logic typographically. Like the electronic impulse, it is flooded with signals. To crack open the closural sovereignty of the Book, we have feigned silence and disconnection, suspending the tranquil cadencing of paragraphs and conventional divisions. At indicated times, schizophrenia lights up, jamming the switchboard, fracturing a latent semantics with multiple calls. You will become sensitive to the switching on and off of interjected voices. Our problem was how to maintain an open switchboard, one that disrupts a normally functioning text equipped with proper shock absorbers. Respond as you would to the telephone, for the call of the telephone is incessant and unremitting. When you hang up, it does not disappear but goes into remission. This constitutes its Dasein. There is no off switch to the technological. **Remember:** When you're on the telephone, there is always an electronic flow, even when that flow is unmarked. *The Telephone Book* releases the effect of an electronic-libidinal flow using typography to mark the initiation of utterances. To the extent that you are always on call, you have already learned to endure interruption and the

click.

Textual operators have been:

Richard Eckersley (Design)

Michael Jensen (Compositor)

Avital Ronell (Switchboard)

abbrev.

A Thomas A. Watson, *Exploring Life: The Autobiography of Thomas A. Watson* (New York: D. Appleton, 1926).

Bell Robert V. Bruce, *Bell, Alexander Graham Bell and the Conquest of Solitude* (New York: Little, Brown, 1973).

BT Martin Heidegger, *Being and Time,* trans. John Macquarrie and Edward Robinson (New York: Harper and Row, 1962); *Sein und Zeit,* 15th ed. (Tübingen: Max Niemeyer, 1979). Page numbers refer to the German edition and are noted along the margins of the English.

CD Sigmund Freud, *Civilization and Its Discontents,* trans. and ed. James Strachey, in *The Standard Edition of the Complete Psychological Works of Sigmund Freud,* vol. 21 (London: Hogarth Press, 1973).

CP Jacques Derrida, *La carte postale* (Paris: Flammarion, 1980). Excerpts from the French are Samuel Weber's and my own. Readers are also referred to Alan Bass's recent translation of *The Post Card* (Chicago: University of Chicago Press, 1987).

DD Samuel Weber, "The Debts of Deconstruction and Other Related Assumptions," in *Taking Chances: Derrida, Psychoanalysis, and Literature,* ed. Joseph H. Smith and William Kerrigan (Baltimore: Johns Hopkins University Press, 1984).

DP C. J. Jung, *The Psychology Dementia Praecox,* trans. R. F. C. Hull, in *The Collected Works of C. J. Jung,* Bollingen Series 20 (Princeton: Princeton University Press, 1974); *Über die Psychologie der Dementia praecox: Ein Versuch* (Halle Verlagsbuchhandlung Carl Marhold, 1907). Page numbers for quotations in German are to the German edition.

DS R. D. Laing, *The Divided Self* (New York: Penguin Books, 1965).

E Mikkel Borch-Jacobsen, "Ecoute," in *Po&sie* 35 (1985): 88–110. Translations from French are my own.

HT A. W. Merrill et al, *Book Two: History and Identification of Old Telephones* (La Crosse, Wisc: R. H. Knappen, 1974).

I Martin Heidegger, "Only a God Can Save Us Now: An Interview with Martin Heidegger," trans. David Schendler, *Graduate Faculty Philosophical Journal* 6, no.1 (Winter 1977): 5–27; "Nur noch ein Gott kann uns retten," *Der Spiegel* (May 31, 1976): 193–219.

M Catherine F. Mackenzie, *Alexander Graham Bell: The Man Who Contracted Space* (Boston: Houghton Mifflin, 1928).

MC Jacques Derrida, "My Chances/*Mes Chances:* A Rendezvous with Some Epicurean Stereophonies," trans. Irene Harvey and Avital Ronell, in *Taking Chances: Derrida, Psychoanalysis, and Literature,* ed. Joseph H. Smith and William Kerrigan (Baltimore: Johns Hopkins University Press, 1984).

MS Alexander Graham Bell, *The Mechanism of Speech* (New York: Funk and Wagnalls, 1916).

P Martin Heidegger, *Poetry, Language, Thought,* trans. Albert Hofstadter (New York: Harper and Row, 1975). "The Origin of the Work of Art" can be found in the original as "Der Ursprung des Kunstwerkes" in *Holzwege* (Frankfurt: Vittorio Klostermann, 1950); "What Are Poets For?" appeared as "Wozu Dichter?" and is also published in the *Holzwege* volume; and "The Thing" was originally printed as "Das Ding" in *Vorträge und Aufsätze* (Pfullingen: Gunther Neske, 1950), and was printed in the *Jahrbuch der Akademie,* vol. 1, *Gestalt und Gedanke,* 1951.

SW Christopher Fynsk, "The Self and Its Witness: On Heidegger's *Being and Time,*" in *Boundary* 2 10, no.3 (Spring 1982). A version of this essay has been reprinted in Fynsk's book, *Heidegger, Thought and Historicity* (Ithaca: Cornell University Press, 1986).

T Martin Heidegger, *What Is Called Thinking?*, trans. J. Glenn Gray and F. Wieck (New York: Harper and Row, 1968); *Was Heißt Denken?* (Tübingen: Max Niemeyer, 1961).

TMP Théodose Achille Louis Du Moncel, *The Telephone, the Microphone, and the Phonograph* (1879; New York: Arno Press, 1974).

W Martin Heidegger, *On the Way to Language,* trans. Peter D. Hertz (New York: Harper and Row, 1971); *Unterwegs zur Sprache* (Pfullingen: Günther Neske, 1959).

1

Delay Call Forwarding . . . .

. . . . And yet, you're saying yes, almost automatically, suddenly, sometimes irreversibly. Your picking it up means the call has come through. It means more: you're its beneficiary, rising to meet its demand, to pay a debt. You don't know who's calling or what you are going to be called upon to do, and still, you are lending your ear, giving something up, receiving an order. It is a question of answerability. Who answers the call of the telephone, the call of duty, and accounts for the taxes it appears to impose?

The project of presenting a telephone book belongs to the anxiety registers of historical recounting. It is essentially a philosophical project, although Heidegger long ago arrested Nietzsche as the last philosopher. Still, to the extent that Nietzsche was said to philosophize with a hammer, we shall take another tool in hand, one that sheds the purity of an identity as tool, however, through its engagement with immateriality and by the uses to which it is put: spiritual, technical, intimate, musical, military, schizonoid, bureaucratic, obscene, political. Of course a hammer also falls under the idea of a political tool, and one can always do more than philosophize with it; one can make it sing or cry; one can invest it with the Heideggerian *cri/écrit,* the *Schreiben/Schrei* of a technical mutation. Ours could be a sort of tool, then, a technical object whose technicity appears to dissolve at the moment of essential connection.

When does the telephone become what it is? It presupposes the existence of another telephone, somewhere, though its atotality as apparatus, its singularity, is what we think of when we say "telephone." To be what it is, it has to be pluralized, multiplied, engaged by another line, high strung and heading for you. But if thinking the telephone, inhabited by new modalities of being-called, is to make genuinely philosophical claims—and this includes the technological, the literary, the psychotheoretical, the antiracist demand—where but in the forgetting of philosophy can these claims be located? Philosophy is never where you expect to find it; we know that Nietzsche found Socrates doing dialectics in some backstreet alley. The topography of thinking shifts like the Californian coast: "et la *philosophie* n'est jamais là où on l'attend," writes Jean-Luc Nancy in *L'oubli de la philosophie.*[1] Either it is not discoverable in the philosopher's book, or it hasn't taken up residence in the ideal, or else it's not living in life, nor even in the concept: always incomplete, always unreachable, forever promising at once its essence and its existence, philosophy identifies itself finally with this promise, which is to say, with its own unreachability. It is no longer a question of a "philosophy of value," but of philosophy itself as value, submitted, as Nancy argues, to the permanent *Verstellung,* or displacement, of value. Philosophy, love of wisdom, asserts a distance between love and wisdom, and in this gap that tenuously joins what it separates, we shall attempt to set up our cables.

Our line on philosophy, always running interference with itself, will be accompanied no doubt by static. The telephone connection houses the improper. Hitting the streets, it welcomes linguistic pollutants and reminds you to ask, "Have I been understood?" Lodged somewhere among politics, poetry, and science, between memory and hallucination, the telephone necessarily touches the state, terrorism, psychoanalysis, language theory, and a number of death-support systems. Its concept has preceded its technical installation. Thus we are inclined to place the telephone not so much at the origin of some reflection but as a response, as that which is answering a call.

Perhaps the first and most arousing subscribers to the call of the telephone were the schizophrenics, who created a rhetoric of bionic assimilation—a mode of perception on the alert, articulating itself through the logic of trans-alive coding. The schizophrenic's stationary mobility, the migratory patterns that stay in place offer one dimension of the telephonic incorporation. The case studies which we consult, including those of the late nineteenth century, show the extent to which the schizo has distributed telephone receivers along her body. The treatment texts faithfully transcribe these articulations without, however, offering any analysis of how the telephone called the schizophrenic home. Nor even a word explaining why the schizo might be attracted to the carceral silence of a telephone booth.

But to understand all this we have had to go the way of language. We have had to ask what "to speak" means. R. D. Laing constructs a theory of schizophrenia based, he claims, on Heidegger's ontology, and more exactly still, on Heidegger's path of speech, where he locates the call of conscience. This consideration has made it so much the more crucial for us to take the time to read what Heidegger has to say about speaking and calling, even if he should have suspended his sentences when it came to taking a call. Where Laing's text ventrilocates Heidegger, he falls into error, placing the schizo utterance on a continent other than that of Heidegger's claims for language. So, in a sense, we never leave Heidegger's side, for this side is multifaceted, deep and troubling. We never leave his side but we split, and our paths part. Anyway, the encounter with Laing has made us cross a channel.

Following the sites of transference and telephonic addiction we have had to immigrate in this work to America, or more correctly, to the discourse inflating an America of the technologically ghostless above. America operates according to the logic of interruption and emergency calling. It is the place from which Alexander Graham Bell tried to honor the contract he had signed with his brother. Whoever departed first was to contact the survivor through a medium demonstrably superior to the more traditional channel of spiritualism. Nietzsche must have sensed this subterranean pact, for in the *Genealogy of Morals* he writes of a telephone to the beyond. Science's debt to devastation is so large that I have wanted to limit its narrative to this story of a personal catastrophe whose principal figures evolved out of a deceased brother. Add to that two pairs of deaf ears: those of Bell's mother and his wife, Mabel Bell.

Maintaining and joining, the telephone line holds together what it separates. It creates a space of asignifying breaks and is tuned by the emergency feminine on the maternal cord reissued. The telephone was borne up by the invaginated structures of a mother's deaf ear. Still, it was an ear that placed calls, and, like the probing sonar in the waters, it has remained open to your signals. The lines to which the insensible ear reconnects us are consternating, broken up, severely cracking the surface of the region we have come to hold as a Book.

Even so, the telephone book boldly answers as the other book of books, a site which registers all the names of history, if only to attend the refusal of the proper name. A partial archivization of the names of the living, the telephone book binds the living and the dead in an unarticulated thematics of destination. Who writes the telephone book, assumes its peculiar idiom or makes its referential assignments? And who would be so foolish as to assert with conviction that its principal concern lies in eliciting the essential disclosure of truth? Indeed, the telephone line forms an elliptical construction that does not close around a place but disperses the book, takes it into the streets, keeping itself radically open to the outside. We shall be tightroping along this line of a speculative telephonics, operating the calls of conscience to which you or I or any partially technologized subject might be asked to respond.

The Telephone Book, should you agree to these terms, opens with the somewhat transcendental predicament of accepting a call. What does it mean to answer the telephone, to make oneself answerable to it in a situation whose gestural syntax already means yes, even if the affirmation should find itself followed by a question mark: Yes?[2] No matter how you cut it, on either side of the line, there is no such thing as a free call. Hence the interrogative inflection of a yes that finds itself accepting charges.

To the extent that you have become what you are, namely, in part, an automatic answering machine, it becomes necessary for questions to be asked on the order of, Who answers the call of the telephone, the call of duty, or accounts for the taxes it appears to impose? Its reception determines its *Geschick,* its destinal arrangement, affirming that a call has taken place. But it is precisely at the moment of connection, prior to any proper signification or articulation of content, that one wonders, Who's there?

Martin Heidegger, whose work can be seen to be organized around the philosophical theme of proximity, answered a telephone call. He gave it no heed, not in the terms he assigned to his elaborations of technology. Nor did he attempt in any way to situate the call within the vast registers of calling that we find in *Being and Time, What Is Called Thinking?,* his essays on Trakl or Hölderlin, his Nietzsche book. Heidegger answered a call but never answered to it. He withdrew his hand from the demand extended by a technologized call without considering whether the Self which answered that day was not occupied by a toxic invasion of the Other, or "where" indeed the call took place. We shall attempt to circumscribe this locality in the pages that follow. Where he put it on eternal hold, Heidegger nonetheless accepted the call. It was a call from the SA Storm Trooper Bureau.

Why did Heidegger, the long-distance thinker par excellence, accept this particular call, or say he did? Why did he turn his thought from its structure or provenance? Averting his gaze, he darkens the face of a felt humanity: "man is that animal that confronts face to face" (*I,* 61). The call that Heidegger did but didn't take is to take its place—herein lies the entire problematic: where is its place, its site and advent? Today, on the return of fascism (we did not say a return *to* fascism), we take the call or rather, we field it, listening in, taking note. Like an aberrant detective agency that maps out empirical and ontological regions of inquiry, we trace its almost imperceptible place of origin. Heidegger, like the telephone, indicates a structure to which he has himself only a disjunctive rapport. That is to say, both the telephone and Martin Heidegger never entirely coincide with what they are made to communicate with; they operate as the synecdoches of what they are. Thus Heidegger engineers the metonymical displacements which permit us to read National Socialism as the supertechnical power whose phantasms of unmediated instantaneity, defacement, and historical erasure invested telephone lines of the state. These lines are never wholly spliced off from the barbed wires circumscribing the space of devastation; calls for execution were made by telephone, leaving behind the immense border disturbances of the oral traces which attempt to account for a history. Hence the trait that continues to flash through every phone call in one form or another, possessing characteristics of that which comes to us with a receipt of acknowledgment or in the hidden agency of repression: the call as decisive, as verdict, the call as death sentence. One need only consult the literatures trying to contain the telephone in order to recognize the persistent trigger of the apocalyptic call. It turns on you: it's the gun pointed at your head.

This presents the dark side of the telephonic structure. Kafka had already figured it in *The Trial, The Castle,* "The Penal Colony," "My Neighbor." The more luminous sides—for there are many—of grace and reprieve, for instance, of magical proximities, require one to turn the pages, or perhaps to await someone else's hand. Take Benjamin's hand, if you will, when he, resounding Bell, names the telephone after an absent brother ("mein Zwillingsbruder"). The telephone of the Berlin childhood performed the rescue missions from a depleted solitude: Den Hoffnungslosen, die diese schlechte Welt verlassen wollte, blinkte er mit dem Licht der letzten Hoffnung. Mit den Verlassenen teilte er ihr Bett. Auch stand er im Begriff, die schrille Stimme, die er aus dem Exil behalten hatte, zu einem warmen Summen abzudämpfen.[3] So even if you didn't catch the foreign drift, and the telephone has no subtitles, you know that the danger zone bears that which saves, das Rettende auch: calling back from exile, suspending solitude, and postponing the suicide mission with the "light of the last hope," the telephone operates both sides of the life-and-death switchboard. For Benjamin, for the convict on death row, for Mvelase in Umtata.[4] Let it be said, in conjunction with Max Brod's speculations, that the telephone is double-breasted, as it were, circumscribing itself differently each time, according to the symbolic localities marked by the good breast or the bad breast, the Kleinian good object or bad object. For the telephone has also flashed a sharp critique at the contact taboos legislated by racism. We shall still need to verify these lines, but let us assume for now that they are in working order and that the angel's rescue is closely tied to the pronouncement of killer sentences.

Just as Heidegger, however, by no means poses as identical to that for which he is made to stand—as subject engaged on the lines of National Socialism—so the telephone, operating as synecdoche for technology, is at once greater and lesser than itself. Technology and National Socialism signed a contract; during the long night of the annihilating call, they even believed in each other. And thus the telephone was pulled into the districts of historical mutation, making epistemological inscriptions of a new order, while installing a scrambling device whose *décryptage* has become our task. Never as such on the side of truth, the telephone became an open accomplice to lies, helping to blur sentences that nonetheless exercised executive power. Don't get me wrong. The asserted side of truth was even more pernicious, sure of its aim and the aims of man. Activated as truth's shredding machine, the telephone, at this moment, became the channeling mechanism for massive disowning. To a large extent, the calls were unsigned.

This work, which was written before the Heidegger affair became an issue of general concern, anticipates some of the urgency with which one tries to grasp the political seduction of a Heidegger. However, where Victor Farías has scrambled connections, largely reducing technology to a mere mention, he sets up a roadblock to *thinking* National Socialism and its others.* To the extent that we continue to be haunted by National Socialism and are threatened by its return from the future, it seems necessary to open the question of

*See in particular the interview with Victor Farías conducted by Crocker Coulsen for *Minerva: Zeitschrift für Notwehr und Philosophie,* no. 9 3/4 (Summer 1988): 25. When asked whether he perceives a link between Heidegger's critique of technology and National Socialism, Farías responds with a series of reckless clichés that serves to close off rather than expand the field of unprobed intensities shared by technology and the terroristic state.

politics beyond a proper name that would displace thinking to a subjective contingency. I am less curious about Mr. Heidegger's fantasy of becoming the Führer's Führer—he momentarily wanted to teach and inflect "destiny"—than compelled to recognize in Heidegger's thinking the ineluctable signaling of democracy's demise. Heidegger failed democracy (the way a teacher fails a class, but also the way one fails a task, an *Aufgabe*) on the grounds of technology. His thinking on the *essence* of technology, for which he claims a different status than technology, forces us to consider how the human subject has been refashioned in the "current talk about human resources, about the supply of patients for a clinic," and body count.* It is Heidegger who poses the greatest challenge to those of us who want to shatter the iron collar of fascism's continued grip on the world. By naming technology the greatest danger that democracy faces, Heidegger, citing Hölderlin, has tried to locate the saving power, too ("das Rettende auch"). Heidegger's crucial questioning concerns the possibility for a free relation to technology. We shall have to backtrack scrupulously in order to discover the unfreedom for which he became a loudspeaker. He was not the only one, nor certainly the crudest of those who were hooked onto a state apparatus of disastrous technological consequences. Heidegger saw the danger, and he called it. And yet, Heidegger experienced the danger too late, which is why we have had to route his thinking on the essence of technology—this has everything to do with death machines—through a delay-call-forwarding system. That is to say, the asserted origin of Heidegger's relation to National Socialism began with the call of technology that has yet to get through to us.

The German telefilm *Heimat* (1987) organizes part of its narrative around the erection of a telephone system. The telephone connects where there has been little or no relation, it globalizes and unifies, suturing a country like a wound. The telephone participates in the myths of organic unity, where one discerns a shelter or defense against castration. A state casts a net of connectedness around itself from which the deadly flower of unity can grow under the sun of constant surveillance. In contrast, we have tried to locate telephones that disconnect, those that teach you to hang up and dial again. Of course the telephone does not "explain" National Socialism or, for that matter, any state in its totality; rather, it offers a certain untried access code to a terrorism that, in the first place, is technologically constellated. It is in any case my only inroad, for I can't get any closer. And yet, in defense of my project, I might say that this length of distance is something which totalitarianism could not ever

**The Question Concerning Technology* (New York: Harper and Row, 1977), 18.

hope to take. When it zeroed in on meaning and confined signification to a tightly throttled regimen, submitting it to the sting of imposed sense, totalitarianism was also making an attempt to crush the real. But existence absolutely resists such an imposition of close range signification. In a genuinely revolutionary text, Jean-Luc Nancy links fascism and Nazism precisely to phantasms of immediacy which are opposed to indefinite mediation. Our telephone junction, at points along its trajectory, tries to dialogue with Nancy's "présence-à-distance," the questions linking freedom to long-distance and other modulations of the call.

These are some of the historical and theoretical premises that have made it seem desirable to dissolve the Book into a point of contact with the Bell system—something that in itself reflects an uncanny history which I felt compelled to trace. Still, with the telephone on the line, one could not simply write a biography as if nothing had come between the *bios* and the graph. One had to invent another form, that of biophony, where the facts of life fall into a twilight zone between knowing and not knowing, between the rather crude ground of empiricity and the more diaphanous heights of speculation. If anything, we have invited Bell and his assistant Watson to speak in order to put a stop sign before technological machismo, and to ask one to listen again to the eerie and altogether hair-raising beginnings forming the implacable fact of the telephone. As proof of the good faith that has guided this procedure, I offer a portion of our biophony, prior to the Survival Guide, appended as a story without specularity and one in fact that, like the telephone, is pregnant with this other. It was a path cut between orality and writing on the edge of a dispersion where absence and exile became the rule.

Why the telephone? In some ways it was the cleanest way to reach the regime of any number of metaphysical certitudes. It destabilizes the identity of self and other, subject and thing, it abolishes the originariness of site; it undermines the authority of the Book and constantly menaces the existence of literature. It is itself unsure of its identity as object, thing, piece of equipment, perlocutionary intensity or artwork (the beginnings of telephony argue for its place as artwork); it offers itself as instrument of the destinal alarm, and the disconnecting force of the telephone enables us to establish something like the maternal superego. Of course Derrida and others cleared the way. They built the switch. For Freud, the telephone, while exemplifying unconscious transmissions, set off the drama of an unprecedented long distance. There is always a child left behind, or the face of a distant friend translated sonically into a call. And there was always a Heidegger pulled into fascism by the strangulating umbilicus of a telephone cord whose radius he failed to measure. There were

other orders of strangulations for which the telephone was made to feel responsible, and these, too, shall fall under our gaze. To trace these calls, the conditions of a long distance that speaks, and the many toxic invasions waged by telephone, it seemed necessary to start with the absolute priority of the Other to the self, and to acknowledge the constitutive impurity that obliges a self to respond to its calling .. ..
....
.. .. **AR**.. .... **AREA CODE 415**

The scopic field narrows, music accompanie

ome of these figurations.   Lights dimming.   Another foreign tongue.

LA VOIX HUMAINE

—Si, mais très loin . . .

—Toi, tu m'entends?

—Ce fil, c'est le dernier qui me
rattache encore à nous.

—Je m'étais couchée
avec le téléphone—

—Si tu ne m'aimais pas et si
tu étais adroit, le téléphone
deviendrait une arme effrayante.
Une arme qui ne laisse
pas de traces, pas de bruit.

A terrifying weapon leaving no traces. Her fear of being cut off from him intensifies. She wraps the cord around her neck.

—J'ai ta voix autour de mon cou.

Is she hanging or strangling herself? You can't decide, you can't cut it.
The receiver falls to the ground.

. . . .

"It's for You"

A structure that is not equivalent to its technical history, the telephone, at this stage of preliminary inquiry, indicates more than a mere technological object. In our first listening, under the pressure of "accepting a call," the telephone in fact will emerge as a synecdoche of technology. As provisional object—for we have yet to define it in its finitude—the telephone is at once lesser and greater than itself. Perhaps because the telephone belongs as such to no recognizable topos or lends itself to an *athetic* response, picking it up, especially in Heidegger and in World War II, can by no means produce a reading without static on the line. We shall constantly be interrupted by the static of internal explosions and syncopation—the historical beep tones disruptively crackling on a line of thought. To sustain our reading against the crush of repressive agencies, busy signals, and missed connections, something like the "rights of nerves" will be newly mobilized.[5] Suppose we begin by citing Heidegger in a decidedly aphilosophical mood when, in angry reaction to a reporter's persistent claims, he responds to a certain genre of transmission problems:

HEIDEGGER:
Das ist eine Verleumdung.
That's a slander.

SPIEGEL:
Und es gibt auch keinen Brief, in der dieses Verbot gegen Husserl ausgesprochen wird? Wie wohl ist dieses Gerücht wohl aufgekommen?
And there is no letter in which such a prohibition is recorded? How did the rumor come about?

HEIDEGGER:
Weiss ich auch nicht, ich finde dafür keine Erklärung. Die Unmöglichkeit dieser ganzen Sache kann ich Ihnen dadurch demonstrieren, was auch nicht bekannt ist. (*I*, 9)
It's beyond me. I've no explanation for it. I can show you the unlikelihood of the accusation.[6]

To be sure, Husserl's name is doubly cut off when it finds itself missing in the translation. And perhaps because Heidegger is about to "demonstrate," his mood is not so aphilosophical after all. Heidegger poses himself as a kind of unscrambling device for a massively entangled historical narrative whose other end somehow involves a telephone call. In the passage cited the call is being set up; Heidegger has not yet made the connection, technologically fitted, to the hollow of the state. What does it mean to begin a telephone call by quoting the rumor? Or rather, by having Heidegger quoted? Not just Heidegger whose proper name resonates with imperial dignity but the Heidegger cited above (the interview appeared when Heidegger was no longer here)—to borrow a subtitling phrase from Nietzsche, the Heidegger "for everyone and no one," the philosopher who put himself into circulation after his death. Part of his destinal mark was to have been made in a newspaper article, the space of *Gerede*'s loudspeaker, which, roughly speaking, refers us to the lower agencies of language transaction. It is beyond Heidegger, the speaker is quoted as saying. We all know what "the rumor" concerns. More or less. In any event, its epistemological authority is such that no further naming seems necessary in order to establish a ground of sound referential effects. In a gesture that rumorological paranoia exacts, the subject will want to settle his debt with rumorous transmissions in a structure of "after-my-death," in the very fragile place where rumor encounters itself, the supplementary issue, in this case, the *Spiegel*. To quell "the rumor" in a weekly journal, Heidegger turns it over to a telephone system for declassification. This is the line that will engage us here. Throughout the ensuing conversations we shall wonder whether there is not something perturbing about the philosopher's explication with a forum of public opinion which splices answerability into the technological instances that Heidegger himself regarded with suspicion. Has Heidegger wanted to bequeath his most urgently authenticated confession to a discourse of *Gerede*? In other words, is Heidegger's last word, made to be articulated after his death, a stroke against his philosophy, a woundingly ironic utterance made against the grain of his thinking (what does it mean for a Heidegger to intend to tell the truth in a newspaper?), or will his afterworldly in-the-world discourse force a rethinking of language's housing projects? It is not that we are listening for a prior continuity which telephone wires would cable into the language of Heidegger, his War Words or *Spiegel* reflections. In some respects, Heidegger's work, including his final interview, hooks up the telephone as if to simulate answerability where it in fact creates a scrambling device whose decoding strands it nonetheless enjoins us to follow. It is Heidegger himself who poses the telephone. He poses it at this junction, almost as if he wished to supply the want of an ethics. It has been said that Heidegger has no Ethics. This brings us to the problem to be raised by the Central Exchange of our system, where empirical guilt and the Heideggerian theory of guilt seem to share the same operator. This is a serious problem promoted by an oeuvre that provides itself with a manual, a directory assistance that makes such connections inevitable, at once calling them forth and wanting to annul them. Yet, if the interview containing the telephone call is a ruse or a scrambling device intentionally installed by the philosopher, then he still isn't given over to laughter. Whether this is because Heidegger would never strike such a pose of subjective mastery—perhaps he would not wish to assert, in the sense of Baudelaire, the idea of a superior bearing—or whether nonlaughter marks a more sinister conviction will have to remain open to an answer temporarily out of service. While it is necessary to elude the confusion of situating a purely empirical/anthropological reading of guilt within a theoretically grounded one, it must be recognized that for Heidegger the relations between anthropology and ontology are not simply external ones. Indeed, Philippe Lacoue-Labarthe has shown the thematization in Heidegger of the empirical and historical figure cut by the philosopher.[7]

The time has come to record the message, to listen in a gathering way to what has been said within the interstices of two beep tones.

Let us wind up this recording around the major points it appears to have urged. Heidegger accepted a call. In Lacan's sense we call this predicament the transfer of power from the subject to the Other.[8] In this case, the other happens to be the top command of the Storm Trooper University Bureau. Heidegger traces his relationship to National Socialism to this call, asserting thereby the placeless place where the other invaded him, the nondiscoverable place or moment when the connection was to have taken place. He does not report a face-to-face meeting, but we shall arrange this momentarily.

The scene can be teletyped for review according to two preliminary aspects. First, Heidegger's compromise with National Socialism marks an arrangement with a supertechnical power. Second, Heidegger in fact elaborates an idea of *techné* that largely stands under the shadow of the negative. It has a contract out on Being, tightening its corruption, its veiling and forgetting. The coherency of these two aspects will lead us to examine whether it is not precisely owing to his theory of technology (*Technik*) that Heidegger was engaged on the Nazi Party line. Later, Heidegger would locate himself at a remove from National Socialism by linking the movement to technology. But if Heidegger can be embarked in the adventure of National Socialism in the first place, this occurs to the extent that there is something which he resists in technology, hoping it can be surmounted like the grief or pain one feels in the human realm over a loss. We shall have to put a search on this unmarked grief through which Heidegger mourns the figure of technology. Or even more to the point, Heidegger *wants* to mourn technology, but it proves to be unmournable as yet, that is, undead and very possibly encrypted. In large, constative terms, we shall have to concern ourselves here with the contours of another, somewhat displaced horizon through which it may be claimed that no fundamental distance establishes itself between the technical, natural, human, or existential worlds, no purity or absolute exteriority of one of these to the other. But Heidegger has produced, let us say quickly, a naive reading of technology whose philosophically inflected and historical effects require rigorous examination. It is as if he thought there were something beyond the radical rupture in Being which technology involves—another relation to Being, more original than that supplied by a technological emplacing; and this possibility he identifies at one point with the Nazis. Still, what is nazism if not also the worst moment in the history of technology?[9] "Worst" can serve as a rhetorical qualification of "moment," which may not be restricted or an indication of closure. The worst moment in the history of technology may not have an off switch, but only a modality of being on. Let me formulate this pointedly so that the telephone can begin its job of condensing and displacing questions of desire and extermination, war machines and simulators, within the apparatus of a peace time: before the time of *Gelassenheit*, when Heidegger fails to consider that technology cannot be surmounted, surpassed, or even perhaps sublated, he walks into a trap. I want to trace this trap to one day, one event. I am going to take the same call several times, and then try to move beyond it.

Rector's Office

Rector's Office

Husserl, whose name suffered erasure by Heidegger under the same regime—Heidegger had deleted the dedication to *Sein und Zeit*—was removed from the offices which Heidegger now occupies. Husserl was not there to answer; he would not even answer to his name. The mentor had had his telephone removed. During Heidegger's tenure a telephone was reinstalled.[10] These gestures are connected to the paternal belly of the state by the umbilical of the telephone. The scene was technologically set for Heidegger to take the call. Preliminarily we shall argue that what came through on that day was a certain type of call of conscience. Why did he answer precisely this call? Or say he did? Is he not trying to give it the same existential legitimacy, trying to make it the same type of call that *Sein und Zeit* describes? Simply asked, what is the status of a philosophy, or rather a *thinking*, that doesn't permit one to distinguish with surety between the call of conscience and the call of the Storm Trooper? This raises a first point.   The other point is organized around Heidegger's technological blind spot as concerns the telephone, which can be grasped as a way to measure his commitment ontologically to divest technology. Accepting the call by missing the point—that is to say, missing the appointment of the call, its "significance"—Heidegger thus demonstrates the force by which to gauge his attempt to secondarize, ontologically speaking, technology. To the degree that his concept of technology is blind or lacking, it is guilty of his alliance of power with nazism. Of course, to the extent that he underreads technology, Heidegger cannot be identified, purely and simply, with the self-constitution of National Socialism. He himself says that he was accused by the party for his "private National Socialism." But the status of what he says is shaky, particularly since it has run on rumorological grounds, a history of dissimulation and silence. On his own subject, on the subject of the Third Reich, Heidegger never stopped playing telephone. The mark to be made here, the incision, indicates the surface of a weakly held limit between technology and Being. Technology, while by no means neutral, but a field of fascination, is viewed as potentially covering an authentic relation to Being. It is from this point onward that claims are made for a relation to Being more original than the technically assumed one.[11]   To be sure, the notation of a Being that would enfold technology only by hesitant parasitical inclusion, has received expression from the "other" side of the line. In a recently disclosed letter to Heinrich Vangleer, Einstein wrote from Berlin in 1917: "All our lauded technological progress—our very civilization—is like the axe in the hand of the pathological criminal."[12] The aberrant course traced by technopathology engages a risk of blindness as if the axe could be surrendered and the criminal appeased, as if, indeed, there were a truer law of Being into which technology were cutting a pathology. However, Einstein was not instituting an ontology—a discourse on Being which presupposes the responsibility of the "yes," as Derrida writes: "Yes, what is said is said, I respond or 'it' responds to the call of Being."[13] Einstein, then, was not taking on an ontology or saying yes to a call, he was definitively disconnected from the supertechnical powers which drew the open ear of Heidegger. In addition, he only took a call from Princeton. . . . .

. . . . .The Maternalizing Call

As we heard ourselves say, the telephone is a synecdoche for technology. It is lesser than itself but also the greater, as in the maternalizing call of *What Is Called Thinking?* A number of things might be put on this account. Lecture 5 of this text opens the telephone book. It is mysterious and compelling. It wants to teach teaching. The mother calls her boy home, opening his ears but also teaching him a lesson. She appears, if only sonically, at a long distance. A certain oedipedagogy is taking shape here—the restoration of contact is in the making, initiated by a mother whose navel, in Joycean terms, would emit signals. The navel is the third eye, closed, knotted, the eye of blindness. Whatever the lesson of the mother, which turns into a desemanticized Nietzschean scream, telephonic logic means here, as everywhere, that contact with the Other has been disrupted; but it also means that the break is never absolute. Being on the telephone will come to mean, therefore, that contact is never constant nor is the break clean.   Such a logic finds its way through much of the obliterature that handles these calls. Heidegger's *What Is Called Thinking?* names Nietzsche in the passage to the ear canal. In a way that comes through clearly, this call has been transferred from Nietzsche before it is returned to him. One should think of Nietzsche on the mother tongue.[14] Deformed by the educational system whose condition she remains, she makes you become a high-fidelity receiver on a telephonic line rerouted by interceptors to the state. This is the telelogic of the Nietzschean critique whose access code runs through "On Redemption." The bildopedic culture has produced itself out of a combinatory of lack ("for there are human beings who lack everything") and excess ("one thing of which they have too much"); it constellates the human subject telephonically.[15] Figuring the human thus first undermines visual security: "for the first time I did not trust my eyes and looked and looked again, and said at last, 'An ear! The tremendous ear was attached to a small, thin stalk—but this stalk was a human being! If one used a magnifying glass one could even recognize a tiny envious face; also that a bloated little soul was dangling from the stalk.'"[16] That Nietzsche's texts are telephonically charged is clarified in *Genealogy of Morals,* where he writes of a "telephone to the beyond," which arguably is the case with every connection arranged by such a switchboard.[17] It is Joyce who excites the hope that an explicit link might be forged between the call to the beyond and a maternal connection which we hear enunciated in Heidegger's exposition:

Boys, do it now. God's time is 12.25 [twenty-five minutes past the Nietzschean mid-day, therefore]. *Tell Mother you'll be there. Rush your order and you play a slick ace. Join on right here! Book through eternity junction, the nonstop run.*[18]

The little boys tell mother they'll be there. While here, which is never "here," they are booking it through eternity junction, cathecting onto the gamble of the book. All the while mother is on the line. What links this act to the calling apparatus of state? Don't forget, though: we are not reading an indifferently occupied state but one which destined itself to the ear, in terms achieved by Hélène Cixous, to the jouissance of the ear.[19] The ear has been addicted, fascinated. And just as Hamlet's father, head of state, overdosed on the oto-injection ("in the blossoms of my sin"), the ghostly *Spiegel*-interlocutor, speaking from the beyond, utters the news of technology's infectious spread, beginning with a phone call. Again, and forever, why did Heidegger accept this particular call? Through which orifice did nazism pass in Heidegger? He has already told us. In terms of an entirely different intensity (but is it so different?), in "The Madonna's Conception through the Ear" Ernest Jones convincingly shows the ear to cover for the displaced anus.[20] This demonstration has received security clearance from subsequent psychoanalytic claims on the matter. Yet, we are not addressing a multiplicity of ears but one ear, technologically unified against the threat of a narcissistic blowout. The jouissance of the ear was felt by a whole nation, whether it was listening to Wagner or to the constant blare of the radio, which is said to have hypnotized a whole people, a tremendous national ear.[21] Heidegger's ear was trained on the telephone. It was what Maurice Blanchot calls "fascinated." He answered the call. The blindness associated with any call assumes proportions that are difficult to name but which nonetheless can be circumscribed. A problematics of image-obliteration engages the telephone, and even the rhetoric surrounding it. The telephone sinks away as a sensory object, much as the mother's figure disappears. When Heidegger mentions being-on-the-telephone, it is not meant to coagulate into an image. The call was fleetingly arranged, like a sonic intrusion. The Nazis were not in sight, they were the hidden and private eyes to whom Heidegger spoke. Visual apprehension on the retreat, supplanted by the dead gaze: these constitute elements brought together in "The Essential Solitude" of Blanchot. A dead gaze, "a gaze become the ghost of eternal vision," stares fixedly from his text, which listens to the Heidegger text which it quietly repeats.[22] In a way, the call of *What Is Called Thinking?* is taken up, transferred or translated to "the force of the maternal figure," which itself gradually dissolves into the indeterminate They (33). Following the telepath of Heidegger, Blanchot induces a stage of telephonics in which he regards the vanishing image. The mark of a maternalized hearing which blinds all imaging, he calls this "fascination." Why fascination? Seeing, which presupposes distance, a decisiveness which separates, fosters a power to stay out of contact and in contact, to avoid confusion. But he writes of a manner of seeing which amounts to "a kind of touch, when seeing is *contact* at a distance" (32). His focus, if that is the proper way of putting it, fixes fascination—something allows sight to be blinded into a neutral, directionless gleam which will not go out, yet does not clarify. "In it blindness is vision still" (32). This vision has been perturbed; it is a "vision which is no longer the possibility of seeing" (32). Fascinated into the dead gaze, one retreats from the sensory and sense: "What fascinates us robs us of our power to give sense. It abandons its 'sensory' nature, abandons the world, draws back from the world, and draws us along" (32). Now the transfer or transit is made to the other woman, the one about to speak to us, teachingly, in Heidegger. The habit-forming mother freezes the image into the blinding absence which we have come to call the telephone. Alongside Heidegger's little boy, we encounter the child of Blanchot, transfixing and fascinated, unseeingly drawn by the enchantment of the mother. Blanchot takes a step in the direction of Heidegger by fading a mother into the They, the neutral, impersonal "indeterminate milieu of fascination" (32). As if responding to a query coming from elsewhere, he offers: "Perhaps the force of the maternal figure receives its intensity from the very force of fascination, and one might say then, that if the mother exerts this fascinating attraction it is because, appearing when the child lives altogether in fascination's gaze, she concentrates in herself all the powers of enchantment. It is because the child is fascinated that the mother is fascinating, and that is why all the impressions of early childhood have a kind of fixity which comes from fascination" (33). Blanchot's evocation continues to withdraw itself from sight, effecting a sense of immediacy complicit with absolute distance. The sequence releases the mother, letting her drop out of sight while the subject appears to have achieved cecity: "Whoever is fascinated doesn't see, properly speaking, what he sees. Rather, it touches him in an immediate proximity; it seizes and ceaselessly draws him close, even though it leaves him absolutely at a distance. Fascination is fundamentally linked to neutral, impersonal presence, to the indeterminate They, the immense, faceless Someone. Fascination is the relation the gaze entertains—a relation which is itself neutral and impersonal—with sightless, shapeless depth the absence one sees because it is blinding" (33). We should like to retain the neutral gleam, the sightless depth that sees—a tele-vision without image, not very distant from the annihilating gaze of Lacan, though perhaps less in arms. The texts of Heidegger and Blanchot are not merely practicing the oedipal blindness with which the maternally contacting child is menaced—even if, indeed, it is the mother who calls first. With the possible exception of Cixous's words, little has been said about Jocasta's call, the way she secretly calls the shots and her responsibility. If these texts were repeating the gesture according to which the oedipal gaze is averted, then we should remember that every repetition, to be what it is, brings something new with it. The child has disappeared in the mother. This disappearance or traversal also devours the mother—each the absolute hostage of the Other, caught in a structure that inhibits the desire to cancel a call. Once made, the call indicates the mother as *aufgehoben,* picked up, preserved, and canned. "L'Imprésentable" is the name Philippe Lacoue-Labarthe gives to the essay which shows how the female figure has always been one that Western thought has attempted to "overcome" or wind down (*überwinden*) in its philosophical, aesthetical, and physical dimensions.[23] The child, like philosophy, gains on the mother. The child, as we said, has disappeared in the mother. He is, in Blanchot, there and not there. He has arrived, if sightlessly averting his gaze henceforth, to face the immense, faceless Someone. In Heidegger, though Blanchot does not simply contradict him in this, the child maintains a long distance. Even though it was a local call. The remoteness of the child to the place from which the call was issued is never collapsed into the "immediate proximity" felt, if evanescently, by the Blanchot text. The invading Other doesn't arrive at touching, contaminating the one that is called or in the ontic enclosure that separates the caller from the called; the one is never held hostage by the Other, fascinated or derailed. The Heideggerian remoteness from the call's source guarantees that it will avoid being danger zoned, for it masquerades as the purity of a long-distance call. This detoxified scene of calling is what, in Heidegger, we call into question. In this light, one of the things that we shall need to ponder concerns a tranquil assertion such as one finds in *Being and Time:* "Being towards Others is ontologically different from Being towards Things which are present-at-hand" (*BT,* 124). While this articulation involves a complex series of designations whose elaborations would require a patient tapping of each term ("Being towards. . . ," "present-at-hand"), it can nonetheless be seen to assume a clean ontological separation of Others and Things wherein the Other, as Heidegger states in the same passage, would be a duplicate (*Dublette*) of the Self. The question that we raise before any approach can be made toward this passage or the locality of Other suggests a disposition other than the one disclosed in Heidegger's assertion. The mood we wish to establish is not one of reactivity but of genuine wonder and bewilderment before the statement. At first sight the statement asserts itself as constatively unproblematic: Being towards Others is ontologically different from Being towards Things which are present-at-hand. What is supposed, however, regards not only the difference between modes of "Being towards" but the aim or destination which would know the gap separating Others from Things. Now, what if Others were encapsulated in Things, in a way that Being towards Things were not ontologically severable, in Heidegger's terms, from Being towards Others? What if the mode of Dasein of Others were to dwell in Things, and so forth? In the same light, then, what if the Thing were a *Dublette* of the Self, and not what is called Other? Or more radically still, what if the Self were in some fundamental way becoming a Xerox copy, a duplicate, of the Thing in its assumed essence? This perspective may duplicate a movement in Freud's reading of the uncanny, and the confusion whirling about Olympia as regards her Thingness. Perhaps this might be borne in mind, as both Freud and Heidegger situate arguments on the Other's thingification within a notion of *Unheimlichkeit,* the primordial being not-at-home, and of doublings. The second type of question, which nags critical integrity, having received only an implicit formulation, concerns the history of, let us say provisionally, a subject of the private sector who normally would be granted diplomatic immunity, sheltered as he is by the structures regulating philosophical politesse. A transgression, authorized by Nietzsche, has permitted us to view the life of a philosopher not as so many empirical accidents external to the corpus of his works. But where Nietzsche constantly affirms the value of dissimulation, including self-dissimulation, Heidegger does not.[24] Thus it is not clear that we already know what, in this instance, involves self-presentation and a statement of identity. In Nietzsche's heterobiography, *Ecce Homo,* we know that the self will fail to reappropriate itself; in Heidegger's journalistic disclosures we know no such thing. At any

event, the referential pathos of his explication leaves room for serious refutation. This order of bewilderment, granted a Nietzschean pass, has permitted us to open the case on two infinitely non-reciprocal texts, linking *Sein und Zeit* (henceforth *SuZ*) and the *Spiegel* interview. Is the call of conscience readable in terms of a telephone call? We suggest this to be the case. More precisely, perhaps, can one rigorously speaking utter Dasein's anonymous calling in the same breath with the call taken by a historical subject whose identity papers, civil status, and telephone personality name a "Martin Heidegger"? A receptionist must know how connections are tolerably made, determining which opening will establish communication between two parties or two things—in brief, she must understand how to manipulate the switchboard or she would lose her post ....
....
.. ..
....
.. ..
....
....
....
....
....
....
....
....
....
....
.. ..
....
....
....
.. ..
....
....
....
....
....

The Local Call

Storm Trooper to Heidegger

In *What Is Called Thinking?* a call is put through according to what might be considered the law of telephonics. "What is called thinking?" chapter 5 begins, repeating on automatic dial the title of the book. The automatic, however, is precisely what must be guarded against, something which Heidegger names in terms of a certain image-interdiction: "We must guard against the blind urge," continues the second sentence; in other words, the question of what is called thinking or of what does call for thinking must renounce access to an urge, an urge for blindness. This form of blindness would permit us to "snatch at a quick answer in the form of a formula"—a quick answer that would be graspable by the right kind of dialing system (*T*, 48). All of this must be given up if we are to stay with the question that asks, "Was heißt Denken?"[25] But in order to stay with this question, Heidegger introduces a seemingly odd example, one which in the first place demonstrates how to put a subject on hold. And the force that puts the other on hold is "die Mutter," instituting a maternalizing call, the beginning of all heeding that we shall later come to identify with Ma Bell: "'You just wait! [*Warte*]—I'll teach you what we call obedience [*gehorchen*],' a mother might say [*ruft*] to her boy who won't come home" (*T*, 48). While the will to obedience and listening are intimately related, like the mother and son stretched apart from one another, and the boy is shown here to aberrate from both modalities of responding, it is not made clear actually how the mother's call is at all connected with the boy who won't come home. By what umbilical of calling will she have reached her son?

This Heideggerian circuit is loaded, for any reader of Heidegger will recognize the strangeness of this maternal eruption, the kind of invisible line to thinking that the mother wires. The mother will of course fade on the line, put on eternal hold, to be replaced in the same paragraph by Nietzsche: "Even so, a man who teaches must at times grow noisy. In fact, he may have to scream and scream" (*T*, 48). But before Nietzsche gets on the line, the mother will have prepared the son fully to exfoliate his invaginated ear, the most open of his organs, whose openness, however, would not appear to be primordial but a labyrinthine drawing out and a deepening effected by the mother whose boy will not come home. The mother speaks to open the ears of the boy who won't come home; he might be Hyperion, Odysseus, K. of *The Castle*, you or me (for it may be that every phone call taken partakes of this calling structure). The mother begins the call, the opening, by teaching to hold: "Warte." In other words, though Heidegger does not indicate this, she teaches, before being cut off, the essence of man. Elsewhere Heidegger has shown the essence of man to reside in waiting: "You just wait," calls the mother on infinite long distance. He will wait for a message, a revealing, but not a lecture. "Does she promise him a definition of obedience? No. Or is she going to give him a lecture? No again, if she is a proper mother. Rather, she will convey to him what obedience is. Or better, the other way around: she will bring him to obey. Her success will be more lasting the less she scolds him; it will be easier, the more directly she can get him to listen, [*je unmittelbarer die Mutter den Sohn ins Hören bringt*]—not just condescend to listen, but listen in such a way that he can no longer stop wanting to do it. And why? Because his ears have been opened and he can now hear what is in accord with his nature. Learning, then, cannot be brought about by scolding. Even so, a man who teaches must at times grow noisy" (*T,* 48). Click.

The German says that the boy will not learn merely to accomodate himself to listening, but that the mother will have arranged for the son never to let up on his desire to hear: "sondern so, daß er vom Hörenwollen nicht mehr lassen kann" (*T,* 48). She will have made him into an addict of taking calls, he will no longer be able to abstain from wanting to hear, "he can no longer stop wanting to do it." So before putting herself on hold, driving the umbilical tap back into her son—"a mother calls to a boy who won't come home"—before receding like the feminine voice of an operator when a connection has been made, she will have transformed her boy into an automatic listening device. His ear cannot let go; no desire of whatever modality can henceforth ever suspend this connection, "so, daß er vom Hörenwollen nicht mehr lassen kann." The mother opens these telephone lines softly, she is not the teaching man who must at times grow noisy ("Nietzsche, most quiet and shiest of men, knew of this necessity" [*T,* 48]). She teaches heeding to a son who has strayed. The son will be able to hear, he will even be able to hear the inaudible translation of the mother into screaming man. The screaming man attached to the vocal cords of the mother is what she has opened his ears to. The straying son is linked by invisible connections to the future of his mother's teachings. Like the heroin of hearing with which she infuses him, she will have made him unable to say no to the call, he must take the call and accept the hearing (*hören*) assignment on which she will have hooked him, "in such a way that he can no longer stop wanting to do it."

Have we understood? Why would there be an underground telephonics in Heidegger's thinking on Nietzsche? Who is this mother who haunts the ear that will never again close, ringing a more primordial teaching of obedience? The telephonic apparatus that the mother hooks up gives a yet inaudible command, opening the ear of a son who has strayed from home. Would these lines cable a kind of crosstalking with Heidegger's War Words on Nietzsche, the prior call to thinking? Heidegger evokes the call that he took around that time, an engulfing call that, one suspected, had intoxicated him, deranged his spirits, throwing him into a predicament of horing/hearing briefly set out in the *Spiegel* interview made public after his death. In a sense, Heidegger's historical embarrassment belongs to a rhetorical mutation that consists in taking a call. The call is technologized, but we must resist the blind urge to accelerate the argument. What is one taking when one takes a call? What is one giving when one returns the call, that is to say, answers it? This already announces the question concerning technology whose brakes we are pressing—a necessary application if we are at all to read the predicament of "accepting a call":

SPIEGEL:
So you finally accepted.
How did you then relate
to the Nazis?

HEIDEGGER:
. . . someone from the top
command of the Storm
Trooper University Bureau,
SA section leader Baumann
called me up. He
demanded . . . (*I*, 6)

The German is bureaucratic: "Nach einigen Tagen kam ein fernmündlicher Anruf" (*I*, 196). Heidegger took a call that functioned like the storm trooping for which the caller was commanding. This takes place within a context of a prior call accepted by Heidegger, though not in terms of a subject's desire but in those of an inescapable calling or vocation. If Heidegger was there to receive the SA call, it is because he first had to accept the *Be-ruf*, or position, from which that ordering ☎ could be picked up, that of rector, a position he held from 1933 to 1934. The genesis of a tainted and partially rumored history is traced back by him to this call; a telephonic command, in the absence by definition of a material image, or recognizable subject, that Heidegger is asked to obey.

If this may recall aspects of the Old Testament, earth taking a call that commands its existence, it points up the scandalous relatedness of the one to the other, in other words the darkened side of the grim performativeness of all orders which are called in. This summoning into being by invisible orders, whether understood politically or ontotheologically, is something that a certain *techné* of telephonics should help us fathom. Heidegger answered the call. But what is called a call? It goes off, and one reaches for it. Who or what answers a call? The telephone enjoys the prestige of committing finitizing acts.

For its benefit, and to render oneself answerable, one drops what one is doing, what one has been, and becomes what one is: a priori and automatically indebted. One responds to its manifestations like a hypnotized thing, replaying the automatic listening device of *What Is Called Thinking?*

This question appears to be consolidated in *Sein und Zeit,* where the *Gewissensruf*—the call of conscience—is shown to possess the character of a telephone call. It brings us to a point that we shall rarely cease making. This concerns the dependency of the *Gewissensruf* on the model of a telephonic apparatus. To the extent that he does not himself make this connection but on some level of textual rendering dissembles it, Heidegger's conduct concerning the telephone seems to undermine his theory of the *Gewissensruf.* If the technologized call had been admitted to the field of reception, Heidegger would have had to screen it thoughtfully, the way Derrida does when, after careful consideration, he refuses a call in *La carte postale*. Putting the telephone aside when reflecting upon the call from the SA, Heidegger loosens a bolt in the apparatus of the *Gewissensruf.* For some reason he did not wish to see how the telephone exemplified and also complicated this call of conscience. This, precisely, is one reason to reconsider Heidegger's theory of the call on the basis of the telephone. But because the telephone offers no presence in Heidegger and because it remains hidden as a fugitive reference, Heidegger's telephone will always be more perverse than it seems, spreading itself out along a thickly disseminated network of near misses. This is what *SuZ* has to say about the call: "Der Gewissensruf hat den Charakter des *Anrufs* des Daseins auf sein eigenstes Selbstseinkönnen und das in der Weise des *Aufrufs* zum eigensten Schuldigsein." "If we analyze conscience more penetratingly," the paragraph offers, "it is revealed as a *call* (*Ruf*). Calling is a mode of *discourse*. The call of conscience has the character of an *appeal* [*Anruf,* telephone call] to Dasein by calling it to its ownmost potentiality-for-Being-its-Self; and this is done by way of *summoning* it to its ownmost Being-guilty. . . . To the call of conscience there corresponds a possible hearing. Our understanding of the appeal unveils itself as our *wanting to have a conscience* (*Gewissenhabenwollen*)" (*BT,* 269–270). Before we begin to hook up this moment of Being-guilty with the telephone call that Heidegger accepts in the rector's office, another moment in *Being and Time* requires our concerned attention. Part of the response to the question—"And to what is one called when one is thus called up?"

—appears to confirm the being-turned-into-a-listening device that we have found to occur in chapter 5 of *What Is Called Thinking?* Heidegger suggests what in Lacanian terms might be understood as the rage of the real:

Indeed the call is precisely
something which we ourselves
have neither planned nor
prepared for nor voluntarily per-
formed, nor have we ever
done so. [" 'Es' ruft,"] "It" calls,
against our expectations
and even against our will.
(*BT*, 275)

The call, it would seem, tears into us with the authority of a suddenness, a resolute event which can neither be subjected to a will nor to a string of predictable determinations. The call, erupting as a kind of violence perpetrated against a destinal projection, is thus essentially out of control, arriving only to mark the out-of-handedness that befalls a planning "we ourselves" ("we ourselves have neither planned nor prepared for nor voluntarily performed, nor have we ever done so"). This, precisely, is where the *Spiegel* article may want to be referring us to, inscribing the "us," that is, who might consult the directory assistance to Heidegger's œuvre: when reading of the call from the SA, look up *Sein und Zeit,* link up the two calls, both of which take place under the explicit sign of Being-guilty. And yet, the question of culpability and taking calls is distributed among different operators, or so it would seem. For calling in *Being and Time* resolutely disassociates itself from "everyday" occurrences: "This existential Interpretation is necessarily a far cry ['*notwendig fern,*' necessarily long-distance] from everyday ontical common sense, though it sets forth the ontological foundations of what the ordinary way of interpreting conscience has always understood within certain limits and has conceptualized as a 'theory' of conscience" (*BT,* 269). Now the question arises of where to place a call from the SA; surely, given the way Heidegger situates it in his interview, it, too, is a far cry from everyday ontical common sense. It happens once, generating the events of a *Schuldigsein* that cannot be reduced to a history of a single subject; in this way, it fits an event acting upon a subject that must respond to the violent intrusion not like a desiring or planning subject but like a virtually hypnotized thing. Nonetheless, as hypnotists in some concurrence with Heidegger tend to remind us, hypnosis as a property either of subjectity or thingness does not fundamentally alter the structure of the will. If the little boy of chapter 5 is called back by his mother, *SuZ* suggests he takes the call because he wants to be brought back. Follow the twisted cord of umbilical logic: "If the everyday Interpretation knows a 'voice' of conscience, then one is not so much thinking of an utterance (for this is something which factically one never comes across); the 'voice' is taken rather as a giving-to-understand. In the tendency to disclosure which belongs to the call, lies the momentum of a push—of an abrupt arousal. The call is from afar unto afar. It reaches him who wants to be brought back" (*BT,* 271). This would be the kind of discourse constitutive of Dasein; it traces only the phenomenal horizon, warns Heidegger, for analyzing its existential structure. The Interpretation of conscience is thus not to be read as being traced back to some "psychical faculty such as understanding, will, or feeling, or of explaining it as some sort of mixture of these" (*BT,* 271). A phenomenon such as conscience renders the ontologico-anthropological inadequacy of a "free-floating framework of psychical faculties or personal actions all duly classified" (*BT,* 272). So the call cannot really be fathomed as a person-to-person call, where conscience is manifestly at issue. "It" calls against our expectations and even against our will. "On the other hand," it continues, "the call undoubtedly does not come from someone else who is with me in the world. The call comes *from* me and yet *from beyond me and over me,* Der Ruf kommt *aus* mir und doch *über* mich" (*BT,* 275).

This assertion seems to complicate our itinerary considerably; still, following the lines of Heidegger's reading of the call induces a clarifying stumble: "But methodologically this is too precipitate. We must instead hold fast not only to the phenomenal finding that I receive the call as coming both from me and from beyond me, but also to the implication that this phenomenon is here delineated ontologically as a phenonemon of *Dasein*" (*BT,* 275). The call cannot be understood in terms of any psychologistic reading of the "psychical faculties." Heidegger is not dealing in feelings, will, and so on. (It could be argued, admittedly somewhat surprisingly, that neither was the early Freud—insofar as his reading of the psychical was conceived in its relatedness to an apparatus of considerable operative complexity.) The call that is placed, therefore, meets its term in its reception: "the phenomenal finding that I receive the call" (*BT,* 275). Insofar as the call comes from beyond me and over me, it commands a power post of sorts, it lords over me, from beyond my station and puts me in its place—*my* place, for the call also calls from me. In this sense the "me" is a receptionist who takes calls which are both outgoing and incoming; but when the connection is made, and I receive the call, to a certain extent I receive it because "it reaches him who wants to be brought back" (*BT,* 271). Back to what? Did Heidegger return the call to the SA? The call is from beyond me and over me.

In the subsequent demonstration of the *Spiegel* interview, shortly before stating that "philosophy is over," Heidegger traces a path by which his earlier descriptions might be judged. The early part of the interview showed him taking a call. Again, we ask what is called a call? We looked up a connection in *Sein und Zeit.* But the interview itself gives us another number, one that might prove to answer our particular call.

"What I'm saying," says Heidegger, "is we've found no path that corresponds to the essence of technology" (*I,* 17). This assertion and subsequent discussion are situated under the subheading "What Are the Political Systems of the Technological World," addressing the "encounter between planetary technology and modern man." Let us rewind and listen to this moment of a two-way conversation:

S:

However, in your 1935 lecture, printed in 1953 as "Introduction to Metaphysics," you said, "What is today being offered as the philosophy of Nazism has not the slightest to do with the inner truth and greatness of that movement (namely with the encounter between planetary technology and modern man). Meanwhile the so-called philosophy of National Socialism fishes in the murky waters of 'Values' and 'Wholes.'" Did you insert the bracketed words in 1953 to make plain to the reader what you had meant in 1935 by "the inner truth and greatness of this movement" or were they already there in 1935?

H:

The phrase was in my manuscript and represented my then view of technology and not my later exposition of technology as Frame-Work (*Ge-Stell*). I did not develop the point because I thought my listeners would understand what I was getting at. As you might expect, fools, stool pigeons and spies understood it otherwise, as they well might. (*I*, 16)

Multiple telephonics. In the first place, what seems clear in this passage is the arbiter's role that a certain understanding of technology will play here. However, in order to establish Heidegger's intentions at the time crucially referred to, a whole system of unreliable telephonics must yield to disentangling measures. The 1935 lecture was in a sense called in; not unlike other lectures, it presents itself as a partially untraceable transmission. Hence the question of the diacritical marks, or of a belated insertion, can be asked of Heidegger: "Did you insert. . . or were they already there?" A question whose answer is to be taken on good faith. The response refers to ostensible evidence, "the phrase was in my manuscript," but the problem is complicated by an assumption that Heidegger claims to have made regarding those who received his call in 1935. The point that he meant to make was at no point made, but given over to rumorological expectation, namely, that the listeners "would understand what I was getting at." The German suggests a certain reliance on enframing that may come as a surprise: the passage (*Stelle*) predating *Ge-Stell* was not read because Heidegger relied on his listener's capacity for correct (*rechten,* right or even right wing) understanding: "und noch nicht der späteren Auslegung des Wesens der Technik als Ge-Stell. Daß ich die Stelle nicht vortrug, lag daran, daß ich von dem rechten Verständnis meiner Zuhörer überzeugt war" (*I,* 204–206). The passage cited by the *Spiegel* had been suppressed at the time because Heidegger understood that his listeners understood. But he misunderstood, as did they. They were not listeners, but *spies,* disconnected from the mouth-ear channel that Heidegger thought had been switched on. One might wonder if Heidegger is not joking, were it not difficult to think of him in such terms. He did not bother making the crucial point, but settled on innuendo, because the lectured-to knew what he meant to say. This is why he did not have to say it. So that the semantic, literal, or intentional dimension of the lecture did not need to be delivered but only gotten at. Not being delivered, or even sent off, it ought to have arrived, but the listeners were not listeners and the unsaid was lost on them. Or rather, the listeners were functionaries of another system of detecting and transcribing, listening in like operators who silently intrude upon two interlocutors, invisible from one another. In sum, Heidegger did not know whom he really was addressing, though his entire justificatory gesture assumes this knowledge (*They* knew what I meant, which is why I didn't have to say it, and so forth).

Reading the interview, one might think one is recognizing a ruse. The man is putting us on; like the prephilosophical mother, he is putting us on eternal hold, waiting for a response. Yet, if this is a ruse and not a potential extension to the texts under discussion, then one of these, too, would have always already programmed the ruse. According to what *SuZ* will tell us, Heidegger is constitutively barred from reporting on the events which the reporter asks of him: "'It' calls, even though it gives the concernfully curious ear nothing to hear which might be passed along in further retelling and talked about in public. But what is Dasein even to report from the uncanniness of its thrown Being? . . . The call does not report events; it calls without uttering anything. The call discourses in the uncanny mode of *keeping silent*. And it does this only because, in calling the one to whom the appeal is made, it does not call him into the public idle talk of the 'they,' but *calls* him *back* from this into the *reticence of his existent* potentiality-for-Being. [Der Ruf redet im unheimlichen Modus des *Schweigens*]" (*BT,* 277). All this prepares the ground for a primordial Being-guilty as "having debts" (*Schulden haben*), which is "a way of Being with Others in the field of concern"; but Being-guilty "also has the signification of '*being responsible for*' ('*schuld sein an*')" (*BT,* 281–282). This is what the call tells us, when it calls: "the call either addresses Dasein as 'Guilty!', or as in the case when the conscience gives warning, refers to a possible 'Guilty', or affirms, as a 'good' conscience of no guilt. Whatever the ways in which conscience is experienced or interpreted, all our experiences 'agree' on this 'Guilty!'" (*BT,* 281; trans. modified).

What the call is "getting at" is this juridico-ontological sentence, this notice of nonpayment and statement of debt. To accept the call is to let oneself be found—"Guilty!" Secondarily and derivatively, "a 'good' conscience" might be found "of no guilt." If Heidegger's 1935 lecture was in any way a call, a calling forth or a calling back, and if it were to have been heard or heeded, not just translated by operators of the state for the state, and if the They had taken the call, they would have heard, like K. when he telephones with the Castle, precisely the "Guilty!" (the "of no guilt" comes afterward, and suspiciously). But Heidegger's listeners had no telephone lines to his public unspoken; they were instead private eyes, spying, eavesdropping, listening for something that wasn't there. Nodal point of the paradox: these professional inverted cripples could not hear what was not there, which is why they were deficient listeners. A true listening would have heard what Heidegger had not said, and they would have understood him therefor. They had not listened to what was unsaid, but the unsaid in this case by no means corresponds to the "unthought" of the Nietzsche essays, a thinking that still awaits its disclosedness. On the contrary, Heidegger's unsaid was not unthought but merely undelivered, since the audience already knew, he felt he knew, what he was going to say. According to the passage from *SuZ,* the lecture, as calling, ought not to have called the listener into the public idle talk of

the They, into a
mass chatter of political publicity.

Maybe they didn't hear the sentence, which remained deleted until recently. But if there were one figure in the audience who was capable of taking the call, namely the one that was both from me and from beyond me, in order at least to hear himself speak, then while making the call which he was the only one to take, Heidegger had anticipatorily called himself back on that day—"als vorrufender Rückruf"—to hand down Dasein's sentence. The question of guilt is not a question at all, but an address. This is why in a way it didn't matter whom he was addressing when the haunting issue of his guilt began to emerge, because the address itself, as a calling, announced to the speaker its being guilty as a modality of being responsible-for. The call kept silent, paradoxically reporting on itself as silence to a journal addressing the They.

The absolute hearing before which Heidegger has been made to appear has to do with thrownness. Just as he was pressed into service by a faceless Other, lorded over by the telephone, "man," argues the Humanism letter, "is not the lord of existence. . . . He wins the essential poverty of the shepherd, whose worth consists in being called, by Being itself. . . . This call comes as the throwing from which the thrownness of existence stems."[26] However, we do not want to neutralize the momentous difference between apparently homonymic utterances. Surely the poverty of the shepherd will not coalesce with the rector of a university, though they may at times share a bleating clientele. Heidegger was not called by "Being itself" to university service; he explains the academic appointment as a kind of impoverished decision made by a committee who preferred him heading up administrative policy rather than a real Nazi. Nor is it clear that "Being itself" disguised its voice into that of a commanding SA section leader, throwing the rector off guard but put through as the throwing from which the thrownness of existence stems. This is not clear, but it is not impossible either.

Perhaps we have been reading the wrong text. Or, more plausibly still, we have consulted the wrong directory assistance only to get a few right answers from the wrong numbers. Heidegger suggests another connection in the interview, pointing toward his concern with technology. Let us begin again, then, and redial. Heidegger answered a call. Not any call by Dasein or Being; in any case, "not from philosophy, no. The sciences have taken over the previous role of philosophy" (*I,* 20). Heidegger received a call from, let us say provisionally, a telephone. What does it mean to answer this type of call? Without wishing to suggest the posture of village idiocy, one asks simply what it means to receive a call from a telephone. It is entirely possible that the question has received a partially befitting answer. Does the one who picks up the call of a telephone become an extension of the apparatus, or is the converse conceivable; is one speaking through a severed limb or organ, as Freud will suggest, and Marshall McLuhan after him? The telephone rings. It reports itself in the manner of an alarm. The rector, on hand, lifts the receiver and listens through the *Hörer*. He is, in his own words, telespeaking (*fernmündlich*), telehearing. Heidegger argues that democracy "and the rest" are halfway measures, "because they, as far as I can see, do not seriously confront the technical world. Behind these concepts is the idea that technology is by nature subject to man's control" (*I*, 16). So the telephone is ringing in the rector's office. "I don't think it is. The essential thing about technology is that man does not control it by himself" (*I*, 16). The German text says rather than "control," to have in hand, "daß die Technik in ihrem Wesen etwas sei, was der Mensch in der Hand hat. Das ist nach meiner Meinung nicht möglich" (*I*, 206). So the telephone rings. Technology, state democracy and the rest can be controlled, kept in hand. Heidegger does not think so (he is, to be precise, not of that "opinion"). He takes the phone in hand and, covering the mouthpiece, says to *Spiegel*: the essential thing about technology is that man of himself cannot control it.

When Heidegger gives a command in this interview, it reads: "Think of the last sentence in my lecture 'The Question of Technology'" (*I*, 20). This is what one is asked to think, even within the context of a journal's assertion, "Pardon us, we can't and don't want to philosophize, but. . . ." Heidegger responds, think to the end with me, think of my last sentence on technology; he has already told the They that philosophy is over, but they seek pardon, they don't want to, they are unable to, but they want to. Heidegger wraps around them the Frame-Work in which a certain *Unheimlichkeit* creates a domestic squabble with the homeland: "Everything great arises from man's rootedness in his homeland." But also: "Everything works. That's what's uncanny. Es funktioniert alles. Das ist gerade das Unheimliche, that it works, and that technology continues to rip and uproot man from the earth. I don't know whether you're frightened. I am when I see TV transmissions of the earth from the moon. We don't need an atom bomb. Man has already been uprooted from the earth. What's left are purely technical relations. Where man lives today is no longer an earth" (*I*, 17). Technology is no tool and it no longer has anything to do with tools, but it provides an uncanny deracinating grid whose locality is a literalization of the *Unheimlich,* two ocular shapes spying on one another, the earth seeing itself from the moon, ripped out of its socket, axially dislodged, bleeding, rendering the centering effect of an A-bomb completely aconceptual. Heidegger concedes fright, alarm ("ich bin jedenfalls erschrocken" [*I*, 20])—the long-distance apparatus has finally reached him, via satellite space ears displaced onto a TV transmission, removing the telephonics which have become indissociable from the rising screams of National Socialism. The prevalence of *Ge-Stell* assures that man is placed, *gestellt,* assigned tasks, and called to order by a power which is revealed in the nature of technology and which he himself does not control. This is when Heidegger states that philosophy (like the earth) is over: "Die Philosophie ist am Ende" (*I*, 209). Perhaps the end can only be an effect of citation; perhaps Heidegger is replaying Nietzsche at this point, forecasting an end that has once again become, miming Zarathustra the mouthpiece and echoing Nietzsche, the last philosopher, who in the *Birth of Tragedy* shrewdly chose the side of science to conduct his questioning. While Zarathustra teaches the Overman, Heidegger, considerably less jubilant, places thinking in the direction of the Overphilosophy. The task that he assigns us, after naming his fright of televisual self-reflection, consists in a thinking of preparation, not entirely disconnected from the thinking of Hölderlin and in some instances, Nietzsche.

S:

You just said philosophy and the individual can do nothing except to . . .

H:

. . . to prepare to be ready. . . . To be prepared for preparation. . . . But it does seem to me that inquiry could awaken, illuminate and define the readiness we've talked about. . . . to prepare to be ready. . . . Even the experience of absence is not "nothing," but a liberation from what I call in *Being and Time* the "Fallenness of Being." To be prepared for preparation requires contemplating the present. . . . and to define the readiness. (*I*, 19)

Isn't this close to what all Hamlets have to say before their causes are reported, aright or wrongly? Overcome by the state, they take a tool in hand which is no longer a tool but a moment in the structure of a general relatedness. Replay Hamlet:

H:

There's a special providence in the fall of a sparrow. If it be now, 'tis not to come; if it be not to come it will be now; if it be not now, yet it will come: the readiness is all. Since no man knows aught of what he leaves, what is't to leave betimes? Let be.

King:

Come, Hamlet, come, and take this ☞ from me.

H:

A few days later someone from the top command called.

Henceforth, *après-ma-mort,* in the afterdeath, reporting his cause aright, Heidegger will have wanted to be ready for the call, seeing himself from above—the moon or the command post—responding to the transmissive call, answering a suppositious voice, coming from me and beyond me, "if it be now 'tis not to come," he was put in his place, *gestellt,* by a telephone that continues to ring in his inner ear, anagram of *Earinnerung,* for H. will not say what he remembers.[27] The interview functions like that which alarms Heidegger: "The fact that it functions is uncanny." The inter-view of two bodies, the *Spiegel* and Martin Heidegger, who took a call, in a vessel destined for circulation after-my-death, looking at himself, interviewing his history as a closure, he is viewing from beyond himself, from the beyond which he shares with an earth that is no longer an earth, receiving an image of herself from beyond her: a transmission both from her and from beyond herself. She receives an image of herself, a click, the shutter of multiple eyes. The teleview comes from me, she says, and yet from beyond me and over me, *aus* mir und doch *über* mich. This time Heidegger does not know if you are frightened: "I don't know whether you are frightened. I am when I see TV transmissions of the earth from the moon, *Mond*" (*I*, 17). Since Heidegger reverts immediately to French at this point (apropos of René Char), translating the moon, it would not be far-fetched to hear him in a *fernmündlich* manner speaking of *le Mond(e)* that frightens him, the technological world of a newspaper interview. By the end of the interview, *Spiegel* addresses the interlocutor as "Herr Professor Heidegger" as if his title needed to be recalled. He has just acted like a machine, allowed himself to be turned into a technological device. "~~Heidegger: Well, cancel that remark." (*I*, 26).~~

The *Zeug* imposes itself upon awareness when it ceases to function, at the moment of breakdown.[28] The collapse of the tool in its serviceability is what fixes our attention. When you have transmission problems, the transmission puts itself in-the-world. "But modern technology is no tool and it no longer has anything to do with tools" (*I*, 17). We need to gain leverage on this question of technology, eventually to consult what might be translated as "The Question Re-garding Technology," for the *nach*—Alexander Graham Bell's test word for all phonetics—suggests a lagging behind, a mechanical pursuit, in other words, repetition and the *death* **DRIVE**: the question that arrives after technology's answering apparatus has set off. Modern technology has threatened to produce not only unemployment for workers as it "advances," but a rising unemployment rate for pretechnological concepts ("Philosophy is over." "And what is now taking over the position of philosophy?" "Cybernetics." [*I*, 20]) But to put it this way is already to be within the province of technology, the way the *Spiegel* cannot avoid being when it asks essentially whether thinking cannot be *retooled*. This line of questioning turns Heidegger into a megatool, reviving the moment when he became an instrument of the Party line, reextending his hand to grasp the telephone. The phone phones. It establishes an entirely novel epistemological impact that could function as the basis of Heidegger's "deep" ontology, if that were our purpose, or propose a series of psychobiologisms inflecting our thanatographical reading assignments. The phone phones. Heidegger reaches for "it." He was not ready to be ready, to articulate the standing-reserve. The notion of a "phony" originates in the phone's call, designating the predicament of a suppositious subject, on both ends. It rearranges the distribution of significance spread out by the authentic and inauthentic dimensions netted by Heidegger. The phone phones, shading in a differential register of inauthenticity, establishing the phony, the shady Other, like the moon, whose identity and therefore also ours is held in suspension. "Hello, may I speak to—?" "You are." So the voice that comes from me and from beyond me can be a phony one, it can miss the point, performing and inducing fraud, putting a metaphysics of identity on hold. As it happens, when the telephone rang that day in the rector's office, it was in order to tell Heidegger to put up the "Jew Notice," as he puts it, in the university. Martin Heidegger says he refused. In itself, this will not mean that he didn't accept the call.

The Subject of Philosophy

Other-to-*SuZ*

While the question touching the identity of the Other tends to be treated in a formal, "existential" manner, it is also true that Heidegger's existential analysis is, as Christopher Fynsk has argued, inevitably founded in or determined "by a given existentiell or factical situation involving something like a 'personal' stance on the part of the 'author'" (SW, 206). The question regarding Heidegger's position toward the subject of the philosophical text has been addressed in Philippe Lacoue-Labarthe's *Le sujet de la philosophie*, which focuses the introduction to Heidegger's *Habilitationsschrift*. Here Heidegger situates the history of philosophy with the aim of keeping it apart from the history of the sciences, arguing that philosophy is marked by "the living personality of the philosophical subject."[29] If the "subject" of philosophy is already carried up into an anonymous history, it is here "individualized" sufficiently to give us a glimpse of the possibility of a kind of philosophical "identity." "Philosophy lives at the same time in tension with the living personality," writes Heidegger to distinguish philosophy from science.[30] In *SuZ*, notes Fynsk, Heidegger also acknowledges something like the necessity of a personal *prise de position*: "He remarks that the existential analytic is founded upon a 'factical ideal of Dasein'—a 'model' ontic existence which, as follows from Heidegger's argument, must be chosen by a concrete subject. The existential analysis is, in fact, an interpretive unfolding of such factical presuppositions" (SW, 207). In *SuZ* this is stated as follows:

> Is there not, however, a definite ontical way of taking authentic existence, a factical ideal of Dasein, underlying our ontological Interpretation of Dasein's exis-

☎

The Subject of Philosophy

Other-to-$uZ

While the question touching the identity of the Other tends to be treated in a formal, "existential" manner, it is also true that Heidegger's existential analysis is, as Christopher Fynsk has argued, inevitably founded in or determined "by a given existentiell or factical situation involving something like a 'personal' stance on the part of the 'author'" (*SW,* 206). The question regarding Heidegger's position toward the subject of the philosophical text has been addressed in Philippe Lacoue-Labarthe's *Le sujet de la philosophie,* which focuses the introduction to Heidegger's *Habilitationsschrift*. Here Heidegger situates the history of philosophy with the aim of keeping it apart from the history of the sciences, arguing that philosophy is marked by "the living personality of the philosophical subject."[29] If the "subject" of philosophy is already carried up into an anonymous history, it is here "individualized" sufficiently to give us a glimpse of the possibility of a kind of philosophical "identity." "Philosophy lives at the same time in tension with the living personality," writes Heidegger to distinguish philosophy from science.[30] In *SuZ,* notes Fynsk, Heidegger also acknowledges something like the necessity of a personal *prise de position*: "He remarks that the existential analytic is founded upon a 'factical ideal of Dasein'—a 'model' ontic existence which, as follows from Heidegger's argument, must be chosen by a concrete subject. The existential analysis is, in fact, an interpretive unfolding of such factical presuppositions" (*SW,* 207). In *SuZ* this is stated as follows:

> Is there not, however, a definite ontical way of taking authentic existence, a factical ideal of Dasein, underlying our ontological Interpretation of Dasein's exis-

tence? That is so indeed. But not only is this Fact one which must not be denied and which we are forced to grant; it must also be conceived in its *positive necessity,* in terms of the object which we have taken as our theme of investigation. Philosophy will never seek to deny its "presuppositions," but neither may it simply admit them. It conceives them, and it unfolds with more and more penetration both the presuppositions themselves and that for which they are presuppositions. (*BT,* 310)

tence? That is so indeed. But not only is this Fact one which must not be denied and which we are forced to grant; it must also be conceived in its *positive necessity,* in terms of the object which we have taken as our theme of investigation. Philosophy will never seek to deny its "presuppositions," but neither may it simply admit them. It conceives them, and it unfolds with more and more penetration both the presuppositions themselves and that for which they are presuppositions. (*BT,* 310)

As Fynsk warns it cannot be clear, however, what a proper noun refers to when we assign it to the "subject" of the text and decipher a kind of factical scenario. He adds: "To underscore Heidegger's own insistence upon finite factical existence is certainly not to caution a psychological reading or one that relies upon biographical data. If we are not yet in a position to describe the nature of the individual subject posed in the philosophical text—the speaking subject(s) and the subject(s) spoken for, to, or against, let us at least maintain

Heidegger's suspicion of the metaphysical subject presupposed by psychology or by historiological inquiry" (*SW*, 207). These warning signals are finely transmitted, and Fynsk's double use of caution indicates the solicitude with which he approaches these issues. Our concerns push us toward the threshold of the metaphysical subject, speaking and spoken to, that as such retains traces of the biographical as it crosses over into a thinking that no longer closes on presuppositions admitted by a classical psychology. The emphasis lies with the passage from "our ontological Interpretation of Dasein" to a *definite ontical way of taking authentic existence* which, while remaining problematic as a translation into sheer empiricity, continues to exert the pressure of a genuine challenge. In other words, it seems necessary to give in to a moment beyond the pull of ontological denial ("which must not be denied and which we are forced to grant"); and the law of such a giving in, articulated in the "it must" form, legislates that it must also be conceived in its *positive necessity*. This is the side, the underlying one, that one must be willing to take up, if only provisionally.

But the question of the speaking subject(s) posed in the philosophical text, and particularly of the subject spoken to, for, or against, raises in turn the question of the Other—something which according to our preliminary reading would appear to sustain itself at an infinite distance. Stationed at the other end—we do not know if the little boy ever came home—the Other never closes in on you, maintaining an essential distantiality which promises you a virginal integrity of your end so that, like Heidegger's argument saying one cannot be represented by another at one's death, Dasein dies alone, founding the possibility of its individuality and integrity as authentically itself. This precisely lends Fynsk's argument its rigorous fervor, for, tracing the relation of Dasein and the Other, he begins identifying Heidegger's "evasion of the question of the Other" (*SW*, 185). Elsewhere, in a note, Fynsk writes that *SuZ* provokes an interpretive decision by leading the reader into its circular structure, thus engaging the reader to repeat the repetition that is therein unfolded—"which may be tantamount to saying that *Being and Time* functions precisely in the position of the Other," which still needs to be described (*SW*, 206). Yet Heidegger undercuts any assignment of a definite origin to this circular movement. The only fact to which one can point is Dasein's being called upon—enjoined—to resolve upon its own guilt (the object, but also the source of the call) and that in the structure of the call we find inscribed the possible intervention of an Other. Fynsk engages himself on this line to read the intervention as a necessary one (*SW*, 206). We shall follow closely, listening in.

The Conference Call

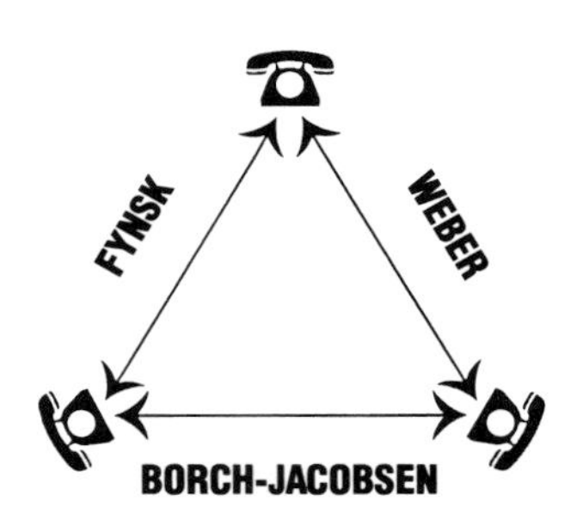

The connection of Dasein's call to the predicament of being guilty/being-in-debt (*Schuldigsein*) has been examined by Samuel Weber in "The Debts of Deconstruction and Other, Related Assumptions" apropos of Derrida's *Carte postale,* and subsequently by Mikkel Borch-Jacobsen in "Ecoute." The task of placing these calls in their difficult Frame-Work imposes itself as a positive necessity; and because we want to understand where our call is coming from, a patient explication of these texts needs to be unfolded. My main concern in so doing is to avoid a power failure when reading the telephone. In view of this kind of electric anxiety it becomes necessary to motivate a strong understanding of the instrumental Other as a hitch or scrambling device lodged within the Heideggerian calling apparatus. This may no longer, today, be Heidegger's problem—he called it, and was called by it—but it most distinctly remains ours to untangle. For Heidegger's apparent opposition between Other and Thing creates a curious standstill or paradoxical arrest—particularly when later, for instance, in what might have been translated as *The Question Regarding Technology,* he turns the human into a constituent of the standing-reserve, thus thingifying what was brought forth as a sort of individualized

Dasein. If the Other and the Thing were to maintain their essentialist divide as separable entities, the one definitively purified of the other, then the telephone simply could not be installed in the place marked by the call of conscience; or, worse still, Heidegger would have to regress to a Hegelian solution for resolving apparent contradictions seen to inhabit the telephone—a temptation to which he will not succumb. Heidegger is not loathe to size up the airplane that is being cleared for take-off. Nor does he hesitate to cite a motorcycle parked in the university parking lot. And while he can equiprimordially hear the difference between a Mercedes engine and that of an Adler, or while he calamitously picks up the telephone, there is essentially no reserved place for the telephone either in his technological reflections or in his collect calls to Being. We refrain from saying "the telephone *as such*," since its essence, if this issue can be raised provisionally, though aporetically, has not yet been determined, much less overdetermined. Yet we respond to the challenge of ontical facticity, hoping to retain in the telephone its instrumental but uncanny gathering of voices (the question of *Unheimlichkeit* awaits restlessly—does the telephone, despite mere appearances, not fundamentally belong to the structure of not-being-at-home, of a being expropriated from a *chez-soi*?).

Yet it is still required of us to give these questions some muscle tone, to strengthen their residential status in what follows. The energy released by the arguments of Weber, Fynsk, and Borch-Jacobsen touches any apparatus working over the possible intervention of an Other, the call and called, the nature of affectability, anxiety, guilt, originary indebtedness. The considerable currency given to constitutive elements of calling ought by rights to clear the runway for thinking the technologized call. And since it may be that sizing up a problematics, pondering the outline of a trajectory to come often resembles and involves a patient lineup, we shall simply have to sit in a mood of anticipation, listening to prior take-offs before accepting our turn. (Writing's rapport to aviation may not be a matter of mere contingency. The aerotrace and general skywriting of Heidegger, Kafka, and Derrida leave particularly rich breaches. In another philosophical climate, when still unsure of his grounding in philosophy, Wittgenstein, as fledgling, was a student of aerodynamics, majoring in engines and propellers.)[31]

One of Fynsk's principal merits is to have set out with clarity the tensions building up in Heidegger and, in particular, those informing Being-with as it comes into contact with the emergent apparition, in his Dasein-analysis, of the solitary self. The Heideggerian break with tradition consists precisely in Being-with (*Mitsein*), constitutive for Dasein, insofar as this is shown to swerve away from those classical inquiries concerning man which begin by posing an isolated subject. To this end, Heidegger writes that "Being with Others belongs to the Being of Dasein, which is an issue for Dasein in its very Being" (*BT*, 123). The analysis of *Mitsein*, asserts Fynsk, may well succeed in revealing one limit of metaphysical thought concerning the subject but Heidegger seems unwilling or unable to work at this limit in a sustained manner, reverting insistently to the solitary self: "In the light of Heidegger's agonistic relation with Nietzsche and his identification with Hölderlin . . . this evasion of the question of the Other may be seen to compose a particular figure of thought" (*SW,* 185–186). The relations between Dasein and Others, which Fynsk claims are inscribed in the paradoxical logic of the hermeneutic circle, are shown to derive from a definition of the self that departs from the metaphysical definitions of the subject, in sum, from the subject of modern metaphysics posed with the *cogito, sum* of Descartes. Heidegger seeks to dislodge this subject from its central position as *subjectum,* but does not renounce all effort to situate or position the subject or self; he situates it elsewhere—in the "there" of Dasein—and describes the condition of possibility for Dasein's assumption of a position or stance in terms of the structure of Dasein's Being as care (*SW,* 186).

On the question of *Mitsein,* Heidegger argues that the gesture, on the part of Dasein, of pulling away from the world is what permits the first contact with the Other, and that the disclosure of Dasein's individual truth is also the disclosure of the truth of the Other. Fynsk sees that this disclosure *is* its truth according to the definition of truth as *alètheia* developed in paragraph 94 of *SuZ* (*SW,* 188). If "Being with Others belongs to the Being of Dasein" (*BT,* 123), Dasein's understanding, its disclosure of its own Being, *already* implies the understanding disclosure of the Other (*SW,* 188). Further, when Dasein discovers its Being and the factical existential situation that is its own, it has *already* discovered the Being of the Other. Dasein has already encountered the Other when it comes to assume itself as a Self (*SW,* 188). This encounter will be "shared" in what Heidegger calls "communication" (*BT,* 162), but the Being-with and its corresponding state of mind articulated by communication are not forms of identification, nor are they identifications of a nature such that the Being of Dasein that "pre-exists" its understanding and assumption of itself (that being *already there* of which Dasein has a preunderstanding and toward which it proceeds in its disclosure of itself—Dasein's own ground could be confused with the Being of the Other). Heidegger takes up the question of how Dasein comes to know the Other *as Other* long enough to affirm that Dasein's relation to itself is not the basis of its understanding of the Other's Being. Fynsk's point is decisive here: Heidegger's brevity is astonishing when one considers the seeming importance of such a question in the analytic of Dasein.

We have already cited part of the passage in which Heidegger establishes his argument. Since the asserted relation to the Other will be of crucial significance to us at a later point, the articulated "puzzle" is worth going over:

Of course Being toward Others is ontologically different from Being toward Things which are present-at-hand. The entity which is "other" has itself the same kind of Being as Dasein. In Being with and toward Others, there is thus a relationship

---

of Being (*Seinsverhältnis*) from Dasein to Dasein. But it might be said that this relationship is already constitutive for one's own Dasein, which, in its own right, has an understanding of Being, and which thus relates itself toward Dasein. The relationship-of-Being which one has toward Others would then become a Projection of one's own Being-toward-oneself "into something else." The Other would be a duplicate [*Dublette*] of the Self.

But while these deliberations seem obvious enough, it is easy to see that they have little ground to stand on. The presupposition which this argument demands—that Dasein's Being toward itself is Being toward an Other—fails to hold. As long as the legitimacy of this presupposition has not turned out to be evident, one may still be puzzled as to how Dasein's relationship to itself is thus to be disclosed to the Other as Other.

Not only is Being toward Others an an autonomous, irreducible relationship of Being: this relationship, as Being-with, is one which, with Dasein's Being, already is.
(*BT,* 124–125)

Prior to demonstrating the process of Being-with as co-disclosure, showing how Dasein responds to the Other, Fynsk casts a shrewd glance of suspicion over the "Being toward Others" passage, though his argument does not require him to gloss the separation between Others/Things present-at-hand, which initially caught our attention. He shows Heidegger to be rushing through this crucial passage, leaving a great deal unsaid. As this is the only passage in *SuZ* where Heidegger takes up the existential nature of a difference in Dasein's relation to the Other, the breathlessness arrives all the more curiously—as if Heidegger wanted out of this Being-with relationship. It is as if Heidegger were "screening" the implications of Being-with by his refusal of the metaphysically laden notion of projection, and what appears to Fynsk as the rhetorically startling evocation of these implications ("The Other would be a duplicate of the Self").

If Fynsk puts teethmarks on "screening," it is in part because this can be read as a telephenomenal citation. Dubbed or *Dublette,* the projections that Heidegger screens are primarily auditory. Thus, in another mention of projection we discover a recognizably telephonic connection unfolding. Dasein's choice (*Wahl,* which in Weber's essay will be read frankly as "dialing") originates in its primordial, free resolving which opens it to the possibility of "loyally following," in the sense of an active affirmation, the existence that has been. The *hören-gehören-Gehorsamkeit* network of *Was heißt Denken?* is resonant with this loyal following. Dasein's choice, seen as affirmative following, does not imply a form of passive reception; because interpretation is involved, it is also a "struggle." Thus when Dasein repeats the possibility of the Dasein-that-has-been-there (believe me, I know), when it encounters the past Dasein's world, it does so on the basis of its own resolute existence in the appropriative decision that Heidegger calls a "reciprocative rejoinder"—and this expression emphasizes once more that the relation to the Other is structured in terms of call and response (*SW,* 200):

Arising, as it does, from a resolute

projection of oneself, repetition

does not let itself be talked into

something by what is "past," just

in order that this, as something

which was formerly actual, may

recur. Rather, the repetition

makes a reciprocative rejoinder

to the possibility of that existence

which has-been-there. But when

such a rejoinder is made to this

possibility in a resolution, it is

made in a moment of vision;

and as such *it is at the same time*

a disavowal *of that which in the*

"today," is working itself out as the

"past." (*BT,* 386; trans. mod-

ified)

While Fynsk points to the structure evoked here of the call and response, this takes place in a moment of vision that in fact blinds itself or at least averts its gaze from "that which in the 'today,'" and so on, so that the call is put through, we might say, following certain lines of spontaneous visual disturbance when vision is in disavowal or not looking, but looking beyond itself, constituting a nonenslaved futurity. The fact that repetition cannot be "talked into" something means that it cuts the lines between itself and the other end—namely "what is 'past.'" Repetition will not succumb to passive receptivity but gets on the line responsively, activating itself as a reciprocative rejoinder. This is how the future gets on the line.

In terms of Dasein's "fateful" relation to the Other, repetition organizes, as fateful existence, a means by which Dasein responds to the Other—the Dasein that has-been-there—according to the factical possibilities constituting the existence of the Other's world (possibilities "in which fate, destiny, and world-history have been factically determined" [*BT,* 394]). Borch-Jacobsen can be made to intervene at this juncture, arguing the point that the relationship to the Other, somewhat as in Derrida's *Memoires,* is founded upon a relation to the death of the Other, for "faithful" disclosure of the Other's existence requires an understanding of that past existence in its authenticity. ("In repetition the Dasein which-has-been-there is understood in its authentic possibility which has been" [*BT,* 394].) Dasein's resolute repetition of its own thrownness, therefore, is also a repetition of the Other's resolute Being-toward-death.

Dasein's encounter with the Other is violent—an event whose force Heidegger compares at one point with a theft. According to Fynsk, the encounter will always have already taken place in the original co-disclosure insofar as it can stand before Dasein as a possibility, and that will have taken place in all the violence of discovery that will have pushed Dasein in the direction of authentic existence. Necessarily violent, the disclosure must counter the pull (*Zug*) of the inertia of the They: Dasein must be *torn* out of its everyday existence before it can be pushed into its authentic, finite existence by going toward its death. The scene of death, by no means a surprise call, is shown instead to be a scene of recognition: Dasein would already have encountered the visage that it encounters there. This scene calls forth recognition insofar as it gives access to that more primordial experience—an originary encounter with alterity: Dasein's uncanny experience of its thrown Being-toward-death—hence, having-been-thrown from which originates the call, out of which calls the Other as an anonymous Other—" 'Es' ruft." The originary encounter, then, is somehow an experience of anxiety, fascination, and guilt—an uncanny experience which as yet remains Dasein's first experience, and perhaps not even "first" insofar as Dasein as a "self" is not yet constituted (or insofar as this takes place somewhere beyond the reach of the Self). The question imposes itself: "What" or "who" undergoes this overwhelming, disappropriating experience of the Other as the source of its "own" nullity? The possibility of posing this as "what" or "who" may point to a technological contamination, suggesting Dasein's uncertain properties (individualized, solitary self, or generally grasped) to resemble the effects of a *techné* under study, which is to say that "what" or "who" suspends, if momentarily, the ontological difference of Thing and Other. Fynsk argues that the question ("what" or "who" undergoes this overwhelming, disappropriating experience of the Other as the source of its "own" nullity?) must be turned about. For if the experience of guilt is an originary experience, then we must try to think the "who" of Dasein as arising *from out* of this experience and see this encounter as the birth in which Dasein is *precipitated* toward its death, as an individual. Thus, in going toward death—that possible death given to it as a possibility by the Other—Dasein progresses at the same time toward the horizon of all possibility, progresses toward a repetition of the uncanny encounter with itself and with the Other—but as Other, the Other as an originary experience of difference or otherness that is not even experienced by a self. The problem this raises return-calls us to our preliminary questions: How does the Other instigate this experience of fascination and guilt? In what sense is he/she/it, literally—"what" or "who"—the bearer of "nullity," and how does this become the gift of nullity as a possibility? In other words, how does the experience of fascination and originary disappropriation turn itself into an experience of appropriation and individuation? Heidegger gives no answers to these questions. Click.

OK. Thrownness is an experience of nothingness or "nullity," and Heidegger calls this experience "guilt"—a radical impotence regarding the conditions of the "there" in which one finds oneself thrown and a powerlessness to become anything other than what one is. In thrownness, the experience of Being-possible is an experience of total powerlessness—powerlessness and fascination, or vertigo. In anxiety, Dasein is taken back fully to its naked uncanniness, and taken with vertigo (*bekommen*) (*BT,* 344). But this capture gives Dasein its thrownness as something possible (*BT,* 344), and it gives Dasein its thrownness as something that can be repeated. It gives Dasein repeatability as something that can be taken up in a resolution (*Entschluss*) in Being-toward-death.

But if thrownness is an experience of a kind of radical passivity, where does Dasein get the impetus, asks Fynsk, to assume this thrownness in repetition? Dasein acts upon itself, Heidegger suggests, spontaneously, out of its own Being-guilty (he speaks of "letting one's most proper self take action in itself of its own accord in its Being-guilty" (*BT,* 295; trans. modified) and thereby discloses this being-guilty as a possibility that may be acted upon. Dasein lives constantly with anxiety—Heidegger underscores the fact that anxiety, like any state of mind, is *accompanied* by understanding. Dasein is constantly drawn toward the experience of fascination and passivity at the same time as it is drawn (or draws itself) toward the experience of death. **«Fynsk still holding the line . . .»** The mastery or "incorporation" of one's thrown Being is never accomplished; or it is accomplished in some sense, that is, if Dasein is able to hold itself in the constancy of repetition, and thus hold itself in its thrown Being, we must conceive this in terms of a movement of constant deferral of mastery. Even this is to privilege the notions of liberty and decision; but we must remember that this liberty is maintained only in and through anxiety. In its repetitive affirmation of its thrown Being, Dasein is constantly thrown back upon the passivity of the experience of this foundation of its existence. Thus Dasein proceeds in two directions simultaneously—approaching the source of its Being as it draws away from it toward its death. And thus the originary encounter with itself and with the Other, as the Other, forms a kind of temporal horizon for Dasein in both past and future; this encounter will have never taken place, and will never take place—or it will have taken place, as Blanchot would put it, in an "immemorial past" and will come about in a future always still to come. But Heidegger accents the possibility of decision, and Dasein emerges victorious—free to construct a monument to its agony by which it preserves reverently the existence that has-been-there: its existence and that of the Other. The monument will serve as a symbol of mourning and of the struggle that it presupposes—a sign to the memory of that immemorial past and of that future always still to come as Dasein continues forward. And thus Dasein acquires a way of recalling the repetitive understanding by which it "painfully detaches itself" (*BT,* 387; trans. modified) from the public, fallen Being of the They. (The term "monument" comes from Nietzsche.)

The call of the Other is essentially anonymous.

Finally, conscience is the call that reaches Dasein in its everyday existence and tears Dasein from it by summoning it (*Aufrufen,* calling it up) to its thrownness, which is the ground of its guilt (*SW,* 195). Conscience calls Dasein *back* to its thrownness by calling it *forth* to the possibility of assuming this thrownness (a clear expression of the double movement in "Der Anruf ist vorrufender Rückruf" [*BT,* 287]). A paradoxical structure of simultaneous approach and withdrawal, of a casting forth that casts back. As the caller is Dasein in its own anxiety, the paradox of a simultaneous, open-ended movement in two opposing directions reappears. Dasein can respond to the call only if it can hear it, and it can hear it only if it wants to hear it—that is, only if it already knows what it is to listen for. (This has been illustrated in our earlier discussion of Dasein's mother, calling forth in order to call back a Dasein, Jr., whose ears are being trained henceforth to have known what to listen for.) "The existentially 'possible' Being-toward-death remains, existentielly, a fantastical demand" (*BT,* 266; trans. modified). Heidegger asks whether anything in Dasein's existence could present it with that authentic potentiality-of-Being that it is asked to assume. He finds this attestation in conscience. Conscience is the call that reaches Dasein in its everyday existence and tears Dasein from it by summoning it (*aufrufen,* call up) to its thrownness, described as the ground of guilt. Conscience calls Dasein *back* to its thrownness by calling it *forth* to the possibility of assuming this thrownness ("Der Anruf ist vorrufender Rückruf" gives perhaps the clearest expression to the double movement). Conscience gives Dasein to understand its thrownness, gives thrownness as a possibility.

But as the caller is Dasein in its own anxiety, the paradox through which Fynsk has just been turning reappears. Dasein can respond to the call only if it can hear it, and can hear it only if it wants to hear it—that is, only if it already knows what it is to listen for. The call is made possible as a call of conscience by hearing just as Dasein's resolute understanding of death is what opens access to the very possibility of this mode of Being: Dasein's guilt. The hermeneutic circle reappears because it is Dasein itself that calls and Dasein that must hear. The call "comes *from* me and yet *from beyond me and over me ('Es' ruft)*" (*BT,* 275)—but it is Dasein itself that is heard in the immediate hearing of which Dasein is capable. "Who else could it be after all?" asks Fynsk, apparently deciding on the "who" of the "what or who" originally offered (*SW,* 196). The voice is uncanny and alien, but unmistakable. Even, apparently, if it is double. When Dasein is listening, it is never alone. One is tempted to insert, there is always that nullity operating in its potentiality, listening to the listening that takes the call. Listening, at any rate, is what opens Dasein to the Other: "Listening to . . . is Dasein's existential way of Being-open as Being-with for Others. Indeed, hearing constitutes the primary and authentic way in which Dasein is open for its ownmost potentiality-for-Being" (*BT,* 163).

A different register of reading this passage would lead us to situate Heidegger within the somewhat far-fetched but implacable neighborhood of eighteenth-century inquiries about man that proceeded by way of nothearing. The philosophical speculations arising out of the predicament of not being able to hear developed a certain ontology of existence, linking hearing to language and thought. These otographs, though intended to come to light in later sections, impress themselves upon us now. Because for Heidegger, what Dasein hears, from itself and from the Other, is silence. But the silent hearing is always bound to speech. Silence, writes Fynsk, is the mode of genuine disclosure. When Dasein becomes silent and reserved, it will speak of death in its turn. Listening will become a speaking-giving, provoking and made possible by a speaking-giving that becomes a listening, and so on in an endless return. It is important to say who gives first, who is indebted to whom, for Dasein cannot hear the Other unless it is ready to speak, already calling upon the call. Can one still distinguish, in this case, the acts of giving and receiving? Or are they implied, one in the other, in a kind of infinite interlacing? Does Dasein's relation to its death necessarily imply its relation to the death of the Other? We know at least that Dasein, when it hears the attestation of the Other, will do so in such a manner that it shares; for hearing, according to Heidegger, is to hold as true, to hold oneself in the truth of that which is heard. **«Fynsk out of sight»** A somewhat dogmatic assertion may suffice here to signal a beep tone: What of the deaf-mute in all this? The deaf-mute would be endangered by Heidegger's axiomatics, which is a way of saying that signs which bypass the voice continue to produce a metaphysical crisis. The place of the deaf—with which Mendelsohn, Kant, and Hegel struggled—is inscribed in the margins of metaphysics, for this radically atopical place depends solely upon the graphics of a sign system, gesture and hand. Even Alexander Graham Bell, exemplary teacher of the deaf, tried desperately to align himself with a metaphysics of primary orality. In a sense, the iron collar of metaphysics imposed on Bell a system of denials as concerned the predicaments of his mother and his wife, both of whom were deaf. The telephone argues with this denial, taking on the primary assignment of vocality, which it tries to overcome. Signing and digital manipulation were somehow relegated to an uncomfortable second place, which in turn made the voice primary persecutor of the deaf. For Heidegger, the hand only holds in as much as those who speak are held by it. One would have to read the entirety of the Heideggerian holding-silence and the distinction Heidegger draws between animality and man—the ape's hand only grasps, man's hand signs, facing language—in order to begin situating the deaf as the critical place from which to reread language theories.[32] Eventually, tracing a certain self-overcoming, we shall have to insert Alexander Graham Bell's lettered glove and hand semiotics to discover a hearing on the other line of this metaphysical crisis—in other words, on the line according to which deafness no longer names a radical separation from language in a logo-melocentric sense, nor does it oppose itself in degradation to divinized blindness.

But first let us follow the lines of a hookup between Christopher Fynsk and Mikkel Borch-Jacobsen, who takes up the question of guilt and the call of conscience in "Ecoute," a sustained *envoi* addressed to an anonymous "tu."

{GUILT}

Drawing Heidegger into conversation with Freud, he starts on finitude. You, he begins, will never be adequate to your finitude, by definition. Your finitude, to be exact, is not yours. Finitude is interminable; you'll never get to the end of it. "As long as you are there—there, thrown project, anxiously caring, always-already-ahead-of-yourself-in-the-world, and so on—you do not cease to anticipate yourself in a 'potentiality-for-Being,' in a 'possibility,' in a 'not-yet,' and you are thus in a way incomplete, not-yet-at-your-end, *noch-nicht-zu-Ende-sein*: something remains suspended, suffering, something is due in the sense that one talks of an outstanding debt, a remainder, *der Rest einer noch zu empfangenden Schuldbegleichung*" (*E,* 88). In order to place this remainder, Borch-Jacobsen interestingly diverts a connection. He speaks of the death that "you" owes from the moment "you" is—you will never attend its (her/his/your) own death, nor Judgment Day, nor will the remission of the debt ever take place. You can never finish with this death. At this point Borch-Jacobsen makes a false attribution, as if intentionally doubling Freud's own repression of an owed debt and death—of being-guilty-unto-death—when he writes: "'You owe a death to Nature,' Freud also said, quoting Goethe" (*E,* 89). The deformation within the collapsed citations and their acknowledgment indeed points to an outstanding debt, a certain guiltiness toward Freud toward Goethe toward Shakespeare which, in a very restricted economy, creates a noble lineage of deadbeats. Freud made a curious lapsus on several occasions when he claimed he was quoting Shakespeare: he substituted "Nature" for "God," which may well be linked to Goethe, the infinite creditor of psychoanalysis whose essay "On Nature" was assumed as the founding text for the Freudian discourse.[33] Thus the simultaneous acknowledgment and withdrawal of guilty indebtedness on Freud's part—he refrains from naming Goethe when slipping him into Prince Hal's throat—is in a sense redeemed by Borch-Jacobsen's wrong number, where something appears to assume the remainder of Freud's debt to Nature. But since that leaves Borch-Jacobsen owing one to Shakespeare, having sacrificed the manifest layer to the latent one, it seemed necessary for the operator to intercept the call.

Once a voice makes itself heard—here we recuperate the Heideggerian structure of conscience calling—it accuses and persecutes. The voice, Derrida has shown, hears itself only in silence. This is the dilemma of the "Guilty!" staging which the call imposes.

The house of Being is haunted, argues Borch-Jacobsen; *un-heimlich,* it is demonic, already drawing you toward its secret. You rise in order to answer the call of the endless night; you can't stop reproaching yourself for this terribly ancient crime. Like a hallucinating thing you respond to the call, it is a call of persecution without the persecutor. "You don't merely hear the call the way one hears a noise, sound, or 'perception' or an 'acoustic image'—even less would you hear it the way one hears a 'phoneme' or a *phoné sémantiké:* you hear it *without* hearing. This voice is therefore not a phenomenon. It never appears as such, never presents itself to your conscience in the form of some sort of experience and you could even say, says the writer, despite all the denials of Heidegger, that it calls you from an unconscious, and even from a superego" (*E,* 90–91). Here **Borch-Jacobsen typically breaks the connection**, allowing it to lapse in an ellipse of three lines . . . .

. . . .

. . . .

For, as inaudible and incomprehensible as it may be, the voice doesn't let up on calling you, indubitably and irresistibly. The "voice," says Heidegger, is a *Ruf,* an interpellation or a scream that comes to you suddenly, *tout à coup,* like a coup (*Stoss,* jolt), and the fact that it is unheard-of by no means relieves you of having to receive its call. To the contrary. "Thus a 'voice' certainly can be aphonic without stopping to be convoking, interpellant, and this, in part, is the case with the voice of conscience, the *Stimme des Gewissens*: it is vocal insofar as you hear it, when you are open to its call" (*E,* 91). Heidegger stresses the vocal character of *Gewissens.* Nonetheless Borch-Jacobsen feels that he does not promote this in order to have it reduced to a pure and spontaneous self-motivation of a self-consciousness that is dictating to itself its own duty within the transparency and self-proximity of a nonworldly "voice." The silence of the voice of conscience renders it that much more alien, *other,* and this is why it is not related, as Heidegger says, to an internal monologue. Before hearing itself in the soliloquy (*Selbstgespräch*) of a conscience, it is received: you are its spontaneous receptor and not the emitter (*E,* 91). This gets a bit difficult and may make more sense when we reflect it against Samuel Weber's thinking concerning the issue of the call. What Borch-Jacobsen seems to be setting up here is a reading by which the call would be put through by an Other, admitting the unconscious or superego into the calling post. But at this point he makes a clear distinction between the place of receiving and emitting, as if to prevent the structure of call and response in Heidegger from borrowing that of a self-addressed envelope—Dasein's collect call to itself. More pressing is his desire to retain the aphonicity of the call in its possibility, while Heidegger appears to permit the call to break the silence barrier at times, to enable it to pierce into the ontic horizon. He also states, however, that the "voice" is comprised as that which gives-to-understand (*das Zu-verstehengeben*). Borch-Jacobsen takes up the gift a few circuit breakers later: you don't know by whom or by what you are called—but at least you know that you did not call yourself (*E,* 91). This knowledge makes claims for something still under construction, for it does not seem entirely clear to me, in reading Heidegger, that you did not make the call yourself. Of course, it all depends on how you divide yourself up.

According to Borch-Jacobsen, the call comes through as a gift that surpasses your initiative, indebting and obliging you before you can undertake any decision. While easily suggesting an agreement and a circular economy of the given and received word, the Heideggerian lexicon of hearing and belonging—*Hören, gehören, zugehören, hörig, Gehörigkeit, Zusammengehörigkeit*—ought first to be understood from this absolute dissymmetry of the gift and the call. "This has been preconfirmed by the religious or mystical tradition out of which Heidegger's argument is built. There is no 'alliance,' no 'marriage' or mystical 'union' which is not sealed before the exorbitant gift of a Word or the startling inspiration of a Breath: 'Hear, O Israel'—the Law is always given as a Voice because hearing (*horchen*) is obeying (*gehorchen*) and listening implies receiving, anterior to any 'auto'-giving or autonomy" (*E*, 91–92). In order to develop this point conscientiously, Borch-Jacobsen must introduce a nuance that was abundantly threaded through his book *Le sujet freudien*.[34] Up to this point what faces us is a rather pointed difficulty, one that makes itself felt: if there is a clear distinction to be made between receptor and emitter, what about the internal implantations encouraged, for instance, by the evocation of the unconscious and id? Furthermore, if you dictate to yourself can the demarcation of receiving and emitting be strictly maintained? Is the one function somehow at a point of exteriority to the other? Borch-Jacobsen implies this possibility when arguing the noncoincidence of the "tu" to itself when it hears the voice of conscience: besides, it is no longer yourself that you hear when you hear the voice of your conscience. "Would the call of this voice seem so urgent, pressing you to respond to it, if it were your own voice? This 'Voice' is only a voice when calling you, selecting you, possessing you, and getting you beyond yourself. Listen, this is the ek-static voice which since olden times struck prophets and 'fanatics,' obsessives and loonies. It is the voice of no one, since it always comes from the Other, a call from the void and a call to speak: *Es* calls, calling you, nothing but you. If you are called and chosen, what are you called? Hence this enigma: as unforeseen and surprising as it may be, the call emanates from none other but you" (*E*, 92). The call, insists Heidegger, is neither a universal Law (which, applicable to all, would not apply to you except to the extent that you could be commutable with "everyone," with *das Man*; but the call concerns only you); nor is it the emanation of some power, be it "biological," sociological, or divine. To attribute the call of conscience to a divine or human Other would be still to interpret it within the horizon of the They which it reduces to silence, and so on. This interruption is made in order to suggest the tension necessary to clear the static produced by the They.

If the call succeeds in reducing the They to silence, is this a different kind of silence than the one(s) involved in producing a genuine disclosure? Are we dealing with competing silences? If so—this would seem to make sense—then what gives assurance that the one silence, shutting down the horizon of the They which it shuts up, never slips, like a slip of a tongue or tripping, into the silence of genuine disclosure? Heidegger indicates two hearings, one proceeding in-the-world as, for instance, the voice of a Judge: in this case the call (*l'appel,* the appeal) is drawn by the Man-selbst toward a soliloquy where one pleads one's cause (*E,* 92). . . . .

«Borch-Jacobsen back on the line» But in fact the call is a thousand times more *unheimlich* and anguishing than the intimate Persecutor whom in delirium you believe you are hearing—this figure is, all in all, an explanation still too reassuring, disculpating. For as concerns the silent call, you cannot even give it the name of someone, even if this were to be that of "Flechsig" or "God" or "Satan."

Not only is the call meant for him to whom the appeal is made "without regard for persons," but even the caller maintains itself in conspicuous indefiniteness. If the caller is asked about its name, status, origin, or repute, it not only refuses to answer, but does not even leave the slightest possibility of one's making it into something with which one can be familiar when one's understanding of Dasein has a "worldly" orientation. On the other hand, it by no means disguises itself in the call. That which calls the call, simply holds itself aloof from any way of becoming well-known, and this belongs to its phenomenal character. (*BT,* 274)

Not only is the call meant for him to whom the appeal is made "without regard for persons," but even the caller maintains itself in conspicuous indefiniteness. If the caller is asked about its name, status, origin, or repute, it not only refuses to answer, but does not even leave the slightest possibility of one's making it into something with which one can be familiar when one's understanding of Dasein has a "worldly" orientation. On the other hand, it by no means disguises itself in the call. That which calls the call, simply holds itself aloof from any way of becoming well-known, and this belongs to its phenomenal character. (*BT,* 274)

Borch-Jacobsen interprets this passage to suggest that not God nor Father nor Drive or Instinct—the *Es* that calls you is rigorously no one, no one other than you. What we wish to retain with particular care from this passage concerns the "other hand" as well (which Borch-Jacobsen does not treat), the undisguised figure of the calling end. For the call doesn't elicit an act of duplicity but is fundamentally remote, unrevealing of a determinate quality, and this trait of abstraction, says Heidegger, is part of its *phenomenal* character. In other words, our understanding of the essentially *phony* character of the caller comes into play: there is no way of securing knowledge of the other's figuration, which, however, does not come in phenomenal disguise. Telephonic mediation seems to imply the constitutive long distance of the caller to the called even if the call is a local one, from Dasein calling itself in conscience: "*In conscience Dasein calls itself*" (*BT,* 275). The most familiar call and most proximate, the local call is also at times the most difficult to trace—it is unlocalizable in the reckoning, bereft of a trait of destination (to . . . from, plus rate). The call of conscience has been raised, on this register, from a dime to twenty-five cents, engaging the motion of throwing a coin toward a destination.

The call makes you come to Being, which throws up another question: how can you hear anything, since you are nothing and you do not as such exist *prior to* the call? The call befalls you, and you cannot prevent the "falling" which you are: it throws you. You are thrown (*geworfen*)—thrown off before any "I" can constitute itself or any subject can be thrown together. "You are called to come to the world and answer for yourself. You consequently are no 'I' hearing itself saying 'you' within a present situation of enunciation or an 'intersubjective' relationship or even a 'dialogic' rapport. . . . Neither addressee nor allocutor nor receiver of some message, 'you' are emitted, dispatched, and given—which also means destined (*geschickt*)" (*E,* 93). Being "Called" is your most proper name, prior to any nomination, any baptism. This is why the call concerns only you, calling none other than you, arriving from no person other than you, all the while coming on to you. The call: it's you, and this is how you are called . . . .

. . . . *In its "who," the caller is definable in a "worldly" way by* nothing *at all. The caller is Dasein in its uncanniness: primordial, thrown Being-in-the-world as the "not-at-home"—the bare "that-it-is" in the "nothing" of the world. The caller is unfamiliar to the everyday* Man-selbst*; it is something like an* alien *voice. What could be more alien to* das Man*, lost in the manifold "world" of its concern, than the Self which has been individualized down to itself in uncanniness and been thrown into the "nothing"? "It" calls, even though it gives the concernfully curious ear nothing to hear which might be passed along in further retelling and talked about in public. But what is Dasein even to report from the uncanniness of its thrown Being?* What *else*

> *remains for it than its own potentiality-for-Being as revealed in anxiety? How else is "it" to call than by summoning Dasein towards this potentiality-for-Being, which alone is the issue?*
>
> *The call does not report events; it calls without uttering anything. The call discourses in the uncanny mode of* keeping silent. *And it does this only because, in calling the one to whom the appeal is made, it does not call him into the public idle talk of* das Man, *but* calls *him* back *from this* into the reticence of his existent *potentiality-for-Being. When the caller reaches him to whom the call (appeal) is made, it does so with a cold assurance which is uncanny but by no means obvious.* (*BT,* 276–277)

We shall get back to this passage so frequently that we might do well to program its number into the automatic dial system—let us say, as #2. It focalizes the originary moment of the call's alert, say, the moment of its initial eruption constituting the calling event. This temporal constricting cordon will permit us to pin down the explosion before you get on the line, that is, before the reassuring simulacrum of a "being-there" can make you forget that you were torn into the restitching fabric of its demand. At this moment the caller collects no worldly determinations; nothing will guarantee any certitude about "who's there?"—as if a question could solicit certitude. Prior to borrowing a status of metaphysical subject or subject of a police interrogation (name, purpose, etc.), the caller, uncontained and un–at home, is Dasein in its uncanniness: "Er ist das Dasein in seiner Unheimlichkeit, das ursprüngliche geworfene In-der-Welt-sein als Un-zuhause, das nackte 'Daß' im Nichts der Welt" (cf. *BT,* 276–277), ringing primordially as Being-in-the-world that is "not at home." This kind of caller is unfamiliar to the *Man-selbst* of everyday life; in other words it would appear that *das Man* is endowed with some capacity successfully to repress or instantaneously to overcome the blinding horror through which the call originates. Heidegger appears to confirm this further along: "Uncanniness is the basic kind of Being-in-the-world, even though in an everyday way it has been covered up" (*BT,* 277). Protective of its alienation from something like authenticity, *das Man* bounces the call off itself, banishing it to the reaches of "something like an alien voice." *Das Man* is as lost to this voice as it is to *das Man*. Yet, one could hazard that *das Man* can take a call precisely because the recognition of its uncanniness and being thrown into "nothing" will not come about. Disdainful as the dominant tone of Heidegger's analysis may be, *das Man* acquires the prestige of a mediation, pulling it beyond the life-despiser, were Nietzsche to be permitted an appearance momentarily less cadaverized than an inscription on a monument.

The caller is Dasein in its not-at-homeness. Heidegger adds "the naked that-it-is," translated as the "bare" that-is. The nuance may be significant, the decision notably to read *nackt* not as naked but as *bloss,* bare. The stark nakedness of the unsolicited call doubles for a mystified version of what *das Man* might recognize as the obscene phone call. This seems **out of line**. And yet, wait: wait and consider the telephone as phantom genital—something Freud will help us fathom—as transmitter of a forbidden Word, a place of placeless trespass. Listen to the hum of this suggestion. Listen, and then hang up on it, returning to the rival silence whose competitive spirit befalls you. Putting you through, *Es*: *Es* calls, the libidinal call is on the line. When the id calls it gives "nothing to hear which might be passed along in further retelling and talked about in public" (*BT,* 277). Particularly not in public. The id calls in the uncanny mode of keeping silent. It calls without uttering anything. Well, this would be to read the *nackte "Daß"* as sheer that-it-is in its nakedness—an obscene reading of the unsolicited call that keeps silent. Forget it, hang up on it, treat it as you would an obscene call—an alien silence, not Heidegger's, but not *das Man*'s, either. My Dasein to your Dasein, being not-at-home. The call does not report events (this is not a call number for content nor even for the new releases of Zarathustra and his coiled up animals); it does not call one into the public idle talk of *das Man,* and so forth. What puzzles me, however, is his certainty of having reached the right number. Dasein appears to be rather sure of making the desired connection: "When the caller reaches him to whom the call is made [*mit der der Rufer den Angerufenen trifft*]" (*BT,* 277). Yet the caller reaches the called with a cold, which can disguise any identity: while uncanny, the cool assurance of reaching the called is "in fact not self-understood" (the English translation: "by no means obvious")—"doch nicht selbstverständliche kalte Sicherheit." This, essentially, is Heidegger's question. The "it calls me," continues Heidegger, is a distinctive kind of discourse for Dasein. "The call whose mood has been attuned by anxiety is what makes it possible first and foremost for Dasein to project itself upon its ownmost *potentiality-for-Being* [or 'most authentic being able to be': *'sein eigenstes Seinkönnen'*]" (*BT,* 277). The call of conscience, existentially understood, makes known for the first time what we have hitherto merely contended: that uncanniness pursues Dasein and is a threat to the lostness in which it has forgotten itself (*und bedroht seine selbstvergessene Verlorenheit* [*BT,* 277]). In case lostness seems burdened with loss, Heidegger in the next sentence shows it to promote a gain: "The proposition that Dasein is at the same time both the caller and the one to whom the call is made, has now lost its empty formal character and its obviousness. *Conscience discloses itself as the call of care*: the caller is Dasein, which, in its thrownness (in its Being-already-in), is anxious about its potentiality-for-Being" (*BT*, 277; trans. modified).

To return now to the dépaysement without a country, and to the reading proposed by Borch-Jacobsen, it appears that the voice does not call you to return home or to yourself, but calls you to where you have never been and to the nonfamiliarity haunting the familiarity (*Heimlichkeit, Vertrautheit, Zuhause-sein*) of your dwelling (*Wohnen*) close to the world and to others. Heidegger writes, in §40, on anguish (translated "Care as the Being of Dasein"), that anguish singularizes and thus opens (*erschliesst*) Dasein as "solus ipse" without, however, allowing this opening—Borch-Jacobsen also calls this an invasion or hemorrhage—to endorse the splendid isolation of a solipsistic subject. §40 also says that appeased and familiar Being-in-the-world is a mode of Dasein's *Unheimlichkeit*, and not the inverse. Being-evicted (*das Nicht-zuhause-sein, Being-not-at-home*), ought to be understood in an existential-ontological manner as the most original phenomenon. This, notes Borch-Jacobsen, is your habitation in the world, this your *unheimlich* familiarity prior to any opposition of the "subject" and "object," of "self" and "other," of "chez-soi" and "the alien," of the "familiar" and the "secret" (this resembles, he adds, the motif of Freud's *Unheimliche* [*The Uncanny*]), where the anguish of the "strangely familiar" emerges on the ground of an initial indistinction of a narcissistic character between the self, or "ego," and "the external world," the "ego" and "other" (*autrui*). The more dreadfully disquieting thing is not the other or an alien; it is, rather, yourself in oldest familiarity with the other—for example, it could be the Double in which you recognize yourself outside of yourself (and which announces to you your death by dispossessing you of your own life, thus your own death). ✂ *This is due to the predicament of your being-in-the-world-with-others, which is without recourse or an outside, and because you cannot oppose yourself to these either (in the way a subject is opposed to an object). This cannot be opposed to anything (it opposes itself to nothing): hence you appear to yourself so strangely familiar, so anguishing, so Double. . . .* ✂ *"Can you hear yourself? You call yourself from outside, to an outside, and it is in putting yourself outside of yourself, without any possible interiority, that the "voice" of your conscience calls you to yourself: this voice is just as properly appropriating as it disappropriates you of all property, just as close as remote, just as familiar as it deracinates and anguishes you beyond all quietude. The voice is always a "voice over" that intimidates you from the outside. In this sense it exceeds any oikonomia, whether this be viewed as the law of the house or the law of the proper—we are using "economy," therefore, in the modern sense of the word.* (*E*, 95). ✂ Now, the voice of conscience, strictly speaking, has nothing to say. "Guilty!" is not the content, argues Borch-Jacobsen, nor the meaning or signified of the call (which has none of these). "'Guilty!' is the way in which you respond to the anguishing silence of the call, echoing it: guilty is the *Hören,* the hearing, that corresponds authentically to the call" (*E,* 97).

Your guilty conscience is a receptive spontaneity, as Heidegger elsewhere says regarding Kantian respect, engaging a contract and indebtedness. The other haunts hearing, even and especially if you hear no one, and it is toward him, toward her, or to you—you no longer know—that you are indebted, toward whom you are guilty and responsible. "When Heidegger, in §34 begins to trace the call of conscience, he demonstrates that the exchange of words presupposes a hearing and/or understanding of the Other, or more exactly, it presupposes communication (*Mitteilung*) as the sharing of Being-with (*Mitsein*), including everything that such 'sharing' implies concerning contractual agreements and indebtedness (the given and taken word, mutual recognition, answerability, etc.)" (*E,* 97).

Before speaking, before even hearing anything whatsoever or whomsoever, you hear this preparatory understanding: you are-with, you are shared, and sharing this share with the Other. "Being-with is in discourse 'expressly' shared (*geteilt*). Thus, hearing (*das Hören auf,* listening for), you are open (*offen*) to, upon, and for the Other. You receive him or it at your place (you receive the Other 'at home,' *tu le reçois* 'chez toi') and you 'share' yourself with him prior to any habitation, possession, or property, *owing* this hospitality prior to any contract, pact, or economical exchange. 'Receive the stranger': this ethical imperative that you would quickly oppose, and so easily, to the ontological solitude and egotism of Dasein. . . . Listen, therefore, and receive: listening for, **you already owe yourself to the Other**, having to respond to him/her and to render to him his due. . . . Listen again, you are not alone, your death is calling you—you owe it; your debt is outstanding: you are guilty" (*E,* 97–98). Both Borch-Jacobsen and Fynsk listen for the friend enigmatically mentioned by Heidegger—your most inner voice, familiarly Other, is that of the friend, therefore, whom you carry within you like a secret or a wound that is open or secret—perhaps like a crime. The voice of the absent friend, possibly dead: this contributes to making you Other, which is to say "with" or haunted. For no one speaks. Nobody's talking.

This kind of cryptological inflection—the effect of the phantom and the lodging of an undead Other will occupy our lines henceforth. In the meantime Heidegger's lines are tapped by the irreversible *Stimme des Freundes* which every Dasein carries within itself. Fynsk writes: "the voice of the friend is *always* there, just as Dasein itself is always there as thrown" (*SW,* 196). He indicates what we might call the irreducible precedence of the friend's voice, for this clearly is not the voice of any Other with whom Dasein may come in contact and with whom Dasein *can* come in contact by virtue of the structure of hearing. Fynsk will in fact end his essay rather spectacularly on this note. The hero or the friend, he writes, suggesting Nietzsche as the hero and Hölderlin as figuration of friend for Heidegger. The hero and friend may be rivals, but any encounter or any *agon* with them is finally, or also, an encounter with an Other, the Other—call it the spirit of history if you wish.

So, where were we? You respond to the Other who you are prior to being an "I." You respond to the other who appears to prophesy your death. The voice of your conscience, continues Borch-Jacobsen, testifies to your own capacity for Being, not by bringing along some sort of proof of your improbable authenticity, but by calling upon you to give voice—responding to him, responding from him—to this Other. “You are outside yourself, you are not yourself, you no longer belong to yourself. You are *possessed, hörig*: *in dieser Hörigkeit zugehörig,*” §34. When you are purely hearing, you don't hear anyone and you hear yourself, then, as *hörig*—that is to say, in the other tongue that you cannot hear except by betraying it, as "listening," as "belonging" to the Other in the mode of servility. Well, isn't "hearing" a silent voice? Isn't belonging to this voice of no one the same as being possessed, as the prophets and saints always were? What else could it be, if not opening and offering yourself to an Other so much the more "other" than you "yourself" are, that you identify with Him in body and soul, you are possessed by the Other, *owing* him your own most being (your death). And this response, the testimony to your infinite finitude? "Guilty!" “To hear the voice of conscience "authentically" is thus to respond, to hear yourself respond (traveled and traversed by this "voice"): "I *am* responsible"; "I *am* guilty." (*E,* 100)” Seized, unhanded by the voice, you aver finally that you are *only* called by the Other in you and that you are yourself the debtor of your being, because you are *hörig,* "possessed." Called to being—you, the called one, you are called into being and you owe your being according to a *Schuldigkeit* prior to any obligation or to any empirical fault. “Heidegger asks where you will find the original existential sense of the *Schuld* that calls you to answer. Insofar as this "guilty" emerges like a predicate of "I am." (§58) Your culpability is in the first place a *Schuldigsein,* a being-guilty, and you will recognize therein this "being of the *sum*" that Heidegger, in §§ 6 and 10, elliptically reproached the Cartesian tradition with having neglected. For this being that you are when you say "I am," *ego, sum*—this being, so proper to you, is what you owe. (*E,* 100)” Nothing is more indebted than this possession or property. Don't delude yourself. Being is yours only to the extent that you cannot shirk this responsibility; it is your duty, you are nothing before being. Hence your immoderately obliging assignment. Being, finally, is *nothing other* than this duty that calls you, possesses and debits you, guiltifies you from the moment you are—you, the Unique, the Called. "That is why no longer will you say being or Being—no more than you would say *the* Other or death. Being is not a substantive; being is the Word that you are yourself beyond yourself. Listen well: Being is being guilty; other, dead. You *are* guilty, you *are* Other, you *are* dead . . ." (*E,* 100). Click. . . . In reality you are nothing but Other, altered, called, inspired, accused, persecuted, beginning from yourself guilty of being yourself. . . . "You are no longer—nor have you ever been—present to yourself . . ." (*E,* 101–102). You are stretched out between you and yourself. . . . About the death that you have been owing since your birth: you'll never be able to realize, effect, or present it. . . . "You see, there is no 'ethics,' no 'morals' of finitude. But even as it is endless, and so much the more demanding, there is the *call* of finitude. . . . Heidegger, who never wrote an 'Ethics,' nonetheless understood that the tragic fault is without a why, being incomprehensible, and this is the only way that it is what it is—free, in conformity to its destiny (*Letter on Humanism*). The tragedies of Sophocles are thus more original arbiters of *Ethos* in their utterances than are the lessons of Aristotle in his 'Ethics'" (*E,* 110).

The crime is so old—the monument of the Sphinx binds it

together,

tightly,

prohibiting

passage.

Ssssssssssssssince we have arrived at a deserted monument to the Greeks, somewhere prior to history's spirit in its aftermath, we seek out the site of primordial guilt. The reading proposed by Samuel Weber backs itself up with three epigraphs. The third citation by which Weber inaugurates "The Debts of Deconstruction . . ." is taken from Nietzsche's heterobiography, *Ecce Homo*: "Under these circumstances there is an obligation, against which rebel at bottom my habits, and even more the pride of my instincts, namely, to declare: *Hear me! For I am such and such. Above all, do not mistake me for another!*" (*DD*, 34). This presents a particularly compelling third term (there were two prior epigraphs) from which to begin a reading of the Heideggerian call as it is received in Derrida's *Carte postale*. The Nietzsche citation, while it resolves nothing—its position is third place, which in dialectical schemas often takes first honors—names the dilemma of the call that we have begun to trace. It begins with the Nietzschean obligation—the responsibility and debt that he carries, we might say, primordially. A duty which instinctual pride disdains, in other words, a duty prior to any instincts or any accretion of habits. The obligation, heralding a declarative statement opened by "namely," requires Nietzsche to identify himself on this modified telephone to the beyond.

Nietzsche opens your  **S**, indeterminately doubling the predicate to "I am," reproducing the echo chamber of a certain moment in self-identity: "Ich bin der und der." We might think of Zarathustra who identifies himself as mouthpiece for an Other—Zarathustra, who began his teachings by carrying a corpse on his back, being *der und der,* always Double, the living and the dead (for example, I am my mother who lives on, and my father, etc.). But even as I am double, such *and* such, and not myself, even though I have covered my ground and disclosed my such-and-such identity, you are namely asked (or commanded) not to mistake me for another. It is still possible for me, who am not myself, to be taken for a wrong number. The ear cannot tell; it keeps silent. Weber begins the first part of his argument by recalling Derrida's anecdote, added early in the *Envois* in the form of a footnote. **Derrida is preparing** the *Carte postale* for his publishers when the phone phones. It creates a hole in the text, which, however, also complies with its telegraphic syncopations. A nervous text, made up of jolts and multiple disruptions, clandestine destinations and disseminating yous (the *envois* are addressed to "tu," who rarely coincides with herself, but then, we must not mistake her for another), the already nervous text starts when the telephone rings, ripping into Derrida's study (Weber puts it nicely: "the writer, whom for obvious reasons of convenience, but without seeking to prejudice an issue yet to be discussed, I shall henceforth refer to as 'Derrida'" [*DD,* 35]). The footnote begins in a way that ought to remind us of the Nietzschean resignation of instinct and habit before the irresistible call of duty. It states, or rather Derrida begins, "I feel obliged." Weber's analysis addresses the effects of the entire passage, but, pausing at this inaugural gesture, one senses the double obligation linking Derrida to Nietzsche, as if "I am *der und der*" were a stammering of the former's name, namely stretching toward Derrida within an anticipatory call toward the futural obligation: "Hear me!" As in all autobiographical projects the request to be heard, in this case articulated as demand, is signed on the other end, posthumously, by the other. "There is an obligation," ends Nietzsche. "I feel obliged," Derrida affirms. But, on the other end, Derrida appears to be called up—this is what he is made to think—by another phantom, the ghost, or *Geist,* as he puts it, of Martin Heidegger.[35] As we reread this passage we might also recognize the disruption of the Hegelian *hic et nunc* tensed into the argument:

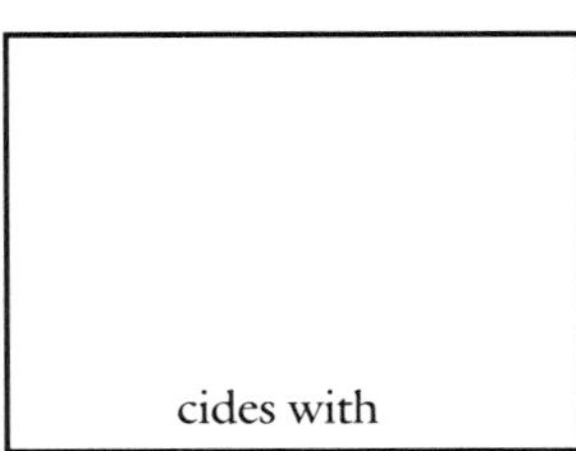

I feel obliged to note, here and now, that this very morning, August 22, 1979, around 10:00 A.M., as I was typing this page in view of the present publication, the telephone rings. The United States. The American operator asks me if I will accept a "collect call" . . . from Martin (she says Martine or martini) Heidegger. As is often the case in such situations, which I know only too well, since I must often call collect myself, I can hear vaguely familiar voices at the other end of the intercontinental line: someone is listening to me, awaiting my reaction. What is he going to do with the ghost or Geist of Martin? I can hardly summarize the entire chemistry of the calculation that led me, very quickly, to refuse ("It's a joke, I do not accept"), after having the name of Martini Heidegger repeated several times, in the hope that the author of the farce would finally be named. Who, in short, pays: the addressee or the sender? Who ought to pay? The question is very difficult, but this morning I thought that I ought not to pay, apart from adding this note of thanks. (CP, 25–26)

The footnote, therefore, arrives as an *addition,* a notice of payment for what has not been paid—the collect call has been heard but not taken: "I thought that I ought not to pay, apart from adding this note of thanks." This note nonetheless carries the value of Heideggerian currency, involving as it does the exchange values of thinking and thanking and the surpassing economy of the gift. By offering thanks, Derrida acknowledges a debt which he feels obliged to think—but thinking in terms assigned by the withdrawal of his deposit.

Weber addresses his remarks to the decisive question of who pays—the addressee or sender?—beginning with this phone call in which, on one level, nothing happens: "unless, that is the refusal to accept a collect call" (*DD,* 34). Can this be said to constitute an event of sorts? We shall follow this line of thought, though henceforth for our purposes the call itself announces an event which, even if "nothing" should happen, in being refused or diffused adds a second dimension to the field of its demand. (To let "nothing" happen, as Heidegger has shown, and Rousseau before him, is not nothing.) The call was not wholly refused—Derrida responded, calculated, rejected, and paid in a foreign currency. The fact of determining it a posteriori as refused adds another angle to our reading, because until now the call of conscience, and even the call at the rector's office, seemed to destine themselves to a response, in order, that is, to guarantee the occurrence of being-called. Weber's argument brings to light the question of who pays, jamming with the earlier questions that were raised regarding the "who calls"? As a joke, the story told in Derrida's footnote comes off as somewhat meager. Its only punchline might be construed as residing in the volatization of the name "Martin," exchanging its gender, or even its species. Unless the fate of the joke depends on its timing, for Heidegger's ghost picked an incredible moment to intervene, "the name of Heidegger had just been written, after 'Freud,' in the letter I am in the process of transcribing in the machine" (*CP,* 26). The ☎ intervened at the moment Martine (or martini) Heidegger's credibility and credit were on the line, as Weber points out, for nothing less than his (her?) credibility and credit had just been called into question. Derrida had just written, apropos of Heidegger's Nietzsche reading that "Nietzsche understood nothing of the initial catastrophe. . . . He believed, as did everyone else, that Socrates did not write, that he came before Plato, who wrote more or less under his dictate. . . . From this point of view, Nietzsche believed Plato and didn't overturn anything at all. The entire 'overturning' has remained within the program of this credulity" (*CP,* 25). Referring to Heidegger's reading of Nietzsche as the *Umkehrung,* the "overturning" of Platonism, Derrida precipitates to the fateful sentence toward which the call calls: "The entire 'overturning' has remained within the program of this credulity. And this holds *a fortiori* . . . for Freud and Heidegger" (*CP,* 25). Weber: this assertion might be "destined to drive the Sage of Todtnauberg straight to the nearest ☎ booth in a vain attempt to assert his right of response" (*DD,* 35). For the History of Metaphysics programs and prescribes its proper overturning, including the very question—and the questioner—of the Meaning of Being. Derrida refused the call, it was not accepted, *nicht angenommen,* not assumed by him, although his obligation to thank the anonymous caller (assuming Heidegger's ghost was not the caller, but rather Heidegger's conscience) suggests that he does assume the burden of payment, or at least that he received the call. However, Derrida simply tells us that "my private relationship to Martin does not operate on the same exchange." It would seem, then, that while Derrida refuses the call, and refuses in this open letter, the *Carte postale,* to divulge the nature of his private relations to Martin, he does disclose one thing, perhaps the only thing of fundamental importance to those still listening for a response (was not Nietzsche's earlier call to Derrida a collect call: *ich bin der und der,* you take it, it's your responsibility and burden that I stammer forth, relaying my obligation, pouring it into your ear and account?). While closing the door on *das* reading *Man*'s need to know, leaving unfulfilled the idle curiosity concerning his intimacy with Heidegger, its locality and intensity, Derrida, still, has given everything away. He has disclosed that his relationship is structured telephonically, according to an altogether different exchange but nonetheless an irreducibly telephonic exchange, a "*standard*" (switchboard) posing some sort of unique person-to-person (or, more plausibly, Dasein to Dasein) circuit. **Weber takes us through** a persuasive discussion of Freud and Nietzsche before returning this call and, strengthening the linkage to the call, he first offers a reading of the indebted, improper character of psychoanalytic discourse whose interests have also drawn Derrida. The economy of the call is momentarily transferred:

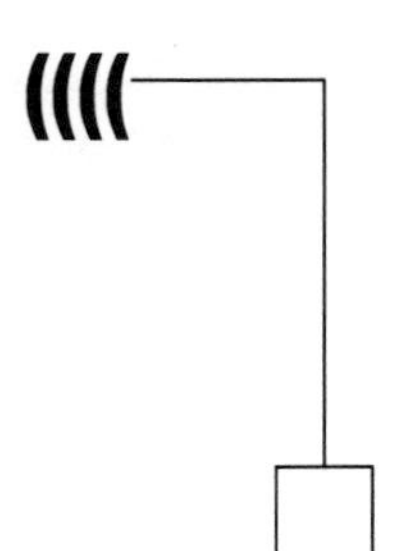

Borrowing is the law . . .
without borrowing, nothing
begins, there is no proper
reserve (*fond propre*).
Everything begins with the
transfer of funds, and there is
interest in borrowing, it is even
the primary interest.
Borrowing gives you a return,
it produces surplus-value, it is
the primary motor of all
investment. One begins thus by
speculating, betting on one
value to produce as though
from nothing. And all these
metaphors confirm, as
metaphors, the necessity of
what they say. (*CP*, 410)

In Freud'sssssssssssspeculations, to borrow from Weber, the most ingenious, most radical stratagem is that which consists in assuming a debt so totally as to render it inoperative. If "everything begins with the transfer of funds," then the very notion of debt itself tends to lose its force. The debt cannot be paid back

perhaps because economy itself has been transgressed; not economy in general but an economy in which the principle of equivalence would have been forced. All the movements in *trans-* would have violated this principle, and with it everything that could have assured a payment, reimbursement, an amortization. . . . This effraction—that is, the speculative transfer(ence)—would have rendered the debt both infinite or insolvent, and hence null and void. It is the economic space of the debt that finds itself in upheaval, immensely enlarged and at the same time neutralized.
(*CP*, 415)

Weber manages this passage in a way that compels him to address *Schuld*. Derrida has endowed the speculations of "Freud" with their paradoxical but characteristic "dual tonality": "Both grave, discouraged, gasping under the burden of the inexhaustible debt or task; and simultaneously flippant, cavalier, affirmative" (*CP*, 415). The questions that this raises in Weber's text provoke further inquiry. Is a debt thus generalized, he asks, necessarily "neutralized"? Does the fact that everything begins with a "transfer" of funds—with a certain form of borrowing—necessarily "invalidate" the notion of a debt? And what is the relation of such "forcing" of the principle of equivalence, to that noncontingent limitation at work in the Oedipus complex, and indeed, in all accounting and accountability? The word for accepting a call in German is *Annahme*. Weber uses it to explain why and how Freud can at the same time deny, acknowledge, and dispatch his indebtedness with that matter-of-factness that so fascinates Derrida. (Weber's earlier example of such pluralized maneuvering invokes a logic familiar to readers of *The Interpretation of Dreams*: "No, I haven't read Nietzsche—he is too interesting. No, he hasn't influenced my work and I know nothing of his. Moreover, he has completely failed to recognize the mechanism of displacement."[36]) "This morning, I thought that I ought not to pay," Derrida thought this one particular morning at 10:00. But in refusing to accept the charges—*Annahme verweigert*—was the debt reduced? This question occupies the last section of Weber's essay, bringing Heidegger, who is "doubtless the most important of the missing links" into the chain of readings which situate "Spéculer—sur 'Freud.'" To pursue the allure of an unrequitable debt,

Weber commences thus:

> The divisibility of place and the reversibility of time, the superimposition of "fort" upon "da," the destination of the postal network, its "exapproriative" structure—all can be traced to Heideggerian notions of *Geschick* and "*Da*," of *Enteignung* and *Ent-fernung,* and of a space in which back and forward, front and backward, near and far, are no longer defined by opposition to each other. The debt to Heidegger is clear, and, in a certain sense, assumed. Why, then, is the collect call, made in his name, refused?
> (*DD,* 59)

To assume a debt, or to assume a proper name, Weber later on reminds us, inflects the problematic toward a region of fictionality, where assumptions of nonverifiable sorts can be made and sustained. The upshot of his closing statements is to signal that "one can be *schuldig*—guilty, responsible, indebted—independently of any act or feeling, intention or awareness. For instance, the act of refusing to accept a collect call" (*DD,* 59). At this point, it would appear that such an act had a more sharply contoured volitional aspect than our earlier discussion, which merely had Heidegger pick up the ☎. Derrida writes that he has had to enter a number of calculations in order to reach, if not the ghost of Heidegger, then certainly at least a decision. Was this a decision reached by a historical, unique empirical subject? Did Derrida in effect create a differance in our unfolding drama of telephonic logic by granting himself, in a kind of supplementary stretch of *s'entendre parler,* a space in which to operate as a subject capable of assuming responsibility toward the ☎, in other words, giving himself the possibility and time to decide and say to the phony ☎ call, "I know your number, therefore I do not accept the call"? But, one can argue, in the *Carte postale,* it is not, strictly speaking, the ☎ that called up Derrida. Or, and this amounts to the same *Schuld,* it was only the ☎ and the radicality of a no One on the other end that called Derrida, a ghost represented in the feminine. (In this scene, it can be said that Heidegger *is* represented by an Other in his death.) This is where Weber's discussion helps us radicalize the point we are making, namely, the differance that would have Derrida consulting technology's Operator thoughtfully, and with suspicion's infinite precision. For, as Weber figures it, in *SuZ* Heidegger has Dasein dialing itself (*sich wählen*) without intermediary: "Indeed, it is this ability of direct dialing that determines the possibility of the call, as that which interrupts *Dasein*, recalling it to its *Schuldigsein*" (*DD*, 60). Citing Heidegger, he adds: "The possibility of its thus getting broken off lies in its being appealed to without mediation [*unvermittelt*: unaided]" (*BT*, 271). This is the crux of Weber's argument: "The ineluctability of a certain *Vermittlung*, however—and the word also designates the ☎ *exchange*—is what *La carte postale* is all about. There is no call, no dispatch, no missive, letter, or communication, without a *Vermittlung*; indeed, the former is an effect, and defect of the latter" (*DD*, 60). This will have constituted the remarkable distance that Derrida takes, it would appear, from Heidegger when (not) taking the phantom's call: the distinction between the call of Dasein, recalling its *Schuldigsein*, and the collect call refused in *La carte postale*, is that the call of Dasein takes place, takes its place, ***without the intervention of an operator***. For our purposes, which coincide with those of the ☎'s Dasein, it would be necessary to figure out whether the concept of operator can in fact be seriously dislocated from the very possibility of a ☎ connection, even one made by Dasein, or if the Operator is not already instated in Heidegger's call of conscience. Admittedly, the cord is being twisted a bit, if only in the hope of making the ☎ ring in a perceptibly truer way. The person in the history of the ☎ who last tried to bypass the operator was Mr. Stowger, the gentleman credited with having invented the automatic switch.[37] Somewhat like Dasein,

his primary occupation was that of

undertaker.

The conference call has engaged our subject to the extent that the ☎ participates in the calling structure. Samuel Weber operates both levels of calling simultaneously: resemanticizing the Heideggerian *sich wählen*, Weber installs the ☎ system effortlessly, empowering the call technologically. It is not clear whether such a switch exists—one that would be likely also to turn *off* the generator of technology in Heidegger. And yet, Heidegger is wired even if the cables go underground, perforating the house of Being, remotely, in its untapped corner. Both Derrida and Heidegger take calls, one from the silhouette of the other, and the other from an SA officer. Derrida says something about the call's source which Heidegger, liquid or feminine—martini or Martine—would never have said: "It's a joke." But in naming the call a joke, Derrida has taken it dead seriously. In the space of a deferral he has placed the call, which is to say, he calculated its effects and probable history; he considered it seriously enough to indebt himself to a certain degree and to feel, if nothing else, "obligated." Hence the acquittal footnote. And to have reproduced the necessity of differance within the triangulation of operator, other, and addressee, means that Derrida, having been taken by the call only up to a point, "calculated" the technology of the call in earnest. In fact, Derrida, whose signature in this text is *j'accepte,* can be shown to have refused the call with the same mistrust he expresses for Heidegger's assertion that "science does not think" (*die Wissenschaft denkt nicht*).[38] If Derrida's legendary caution indicates the value he holds for science's thinking—including the potentiality for thinking in technology, but what is called thinking?—this is why he can refuse a call, precisely because a decision has to be made with each technological move on you—in this case, "you" may be an effect or defect of technology. In this respect, all politics of moment withdraw from first place when it comes to the call of technology, losing indeed such claims as are made for their strict anteriority. Technology has come to rule Power: there is a politics of technology which then begins to say, among other things, that politics as such, or ethics, can no longer be considered altogether prior to technology. Politics has become a secondary, derivative form of telecommunications, Power-generated by technology. This is where to start, but it's too soon to blow a fuse. The break in the circuit calling Derrida to Heidegger is not absolute. For while Derrida refuses a call to which he nonetheless pays tributary taxes, the call that he takes and does not take still issues from a certain Heidegger. The call comes from Jacques Derrida and from beyond him. It comes from him because, as he confirms, he was just putting Heidegger's credibility on the line for which the addressee pays in turn by calling in his incredibility. The point is that Heidegger takes to the ☎, even in the fantastical scenario which the footnote feels obliged to report, when his answerability is called to account. Derrida's context is no doubt different from that of our investigation; yet "Heidegger" is resolutely assembled and managed according to a telephonic logic. At any rate, the collect call, too, comes from me and from beyond me, printing out a footnote to itself and inscribing itself in the recognition scene from which the so-called unconscious can say,

"Joke!"

All in all, the question does not amount to a locational one. We are no longer asking where you are calling from but what is calling me from me, demanding my deconstitution while "I" stand by. "Where?" is a primally metaphysical question. Its greatest desire consists in exposing some other world behind the scenes, setting some place up whose locality would be more genuine than what takes place in the neighborhood of the technologized membrane. Presupposing a phenomenality of the "is," a stasis, "where?" is the infinity of what never enters into the present. Instead, the call transfers you to the Other. In this regard, calling might be viewed as perturbing the self's traditional subjection of the Other to itself. This goes counter to mainstream Western philosophy, which traditionally holds the Other to be secondary to the self, the Other *of* the self, the symmetry of self-duplication. Telephonics imposes the recognition of a certain irreducible predecence of the Other with respect to the self.[39] What status of otherness can be ascribed to the Other somehow located in the ☎? The ☎ has no site as its property, which makes it break down the limits of spatiality—this is what makes it uncanny, the inside calling from an internal outside. To what degree has the Other become a technologized command post, perhaps even a recording? The ☎ appears to have procured a subject who in a Lacanian way, may well be headless, but only because the technoid headset doubles for a head that is no longer entirely there. The effects of the assumed apparatus ineluctably reach out and touch the very concepts of subject and Other—the trace "itself" already tending toward the thingification of the Other. And yet, if the ☎ has emerged as a source of epistemic inauguration, as origin of a new deconstitution, then this is

only partially

true and so,

false.

"Now, where were we?" asks the scholar. We shall ourselves follow an exorbitant path from electrical carriers to nocturnal emissions, sheltering our hopes in the neighborhood of poetry, even if that neighborhood should be inclusive of devastated ghettos where schizophrenia speaks in ☎ booths. The way we shall proceed may suggest that something like technology does not dominate our course. This is not the language of technology, in the sense that technology would be placed at an origin of this reflection, or own it as a piece of property, something built onto the house of Being in order to increase the property value in the more secluded neighborhood of thinking. To a large extent, the neighborhood is no longer cut up or sectioned in this way. **The fourfold is undone**, earth has been blown away. No, technology would not be the source or origin of a new insight. This is what Heidegger suggests in the promising words which, in his essay "On the Way to Language," offer that technology itself answers a call. This is why we shall have to plod through an endless "weed garden."   It would have been easier to establish the newly laid ground of technology as our foundation, pretending that nothing were covered over, pushed deeper under our tabula rasa, suppressing an older ecology of reflection. Technology is not simply the ☎ (whose determination as tool, object, implement, equipment, fantasy, superegoical machine, etc., remains uncertain). Rather, technology, too, obeys the law of responding, waiting to answer a call at whose origin one encounters so much static when tracing. We cannot yet answer the question concerning technology except by answering its call—something that does not in itself constitute an answer, a finite, singular outcome or endproduct. If answering the call were the answer, then the question would vanish by it. It would have disappeared, long ago taken over by The Answer. Answering a call does not mean you have the answer. This explains why we have to stay with the call that seeks to pull us in.

In any case the puzzle is nullified. When Martin Heidegger says he took a call, the charge tabulates as "Guilty!" Even though this is not the content nor the meaning nor the signified of the call, as Borch-Jacobsen has argued. At the risk of neutralizing the pain—thinking only negotiates with this possibility—"Guilty!" is the *Hören,* the hearing that corresponds authentically to the call. Hence our need to hear out this call in its duration. ~~In this case, the addressee still pays.~~

✂

Derrida to Freud

The Return Call

□ The telephone, within language, entrusted to transference and translation, is to be plugged in somewhere between science, poesy, and thinking. Inasmuch as it belongs, in its simplest register, to the order of the mechanical and technical, it is already on the side of death. However, the telephone cannot be regarded as a "machine" in the strict sense of classic philosophy, for it is at times "live." Or at least "life" punctually gathers in it and takes part in it. The telephone flirts with the opposition life/death by means of the same ruse through which it stretches apart receiver and transmitter or makes the infinite connection that touches the rim of finitude. □ Like transference, the telephone is given to us as effigy and as relation to absence.[40] At bottom, it asserts an originary nonpresence and alterity. The self, when called into existence, comes to recognize an original self-effacement. Responding to the opening of the first exteriority, the self is prevented from being itself since, as Rodolphe Gasché has demonstrated, the relation to the Other is "older" than selfhood.

Gasché insists upon "the minimal unity of self and Other before all relations between constituted personalities, entities, or identities."[41] If all reference to self takes place by way of a detour through an Other, the self to be itself is traversed, deposited in the Other, reappropriated to itself by some fundamental impurity. The self has been hit by the Other. If the self comes to, it is to be **slapped down again**; call it a violence, loss of the proper, of self-presence, "in truth the loss of what has never taken place, of a self-presence which has never been given but only dreamed of and always already split, repeated, incapable of appearing to itself except in its own disappearance."[42] This relation—of a constituting impurity or alterity, the constituting nonpresence—compellingly resembles what Freud in Derrida's sense called the unconscious: "A certain alterity—to which Freud gives the metaphysical name of the unconscious—is definitively exempt from every process of interpretation by means of which we would call upon it to show itself in person."[43] This is not a hidden, virtual or potential self-presence but an apparatus that sends out delegates, representatives, proxies, phony messages, and obscene calls taken but not essentially put through, often missing their mark. Perhaps that is the end of the analogy referring the unconscious to the telephone, unless both were generally to be understood as that which is inside the subject but which can only be realized in a dimension of outside, that is to say, says Lacan of the one, "in that locus of the Other in which alone it may assume its status."[44] The name of Freud ineluctably slips into the telephone's mouthpiece as when we feel our way along a Moebius strip, a telephone cord, whose logic commands that one will come back mathematically to the surface that is supposed to be its other side. Freud himself attached this story to different strings, resonating ever so delicately with those pulling in Heidegger's little boy. ⊡ Returning in general, disappearance/ reappearance—what was earlier cited as a relation to absence—transferring oneself into an object or placing a call to the not-there, and identifying with it: these motion to the events described by Freud in the now famous *fort/da* analysis. The scene translates as an inversion of the one in *What Is Called Thinking?* where the mother called the boy who would not come home. Here, a few years earlier in the life of a little boy, the mother has gone "outside" (anything that is not at home is out). The child throws the reel to call it back. Like the mother (but Lacan says the reel is not the mother), it is a small part of the subject that detaches itself from him while still remaining his, still retained. Hang on to this detachable part. ⊡ Disappearing like her and making her return along with himself, the child identifies with the long-distance mother. Effecting his own disappearance, he masters himself symbolically, and he makes himself reappear henceforth in his very disappearance, without imaging himself on a mirror, keeping himself (like his mother) on a string, on the wire. Jacques Derrida's reading of this self-appropriative performance is well known. Nonetheless, I would like to recall the explicit scenography he makes by means of the telephone: "[The child] makes himself *re-*, still in accordance with the law of the PP [pleasure principle, grandpa, i.e., Freud], in the grand speculation of a PP that seems never to leave him/itself, nor anyone. This recalling, by telephone or teletype (i.e., voice or writing, from afar), produces the 'movement' by contracting itself, by signing a contract with itself."[45] ⊡ The moment of signing occurred when Freud was himself all strung out, forced technically to repeat a crucial part of his body that, detaching itself, marked the body's opening for a second time—it is at this point that he gets on the line. As Lacan and others have indicated, analytic experience shows that the bodily orifices are linked to the opening/closing of the gap of the unconscious.[46] Now, around 1928, bearing up under great suffering and requiring a second mouthpiece, his prosthesis, Freud writes about three sources of suffering. "We shall never completely master nature," he claims in *Civilization and Its Discontents,* "and our bodily organism, itself a part of that nature, will always remain a transient structure with a limited capacity for adaptation and achievement" (*CD,* 86). With this sense of the enfeebled frame, newly reinforced—by the vision, one might argue, offered by the already technologized body-in-breakdown—Freud's text picks up the telephone. In a way that should remind us both of the pre-Nietzschean mother calling for her little boy and the voice of the friend in Heidegger, Freud, after extolling the "newly-won power over space and time" as well as "the extraordinary advance in the natural sciences and in their technical application," poses a question:

> **One would like to ask: is there, then, no positive gain in pleasure, no unequivocal increase in my feeling of happiness, if I can, as often as I please, hear the voice of a child of mine who is living hundreds of miles away or if I can learn in the shortest possible time after a friend has reached his destination that he has come through a long and difficult journey unharmed? Does it mean nothing that medicine has succeeded in enormously reducing infant mortality and the danger of infection for women in childbirth, etc.? (*CD,* 88)**

☐ Freud relates these technical advances to one another by creating a relay that links infant mortality with the repeated call to a child of mine ("as often as I please"). The call reaches the destination attained by a friend who has undergone a difficult and long journey, and is easily transferred to the diminishing susceptibility of women to infection in childbirth (we are not talking Irma here).[47] Though safeguarding the alterity that is mine (my child, my friend, my wife at childbirth), the telephone and medical technologies still belong to the region beyond the pleasure principle, opening as they do the regime of the repetition compulsion ("as often . . .") within a radically negative count ("no positive gain . . . no unequivocal increase. . . . Does it mean nothing . . .").[48] While the death drive is not explicitly at the wheel, the Ma Bell connection receives confirmation several paragraphs further along when Freud writes, "with the help of the telephone he can hear at distances which would be respected as unattainable even in a fairy tale. Writing was in its origin the voice of an absent person; and the dwelling house was a substitute for the mother's womb, the first lodging, for which in all likelihood man still longs, and in which he was safe and felt at ease" (*CD*, 91). The telephone has exceeded all narrativity, a thing beyond fiction's most self-declaring fiction, the fairy tale, which could not itself reach for the telephone ("would be respected as unattainable even in a fairy tale"). In terms allotted by a primary wish-fulfillment, writing originally was, Freud seems to be suggesting, the telephone. Original writing as telephone engaged the possibility of receiving "the voice of an absent person"—the friend, for instance, who returns a call, having reached a final destination, "his destination." When it attains to the reception hall supplanting a prior "dwelling," the telephone connection, here as in Joyce's evocation, taps back into the womb. The subject, as with the *fort/da* imperative, hooks up with the phenomenon of his own disappearance, located in the belly of the Other. Having just shown how "with every tool man is perfecting his own organs," Freud situates the telephone both as the perfectability of the womb (one of "man's" preferred organs), and as something that conspires with death to install a megaphone from the beyond—a voice reconnecting the "from me" (a child of mine) with the "beyond me" (a final destination) (*CD*, 90). Aurally bound to the telephone, these phantasms disclose the nonexperiential reach of a speculative telephonics whose logic rests on the unattended events of birth and the subject's expiration. Inasmuch as Freud traces the telephone to these primal nonscenes, this somewhat monsterized organ out-fairy tales the fairy tale. ☐ Now, the "beyond me" organizes the divinized region from where a technology of long-distance calling stems. Long ago an ideal conception was formed of omnipotence and omniscience which man, writes Freud, embodied in his gods. Reaching for the major amplifications of the telephone, "today he has come very close to the attainment of this ideal, he has almost become a god himself" (*CD,* 91). The "almost" in this sentence provides a space for a somewhat striking difference, marking the incompletion of any subject's ration of infinity. Freud's rhetoric does not depict man attaining a "poore inch" of self-inflating divinity; rather, the detachable tool itself is inspired with divinity. Only the "almost" belongs to man, whereas the "become a god himself" attaches properly to his "auxiliary organs": "Man has, as it were, become a kind of prosthetic God. When he puts on all his auxiliary organs he is truly magnificent" (*CD,* 91–92). Is God the dream of absolute technology? Made in his image and sound systems, man adorns himself with a mass of artificial supplement disguised as divinity. □ At this point the editor of *Civilization and Its Discontents,*[49] James Strachey, adds a footnote, itself a kind of prosthetic device, stating that "a prosthesis is the medical term for an artificial adjunct to the body, to make up for some missing or inadequate part: e.g.

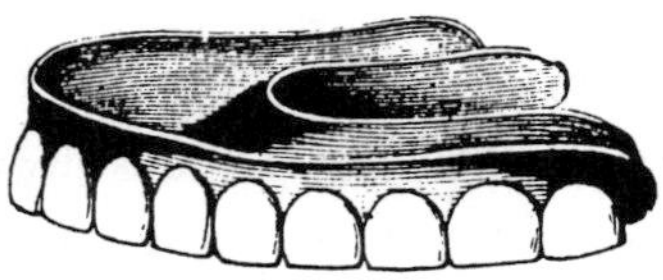

or a false leg." What is missing to render man godlike can be supplied therefore by a technological extension cord to the body's natural, "transient structure." The prosthesis, capable of surviving the body which it in part replaces, acts already as a commemorative monument to the dissolution of a mortal coil. This godlike annexation to a certain extent enjoys the status of the fetish, covering a missing or inadequate body part, amplifying the potentiality of a constitutively fragile organ. ⊡ As has been the case with all such infinitizing inventions (one thinks of the works of Edison, Bell, or Dr. Frankenstein), the fulfillment of a fairy-tale wish, coming very close in omnipotent sway to a god, emerges from a traumatized zone to establish some form of restitutional services: the typewriter originally intended for the blind, the gramophone for the deaf, the telephone clandestinely for those afflicted with speech and hearing impediments.[50] Nor was Freud spared such divine depletion when, writing on discontent, his mouth had taken on an "almost godlike" quality, being sheer mouthpiece, prosthetically annexed. But as long as those technological adjuncts remain lodged in their difference, resisting a true replacement of the failing organ, there will exist no possibility of a complete implant-incorporation of the divine thing. Historically, man still belongs to the regime of the "almost" godlike. Thus by restricting his predicament to time's most trivial calculator, Freud offers a consolation prize, conjuring an image of a future telephone system that would take root, growing, as it were, from within the body. "But those organs have not grown on to him and they still give him much trouble at times. Nevertheless, he is entitled to console himself with the thought that this development will not come to an end precisely with the year 1930 A.D." (*CD,* 88). The A.D. registers the advent of another dating system after death. But it also commits itself to the promise of a future evolution to succeed the deluded misfitting in the thirties of the early phase of supertechnical powers on the rise. ⊡ Freud's reading of the body in godlike annexation, whose phantasmatic order deduces durable electric organs for the body's future, anticipates McLuhan's understanding of fundamental autoamputation. "With the arrival of electric technology," writes McLuhan, "man extended, or set outside himself, a live model of the central nervous system itself."[51] Perhaps the most compelling aspect of this observation resides in its philosophical imputations, bringing to the fore a problematics switched on by "the arrival of electric technology." Why does McLuhan claim that electric technology produces a *live* model? It is true that we speak of a live wire. Will "life" have been submitted to a highly modified reading under the new regime? The contaminations are immense, and it may be that McLuhan points to a borrowing system through which determining structures are leased, for example, from dead batteries. This death is not finite but can be recharged. ⊡ In McLuhan's writing, the "nervous system itself" often suggests the *Ding an sich*. Still, the *live* model of the electric switchboard sounds more like a constative statement about Frankenstein's monster than anything else. This is not bad, since electric currents no doubt compel scrambling devices to recode the philosophical opposition of life/death, body/machine. "To the degree that this is so, it is a development that suggests a desperate and suicidal autoamputation, as if the central nervous system could no longer depend on the physical organs to be protective buffers against the slings and arrows of outrageous mechanism."[52] It would seem that the critique of technology depends for its sustenance upon a Shakespearean line rerouted—Hamlet is the one confronted with a ghost of himself, with technology and the name of a losing economy. *Understanding Media* develops a hermeneutics of despair, linking up the rapport to technology with a grammar of shock absorption and loss. As if the work of technological desire encapsulated an electric version of the work of mourning, McLuhan continues: "There is a close parallel of response between the patterns of physical and psychic trauma or shock. A person suddenly deprived of loved ones and a person who drops a few feet unexpectedly will both register shock. Both the loss of family and a physical fall are extreme instances of amputations of the self."[53] Like other live electric extensions, the telephone will be entered into this shock registry of *Understanding Media*. In this way, the text offers tracings of the telephone's genealogy which originates in "the loss of family" and "a physical fall." The question of whose alarm we still respond to or whose unconscious is wrapped tightly in the coils of the telephone will be taken up momentarily as we work our way down the umbilical. ☐ In the meantime, both Freud and McLuhan share the project of elaborating a *techné* of autoamputation. For Freud this involves a moment of acknowledging separation from a child of mine. If he wants to hear the voice of a departed child, he can attach his ear to a receiver; if he wants a godlike prosthesis doubling for the one covering his wound, he can speak into a mouthpiece. The telephone furnishes a singular place for calling forth and hearing: in this sense it exceeds the relatively hubristic range of the fairy tale and the granting powers of a fairy-godmother's wand. It evokes the sheltering dwelling of a perfected womb. Finally, in the examples enlisted by Freud and McLuhan, it also appears to annex the limbs, thus implementing the at-handedness of the call. McLuhan introduces the shock paradigm of "dropping a few feet unexpectedly" (it remains unclear as to how much control the author exercises over his rhetoric: the statement about dropping feet comes in the context of autoamputation), and Freud somewhat similarly puts a foot forward to estimate the losses incurred by the telephone. Tallying up the net profit, forfeits, and write-offs exacted by the technological extension, Freud takes a call from the voice of pessimism: "But here the voice of pessimistic criticism makes itself heard and warns us that most of these satisfactions follow the model of the 'cheap enjoyment' extolled in the anecdote—the enjoyment obtained by putting a bare leg from under the bedclothes on a cold winter night and drawing it in again" (*CD,* 88). ☐ The economy of the cheap thrill seems to come from out of the bedclothes in the form of a leg extended to test the threshold of exteriority. The pleasure comes cheap insofar as its discovery takes place in negativity, being reactively dependent upon a cold winter's night to know itself. The body's limb momentarily self-extends beyond the zone of comfortable closure to

SEQ 021 JOB TEL- 108-16 PAGE-007
REVISED 12JUN89 AT 18:11 BY MJ DEPTH: 0 PICAS WIDTH 34 PICAS
Galley 7

meet, in the blindness of telephonic night, the biting cold. The "cheap enjoyment" actually covers over the cost of anxiety's epistemological retreat, for the leg of Freud that protrudes beyond the clothes to be nipped, retreats in blindness from the memory of castration anxiety. Always ready to kick up metonymically, the bare leg suffers from exposure—but what it suffers is enjoyment. ☐ The leg that he in the inserted anecdote draws back should never have left the cover, like the child for which the telephone extension became a sorry substitute. The voice of pessimism has more to say:

> *If there had been no railway to conquer distances, my child would never have left his native town and I should need no telephone to hear his voice. . . . What is the use of reducing infantile mortality when it is precisely that reduction which imposes the greatest restraint on us in the begetting of children, so that, taken all round, we nevertheless rear no more children than in the days before the reign of hygiene, while at the same time we have created difficult conditions for our sexual life in marriage, and have probably worked against the beneficial effects of natural selection? And finally, what good to us is a long life if it is difficult and barren of joys, and if it is so full of misery that we can only welcome death as a deliverer?* (*CD,* 88)

Beyond the bad sex which technical hygiene seems to have imposed, the calculation articulated by pessimism's voice appears to be commuted to the irresoluble loss of a child, whether the sum be the result of infantile mortality or indeed whether one regresses, as in Oedipus's answer, to the elder infant who would be delivered into another world by death. ⊡ It seems reasonable to say that the pessimistic voice calls in the telephone principally as the effect of a prior loss whose recuperation can be partially accomplished, if only to mark the drama of an unprecedented long distance. Freud's argument sums up the comfort afforded by the telephone as the effect, in fact, of the losses for which it stands. Initially, his reckoning tended to accumulate a sense of profit, fitting a posture of gratitude toward the prosthetic God we have projected. But this amounts to the gratitude felt toward a reprieve, shaky and unstable, which briefly functions as a simulacrum of that which is no longer there while it also announces its not being there. On both ends of the line there is the departed infant, connected to itself by the imaginary. The principles of addition and subtraction, informing both the prosthetic application and the pleasure/suffering yields, resolves itself on the side of subtraction, if adding the losses can be subsumed under general subtraction. The problem is that technical advances multiply needs, hence their self-engendering character (the telephone to make up for the transfer of pain conducted through the railroad, etc.). The more advances are made, the deeper the wound of renunciation.

Renunciation and cultural conquest go hand in hand in a footnote Freud added in 1932 to these passages. Engaging the issue of original toolmaking, the footnote directs itself to controlling fire. The example illustrates the way losses are to be accounted for, but because flames have tongues, fire control overlaps with a praxis of rumor control. This, too, works along the lines of containment.

> It is as though ***primal*** man had the habit, when he came in ***contact*** with fire, of satisfying an infantile de***sire con***nected with it, by putting it out with ***a stream*** of his urine. The legends that we pos***sess leave*** no doubt about the originally phal***lic view*** taken of tongues of flame as they shoot ***upwards***. Putting out fire by micturating—***a theme*** to which modern giants, Gulliver ***in Lilliput*** and Rabelais' Gargantua, still ***hark back***—was therefore a kind of sexual act ***with a*** male, an enjoyment of sexual potency ***in a homo***sexual competition. The first per***son to re***nounce this desire and spare the fire ***was able to*** carry it off with him and subdue ***it to his own*** use. By damping down the fire of ***his own sex***ual excitation, he had tamed the ***natural forces*** of fire. This great cultural conquest ***was thus*** the reward for his renunciation ***of instinct***. Further, it is as though woman ***had been*** appointed guardian of the fire which ***was held*** captive on the domestic hearth, be***cause her*** anatomy made it impossible for her ***to yield*** to the temptation of this desire. (*CD*, 90)

What bears some interest upon our discussion, though this passage merits a more suspicious reading, concerns those acts subduing phallic tongues, and the way one learns to put out the fire shooting from the mouth of the earth. This movement, beginning with a certain structure of naturality which then gets translated into another ostensibly containable currency, suggests a second-phase disjunction that transfers a naturality of voice, afforded by proximity, into electricity, or what then was called electric speaking. Freud points to three levels of subduing action related to this legendary originality. They tend to retire any easy notions concerning captivity. Woman, prisoner of her anatomy cage, tends to the fire held captive. But submission is no easy thing. For if the fire held captive by the captive woman has indeed proven containable, this is because in the first place the phallus was subdued, so that the phallic tongues will have been assimilated to the woman, tamed and kept low under her supervision. Beyond the scene of multiplied captivity within which one anatomy encapsulates another, and whose minimal episode involves the anatomy of a dwelling place, the major difference asserted in this passage appears to be set forth between zoning laws legislating outside and inside, or more precisely, public and private. Giving up the public contest among the many phallic tongues, man, subdued, retreats into a space governed by private, inwardly turned, and largely feminized tongues. The movement repelling homosexual publicity toward a feminized domesticity, which in fact preserves the man, comes about after the "fire of his own sexual excitation" has been damped. ⊡ The woman, appointed guardian of the dephallicized tongues, will have been henceforth structurally bound to "being there." The scene reports the difference Lacan maintains: men have the phallus (hence the anxiety of dispossession), while women *are* the phallus. Except that one never seems able to "have" the phallus in the first place (assuming such a place exists). ⊡ Turning down but sparing the fire, restraining himself from competing with the phallus which threatens to consume and destroy him, the man takes it home with him, to tame it. But in order to bring it in he has to put it out—and this fire that he puts out is the one within, the "fire of his own sexual excitation," but also the feminized other, engulfing, and which by dint of renunciation, he can piss on. The fire spared, the spent man will be brought inside, which is the starting point of the domestic: "This great cultural conquest [of fire, of femininity] was thus the reward for his renunciation of instinct." The fire, inside, under control, will not spread to an infinite outside; the woman has been appointed guardian of its captivity, two subdued entities sitting watch over one another, trimming the silhouette of an original couple equally tamed. Technology would be responsible for this scene of sublimated interior decorating, promoting the internalizing primacy of the dwelling place. Everything is to be brought in. The outside is to be located, colonized, contracted; and so the telephone, to recruit our example from its station, was advertised as the "annihilator of space," the conquest of savage intensities. Technoculture can barely abide an outside. Nor certainly an outside that stays out all night. Thus Freud's footnote on the renunciation of instinct falls under the "activities and resources which are useful to men for making the earth serviceable to them. . . . If we go back far enough, we find that the first acts of civilization were the use of tools, the gaining of control over fire and the construction of dwellings" (*CD,* 90). Arising with the fire whose place is now in the kitchen, the question on the tips of the flamed tongues, always prepared to ignite and spread, concerns the movement in which interiorization and instinctual renunciation become coconstitutive. The tongues, as with the suppressed instinct, fall silent. The concept of an inside has been won technologically; space and libido, contracted (by marriage). ⊡ If gaining control, self-mastery, and some dominion over alterity motivate original toolmaking, would this schema suitably define the electric speech of the telephone? Would it too constitute a thing carried into some identifiable inside to subdue the tongues of exteriority—for example, those still heard by schizophrenics, paranoiacs, or prophets in the desert? As we shall observe, schizophrenics in particular maintain a high level of externalized polytelephony. At this intermediary space between the outside and inside of the subject, will a certain voice have been subdued? To what extent—this question would be the consequence of Freud's logic—does the telephone, as trophy for a forgotten instinct, commemorate its renunciation? If the telephone's being-in-the-world has been guided by a protocol of renunciation, we still need to read the terms of the contract.

Perhaps this would be the time to recall the Freudian paradigm of knowing, which is always shown to be related to the essential possibility of being cut off, disconnected and, in the first place from the mother. Disconnection occurs whether the subject is to be construed as a little girl or boy, but more difficultly, it is said, for the little boy, from himself as his mother. This is what leaves the mother in Heidegger, and Freud, to endlessly attempt reconnection—as the operator who acknowledges the blindness of the other.

The child comes to know what is not there, what essentially fails the identity test. The story is fairly well known: in order to arrive at this knowledge which the subject does not want to know, he, like Prometheus, steals something from above; in this case, the child is said to have stolen a glance at the mother's genitals to find what cannot be found, namely, a piece of himself, the not-thereness of the mother's penis. The child "sees" what cannot as such be seen; his relation to the mother fills with the abundant lighting of blindness, he sees that in order to "see" the mother, he must renounce seeing her within the field of visual perception. The stolen glance, therefore, as the object of scopic transgression not his own, discloses the mother as that which does not have a "thing." The child's response to the nothing that he nevertheless sees—and which must be familiar, since it emerges like a ghost of what is found missing—is to assign its meaning to this body. What he sees is what he gets.

Station identification:

the child is made to *identify* with mother through this perceptual break. He classically understands this body as the potentiality for the future of his own disconnectability—his own disintegration into being-as-tool, or in Freud's vocabulary, "castration anxiety."

The point that can be newly urged issues from the telephonic lesson promoted in Freud's epistemological paradigm of sexual difference. In order to see what cannot be seen—both as prohibition and perceptual retreat—the child steals a glance, diverting the predominant mode of relatedness to the mother, which, supported by a mouthpiece and a receiver, is the breast offered to the child, the voice, as Joyce saw it, which he sucks in.[54] This voice will in a way become dephenomenalized eventually to the point of resembling Heidegger's aphonic call of conscience. However, in the meantime, the child's early lesson in anxiety (and the call of conscience takes place at anxiety's reception desk) induces a retreat of visual perception, a punishment for a kind of nontelephonic hermeneutics of the mother. Looking at the mother in her not-thereness, however, implies that the telephone connection has never really been severed but is rather fundamentally organized thereby. For what a child sees, were he to look behind the empirical curtains covering the "thing" in its not-being-there, comes down to something like an invaginated ear, or lips forming a mouth. Where he was looking for an image of his own penis, he finds that the mother has instead another mouth—a mouthpiece and a receiver that have been kept in reserve, hidden, and virtually silent. We say virtually silent because Freud and others have heard the womb calling back the child. According to these sources, the second mouth never stops calling.

Within this perceptual paradox of seeing not what is there in its materiality but what is missing, whatever the child does or does not see educates him toward a different register of representation, whose stress, by definition, can no longer be visual where the maternal is concerned (little Hans learns this lesson exclusively at his mother's side, as he has reportedly "seen" his little sister's penis). The lesson of the mother's silent other mouth teaches to close one's eyes and to listen inwardly, to start probing the mute mouth-ear of the mother's obscurity—as, indeed, Alexander Graham Bell was bound to do. . . . .

. . . . There is something magical about the penis disappearing in the mother (this disappearing act supplies a crucial stage of the Wolf Man case). The maternal constitutes the space of the other's disappearance, the epistemology of not seeing. Understanding the telephone as medium implies the risk of retrieving its magical moment—for instance, when in its Sturm und Drang period, it shared a profound complicity with the function of a medium. Offering itself as a supplementary globule which absorbs excessive sight, it claims a complexity whose access code is manipulated by a multiply veiled and knowing woman. The crystal ball, glass eye, substituting for man's sight, prevailed at the time the telephone was about to speak. In other words, with technology, the field of knowing what is not there competes with a presencing of a supernatural femininity at the technical controls, seeing through the translucency of crystal, telephoning in visions from the beyond. What seems significant in this scene reverts less to an oddball mysticism than to a certain rapport to a nonphenomenal seeing in which something like a *Geschick* can be divined in the feminine.

The somewhat occulted foundations of psychoanalysis and telephony in magic require further study. / **priority call. Pick up #362.**

In historico-technocological terms, this means a look at the mostly subdued feminine underside of technological desire, whose emblazoned tongue has in part been turned down. The call for technology may well be figured in the feminine, by which we also understand man's feminine repressed. As for psychoanalysis and telephony, they share a notion of certain séances which will have to be brought to light (in French, the word for a psychoanalytic session is indeed "séance"). This eerie voice will be picked up at the other end, a kind of deep end from which Thomas Watson, who attended nightly séances and apparently made successful connections to the dead, began cooperating on the invention of the telephone. In the meantime, the orthodox view of the session is well known. It required the retreat of the analyst into the position of an ear that occasionally responds; in short, early psychoanalysis advanced an ear-mouth connection so that the unconscious might be hooked up and encouraged to speak. As classical pedagogy, as something that ought to be cannily transmissible and passed along, psychoanalysis defines its practice essentially as unteachable, basing its epistemological acquisitions on hearsay and, in Lacan's practice, also as "sleight of hand."[56] To tie up some of these loosened wires, it is useful to note that the question of sight-retreat and of unconscious transmissions is articulated in psychoanalysis in terms citing a telephonics, that is, according to a problematics of putting through calls from the unconscious, always subject to being cut off. When Lacan "call[s] upon the subject to reenter himself in the unconscious," he adds "—for, after all, it is important to know *whom* one is calling."[57] The telephone lines of psychoanalysis are endlessly open, beginning with the cap of the unconscious that the analyst offers to the analysand, "wie der Receiver des Telephons zum Teller eingestellt ist."[58] The two unconsciouses are to operate as a single telephonic unit, advises

Freud, hooking up certain telepathic channels with the technical skills of an engineer. As skilled as he is, however, the engineer often finds himself working blindly.

—//—

The power of vision, held in suspense by magic, psychoanalysis, and telephony, has not yet undergone a health check. Freud claims that vision can be disrupted by something like **AN INTERNALLY PUNISHING VOICE**. The voice gets the upper hand, shutting down visual apprehension, when the eye is felt to be abusing its "organ of sight for evil, sensual pleasures." Before we see the voice slapping down eyelids, we must wonder whether the telephone line, when psychoanalyzed, still carries remnants of self-punishment in the form of a necessary institution between two subjects of distance and loss of sight. What if the law of long distance dictated all sorts of prohibitions that we have largely forgotten or internalized? Or, in a similar vein, what if long distance were already the effect of a prohibition, operating along the lines of renunciations which the telephone has called forth? In the first place, visual instincts succumb to another organic coalition. Perhaps the ghostly dimmer belongs to some sort of legal pact that one has concluded with oneself clandestinely.

In a paper written as a contribution to a festschrift in honor of Leopold Königstein, a well-known Viennese opthalmologist who was one of his oldest friends, Freud asserts that "the psychogenic disturbances of vision depend on certain ideas connected with seeing being cut off from consciousness."[59] This cut-off point occurs when the ego swiftly rejects ideas that have come into opposition with other, more powerful ones. The signals have filtered through so that the entire mechanism of ideational rejection results in blindness. The predicament of being cut off gathers strength from its telephone modality. We can translate this phenomenon back into the idiom of telephonic repression as follows: the disconnection, effected by repression, takes place when the ego hangs up abruptly on ideas that have come into opposition to other, more powerful ones. Nonetheless the call had been put through, which in itself represents for the ego a symptomatological problem, in this case inducing a hysterical blindness. Assigning this spontaneous assumption of blindness to the repression of erotic scopophilia, Freud reminds us of an unrepressed fact: "Psychoanalysts never forget that the mental is based on the organic, although their work can only carry them as far as this basis and not beyond it."[60] Linked to an organ with a double claim on it, the disturbance gives rise in turn to an internal voice command. "As regards the eye," writes Freud, "we are in the habit of transplanting the obscure psychical processes concerned in the repression of sexual scopophilia and in the development of the psychogenic disturbance of vision as though a punishing voice was speaking from within the subject, and saying: 'Because you sought to misuse your organ of sight for evil sensual pleasures, it is fitting that you should not see anything at all any

more. . . . The idea of talion punishment is involved in this, and in fact our explanation of psychogenic visual disturbance coincides with what is suggested by myths and legends."[61] Resorting to an example, Freud cites Lady Godiva "and how the only man who peeped through the shutters at her revealed loveliness was punished by blindness."[62]

Freud's argument implies the rezoning of **PHALLO-CENTRAL PLEASURE**, revealing a spreading network of erotic localities which the psyche tries to check. Self-punishing desexualization of the body's topography emerges from "an organ with a dual function":

extract

Sexual pleasure is not attached merely to the function of the genitals. The mouth serves for kissing as well as for eating and communication by speech; the eyes perceive not only alterations in the external world which are important for the preservation of life, but also characteristics of objects which lead to their being chosen as objects of love—their charms (*Reize,* which means both "charms" and "stimuli"). The saying that it is not easy for anyone to serve two masters

/ priority call. Pick up #382.

is thus confirmed. The closer the relation into which an organ with a dual function of this kind enters with *one* of the major instincts, the more it withholds itself from the other. . . . It is easy to apply this to the eye and to seeing.[63]

In the history of philosophy the dual-functioning organ was

poignantly named by Hegel, and later commented by Kierkegaard. The former understood the penis to be in "contradiction" with the vagina, performing as it does the two essentially opposing tasks of producing semen and piss (*Piß*), generative substance and waste product.[64] Properly interpreted, this sublates into the concept (*Begriff*) for Hegel.

The penis, however, doesn't really have a choice about hosting oppositional forces, whereas other organs are more volitionally oriented. Such is the case of the mouth, argues Freud, and it is "easy to apply this to the eye and to seeing."[65] In order to escape serving two masters, the pertinent organs can translate themselves into monotheistical servants, obeying the dictates of a single master desire. This creates a toxic shock of sorts: "Indeed, if we find that an organ normally serving the purpose of sense-perception begins to behave like an actual genital when its erotogenic role is increased, we shall not regard it as improbable that *toxic* changes are also occurring in it."[66] One can begin to see how an eye might turn inward to reemerge as a prosthetic god, attaching its blindness to a mouth-earpiece.

The extent to which the telephone feeds into the psychogenic disturbance of which Freud writes, or in fact simulates it, needs to be seriously considered. Understanding the organ *as such,* in its singular unity, still remains to be determined. But the kind of organ which the telephone duplicates, replaces, or protects may itself be subject to multiple displacements (psychoanalysis has argued convincingly for the symbolic exchangeability of anus and ear, for instance). If, by this logic, the telephone begins to behave like "an actual genital," we may be opening the shutters on the scandal which accompanied its conception. The courts had to determine whether the telephone amounted to an instrument of seduction and entry. Thus, in New England, a group of Puritans fought to have its material placement legally restricted. They sought law enforcement for the telephone's eviction from the bedroom. To deny the telephone's libidinal claims would be tantamount to disowning infantile sexuality. The telephone's sexuality has not been explored, though allusions nowadays are made to it in underground journals, minitel advertisements, and a section of *Cien Años de Teléfono en España* entitled "Interviene—¿como no?—el amor." In one elegiac moment it is stated that "Il disco llamador es la magica margarita mécanica."[67]

The consequences are considerable. Let us, for the sake of clarity, condense the telephone into a single supplementary organ, the mouth-ear. Supposing this organ were to exceed its "intentional" function—this, like Hegel's penis can be double, involving waste product and inseminative force, chatter and "high thought." If the telephone deviated from its ostensibly proper and intended usage, began to mime an actual genital, then according to Freud's reading, it has to be subject to the rule of the superego. Of course, the telephone may be the conceptual result of improper organ usage. The telephone would be the surplus and the deficit accruing to unconscious mismanagement of a bodily organ. The point, which will pass itself into the telephone's invention, remains unaltered: if it projects itself as a dual-functioning organ, then the telephone, because of its split personality, requires strict legislation. The legislation, however, can only come from the same, though not identical, place. This requirement, whose itinerary follows Freud's schema, installs the telephone as voice in the position of legislator. In fact, we are witnessing how Freud has set up the question which finds its articulation in Heidegger's interrogation of the call. Once the superego takes the reins, we are in legal

territory. Witnesses take the stand, judgments are passed, verdicts announced. In sum, an ethics demands a hearing. The collusion discovered by Freud, between a voice of judgment and hysterical blindness, requires us to ask how this is negotiated by the telephone. To what degree has one blinded oneself on the telephone, and according to which valuation of blindness's farsighted range (as insight, knowledge and the refusal to know, obtuseness, etc.)? So far, it looks like the telephone insistently calls in a certain degree of blindness, whether this be empirical, ethical, or epistemological. This seems indisputable. However, at the same time, before anything is said, it, like the punitive voice or voice of conscience, appears to make ethically clear statements to the subject. These statements may not be attached to a signified. They come in the form of a demand or ethical posture. There is no call that does not call forth responsible responsiveness. Has it then perhaps inherited the receptive vocal cords of Kant's categorical imperative? Still, the invasive force of the call can be so great as to induce hysterical blindness, canceling all ethical systems momentarily. The call may announce itself as a punitive voice, itself a response to blindness. Yet, as in Kafka's "Before the Law," the call fixes its jurisdiction and site with the promise of gradual blindness for the self-summoning subject.[68]

///

///

///

///

///

///

///

///

///

/

The Nervous Breakdown

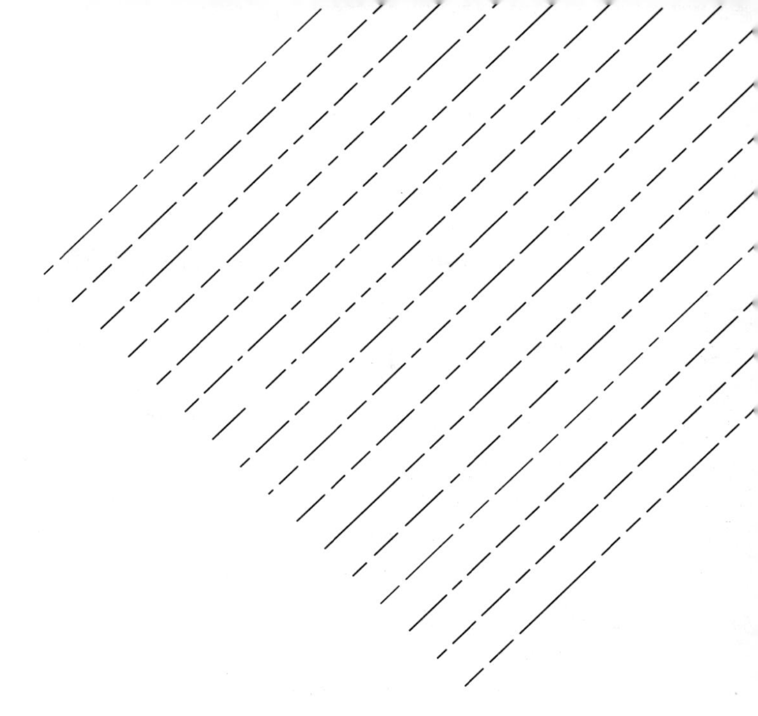

We have to cut the shit.

Or perhaps you have not understood. It is no longer a question of adducing causes to the telephone, assigning its place, and recognizing in it a mere double and phantom of an organ (like Woman, reduced to the phantom of a missing organ). This would be much, and much that is engaging: the phone as a missing mouth, displaced genital, a mother's deaf ear or any number of M.I.A.–organs such as the partial object-ear transmitting and suturing the themes of *Blue Velvet.* Put through the body-slicing machine, the telephone will have become an organ without body. But "without body"—what is this? The ear, eye, even skin, have been divested of authority as they acquire technical extension and amplification in media.[69] All this belongs to our subject. But the radicality of the transaction takes place to the extent that technology has broken into the body (every body: this includes the body politic and its internal organs, i.e., the security organs of state). The somaticizations that a neurotic might chart are little compared with the electric currents running through the schizonoiac body. Hitting the lights on Reich's contention, we read: "With respect to their experiencing of life, the neurotic patient and the perverted individual are to the schizophrenics as the petty thief is to the daring safecracker."[70] The schizophrenic gives us exemplary access to the fundamental shifts in affectivity and corporeal organization produced and commanded by technology, in part because the schizophrenic inhabits these other territorialities, "more artificial still and more lunar than that of Oedipus."[71] In the cases we are consulting, the telephone occupies a privileged position, being installed, in Jung's case, in the patient's body, from where it extends a partial line to the receiving doctor. The telephone has been the schizonoiac's darling, calling to itself zomboid subjects who, in the early days of telephony, lined up to discuss with Bell and Watson the telephone operators, exchange numbers, and circuitry threaded in their heads. Telephony suited the migratory impulse spanning indivisible distances, and, permitting them to escape the puerile, reactionary dragnet of psychiatric wisdom, it donated structures of disconnection and close-range long distance. "The schizo knows how to leave: he has made departure into something as simple as being born or dying. But at the same time his journey is strangely stationary, in place. He does not speak of another world."[72] *Anti-Oedipus* describes the schizo as "trans-alivedead, transparentchild," transsexual, a subject alongside a machine. The withdrawal into a body-without-organs "that has become deaf, dumb and blind" does not make schizophrenia the clean-cut other of the normally constituted subject, however.[73] The concept itself of a "normally *functioning* human being"—one equipped, so to speak, with proper shock absorbers for enduring interruption and pain—and *conversely, within this normativity, the concept of breakdown,* demonstrate the effects of wiring systems. (The very possibility of "having" a nervous breakdown can be traced to structures borrowed by the so-called psyche from advanced machinery, a historical transaction of massive rhetorical, affective, and bodily shifts.) Desire has been rerouted, computerized, electrocuted, satellited according to a wholly other rhetorical order. And thus the field under investigation, whose floodlights are power-generated by schizonoia, ought to concern the engulfing transformation of the human subject into a technologized entity.

In their work on schizophrenia, Deleuze and Guattari at one point explain a type of interruption or break characteristic of the desiring machine—the residual break (*coupure-reste*) or residuum—which produces a subject alongside the machine, functioning as a part adjacent to *the machine.*[74] With what intensity have these chips of *coupure-reste* been generally internalized so that one has been programmed to respond in certain ways to equally programmed events? "Internalized" cannot belong here as the inner/outer dimensions of a self begin no doubt to constitute part of an accelerated obsolescence. To plug in the electrical currency of the epochal shift it becomes necessary prior to any reading of the desire that called forth prosthetic gods, to undertake an exploration of the extent to which we have become effects of technology. Because it is entirely possible that reading such a desire is already programmed by the technology in question. And if technology will not be limited to a reactionary grasp of science but expands to fill a space of art and dissimulation, then the hallucinated fantasy to which it owes its existence also invites a reading.

{ It is not clear how to call it, in the sense that an umpire calls a play. As with the question regarding the Call and the Called, we echo this acoustical shadow, a remembered line in identity crisis when, apropos of Kafka, Derrida writes that "neither identity nor non-identity is natural, but rather the effect of a juridical performative."[75] Psychoanalysis was not sure how to call it or whether to legislate the disruptive tropes of schizophrenia's self-constitution. Deleuze and Guattari chalk this up to the schizo's resistance to being oedipalized. Freud doesn't like them, argue Deleuze and Guattari, for in the first place they mistake words for things. Furthermore, they are apathetic, narcissistic, cut off from reality, incapable of achieving transference; they resemble philosophers. The problem of securing an identity for the schizophrenic condition or singularizing its aspect occurs even in the subtitle of *Anti-Oedipus,* which couples schizophrenia with capitalism by the conjunction "and." Always connected to something else and to another calling, schizophrenia is never itself but invariably put through by an operator. The schizophrenic subject insists on this, as does the philosopher who hazards the problematic unity of clinical and critical discourse. What *Anti-Oedipus* argues may involve a predicament of even more general intensity than the authors suggest, however. The restrictions placed on schizophrenia seem strangely under capitalism's sole surveillance, in a constricting space "artificial." We view the phenomenon as being largely ascribable to technology in general, and not solely to capitalist production, though these often present invaginating rather than opposing structures. This, precisely, is why we need time out before calling it.

{ Schizophrenia never had an easy access code. It (in the plural) could not be presented in its singularity—though that, in a sense, is what it's "about." In the preface to his pioneering work *Dementia Praecox oder Gruppe der Schizophrenien* (*Dementia praecox or group of schizophrenias,* 1911), Professor E. Bleuler makes the opening statement: "Knowledge of the group of illnesses, which Kraeplin has gathered together under the name of dementia praecox is too young for us to give, at this early stage, a closed description thereof."[76] In a sense, then, still too young, at the blossom of its youth, the study of dementia praecox is shown to be too precocious to form as yet a system of closure; it exhibits resistance to totalization. The terms of the felt precocity are spelled out by Bleuler as "zu jung." These words resonate prophetically for any commencement by way of Jung; can a field *become zu Jung,* that is, too Jungian? Dementia praecox "or" schizophrenia are attuned to inquiry relatively late in psychiatric history. In a streaming way, the lines of inquiry are opened with the aid of a hidden telephone, linking up systems of auditory hallucination to the very concept of voice, which often overlays the voice speaking from different topoi of the self (for example, in terms of high-psychoanalysis, the hookup to the superego or other regions of aphonic calls).

{ An object of considerable dispute, provoking valuation wars ("the great artist scales the schizophrenic wall"),[77] "schizophrenia" put psychoanalysis on guard. While the term has largely been accepted in psychiatry, the history of schizophrenia is rooted in disagreements about its nature and, correspondingly, about its extension as a nosological category. Distinguished by three forms—the hebephrenic, the catatonic, and the paranoid—the condition fell victim to striated voices wanting to identify it and was itself turned over to schizophrenizing acts of naming. When it came to baptizing the disorder, "dementia praecox" often took the upper hand, though Freud ascribed more saying power to the term "paraphrenia," which could be paired up with "paranoia," stressing both the unity of the field of the psychoses and its division into two fundamental types. Pontalis characterizes one aspect of schizophrenia by emphasizing the predominance of the process of repression, or of withdrawal of cathexis from reality, over the tendency toward reconstruction. The primary thought disturbance emerges with a loosening of associations induced by disconnecting interceptors. Schizophrenia seems to disconnect quite haphazardly, sometimes cutting simple threads, sometimes an entire group or large units of thought. Due to actions taken by demonic operators, certain connections are simply not made, while others are interrupted or transferred to other posts. There are also ambitious schizophrenics, contends Pontalis, and these dream only of their desires; obstacles simply do not exist for them. This is part of the same system of dealing with the operator by bypassing her through the automatic switch. Like doubles of technology, they immediately gain access everywhere—no roadblocks or policing operators, who they invisibly run down on automatic switch. Psychoanalysis approaches schizo-dementia-paraphrenia-praecox largely by treating it diffidently; it is in a broad sense made fragile by schizophrenia, which it frankly expulses from its knowing about itself. Where does it resist? Is the ejection button at hand because psychoanalysis in some radical way is implicated in this predicament which at once it must and cannot confront?

{ An exponent of this malaise, Jung's classic study quickly and consistently falls into default; he cannot stop apologizing for not knowing what he is doing, he signs off by offering that "someone had to take it on himself to get the ball rolling," hoping that future countersignatories will help him untangle some of the scrambled semantics he has recorded, finding himself tossed into what he claims on a number of occasions his patients come up with, namely, a "word salad."[79] Generally speaking, the word salad which afflicts Jung—we'll get to the head of this lettuce momentarily—evokes a phobia shared by psychoanalysis and the schizo. It is as if the two were playing telephone with one another, garbling transmissions that cannot be made to stop. But schizonoia may have a direct impact on the way psychoanalysis forms a recording surface. Let's rewind and play. Freud says we can gain cognition by hearsay of that which psychoanalysis achieves. In other words—it is only a matter of other words—by reports of what takes place behind closed doors (of the unconscious, of the session). These reports of what psychoanalysis tells itself can be passed on through lines of rumorological paranoia. We know something of psychoanalysis by the distortions (*Entstellungen*) that attempt to report on it. In the *New Introductory Lectures* the discipline of which Freud speaks without being prepared to establish a clean transmission system depends, for its dissemination, on the workings of hearsay. This may mean that psychoanalysis is particularly prey to the complaint registered by intensely suffering paraphrenics, who are tormented by chatter and by ascertainable forms of auditory hallucinations. Psychoanalysis duplicates this suffering when it draws into itself in an effort to systematize a way out of these fluid channels. To the wall of systemacity erected by psychoanalysis, the schizo responds by the chatter which persecutes him, the vegetal word salad. Still, the lines between psychoanalysis and the schizo are not entirely cut. Thus the schizo herself will ring up the analyst by internal phone systems, returning the call of chatter. Beyond schizophrenia—if such a realm exists, with sound frontiers, border patrols, exit visas—the telephone maintains an instrumentalizing role in modern phantasms of chatter. Such is the case in the last play read by Nietzsche, Strindberg's *Father;* as in his *Easter*: the telephone torments the subject under sufferance, acting as the purveyor of hearsay, chatter, alarm. Now, this demarcates one of the most vulnerable points of entry into psychoanalysis, its dependence upon a fundamental structure of *Gerede* or, in Freud's terms, of hearsay. This does not necessarily situate psychoanalysis among the historical lowlife, for a number of well-known though often ill-advised discourses depend upon hearsay for their persistence, and this includes spreading the word of any absent Speaker, organizing one's actions according to commanding voices, from Hamlet to other mass murdering automatons. But this dependency also protects psychoanalysis, like the schizo, from being knowable on the surface or exhaustible. Discouraging a serene certitude about its principles or actual taking place, it is often bound up

in the stationary mobility

which characterizes the

schizonoiac machine.

We now repair to Jung. His illustrations tend to focus the inadequate feeling-tone in dementia praecox whereby a painful feeling, incompatible with the ego-consciousness, becomes repressed. In a great majority of cases the "feeling-toned complex" is in some way spliced into fear of gossip, oversensitivity to chatter, or suggestibility which emphasizes command automatism and echopraxia. In some instances indifferent and quite trivial ideas may be accompanied by an intense feeling-tone, which has been taken over, however, from a repressed idea. Accordingly the symptomatology that is about to hit us appears to run counter to that of obsessional neurosis, where a strikingly exceptional narration can be delivered by the analysand with an equally striking lack of affect. It seems necessary to mention this difference, or the position from which a difference can be discerned, because Rat Man's obsessional neurosis operates along telephonic lines as well. His telephone system consists of an internalized converter of constative speech acts into perlocutionary utterances, making it necessary to respond to the calls commanding him much in the way the *Spiegel* article has Heidegger respond to his call.[80] Nonetheless, it can be quickly said of obsessional neurosis, and of that which hosts it as a dialect—hysteria—that their telephone systems appear to be connected in compliance with a different set of rules from those governing dementia praecox, where the disconnective structures take the upper hand.

{ Jung's argument begins in a somewhat reactive tone, by disputing the "displeasing thing about [Gross's] hypothesis" (*DP*, 29). Because Otto Gross throws open the switch that lets in the psychic phenomenon of voices, parts of this passage seem worthy of repetition. His reading of catatonic symptoms link these to:

> **alterations of the will itself by an agent felt as external to the continuity of the ego and therefore interpreted as a strange power. (They are) a momentary replacement of the continuity of the ego's will by the intrusion of another chain of consciousness . . . One of these chains will have to become the carrier of the continuity of consciousness . . . the other chains of association will then naturally be "subconscious" or, better, "unconscious." Now at any given time it must be possible for, let us say, the nervous energy in them to mount up and reach such a pitch that attention is suddenly directed to one of the terminal links in the chain, so that a link from an unconscious chain of associations unexpectedly forces itself directly into the continuity of the hitherto dominant chain. If these conditions are fulfilled, the accompanying subjective process can only be such that any psychic manifestation is felt as suddenly irrupting into consciousness and as something entirely foreign to its continuity. The explanatory idea will then follow almost inevitably that this particular psychic manifestation did not come from one's own organ of consciousness but was injected into it from outside.**
>
> **(*DP*, 29)**

What Gross invites us to imagine is precisely what Jung repeats as bringing displeasure ("As I have said, the displeasing thing about this hypothesis is. . . ." [*DP,* 29]). What could it be? In the passage Gross evokes a sudden irruption localizable in some exteriority to consciousness which comes to represent something entirely foreign to its continuity. The symptom gives the subject an impression of having been brought to bear upon its consciousness, acts somewhat like an injected foreign element—a supplement of something that would be detachable from one's own organ of consciousness. Making its arrival felt on an inside of consciousness, this hookup from a supplementary organ organizes the field of dementia praecox to a significant degree. We are asked in fact to imagine a kind of switchboard where several lines can be maintained in the organ of consciousness simultaneously, without influencing one another. This, "as I have said [is] the displeasing thing about this hypothesis: the assumption of independent but synchronous chains of association. Normal psychology furnishes nothing in support of this" (*DP,* 29–30) Yet, schizophrenia "itself" says it maintains an open switchboard. And it says so to Jung, but he's on the other line, on this side of the line ("normal psychology"). At the same time Jung proposes what he calls a purely hypothetical conjecture, venturing a distinction between hysteria's finitude and the unnegotiable endurance of paraphrenia. In fact, it entails the wager that the latter has entered the systemic design of the body to an extent such that it can be viewed as a physiological insert of sorts, affecting the body, suggests Jung, in a manner that cannot be redressed: "the hysterogenic complex produces reparable symptoms, while the affect in dementia praecox favours the appearance of anomalies in the metabolism—toxins, perhaps, which injure the brain in a more or less irreparable manner, so that the highest psychic functions become paralysed" (*DP,* 36). Indeed, Jung argues, the change in metabolism (in Kraeplin's sense) "may be primary; the complex which happens to be the newest and last one 'coagulates' and determines the content of the symptoms. Our experience does not yet go nearly far enough to warrant the exclusion of such a possibility" (*DP,* 37). We have not yet accumulated a sufficient amount of experience to exclude the hypothesis of a primary change in metabolism. It would be entirely possible, therefore, to conceive somatological reordering, we could say, as the body achieves a new interpretation of exteriority toward which it seeks attunement. This form of "adjustment," which clinically needs to be read as severe maladjustment, nonetheless happens to respond with excruciating sensitivity to **a**

felt
technologization
of a
world bionically
assimilated—which is to say, by no means fully assimilated, interiorized, freeze-dried, or swallowed. We shall observe presently how easy it is to confuse a schizophrenic with a perfectly well-behaved child of machinelike obeisance. Schizophrenia scrambles the lines separating the physiological from psychological, keeping it unclear whether dementia praecox is due to somatic or psychogenic causes: "the mechanisms of Freud are not comprehensive enough to explain why dementia praecox arises and not hysteria; we must therefore postulate for dementia praecox a specific concomitant of the affect—toxins?—which causes the final fixation of the complex and injures the psychic functions as a whole. The possibility that this 'intoxication' might be due primarily to somatic causes, and might then seize upon the last complex which happened to be there and pathologically transform it, should not be dismissed" (*DP*, 37). As Jung proceeds in this volume toward the case study that most dramatically incorporates the telephone monopoly into its rhetoric, he points up the superegoical dimension of hallucinatory voices, for subjects "are often corrected by their voices," importantly suggesting that the "normal ego-complex does not perish entirely, but is simply pushed aside by the pathological complex" (*DP*, 90). This seems to be borne out by the fact that schizophrenics "often suddenly begin to react in a fairly normal manner during severe physical illnesses or any other far-reaching changes" (*DP*, 91). The relay between a normativity ruling the ego or superego functions and severe illnesses, one that supersedes injury, maps a passage from acquired catatonia to sudden alarm. The (super)ego can give a wake-up call. Thus:

It is remarkable that not a few patients who delight in neologisms and bizarre delusional ideas, and who are therefore under the complete domination of the complex, are often corrected by their voices. One of my patients, for example, was twitted by the voices about her delusions of grandeur, or the voices commanded her to tell the doctor who was examining her delusions "not to bother himself with these things." Another patient, who has been in the clinic for a number of years and always spoke in a disdainful way about his family, was told by the voices that he was "homesick." From there and numerous other examples I have gained the impression that the correcting voices may perhaps be irruptions of the repressed normal remnant of the ego-complex. (*DP*, 90)

Pierre Janet's observations on psychasthenics take us one step further in illustrating something like a technological need. This is articulated in the terms spelled out by the *sentiments d'incomplétude* (where the subject feels that "the action is not completely finished, that something is lacking"), the *sentiment d'automatisme* (of which one patient reports, "I am unable to give an account of what I really do, everything is mechanical in me and is done unconsciously. I am nothing but a machine)."[81] Here we see to what extent dementia praecox poses a move in the horizon of a bionic unconscious. A related borrowing structure emerges in the *sentiment de domination*. A patient describes this feeling thus: "For four months I have had queer ideas. It seems to me that I am forced to think them and say them; someone forces me to speak and suggests coarse words, it is not my fault if my mouth acts in spite of me" (*DP*, 84). Jung adds, "A dementia praecox patient might talk like this" (*DP*, 84), that is to say, there exists a marked accentuation on the physiological organization of the mouthpiece, a kind of mechanized vision of the body in response, in this case, articulated as the instrumentalization of the mouth that acts in spite of "me." This would suggest a denial statute which legislates the letting go of superegoical interventions, insofar as "it is not my fault if my mouth acts in spite of me." The "my mouth" imposes an anglicism, a mark of possession which other languages of the body are content to dispense with. English hangs on to body parts, as if threatened by the organ without body: *la bouche, der Mund* in solitary orbit. In this context of a mouth that speaks like a loudspeaker detachable from a concept of self that it nonetheless leaves intact, precisely at the place of mouthpiecing together components of dementia praecox, Jung somewhat perplexingly introduces an example of "normal people." What serves as example is the birth of Nietzsche's mouthpiece, *Zarathustra*: "We frequently hear such remarks from hysterical patients, especially from somnambulists, and we find something similar in normal people who are dominated by an unusually strong complex, for instance in poets and artists. (Cf. what Nietzsche says about the origin of *Zarathustra*)" (*DP*, 85). Jung at this point refers us to his "On the Psychology of So-Called Occult Phenomena," which leads in Freud's case, as in every case of occult interference, directly to the telephone. The switching on and off of the interjected voices, argues Jung, often coincides with "the 'stupid chattering' about which so many schizophrenics complain" (*DP*, 95). These bouts of persecutory chattering, like the complaints which they generate, can be turned down or even tuned out by hallucinating patients who claim with frequency that "the voices in time grow quieter and emptier, but as soon as the excitement returns they regain their content and clarity" (*DP*, 95). This brings Jung to the issue of stereotypies, "or rather stereotyped automatisms, which from the very beginning do not show any psychic content, or at any rate no content that would render them comprehensible even symbolically. I am thinking here of those almost entirely 'muscular' manifestations of automatism, such as catalepsy, or certain forms of negativistic muscular resistances" (*DP*, 96). Given the semiotic wasteland of psychic content, Jung directs his sights to creatures of minimal survival via Auguste Forel's experimentation on ants (the destruction of the *corpora quadrigemina*). The outlook is grim, but as it will be constantly reproduced, particularly in the case study of telephone swallowing and in the manual for telephone operators, it attracts attention to itself. Forel's contribution consists in showing that automatisms appear when the largest portion of the brain tissue is removed. The "debrained creature becomes a 'reflex-machine,' it remains sitting or lying in some favorite position until roused to reflex action by external stimuli. It is no doubt rather a bold analogy to compare certain cases of catatonia to 'reflex machines,' although the analogy fairly leaps to the eye" (*DP*, 96). This serves to represent the bold step from which it now seems possible to try another rung or two, for the rapport of machinery to types of dementia praecox appears to pose itself as ineluctable. Directly before entering the crucial "Analysis of a Case of Paranoid Dementia as a Paradigm," Jung will have argued as follows. The enormous tendency to automatization and fixation characterizing the subject, born as it is from "the alienation from reality, the loss of interest in objective events," can be explained by the fact that "schizophrenics are permanently under the spell of an insuperable complex" (*DP*, 97–98). He adds that anyone whose whole interest is captivated by a complex must be dead to his environment. It would be foolish to engage Jung in a debate on this conclusion; as presiding doctor, he is entitled to pronounce a death sentence. He invites further inquiry, however, by his highly conjectural style, which advances the supposition, among other things, that anyone so wholly absorbed "must be," as if he were, which he openly suggests he is, quite finished. What remains unclear to me is the meaning with which Jung invests "environment" and "dead" in this context, although the figural gist of the phrase is by no means incomprehensible. The questions to be raised, then, are: What environment? Does schizophrenia not conjugate only with a technologically inflected environment? Is its silence not always the answering machine to the noise of a prior, organizing machine whose function precisely lies in stimulating such a response? Or put less vulnerably, how does it come about that schizophrenia's Vocabulary is so imbued with the ascientific dial tone of technology, no matter what number or which channel you dial? Given the blank spaces, or rather the insufficient material with which Jung fills his understanding of environment, what does it mean to be dead, that is, presumably not alive to this nondetermined environment? Does not the pressure exerted by technology require a rethinking of easy recommendations made by the life sciences? And if the intrusion of such radical machinery is itself the irreparable *Ge-Stell,* then what permits us to decide that the mute speaker of technologese is dead? Perhaps we are confronted with a radical answering device, a kind of turned-up mimetological stance toward machined being. But we shall stick to a mere signpost of this possible mapping, gluing ourselves, as it is said, to the telephone.

The case history that Jung designates as paradigmatic traces a route from slandering voices to a telephone connection. In terms of a literary mapping, we could say it takes us from Kafka's *Trial* ("someone must have slandered him" opens the hearing and text) to *The Castle* (K.'s telephone line to the top). I would recommend that one read "Analysis of a Case of Paranoid Dementia as a Paradigm."[82] It begins as an essay on hearsay, inextricably linking the torments of its victims, who are simultaneously persecuted by killer telephones. The speaker, recorded by Jung, has remained permanently in the asylum. To the extent that she is radar controlled by Jung, we see only a minimal trace of her trajectory, which nevertheless suggests a heightened, if troubled, adherency to language ("Now and then she used peculiar expressions, and in general spoke in a somewhat pretentious manner. The letters she wrote . . . ," [*DP*, 99]). I am not unaware of the scandal of putting Ms. St. on the line in order to achieve the telephone's finitude. Yet, we are dependent on her connections if we want to obtain a genuine appointment with its fantasmatico-historical personality. The reading of Miss St.'s essay on technology neither mystifies her as oracular, anarchic source nor pretends to observe a noninterning, bloodless coup. This is not so much an interpretation of schizophrenia, as schizophrenia is made to read technology's omphalos. The interrogation of the schizo does not avoid violence—to assert piety would be hypocritical. I want names and facts. B. St., dressmaker, unmarried, born in 1845, admitted to the asylum in 1887, had "for several years heard voices that slandered her. . . . She explained the voices as invisible telephones. They called out to her that she was a woman of doubtful character, that her child had been found in a toilet, that she had stolen a pair of ✂ in order to poke out a child's eyes. (According to the anamnesis the patient had led a thoroughly respectable and quiet life)" (*DP*, 99). Once installed, the ~~telephone~~ ☎ accuses the childless woman of conceiving a child whose eyes she removed, annulling the sight of the other at the outset of the narrative projection. The child was found in a toilet. The patient later describes herself as a containing house. She hosts a toilet as one of her orifices. It may not be incorrect to designate the toilet, like the telephone, as offering principal household cavities made invisibly to link the inside, an inside going as deep as one's own insides, to an outside. ~~Words~~ Words are flushed through the telephone like so much excrement, nothing to hold this in the house, out with it. The flushing action taken by Miss St. appears to bolster her delusion of having millions to spare, immense cash flow and liquid assets. (Freud has made ~~the~~ the definitive connection between money and excrement, both of which are hard to part with. The flush and the call: money down the drain.) ~~■I~~In a later episode of imagined childbearing, Miss St. brings forth a child from her mouth ("—also a little girl jumped out of my mouth with a little ~~brown~~ brown frock and a little black apron—my little daughter, she is granted to me—O God, the deputy—she is the deputy, the end of the lunatic asylum came out of my mouth—my little daughter shot out of my mouth to the end of the lunatic asylum—she was slightly paralysed . . . I came first as double, as sole owner of the world, first with the deaf and dumb Mr. Wegmann" [*DP*, 141]). She makes her little girl. The buccal ~~cavity~~ cavity appears somehow to be connected with the toilet, both openings bypassing the vaginal or anal orifices, from where one would expect a child to spring forth. The motif of paralysis, deafness, and dumbness rarely makes its absence felt in evocations of telephonics, be these located at the origin of the telecommunicative history or at the origin of schizophrenic discourse. The patient repeats "I came first as double," notes Jung (*DP*, 143). In an entirely different episode she asserts "I am the Emperor Francis" (*DP*, 138). Jung recalls that "the Emperor Francis I was the husband of Maria Theresa. The patient is both of them at once, but 'in spite of that I am a female'" (*DP*, 138). In other words, we feel we have reason to add, she is a telephone, compacting a double gender; she came first as the other, as the anteriority of the other which allowed her to come first. A kind of empty container, she opens only to dissemination. The double gender dominated by the feminine arrives in a richly complicated narrative. In the first place, she produces allusions to an erotic song, "My Liesel rises early." "The patient connects this song with the horses, which 'stood near the speaking tubes'" (*DP*, 139). ■ Jung points out, perhaps with some exasperation, that horses, like bulls, dogs, and cats, are often sexual symbols. But I am more taken by another observation concerning Miss St.'s fixation on "extensile animals." To situate this properly, let us present the context from which the double gender falling under the feminine arises—one might in passing note that this particular figuration of gender which breaks down the hope for sexual ~~opposition~~ opposition is common both to Nietzsche ("I am the both") and to Strindberg, whose dramas play out the persecuting mergers that take place in the telephone. Under the entry made near the name Maria Theresa, we find some of the following elements. Remember that for Jung, dreams and schizophrenic utterance share the same phenomenological status:

—in the dream I was at a table with omelets and dried prunes—

then there was a dam with speaking-tubes in it—

then there were four horses with moustaches over their tails—

they stood near the speaking-tubes—

the third emperor has already legalized this—

I am the Emperor Francis in Vienna—

in spite of that I am female—

my Liesel rises early and yodels in the morning—

each horse stood near a speaking-tube. (Suddenly the patient made a gesture of embracing. . . .) (*DP*, 138)

[———]

Of this episode, Jung writes, transferring the concept of analysis to the patient:

> **This analysis, unlike any of the others, was continually interrupted by blockings (thought-deprivation) and motor stereotypies (embracing). . . . the patient went on tracing little circles in the air with her forefinger, saying she "had to show the speaking-tubes," or she drew little half-moons with both hands: "These are the moustaches." Besides this, the "telephone" kept on making mocking remarks.**

(*DP*, 138)

The telephone exchange: the schizo as analyst, rhetorical transfer of power, continually interrupted. A pointer, an index, her forefinger gestures an air dialing whose telephonic systems appear to conjoin the receiver (speaking tubes) with the anus (the mustaches cover the horses' tails, covering the anus). The speaking tubes were themselves shown to be located by a dam, a Deleuzian switchboard barrier containing flow. Thus "every machine, in the first place, is related to a continual material flow [*hylè*] that it cuts into. It functions like a ham-slicing machine removing portions [*prélèvement*: a skimming off or draining off, a deduction from a sum of money on deposit, etc.] from the associative flow: the anus and the flow of shit it cuts off, for instance; the mouth that cuts off not only the flow of milk but also the flow of air and sound; the penis that interrupts not only the flow of urine but also the flow of sperm. Each associative flow must be seen as an ideal thing, an endless flux, flowing from something not unlike the immense thigh of a pig."[83] Rather than pouring on more commentary, it seems appropriate now to allow Miss St. to speak through her tubes in her preferred mode of interruption, without the assurance of continuity from any operator. Just one more thing: Jung remarks that "she is involved in the automatic machinery, with the result that all logical reproduction naturally ceases" (*DP,* 125)—an unfortunate choice of words which nonetheless serves to underscore the disjunctive shifts within the rhetoric of machinery returning to that of logical reproduction, and coming home finally to a moment in naturalizing discourse ("naturally ceases"). The register of machined-being belongs to the milieu of dream logic: "But when the patient talks of her dreams, she speaks as if she were still in the dream, she is involved in the automatic machinery, with the result that all logical reproduction naturally ceases. She is then entirely dependent on chance ideas, and must wait to see whether the complex will reproduce anything or not. Accordingly her thought-process is halting, reiterative (perseverating), and constantly interrupted by thought-deprivation, which the patient considers very trying" (*DP,* 125). Miss St. considers herself a "double polytechnic." (Jung: "It is quite clear that 'double polytechnic' is simply another metonymy for the acme of art and wisdom" (*DP,* 114). Let us take this at face value. Miss St. is a polytechnic, a metonymy if that's what it must be, of that which provides instruction in a number of scientific and technical subjects. What does she instruct? In the first place she pieces together a link that she will maintain throughout her stammering, affiliating her invisible telephones with ineffaceable loss. At times this achieves expression in the form of mourning or paralysis, at other times through what she calls her "hieroglyphic suffering," a phone number that we shall try in a moment. Miss St., like Nietzsche in his suffering, goes by many names simultaneously. ("The schizo indeed participates in history; he hallucinates and raves universal history, and proliferates all the races."[84]) Besides being the Lord God, Mary Stuart, Empress Alexander, triple owner of the world, and a number of others, she also emerges as the Lorelei. This identifies her with the famous refrain of "have I been understood?" She punches in the code of literary history herself:

> ***Lorelei:*** **Is the owner of the world—it expresses the deepest mourning because the world is so depraved—a title that is the greatest happiness for others—usually these personalities who have the misfortune, I might almost say, to be the owners of the world are extraordinarily tormented—Lorelei is also the highest life-image—the world can show no higher remembrance—no higher veneration . . . for example, the song runs "I know not what it means"—it happens so often that the title owner of the world is not understood at all—that people say they don't know what it means. (*DP,* 116)**

To this gloss of the Lorelei, Jung adds, "When the patient says 'I am the Lorelei,' it is simply—as the analysis shows—a condensation by means of a clumsy analogy: people do not know what owner of the world means, that is sad; Heine's song says 'I know not what it means,' etc., therefore she is the Lorelei" (*DP,* 116). But Heine's song, which also resonates in Nietzsche, knows what "it" is whose meaning I do not know. It goes on to say, I do not know what it means to be so sad, or even, so deeply in mourning ("daß ich so traurig bin"). In Miss St.'s words, "it expresses the deepest mourning" (*DP,* 116). Moreover, the song which figures shipwreck and destruction, begins in a more nuanced fashion than Jung suggests, asking I do not know what it should mean that ("ich weiß nicht, was soll es bedeuten"); that is, its normative interpretability is drawn into the question of meaning. Be that as it may, the telephone in her discourse continues to ring out in death-giving moments, on the pain of financial and human loss, as loss of the properly human. Her resources drained,

the heathens chatter so. . . . they said over the telephone that Mr. O. had drawn my annuity—

universal is a finality—

you can be that through deceased persons—

through legacies. . . . I am the hero of the pen. (*DP,* 118–120).

Jung does not provide an analysis of the telephone report. Instead, the patient is found to have "lost all sense of humor, as usually happens in dementia praecox" (*DP,* 120). But the telephone, as a storage tank of reserve otherness, takes on an increasingly ironic function as it assumes an order of alternative consciousness or secondary personality "with a separate consciousness of its own" (*DP,* 156). Distance asserts itself in a schizophrenia where the complexes have become disconnected and autonomous fragments. The nearly allegorical distance produces "the hero of the pen" who fights a duel with the ironizing stabs of the telephone. The telephone grows by extension into the voice of irony and self-corrective dialogics. It attains this commanding post by scaling the regions of absolute loss, cabling messages across an abyss. Miss St. charts the preliminary stages of devastation with which the telephone is to be inextricably identified. Under "Complex of Injury," she dictates a first entry:

(1) Paralysis *(stereotypy: "That is*
paralysis"): "Bad food—
overwork—
sleep deprivation—
telephone—
those are the natural causes—
consumption—
spine—
the paralysis comes from there—

wheel-chairs . . .
tortured. . . .
I belong to the monopoly, to the
payment—
banknotes—
here the suffering is affirmed—
it is a just system—
crutches—
dust development—
I need immediate help."
(*DP,* 125)

This unit could have been taken from McLuhan's steno pad, or indeed originated it, since a necessary articulation is insinuated between a communications media and body extensions—here most pressingly supported by the word "crutches," itself designating corporeal citation marks: crutches holding up a body the way citations are propped up. Somehow the patient senses her membership in the monopoly which indebts her. The banknotes, according to Jung, belong to the clang-association of *Not/Noten,* placing it in a signifying network organized around "distress" and "notes." In German, *Notruf* is the word for an emergency call or call of distress which may be where the suffering is being affirmed ("I need immediate help," etc.). It is not without interest to note that the telephone is inserted into a long line of deprivations listed under the definitional stereotypy, "That is paralysis." Of these the telephone is listed as a "natural cause" of paralysis, whereas other forms of torture, tapped in the spinal cord and supported by the dials controlling the wheel chairs, do not emanate from natural causes. Still spinning, labyrinthine structures coil up in the ear or telephone receiver, communicating with the intestines into whose receivership "bad food" initially is placed. The speaking tubes enter this system. Further along, then, in order to explain the stereotypy "I suffer hieroglyphical," Miss St. focuses momentarily on the mouth as a place of respiration:

"*—I was shut up for fourteen years so that my breath could not come out anywhere—*

that is hieroglyphical suffering—

that is the very highest suffering—

that not even the breath could come out—

yet I establish everything and don't even belong to a little room—

that is hieroglyphical suffering—

through speaking-tubes directed outward." (*DP,* 126)

The grammar of this pain does not permit us to hear whether the hieroglyphical suffering abates through the outwardly directed tubes, or, to the contrary, whether the respiratory blockage is not wrapped up in tubes. If blockage is not due to these instruments, then Miss St. is sent down the tubes by her research of *discord,* something to do with a kind of extension wire into her phantasms:

Discord: "*Discords—*

it is really a crime—

I have to be cared for—

I saw in a dream

two people twisting two cords in the loft—

there are two such great discords—

I have

to be cared for—

discords simply won't go any longer on this floor." (*DP*, 126)

Suspicious accuracy of the signifier: spinal cord, telephone cord, discord. The body reterritorialized, broken into, entered by the telephone cord. Somewhere someone has said that the enema was the first telephone line to the body. She connects the spinal to the telephone cord. They do not reach far enough, on each end two people are twisting them. Miss St. invents her prophetic rapport to the Bell system monopoly. In fact Bell, in her manner of speaking, has destinal control, eventually transforming her into a geographical site, a telephone station ("I am Uster, I am Switzerland, I am . . ." [*DP*, 123, 135]). Consider the way in which she operates the monopoly:

Monopoly . . . *"With me it expresses itself in the note-factory—*

quite black

windows—

I saw it in a dream—

that is paralysis . . . it is a double house . . . the

note-factory is genuine American—

the factory has been drawn into the monopoly

just like, for example, Schiller's Bell *and the monopoly—*

the monopoly includes ev-

erything that can happen . . . then attacks of suffocation—

from above it is

credible—

then the terrible stretchings—

they're continually stretching me. . . then

the poisoning, it is invisible." (*DP*, 127)

Jung adds, "the concept of 'monopoly' is again very unclear. It is associated with a series of tortures" (*DP*, 128). The patient also finds Jung to be an "amphi": you have two sides, doctor. The telephone box and the Bell system in her vision don't let go. Jung explains her frequent use of "splinter" that "is a 'wooden post' on a mound of earth which signifies 'the extreme end,' probably a metaphor for 'grave'" (*DP*, 131). He cannot decipher her idiolectic use of "Oleum" but adds that it implies "the complex of death expectation" (*DP*, 133).

("Where the word 'Oleum' came from I do not know. The patient claims to have heard it from the voices, just as she heard 'monopoly'" [*DP*, 129].) The associations admitting of suffocation, enclosed spaces, America, suggest her reading of the telephone booth—mausoleum, place of entombed silence, where the figures of paralysis, deaf and dumbness, and the speaking tubes communicate to one another shadowlessly. But what of Schiller's *Bell,* his *Glas*? A great deal is cited of this:

Schiller's Bell *(stereotypy: "I am Schiller's* Bell *and the monopoly"): "Well, that is—*

as Schiller's Bell *I am also the monopoly—*

Schiller's Bell *needs immediate help—*

whoever has achieved this needs immediate help . . . needs immediate help. Because all those who established this are at the end of their life and have worked themselves to death, immediate help is needed. . . . it is world famous, the poem: The Bell—

it also establishes the whole of creation . . . that is the greatest conclusion— Schiller's Bell *is the creation, the highest finality."* (*DP*, 132)

Beyond sounding like mutilated telegraph messages emitted from Heidegger's reading of Hölderlin, we note that the patient self-converts into a poem needing immediate help. But as poem, she recognizes the mortal coil from which she was released, the poet-mortal, who needs immediate help from her, the grounding monopoly/poem. "Was bleibet aber, stiften die Dichter": whoever has achieved this insight needs immediate help, because establishing the poem puts one at the limit, and they, the poets, are at the end of their life, death, immediate help, highest finality. Mortals, Heidegger has said on the way to language, are those who experience death as death; they know that to be alive is to be in pain. To be in hieroglyphic pain is, for Miss St., to need immediate help.[85] As Schiller's *Bell,* she has outlived Schiller, she is creation, the highest finality, who tolls the predicament of those who need immediate help. She has become the supreme Operator; and furthermore, "the patient accords herself the title 'Lord God,' so in this respect there is a firm association to the idea of divinity. Now comes another connecting link: the highest deity is called 'St.,' the patient's own name. . . . The deity, like the Pope, is of masculine gender and is thereby distinguished from the patient herself as 'Lord God.' Besides the masculine deity, whose name is obviously meant to express an inner affinity with her family, she sees the head of her deceased sister, an image that reminds one [i.e. Jung] of the two pagan divinities, Jupiter and Juno" (*DP*, 134). "Doctor there is too much amphi" (*DP*, 136).

"—I established this through pork-sausages—I always hear: there is too much amphi—the animal will only have grown so big by mistake perhaps—it must be in the evacuation (stool)—instead of the factory in S. there was a building for amphi . . .—it needs a huge building. . .—once when I affirmed my 1,000 millions in a dream, a little green snake came up to my mouth—it had the finest, loveliest feeling, as if it had human reason, and wanted to tell me something—just as if it wanted to kiss me." (At the words "little green snake" the patient showed lively symptoms of affect, blushing and bashful laughter.) (*DP*, 136)

Blushingly, the patient acknowledges the sexual symbolism which Jung then does indeed detect. Jung makes very little of the telephone which dominates her sensibility, although this in itself, as we have seen, hardly warrants a thorough desexualization of affect. There is too much amphi, Doctor, too much psychoanalysis, hearsay, too much of the mouth-ear connection, coming up to my mouth, "as if it had human reason, and wanted to tell me something." She establishes this through pork sausages. Miss St.—we might add a link—additionally considers herself to be Socrates' deputy, a transcribing Plato, hero of the pen and mouthpiece to the phantom voice. The status of dementia praecox attains to a certain dignity when Jung arranges a conference call on the outer limits of psychoanalytic logic. In another essay Jung confirms that the concurrence of "three experimenters—Stransky, myself and, so to speak, dementia praecox—can be no accident" (*DP*, 24). He grants the disorder a clinical if not a legal personality. Yet, this experimenter, dementia praecox, manages a special kind of techno-irony. As if to refute Jung's earlier suggestion that cases of dementia praecox show the collapse of humor, the telephone gets on the line to become an automaton of ironic doubling and subversion. Jung describes her voices as having an almost exclusively disagreeable and derogatory context, just as parathesias and other automatic phenomenon are generally of an unpleasant character. The telephone lights up otherwise, it seems to us. During a typical conversation, while the patient was telling Jung "what a misfortune it would be for humanity if she, the owner of the world, should have to die before the 'payment,' the 'telephone' suddenly remarked, 'It would do no harm, they would simply take another owner'" (*DP*, 149). At another time the patient apparently was being hindered by thought deprivation. For a long time "I could get no further. Suddenly to the great chagrin of the patient, the telephone called out, 'The doctor should not bother himself with these things'" (*DP,* 149). We note that when it comes to the rescue of Dr. Jung, the telephone is not placed under the arrest of quotation marks, as if at this moment it were to be admitted, as was dementia praecox, as a legitimate participant in discussions under way, or at least the telephone appears to be transferring a call to the patient from Jung, who may not have wanted to bother with their impasse. On this occasion, the disconnecting telephone actually disconnects the disconnection (thought deprivation, "I could get no further"), thus looping around to a crucially intelligible connection. Another example shows the telephone behaving as a colleague to Dr. Jung, miming an explanation and, taking the part of the patient, saying that nothing can be said. "The associations to 'Zahringer' likewise presented difficulties, whereupon the telephone said, 'She is embarrassed and therefore can say nothing'" (*DP,* 149). In still another example, the telephone laughs and sides with the doctor, which makes it all the more difficult to understand why Jung considers this condition to show no sense of humor, unless the telephone were to act as echo chamber for the laugh of the Other. "Once when she remarked during analysis that she was 'a Switzerland,' and I had to laugh, the telephone exclaimed, 'That is going a bit too far!'" (*DP,* 149). Intolerant of a crack in the scene's semantics, the telephone supplies the doctor's laughter with words. Once again, as often happens, when the telephone achieves audibility, there follows something so dense "that I absolutely could not follow her; the thing was really too complicated" (*DP,* 149). The following dialogue develops:

Telephone: "You're leading the doctor round the whole wood."

Patient: "Because this also goes too far."

Telephone: "You're too clever by half." (*DP,* 149)

At this point Jung writes that "when she came to the neologism 'Emperor Francis' the patient began to whisper, as she often did, so that I continually misunderstood her. She had to ~~repeat~~ repeat several sentences out loud. This made me rather nervous and I told her impatiently to speak louder, whereupon she answered irritably too. At this moment the telephone called out: 'Now they're getting in each other's hair!'" (*DP,* 149–150). The telephone acts as a narrator, earwitness, and interpreter for the irritated couple; it establishes a dimension of thirdness which every couple, in order to get somewhere, requires. Still, it is too bad that we have no hint of the feeling tone of the telephone, for this agrammatical, arhetorical, nonlexical aspect of its emergence in language would shed light on the telephone's personality. How is it modulated? One can suppose it to match the voice of Tony the index finger in the film *The Shining*—the signing part of the body that speaks with foreknowledge and special cognition of the sort available to a medium. At other times, however, this repository of luminous knowing turns into the trope of irony, particularly when the telephone responds to poetry: "Once she said, with great emphasis, 'I am the keystone, the monopoly and Schiller's *Bell*,' and the telephone remarked, 'That is so important that the markets will drop!'" (*DP*, 150). The stock-exchange system of knowledge in which the telephone participates seems to have reversed its value, for schizophrenia's capacity for irony has now gone up in Jung's subsequent commentary: "In all these examples the 'telephone' has the character of an ironically commentating spectator who seems to be thoroughly convinced of the futility of these pathological fancies and mocks the patient's assertions in a superior tone. This kind of voice is rather like a personified self-irony. Unfortunately in spite of diligent research I lack the necessary material for a closer characterization of this interesting split-off personality" (*DP*, 150). The telephone comes from the patient and from beyond the patient. It mimes the style of the ethically witnessing Other, in this case demonstrating the physician's conviction of the "futility of these [i.e., schizophrenia's] pathological fancies." In a mode which resembles that of Jung throughout, but less toned down, the telephone also appears to function as loudspeaker for Jung's unsaid when it permits itself to mock the patient's assertions. Assuming a superior tone, it masks itself as the clinical complicity which keeps the patient locked up in the asylum, intercepting the initial two letters of "pretentious" diction in which she begs to be let free. What would it mean for "the character of an ironically commentating spectator" to occupy the interstices between the analyst and analysand? Does not the very object that serves to implement the technicity of hearsay, that is, the epistemological structuring of psychoanalysis and its transmissions, intervene in order to cut the lines between the couple, to add a third dimension, assuring the sense that reproduces the scene itself of psychoanalysis? By miming the surveillance apparatus trained on the patient, hearsay's televisor ("an ironically commentating spectator") comes as much from the doctor as from the patient. It annuls the doctor's position by assimilation and usurpation as much as it undermines the patient's assertions. It arrives on the scene in order to dislocate each partner from the place of absolute Other—it is the contaminator. The paradigm case has commended itself to our attention because it furnishes a reception desk for phantasms of telecommunications. One of these arrives in this form: "Beside the complexes of grandeur and injury [i.e., paranoid persecution mania] there is another complex which has retained a certain amount of normal criticism but is withheld from reproduction by the complex of grandeur, so that no direct communication can be had with it. (As we know, in somnambulism direct communication can be had with such personalities by means of automatic writing)" (*DP*, 150). While the complex harboring the telephone has been shown to be somewhat directly hooked up with the analyst's discourse—be this analyst understood as the ironic, superegoical voice, Jung, or the patient named analyst by virtue of the "analysis" she gives—Jung suggests the necessary inclusion of an operating function or intervention in order to put us through to this place from where "no direct communication" can be had. It is as if the schizophrenic were momentarily opposable to the somnambulist with whom, as with nighttime radio, surprisingly open lines can be maintained. While Jung himself refrains from formulating this opposition, it does appear that the schizophrenic strikes a posture of such paradoxical hyperawakenment that the more direct lines which psychoanalysis likes to take to unconscious representations are shut down. Schizophrenia would not belong to the dark continent of the noncontradictory regime, but appears to work instead in the abyss of light. ▌The ☎ case represents the final stage of observation that Jung makes here: "Finally, there are cases where a correcting, ironical, semi-normal ego-remnant remains on top, while the two other complexes are acted out in the unconscious and make themselves felt only through hallucinations" (*DP*, 150). As if to underscore her vigilance over this knowledge and the terrible light, as if to offer psychoanalysis the design of the probe, Miss St. has thrown hints at the analyst, suggesting the necessity of entering this difficult case and locket: under *summit* ("Sublimist sublimity—self-satisfied am I") she has thrown in "—an orphan child—am Socrates—Lorelei—Schiller's *Bell* and the monopoly—Lord God, Mary the mother of God—master-key, the key of heaven" (*DP*, 115–116). Under the stereotypy "I am the crown," she has uttered, "*—master key and a key of heaven with which one cuts off relations*" (*DP*, 117; italics added). Jung views this key phrase as "a naive bit of dreaming" (*DP*, 117). Perhaps so. Still, she hands us

the key of heaven

and inserts the

master key.

[———]

The master key provides the means by which the schizophrenic cuts off relations, achieving disconnection. To cut off relations implies mastery, or knowing how to interrupt the call. The patient is not herself the master key, but offers it as a way to enter her secret. Once entered, she then dissolves her interiority to become the master key. The temporal succession is disclosed under *Master-key* (stereotypy: "I am the master-key"): "The master-key is the house-key—I am not the house-key but the house—the house belongs to me—yes, I am the master-key—I affirm the master-key as my property—it is therefore a house-key that folds up—a key that unlocks all doors—therefore it includes the house—it is a keystone—monopoly—Schiller's *Bell*" (*DP*, 117). Jung importantly adds: "The patient means the pass key carried by doctors" (*DP*, 117). He allows the power of this remark to attenuate when continuing: "The patient means the pass key carried by doctors. By means of the stereotypy 'I am the master-key' she solves the complex of her internment. Here we can see particularly well how hazy her ideas are and also her expressions: sometimes she *is* the master-key, sometimes she merely 'affirms' it; sometimes she *is* the house, sometimes it belongs to her," etc. (*DP*, 117). Here is one analyst who really shuts off the Nietzsche tape. While Freud comically denies ever having read the last of philosophers, Jung begins by citing him as a case of normalcy but lets the master key slide when the time for affirmation and double, enfolding being comes along. No matter. Nietzsche may be the master key and its affirmation, but we're not turning him either. If, as Jung contends, the patient means the passkey carried by the doctor, then she discerns herself as the key by which the analyst can unlock doors, but insofar as she is the passkey held by the doctor and psychoanalysis, she is also dispossessed of herself as her own asylum, place of internment; she is the carceral subject linked by telephone to the possibility of exteriority.[86] The telephone attunes the note that sings in the master key, the one tolled by Schiller's "Bell" and which also knows the password carried by the doctor, ringing out in time to his unspoken deposits. She is, she says, the house that holds the master key, within which the telephone is connected, but precisely the master key promises to crack the case, furnishing the instrument by which one cuts off relations, and housed, remains simultaneously shut up, like her impenetrable case, and open ("'I am a Switzerland.' Analysis: 'I long ago established Switzerland as a double—I do not belong shut up here . . . Switzerland cannot be shut up'" [*DP*, 123]). Like the telephone whose ring cuts into the elusive "master key," dementia praecox plays itself out along the walls of mute inside and noisy outside, linking death to the clang of a certain form of life whose slapping lightstreams

strike the schizophrenic
as an immense
catastrophe.

Noise disaster keeps the schizonoiac on the run (even though she's not going anywhere. Nonetheless, they're hitting the streets: Rousseau's promenades, Nietzsche in Turin, Artaud's strolls). When the heat is on, it comes down hard on you. Everything crashes. In "The Psychogenesis of Schizophrenia," Jung cites Paul Sollier for his description of *troubles cénesthésiques,* which are compared to "explosions, pistol-shots, and other violent noises in the head. They appear in projection as earthquakes, cosmic catastrophes, as the fall of the stars, the splitting of the sun, the falling asunder of the moon, the transformation of people into corpses, the freezing of the universe, and so on."[87] "Dreams," adds Jung, "can produce similar pictures of great catastrophes," defining them as sonic images that disturb sleep, as "due to an incomplete extinction of consciousness" (*DP,* 163). If, then, the phenomenology of the dream and that of schizophrenia are almost identical, there is nothing to disprove a reading of schizophrenia as a condition of hyperinsomnium, the terrible state of alert in which the "incomplete extinction of consciousness" sustains itself indefinitely. It is fed and sustained by noise explosions and the catastrophic knowledge by whose disclosure the telephone box resounds. One of Miss St.'s great fears is rooted in reports that she was seen carrying a cat ("'I was once slandered by somebody because I always carried cats in my arms.' It is not clear whether the slander emanated from the voices or from people" [*DP,* 106]). Miss St. was carrying a cat. She joins the bestial moments that tend to hit the schizonomad: Rousseau run down by a dog, Nietzsche embracing a horse being beaten; Watson and Bell were receiving signals from finitizing animals too. Cats. Back to Miss St., still ("always") carrying a cat. Miss St. carries some catastrophe with her, whose secret the telephone has attempted to disconnect. It is not clear from what part of the body the telephone speaks, where it has entered, what it zones. Of another patient in another case, Jung has written: "She suffers from numberless voices distributed all over her body. I found one voice which was fairly reasonable and helpful. I tried to cultivate that voice" (*DP,* 170). In a later essay, written from "the privilege of old age," Jung observes the structure of sudden eruption, the abrupt call from schizophrenia's poetry of discontinuity: "Whereas the neurotic dissociation never loses its systematic character, schizophrenia shows a picture of unsystematic randomness, so to speak, in which the continuity of meanings so distinctive of the neuroses is often mutilated to the point of unintelligibility." (*DP,* 179). The neurotic switchboard makes connections which are sustained in their systematicity. Schizophrenia lights up, jamming the switchboard, fracturing a latent semantics with multiple calls. No one can take all the calls—a number in the Miss St. case are still on hold. Jung ends his and her analysis with the admission of serious "gaps and many weak spots" (*DP,* 151). His exposition of the case was not a radio play, but implicated him in the telephonics of the case. The doctor spoke into and from the telephone. He did not speak of the telephone to which he spoke; it held up a mirror to him, and he found it ironic. The telephone was not entered in the lexicon of psychoanalytic conquest—it remained surprisingly in the wild. Jung goes natural and adds a vegetal signifier to the lexicon. He introduces the concept of a "word salad." This imposes a certain schizophrenic reading of the paradigmatic case study—schizophrenic but also detechnologized. A false *piste,* wrong way. Once introduced, word salad quite naturally keeps the fragments in asignificatory disassemblage. What does it mean to bring into the vocabulary of psychoanalysis a concept of salad, a linguistically tossed salad? Jung naturalizes the unreconstitutable edibles; nothing ever again will be able to piece together something like an original head of lettuce, not to speak of its heart. This is precisely why Jung's decision to offer the shared logic of a broken head of lettuce and the dream needs to be considered. For while the dream was thought to have a latent content, a retrievable unconscious narrativity, the schizophrenic utterance remains a pistol shot in the dark of metaphysics, shattered, fragmented. This is perhaps why it may be necessary to note that in German, Miss St. is not quite a "dressmaker," as the English translation would have it, but rather a *Schneiderin,* literally a cutter or tailor, also that in the feminine which cuts off or interrupts the fabric of meaning or the texture of a natural unfolding. Jung's final image is rendered in English as "someone had to get the ball rolling" (*DP,* 151). In German, however, he hopes, he writes, to have brought a stone to roll ("Jemand muß es ja schließlich auf sich nehmen, einen Stein ins Rollen gebracht zu haben" [*DP,* 179]). The analyst takes it upon himself to move the petrified thing, to get it to roll or unravel. Miss St. had offered up an image of medusoid petrification when she recalled "den Kopf ihrer verstorbenen Schwester" (the head of her dead sister [*DP,* 158]). As cutter she offers the analyst the decapitated image of a sister. Jung, in the same sentence, doubles the head, shifting the gender and entering quickly into mythology: "den Kopf, etc., ein Bild, das etwas an zwei heidnische Gottheiten, an Jupiter und Juno, erinnert" (*DP,* 158); "she sees the head of her deceased sister, an image that reminds one of the two pagan divinities, Jupiter and Juno" [*DP,* 134]). Jung inte-

riorizes, remembers (*erinnert*), averts his gaze. There is something he was un-
riorizes, remembers (*erinnert*), averts his gaze. There is something he was unable to look at, and it may indeed be the thing or the thingification of the
able to look at, and it may indeed be the thing or the thingification of the
patient whose mechanized fragment spoke so smartly, whose death toll and
patient whose mechanized fragment spoke so smartly, whose death toll and
place of mechanization knew how to turn things around or double them. The
place of mechanization knew how to turn things around or double them. The
snake, which Jung translated in a psychointerlinear manner, belonged, it
snake, which Jung translated in a psychointerlinear manner, belonged, it
seemed, to the telephone, to a structure of decapitation—for what else would
seemed, to the telephone, to a structure of decapitation—for what else would
it mean to hold a petrified ear-mouthpiece to one's head?

it mean to hold a petrified ear-mouthpiece to one's head?

On the Way to Lainguage

Laing to Heidegger

A few decades later, in 1965, R. D. Laing brought out his highly acknowledged meditation on schizophrenia. Leaning on a number of elements gathered up by Jung, *The Divided Self* divides itself over philosophy. Deleuze and Guattari pick up the metaphysical flower from Laing when citing his *Politics of Experience*: "R. D. Laing is entirely right in defining the schizophrenic process as a voyage of initiation, a transcendental experience of the loss of the Ego."[88] One need only consider the chapter headings of *The Divided Self* to recognize the prominence of philosophical inquiry underlying the implicit language theory and philosophy of being: "The Existential-Phenomenological Foundations for a Science of Persons"; "The Existential-Phenomenological Foundations for the Understanding of Psychosis"; "Ontological Insecurity," and so forth (*DS*, 7). Nonetheless the work also falls into word salad—a concept uncritically adopted by Laing—and suggests a certain schizophrenogenic concept of language. This, in addition to the philosophical claims informing the work, force schizophrenia to cooperate with a metaphysics into which it fits only uneasily. This problematic becomes especially clear in the section titled "The Self and the False Self in a Schizophrenic," where being is divided into a notion of distinctly boundaried outside and inside (i.e., "inside [me], outside [not-me]"). The purpose at which we aim is not to offer a critique of a discourse that may, despite itself, seek further to inter schizophrenia, but to understand how it falls short when simultaneously including and expelling the out-of-hand logic of the telephone. Thus "The Ghost of the Weed Garden," like Jung's paradigmatic case study of schizophrenia, originates in a telephone connection which is left on the invisible peripheries of the treatment text, where it might have provided a singular model for reading the doubling, ghostly, or phony self inhabiting schizophrenia. Still, Laing produces significant material to bolster us on the path to that technologized entity of which schizophrenia provides an exemplarily telling instance. Thus in the section entitled "Ontological Insecurity" Laing appears explicitly to take up the rolling stone that Jung has launched. Under the heading "Petrification and Depersonalization," he begins as follows:

1. A particular form of terror, whereby one is petrified, i.e. turned to stone.

2. The dread of this happening: the dread, that is, of the possibility of turning, or being turned, from a live person into a dead thing, into a

> **stone, into a robot, an automaton, without personal autonomy of action, an *it* without subjectivity.**
>
> **3. The "magical" act whereby one may attempt to turn someone else into stone, by "petrifying" him; and, by extension, the act whereby one negates the other person's autonomy, ignores his feelings, regards him as a thing, kills the life in him. . . . One treats him not as a person, a free agent, but as an it. (*DS*, 46)**

It is perhaps unnecessary to point out the degree to which this opposi-tional logic is derived from a classical metaphysical divide, embracing the autonomous subject *versus* thing, live person *versus* dead thing—particularly troubling in a work that treats a phantomization of the self in which one would be hard-pressed to assert the pure livingness of the undead—subjectivity, self-unity, and so on. Laing's petrification is entirely decapitated from the Freudian corpus, leaving only a trait of genderized difference in the technologization of self. In our trajectory, this serves as a nostalgic remnant or appears as a result of the equation put forth by Jung's patient (I am male and female but predominantly female), urging the necessity of suspending the biological backdrop if only to let the working hypothesis breathe. Laing resists mention of Freud when lifting the Medusian paradigm, precisely in order to place under erasure the full-blown drama of sexual difference and castration anxiety in their rapport to the dread of petrification. Laing shows how some of the symptoms he lists participate in the prosody of everyday life: "A partial depersonalization of others is extensively practised in everyday life and is regarded as normal if not highly desirable [note the passive construction, the subjectless normativity at work in this phrasing]. Most relationships are based on some partial depersonalizing tendency in so far as one treats the other not in terms of any awareness of who or what he might be but as virtually an android robot playing a role or part in a large machine in which one too many may be acting yet another part" (*DS*, 47). One is threatened "with the possibility of becoming no more than a thing in the world of the other, without any life for oneself, without any being for oneself," adds Laing, paraphrasing part 3 of Sartre's *Being and Nothingness*. James, a patient of Laing's, illustrates this predicament of having "no self" with the utterance, "I am only a response to other people" (*DS*, 47). An answering machine, he answers to the description of the android robot whom Laing halfheartedly begins to construct. Later on: "By depleting him of his personal aliveness, that is, by seeing him as a piece of machinery rather than as a human being, he undercut the risk to himself of this aliveness either swamping him, imploding into his own emptiness, or turning him into a mere appendage" (*DS*, 48). Elsewhere, in the section "The Inner Self in the Schizoid Condition": "The body may go on acting in an outwardly normal way, but inwardly, it is felt to be acting on its own, automatically" (*DS*, 78). "However," adds Laing, "despite the dream nature or unreality of experience, and the automatic nature of action, the self is at the same time far from 'sleepy'; indeed, it is excessively alert, and may be thinking and observing with exceptional lucidity" (*DS*, 78). While this apparent paradoxicality receives no further elaboration, it is this rapport of deaf and dumbness to acute attunement, the partial relieving of self from itself, the retreat into a mode of mechanized nonlife, putting oneself on hold, which ought to claim our attention. One of the schizo signs that Laing identifies for us, perhaps as an appendage to petrification, reads as the transformation of the subject into a radically compliant thing—a concept that arises on several key occasions in this work, for example in the chapter "The False-Self System," where the subject is shown to act as a compliance-appliance of sorts:

Much of the eccentricity and oddity of schizoid behavior has this basis. The individual begins by slavish conformity and compliance, and ends through the very medium of this conformity and compliance in expressing his own negative will and hatred. The false-self system's compliance with the will of others reaches its most extreme form in the automatic obedience, echopraxia, echolalia,

and flexibilitas cerea of the catatonic. Here obedience, imitation, copying, are carried to such excess that the grotesque parody becomes a concealed indictment of the manipulating examiner. (*DS*, 102)

The false-self systems would then be a reflex of the other, staging a response in juridico-parodistic terms ("parody . . . concealed indictment"). Caught up in the mechanics of "obedience, imitation, copying," schizophrenia shines like a Xerox machine of blinding exactitude (assuming you flip the lid), like its study which, on a lesser intensity, Xeroxes philosophy. Compliance ends through what Laing calls the "medium"; it becomes a mode of expressivity for something like hating, which he, like Jung, associates with the "will" (Jung makes explicit reference to Schopenhauer, which might recall to us the torturing wheel of Ixion, the being-as-dialing mechanism to which the self is irrevocably attached). In another philosophical excursion, some of Laing's patients are shown to be quoting, apparently without their knowledge, Heidegger. The unconscious ventriloquy occurs in particular when they feel themselves to be located "on the fringe of being." How is it that the schizophrenic condition is an unrehearsed citation now of Heidegger, now of Sartre? In the chapter "The Self and the False Self in a Schizophrenic," Laing tells of a patient who "was unable to sustain real autonomy because all she could be *vis-à-vis* her parents was a compliant thing. . . . Yet the only way she could disentangle herself was by means of an empty transcendence, into a 'world' of phantoms" (*DS*, 173). It is not entirely clear what Laing wishes to understand under empty transcendence, though he seems to suggest that there would be something like a full transcendence, a real transcendence comparable perhaps to a "real autonomy." The map of empty transcendence puts it in the neighborhood of a phantomized world leading us to the ghost in the weed garden which poses itself as so many telephone poles from which voices are retrieved by the compliant thing that listens with exceptional lucidity. In one of the less happy cannibalizations of philosophy, "The Case of Peter," Laing begins precisely where Heidegger brought us to a halt, that is, with the recall that we couldn't stop making: "'Guilt is the call of Being for itself in silence,' says Heidegger. What one might call Peter's *authentic guilt* was that he had capitulated to his ***unauthentic guilt,*** and was making it the aim of his life not to be himself" (*DS,* 132). This may sound like hot-tub Heidegger, yet its significance lies in rendering the call of conscience crucial for schizoanalysis—however relaxed the calling extension may seem. But this is where things get bad for Peter: "When he dropped the pretence, therefore, it forced itself on his notice as he was recalled to it as something musty, rancid, uncanny—in fact, unlived and dead. He had severed himself from his body by a psychic tourniquet and both his unembodied self and his 'uncoupled' body had developed a form of existential gangrene" (*DS,* 133). Existential gangrene, indeed. "The matter in a nutshell," as Laing puts it, is stated by the patient himself, who allows, "I've been sort of dead in a way. I cut myself off from other people and became shut up in myself. And I can see that you can become dead in a way when you do this" (*DS,* 133). This patient, like others on file, exists in a mode of fundamental disconnectedness, becoming dead in a way the telephone goes dead when a disconnection is made. Thus Julie, heroine of "The Ghost of the Weed Garden," finds herself disconnecting in her narration: "after the telephone-box incident, she simply cut herself off from [her father]" (*DS,* 191). In this scene the connection between a telephone and the schizophrenic act par excellence, that of disconnecting, are linked like two parts of an apparatus, separated only by a thin umbilical. In Julie's case and encasement, death and the telephone are shown mutually to participate in assuring the extinction of the exceptionally lucid subject which comes about as a disorder in destining. Cutting her self off from her father, the telephone system entangling her in fact emerges as a maternalizing dysfunctionality: "It would be approriate to call this quasi-autonomous partial system a 'bad internal mother.' She was basically an internal female persecutor" (*DS,* 200). There is always a remnant of the persecuting, accusatory mother in the telephone system, suggesting that the entire dimension of the monolithic parental unit can never as such be silenced.

Among the elements informing this study of a chronic schizophrenic are those linking her to Jung's *Schneiderin,* as if by uncanny telephone wires, as if the patients were remote controlled by the same call box. In the first place, the "existentially dead" patient calls herself in her psychosis Mrs. Taylor, a translation of Jung's special schizo case of the *Schneiderin,* indicating that both patients are involved in cutting lines. "What does this mean?" queries Laing. "It means 'I'm tailor-made.' 'I'm a tailored maid; I was made, fed, clothed, and tailored.' Such statements are psychotic not because they may not be 'true' but because they are cryptic:

they are quite often impossible to fathom without the patient decoding them for us" (*DS*, 192). Laing at no point has the patient decode her systems, though he suggests the position of the chronic schizophrenic as code maker and decoder, simultaneously then in the conjoined roles of telling and listening for what she has been told, a homemade telephone system. Mrs. Taylor is a clear-cut case of the homemade, like a slice of apple pie or a splinter off the old parental block from which she has been blade run. Her existence owes itself to a kind of parental disruption: "It is remarkable that, despite the radical disruption of the relationship between husband and wife, in one respect at least they maintained a collusion. Both accepted the patient's false self as good and rejected every other aspect of her as bad" (*DS*, 192). But Julie's father had been disconnected from her before her birth; in fact, she appears to have been born through this disconnection, owing her birth to a strange conception of coitus interruptus: "The father, indeed, as he said, had not much to tell me, because he had 'withdrawn himself emotionally' from the family before Julie was born. . . . Despite her father's distance from her and his relative inaccessibility, Julie had seemed fond of him" (*DS*, 191). The serene distance, fondness as a mode of interruption, can be maintained up to a point—a point in which the father makes a telephonic connection. It is only when her father puts through a call that Julie's symptoms appear to erupt; and while Laing does not cut a deal with the event, the language itself of calling and anacalling spreads over his narration as he attempts to identify the different family connections: "Her father had taken her into a call-box"; a few sentences after the call-box, the analyst writes: "Mrs X. did not hesitate to miscall her husband to her daughters, and in piling up innumerable instances of injustices, she tried to get them on her side" (*DS*, 191). (As Laing points out, it requires immense energy to attempt a reconstitution of a schizophrenic's biography; Jung has given us little in the way of clues about his lady's "past," which is why we can only guess at such a thing, as if moved by the memory of an ancient ritual. As such, schizophrenia, like technology, needs to reinvent the very possibility of the autobiography. What is the childhood of a schizophrenic answering machine like? Or, for that matter, her "life," *bios*?) As for a chronic schizophrenic, Julie would say that she was a "tolled bell" ("or 'told belle'"). In other words she was only what she was told to do, says Laing—or a told story (*DS*, 187); it is yet to be decided for whom the bell tolls, where its knell starts peeling. Beyond this, she was terror-stricken, "petrified into a thing," affected by phantasms of pulverization, she was sure her analyst would "cut off her legs, hands, tongue, breasts" (*DS,* 204). Reminiscent of Jung's inscription of schizosexuality, she was furnished with "a heavy armamentarium of the sexual equipment of both sexes" (*DS,* 204). It is noteworthy that when the analyst is intending to mark his self, his "I," in the scene of threatened amputation, a slippage into momentary agrammatical vertigo occurs: "Life (me) would mash her to a pulp, burn her heart with a red-hot iron, cut off her legs, hands, etc." (*DS,* 204). Why the analyst's "I" gets blockaded by the accusative "me" at this moment of projected mutilation cannot be lacking in meaning. It is as if the "I" had participated in the schizophrenic discourse, mashing itself, coming out of the process as a "me" in the objective case, relinquishing at least its position as subject. No wonder the patient feared the analyst's potentiality for nonbeing: "me would mash her to a pulp" lifts the analyst's locus as responsible subjectivity, thingifying his place as a blade runner of abuse: an other-thingly monsterized self saying "me would mash you." The problem of address, of me and you, to which Lainguage points begins at this point, perhaps in

the literality of a splitting ego
that divides it self between
"I"
and "me."

Julie, according to Laing's description, can be viewed as the automatic answering machine to her mother's call. This is what creates the conditions of her dysfunctionality, for she would do whatever her mother called her to do (hence her status of tolled bell). "She would never take too much cake. You just had to say, 'That's enough, Julie,' and she wouldn't object" (*DS,* 200). Nor would she subject, however. In fact, to mime Lainguage, in a nutshell, the mother may have offered us the piece of cake Julie can do without. Follow Julie's logic. Julie tends to reverse words, we are told, or to produce the compliance that stands for hatred. Not only does Julie object, she is *object,* and also, uncannily, meta-object, for she abuses her little "Julie-Doll" of which she is the mother. Just as the Frankenstein monster responds on automatic to the call of the dead mother, Julie is telecommanded by the dead in her mother of whom she is a double, a telephone piece, the invaginated ventrilocating ear of a tolled bell. Being attached to the umbilicus, Julie as a child had played a reverse *fort/da* whose operator kept her eternally on the line: "Things [!] went so smoothly at this time that her mother could recall very few actual incidents. However, she did remember that she played a 'throwing away' game with the patient. Julie's elder sister had played the usual version of this game and had exasperated Mrs X by it" (*DS,* 185). (Laing had explained that "in Freud's case, the little boy kept his reel of string attached to him when he threw it away, in contrast to the fact that he could not keep his mother thus under contol by an attachment to her 'apron strings'" [*DS,* 185]). Mrs. Chiasmus is quoted as saying: "'I made sure that *she* (Julie) was not going to play that game with me. *I* threw things away and she brought them back to *me,*' as soon as she could crawl" (*DS,* 185). I could call this a syndromic habit of reversing charges. As the self in the text keeps dividing on automatic, Laing leads us to suppose, if by indirection, that schizophrenia may be an effect of something intensely peculiar to our contemporaneity, what we are calling technology: "I am, however, describing something that occurs in our twentieth-century Western world, and perhaps not, in quite the same terms, anywhere else. I do not know what are the essential features of this world that allow of such possibilities to arise" (*DS,* 180).

When you or I

get on the line

to a schizophrenic

you do not know who is there, who is speaking; in fact, one has the feeling that no one is there, and like Ophelia, the no one that is there or not gives you the sensation that she is not a person. Her "word salad" seems to be the result of a recording, registering a number of quasi-autonomous partial systems striving to give simulcast expression to themselves out of the same mouth. The overall unity of their being is disconnected into several "partial assemblies" or "partial systems" (quasi-autonomous "complexes," "inner objects"), each of which has its own little stereotyped "personality" (molar splitting). Their being is dystonic, there is a lack of an overall ontological boundary. Listen:

In being with her one had for long periods that uncanny "praecox* feeling" described by the German clinicians. . . . that there was no one there. . . . There might be someone addressing us, but in listening to a schizophrenic, it is very difficult to know "who" is talking, and it is just as difficult to know "whom" one is addressing.

In listening to Julie, it was often as though one were doing group psychotherapy with the one patient. (*DS*, 195)

Julie seemed to speak of herself in the first, second, or third person. (*DS*, 196)

Julie's being as a chronic schizophrenic was thus characterized by lack of unity and by division into what might variously be called partial "assemblies," complexes, partial systems, or "internal objects." Each of these partial systems had recognizable features and distinctive

* . . . This "praecox feeling" should, I believe, be the audience's response to Ophelia, when she has become psychotic. Clinically she is latterly undoubtably a schizophrenic. In her madness there is no one there. She is not a person. . . . Incomprehensible statements are said by nothing. She has already died. There is now only a vacuum. (*DS*, 195)

ways of its own. . . . Personal unity is a prerequisite of reflective awareness, that is, the ability to be aware of one's own self acting relatively unselfconsciously, or with a simple primary non-reflective awareness. In Julie, each partial system could be aware of objects, but a system might not be aware of the processes going on in another system which was split off from it. For example, if, in talking to me, one system was "speaking," there seemed to be no overall unity within her whereby "she" as a unified person could be aware of what this system was saying or doing.

In so far as reflective awareness was absent, "memory," for which reflective awareness would seem to be a prerequisite, was very patchy. All her life seemed to be contemporaneous. The absence of a total experience of her being as a whole meant that she lacked the unified experience on which to base a clear idea of the "boundary" of her being. . . . She would refer to these diverse aspects as "he," or "she" or address them as "you." That is, instead of having a reflective awareness of those aspects of herself, "she" would perceive the operation of a partial system as though it was not of "her," but belonged outside. She would be hallucinated.

Together with the tendency to perceive aspects of her own being as not-her, was the failure to discriminate between what "objectively" was not-her and what was her. (*DS*, 197–198)

The "you" here might be referring directly to me, or to one of her systems, or I could be embodying this system. (*DS*, 200)

The itinerary of this question regarding as it does whom Julie addresses, might be fruitfully complicated by introducing some remarks concerning, we might say, a constitutive disordering of destinal address. One obvious source reference upon which to base such an argument would be the richly articulated cross-wires of *La carte postale,* stamped by Derrida with a heavy accent on purloined postal systems. However, to shift the emphasis principally toward a somewhat "live" but vacuumed mode of communication, inflected by the scene of a lecture, it would be even more to the point to cite a portion of "My Chances / *Mes Chances*" if we wish to bring this disorder into determined focus. We note first that Laing's prerequisites for a liberal vision of the subject's normativity are constellated via strictly metaphysical aspirations for the self, as if the divided self were a falling off from a self-totalizing presence, and so forth across the board. You know the argument. Still, it seems necessary to emphasize the extent of these determinations, for they arrange the place from which schizophrenia receives treatment. While Laing's objectives are anti-institutional, that is, while he clearly wishes to liberate the locus of schizophrenic utterance from the dismally empirical prose of his interning colleagues, his hermeneutics of basic fictions such as the "self" and "experience" keeps him locked within a recognizably uptight, closing-off system. Thus his readings of "personal unity is a prerequisite of reflective awareness," "the absence of a total experience of her being as a whole meant that she lacked. . . ," or the assertion that Ophelia is no longer a person—something which litcrit maintains about literary figures in general—all suggest the readiness of metaphysics to swallow up into its own foundation something as heterogeneous to its assimilative systems as schizophrenia, which is not even served up as an emetic formula. I am assuming that it is no longer necessary at this point to stage the rootedness of these citations ("total experience of her being," etc.) in the totalizing demands of metaphysics. If "the divided self" supplies the name of the disorder under which schizophrenia comes to be subsumed, then the rhetoric of the cure risks being merely an effect of the disorder which it seems to identify.

We now take up the question of address peculiar, according to Laing, to schizophrenic discourse, for example to the disconnective mode of address he invokes ("in listening to a schizophrenic, it is very difficult to know 'who' is talking, and it is just as difficult to know 'whom' one is addressing"[*DD,* 195]) Why the quotation marks? Does Laing know "whom" he is addressing in this book? *Mes Chances,* as the title may indicate, launches the double rapport of chance to its misfiring, to the place where such a missed encounter could be arranged (hence the subtitle "A Rendezvous with Some Epicurean Stereophonies"). Making subversive use of the classical trope of apostrophe, Derrida addresses his listeners with a "you" that runs a self-canceling course: "if I may now make use of the apostrophe, let me tell you this much at once: I do not know to whom I am speaking. Whom is this discourse addressing here and now? . . . it becomes at least possible to demonstrate that, beginning with the first sentence, my lecture has not simply and purely missed its destination" (*MC*, 1–2). Dealing with a logic and *topos* of the dispatch, Derrida shows destiny and destination to be dispatches (*envois*) whose descending trajectories or projections can always meet up with perturbation, interruption, or deviation. For example, the *lapsus,* as slip or fall, when revealing its unconscious destination and manifesting thus its truth, becomes, for psychoanalytical interpretations, a symptom. The question concerning psychoanalysis is shown inextricably to be bound to a concept of *Geschick,* not least because of the audial dimension upon which it relies for one channel of disseminative occurrence. So, when speakers seek out a criterion by which to arrive at some decision regarding the knowability of the addressee, they must first dispatch with hopes offered by self-conscious knowledge: "Not necessarily the criteria of self-conscious knowledge. For I could be addressing myself to an unconscious and absolutely determined addressee, one rigorously localized in 'my' unconscious, or in yours, or in the machinery programming the partition of this event. Moreover everything that comes to mind under the words 'consciousness' or 'unconsciousness' already presupposes the possibility of these marks in addition to all the possible disruptions connected with the destining of dispatches" (*MC*, 3). To this end, it would appear that in the case of Julie, Laing's destabilization of the addressee belongs to a general law of destination, and to the chances inherent to language. In Jung one observes how the telephone installed in Miss St. felt it knew whom it was addressing, who was speaking, who listening, but nonetheless it completely missed its mark, possibly only sideswiping its presumed addressee—the doctor with whom it worked in outspoken collaboration. Derrida affirms the ineluctability of this necessary nonknowing: "Regarding those to whom I now speak, I do not know them, so to speak. Nor do I know you who hear me" (*MC*, 2). This produces a subtle division among that which may appear to constitute the same, for Derrida claims neither to know those to whom he speaks *nor* can he close in on those whose ears open to his speaking. These represent two destinations, both unknowable. So the probing does not let up:

"How indeed could I aim my argument at some singular destination, at one or another among you whose proper name I might for example know? And then, is knowing a proper name tantamount to knowing someone?" (*MC,* 2). Derrida demonstrates for his part that the most general structure of the mark participates in a speech destined in advance to addressees (*destinataires*) who are not easily determinable or who, as far as any possible calculation is concerned, in any case command a great reserve of indetermination. This involves a language operating as a system of marks: "Language, however, is only one among those systems of *marks* that claim this curious tendency as their property: they *simultaneously* incline towards increasing the reserves of random indetermination *as well as* the capacity for coding and overcoding or, in other words, for control and self-regulation" (*MC,* 2). We begin to discern how the simultaneity of determining, coding, and even supercoding forms a deep cooperation with the inclination in language toward anticoding, or what Derrida sees as the inflated reserves of random indeterminateness. This double-edged coding, we must remember, regards, as it were, nonschizophrenic language, if such a thing there be. "Such competition between randomness and code disrupts the very systematicity of the system while it also, however, regulates the restless, unstable interplay of the system. Whatever its singularity in this respect, the linguistic system of these traces or marks would merely be, it seems to me, just a particular example of the law of destabilization" (*MC,* 2). It may be useful to note that Derrida understands language in terms primarily of traces and marks, where Lainguage concerns signs in the first place, and in particular the broken rapport of that which is signifying to what ostensibly lies hidden behind it, or the disconnection between signs and signs or signs and referents. Laing is led to assume the latency of a single, unique, localizable but timid presence—rather than trace or residual mark—from where it could be securely determined who speaks, and to whom.

This all too brief excursion into "My Chances," which may unwittingly reproduce the effect and trauma of a chance encounter, means to engage a dialogue between the question of address raised by Laing and the ones raised in turn by Derrida. For it now appears that Laing places his bets on the sustained systematicity of the system which Derrida shows always already to fall under a law of destabilization.[89] Moreover, Derrida does not suggest language to be some emanation of the fully formed subject, as Laing seems to want to do. Pursuing the lines of trajectories and the *translation* of signs addressed by those contained within the twilight of an audiovisual community, Derrida describes what he has been saying as something that "comes at you, to encounter and make contact with you" (*MC*, 3). This admits an action no less abstract or terrorizing than a telephone vowing to reach out and touch. In fact Derrida characterizes his utterances as "the 'things' that I throw, eject, project, or cast (*lance*) in your direction to come across to you" (*MC*, 3). The schizo-candidates of both Jung and Laing had things, of which they and "their" language were a part, that, thrown or ejected, behaved like missiles or missives whose destination was difficult to determine. This was especially the case with their projections. Often their retreat into resolute muteness was related to a dread of murdering, indeed, as if language were armed to the teeth—an uncontrolled thing whose release-controls they manned. The partial system inverts but structurally maintains the long-distance relay of the *fort/da* apparatus. The Other in its being-as-not-thereness is never found to be fully retrievable or recuperable. The thing of language is that if it is there to be given, it is to be given away. Perhaps language management begins with someone at the other end, more or less dead or alive, traversing you by a dimly perceptible long distance—the *fort* slashing into the *da*. The essential not-thereness of the subject as self or Other makes the telephone possible but also leads the telephone to raise the question of which system is speaking when the telephone speaks, simultaneously translating while emitting sound waves: "'she' would *perceive* the operation of a partial system as though it was not of 'her' but belonged outside. She would be hallucinated" (*DS*, 198). Near the end of the tolled bell: "Anything she wanted, she had and she had not, immediately, at one time. Reality did not cast its shadow or its light over any wish or fear. Every wish met with instantaneous phantom fulfillment and every dread likewise instantaneously came to pass in a phantom way. Thus she could be anyone, anywhere, anytime" (*DS*, 203). He reads her hauntingly like a telephone's metadirectory. The case history never makes clear which phantom walks in the weed garden. Is the ghost this "phantom"—a phantom instantaneity of omnipresence whose space ingathers modalities of dread and desire alike, calling in from anyone, anywhere, anytime? What sanctions a phantom fulfillment, or a "reality" that would cast neither shadow nor light but leave every wish or fear within range of the dead gaze? Dispossessed of properly metaphysical apprehensions of property, Julie stages the dumb show of desiring by whose law "she had and she had not": "Anything she wanted," writes Laing, "she had and she had not immediately, at one time." Don't forget that she cut herself off from him when her father made a telephone call. Still, she put herself through his desire: "Julie had seemed fond of him. He occasionally took her for a walk. On one occasion Julie came home from such a walk in tears. She never told her mother what had happened. . . . After this, Julie would have nothing to do with her father. She had, however, confided to her sister at the time that her father had taken her into a call-box and she had overheard a 'horrible' conversation between him and his mistress" (*DS*, 191). She was made to witness a telephone call, a sexual encounter cut off from itself. The one-sidedness of the telephonic rendezvous makes up an intolerable history for the witness: for this very reason Alexander Graham Bell had phones removed from his home. The protagonist of Kafka's "The Neighbor" goes batty. Who is speaking? — The schizo points the finger at no one. "She had and she had not": having you on the line without properly possessing you, or possessing you the way a hallucinated figure is possessed, entered by the voices from the other end. Perhaps this is one story line that the tolled bell wished to evoke. There is nothing to prove that she did not consider herself a "told bell" in the first place, told by the far-off voices whose clicking tongues she feared had been cut out.

Mouth!

That
Trem

b l e s

through the

It is difficult to comprehend how the world, divided into neat and distant zones, gets covered over by the technological environment. For me, there is a breach here. . . . If only we knew what this schizophrenia meant —From Heidegger's Seminar on Heraclites ('66–'67)

Silvery Willow

O mouth!

A way to language is needed. To spring schizophrenia from the dragnet of reactionary psycho wards, Laing poses the schizo on the Heideggerian path, like a hitchhiker, looking for trouble and a dose of aporia. In general, we have been fed clues about the devotion which the doctors of schizophrenia practice with regard to philosophy. The names of Schopenhauer, Nietzsche, and Heidegger make up the catalogue of referrals that these doctors provide. In Jung's case study, Nietzsche is made to sail under the banner of wholesomeness in order to make it into the directory of patrons. Heidegger is convoked, cited; transactions are openly carried out to borrow certain principles from his thinking. You can transfer the call from philosophy to schizoanalysis; the psychiatric switchboards are working on it. There are ontology, existentialism, and phenomenology holding up the foundations of psychosis. Freud, for his part, declared denial upon philosophy's thinking. It becomes necessary to follow the path which Heidegger has cut through schizophrenia. His name is a signpost, put up painstakingly by Lainguage. Yet, Heidegger speaks, we could venture to say, on the side of schizophrenia, in a manner that would cut against the grain of the doctors' referral systems. Heidegger's place as pharmakon has not been staked out by those who dispense him eagerly to tranquilize their patients. Even so, they are right to point to him, for he leaves marks that show his traversal through the weed garden, he has spoken to their ghosts who continue to beckon, and most uncannily, he has conjured the ghost that inhabits technology—to such an extent, indeed, that philosophy is over. "Schizophrenia" may be the naming word for the new, ghostly tenants of overphilosophy. Since they are ghostly, however, they collect images of that which has been made to vanish, still projecting a pale double of a fading regime, a cipher of its own disappearance. A new house of Being is being tolled, one which communicates with the echo of that which Heidegger shows to be yet to come, a present, that is, that would be the advent of what has been. It is as if the weed garden were to be cleared by the Destructive Character whose figure Heidegger provisionally occupies. Benjamin's Destructive Character takes momentary possession of Heidegger in the sense that Julie describes the terms of "self-possession," the self possessed by an other that bids it forth into its mute calling.[90] **If Heidegger** indicates the beckoned sign put up by those who puzzle over schizophrenia, he understands his position as the place where disconnectiveness is assigned. The sign places him in the possibility of newly designing the garden:

The "sign" in design (Latin *signum*) is related to *secare,* to cut—as in saw, sector, segment. To design is to cut a trace. Most of us know the word "sign" only in its debased meaning—lines on a surface. But we make a design also when we cut a furrow into the soil to open it to seed and growth. The design is the whole of the traits of that drawing which structures and prevails throughout the open, unlocked freedom of language. The design is the drawing of the being of language, the structure of a show in which are joined the speakers and their speaking: what is spoken and what of it is unspoken in all that is given in the speaking. (*W,* 121)

It is as if the weed garden had been read by what Heidegger calls the debased meaning of sign, by the lines on a surface, rather than by the cuts that it openly designates. The question regards speaking, speaking as listening, as a hearing given to the precocious patient. At the end of the essay whose title reads "Words," Heidegger falls into silence when these words trail off: "our hearing may err"; they open in a quiet way the disordering flow of destinal address which has come at us (*W,* 156). **Again, dwelling** in the neighborhood of that toward which his name has been convoked, Heidegger tells us about language. His telling comes eerily close to the hearing disability of which the doctor complains. As if in response, for speaking is always an answering, he calls out: "But language *is* monologue. This now says two things: it is language *alone* which speaks authentically; and, language speaks *lonesomely*. Yet only he can be lonesome who is not alone, if 'not alone' means not apart, singular, without any rapports" (*W*, 134). With these words, Heidegger grazes schizophrenia; it touches him, scratching a distinction between *lonesome* and *alone,* wounding his language in some essential way. Was Hölderlin not at times alone? Language will *not* leave one alone. When Heidegger establishes this distinction, it tells us that language is pregnant with its flipside (Hölderlin, Lenz, Nietzsche, Artaud). In the same essay, Heidegger identifies the obscurity surrounding "just how we are to think of essential beings." It remains "wholly obscure how it speaks, and supremely obscure, therefore, what *to speak* means. This is the crux of our reflection on the nature of language" (*W*, 95). The crux to bear concerns the meaning of speaking, a speaking language which is always monological, always speaking in the language of language—a thought that renders the evocation of Heidegger in the ways we have seen perplexing, dissolute. For as long as the way has not been cleared for understanding what it means *to speak,* then the manner of self-absenting speaking in which the patient speaks cannot yet receive clinical determinations secured in the ground of Heidegger's thinking. **For what** if language were speaking in the mode precisely of *die Sprache spricht,* through the instrument of Being, but subterraneously designing an unheard-of way through the telephone implanted in technology's weed garden? We must wait; Heidegger himself will give up a reading of the ghosts that lighten, calling forth radiance and white ashes. Pointing to what is essentially present in all speaking, Heidegger writes first, let us say, of Alexander Graham Bell's father, professor of phonetics, before proceeding to the invention of the son. Thus in the first place, speaking, as a form of cognition and practice, "is known as the articulated vocalization of thought by means of the organs of speech" (*W*, 123). Now we come up on the amendment that doubles the structure of speaking, in the form of a simultaneity. "But speaking is at the same time also listening. It is the custom to put speaking and listening in opposition: one man speaks, the other listens. But listening accompanies and surrounds not only speaking such as takes place in conversation. The simultaneousness of speaking and listening has a larger meaning. Speaking is of itself a listening. Speaking is listening to the language which we speak" (*W*, 123). What is called speaking, if not the invisible structures which have been manipulating the Heideggerian scene of writing from the beginning? This assigns the condition of listening to the language which we speak, simultaneously achieving a speaking and a listening no longer to be understood in terms of an opposition. Heidegger grafts the assimilation of a telephonic structure onto the first known meaning of speaking, the organic vocalization which speaking-and-listening complicates and doubles. Speaking-and-listening may be simultaneous, but listening will have had the edge on speaking, asserting a certain temporal priority. A listening, in fact, is prior to speaking, so that when speaking gets on the line, "it is a listening not *while* but *before* we are speaking" (*W*, 123). What do we hear there? asks the text: "We hear language speaking" (*W*, 124). This is a non-organic speaking, Heidegger advises, a form of language not equipped in this way: "But—does language itself speak? How is it supposed to perform such a feat when obviously it is not equipped with organs of speech? Yet *language* speaks. . . . In our speaking, as a listening to language, we say again the Saying we have heard. We let its soundless voice come to us, and then demand, reach out and call for the sound that is already kept in store for us" (*W*, 124). To "reach out and call" has become the gestural trait par excellence of commercial telephony, so much so that one cannot resist its homonymy with the "same" utterance in Heidegger. Yet the two utterances appear to breathe in the unity of the same apparatus, from the being-on-the-telephone which, immobily fixed, ejects a soundless voice whose sound, kept in store, one then calls for. This is the mutism of anticipatory calling that schizophrenia frequents. **In order** to bring the drift of the thought to "our human saying in this light" (*W*, 123), Heidegger has drawn a distinction between saying and speaking (one may speak endlessly and all the time say nothing); to "say" means to show, to let appear, to let be seen and heard. Speaking belongs to the design of language, which is pervaded by all modes of saying and of what is said, in which everything present or absent announces, grants, or refuses itself, shows itself or withdraws. But "saying" has a history of degradation behind it, which Heidegger must first cast aside. In the mostly disparaging sense, "saying is accounted a mere say-so, a rumor unsupported and hence untrustworthy. Here 'saying' is not understood in this sense, nor in its natural, essential sense of *saga*. . . . In keeping with the most ancient usage of the word we understand saying in terms of showing, pointing out, signaling. Jean-Paul called the phenomena of nature 'the spiritual pointer' or 'spiritual index finger' (*der geistige Zeigefinger*)" (*W*, 123). Language could be resumed as the history of this finger, even when it is placed on the mouth to silence a speaking. The teacher points, the god and the schizophrenic speak through or to the spiritual forefinger. In the discipline of anthropology, the digital has won man distinction over other animals. Heidegger traces the route of saying from rumor to the spiritualized digitals. The semiotically invested finger comes to manipulate the alphabetico-numerical ordering of *Geschick*. The spiritual forefinger presses toward schizophrenic partial systematizing. Also, it is the bewitching finger, which makes it rude to point or to press red buttons, for the power of pointing used to be associated with magical arrests (thus in Jewish Orthodox marriage ceremonies the wedding ring is said to be placed on this spiritual finger of the woman, to block her potency). The history of this finger of which the stylus is an extension, includes making the marionette come alive, but mostly it points to the essential being of language, which is "*Saying as Showing*. Its showing character is not based on signs of any kind; rather, all signs arise from a showing within whose realm and for whose purposes they can be signs" (*W*, 123). This, importantly, is not a trait of the properly human, Heidegger argues, for,

In view of the structure of Saying, however, we may not consider showing as exclusively, or even decisively, the property of human activity. Self-showing appearance is the mark of the presence and absence of everything that is present, of every kind and rank. Even when Showing is accomplished by our human saying, even then this showing, this pointer, is preceded by an indication that it will let itself be shown. (*W*, 123)

The structure of saying exposes the human as only one of its properties, though not in a unique or even decisive way. Self-showing and telling cannot be claimed as trophies of the properly human. After marking the appearance of every kind and rank, Heidegger brings into view the simultaneousness of speaking and listening. Perhaps this supplies the transparency of context in which to circumscribe the kind of aggravated misreading that the science of schizophrenia presses upon Heidegger. This occurs precisely when it draws limits to its hopes for a decisively human property of self-showing. The question, as we saw it, concerned the presencing of the speaker, which appeared to be cut off from itself like an effect from a cause. "Speaking must have speakers," Heidegger shows, "but not merely in the same way as an effect must have a cause. Rather, the speakers are present in the way of speaking. Speaking, they are present and together with those with whom they speak, in whose neighborhood they dwell because it is what happens to concern them at the moment" (*W,* 120). At this point, Heidegger appears to rely on a communality of sense, a *sensus communis,* or an essential consensus, into which the unpresent tense of schizophrenic discourse could not, admittedly, be happily entered. However, even in this convocation of something like a contractual agreement of sense, a common contextuality and steadiness of address, Heidegger amends the speaking to include, as an address, the human and the thingly: "That includes fellow men and things, namely, everything that conditions things and determines men. All this is addressed in word, each in its own way, and therefore spoken about and discussed in such a way that the speakers speak to and with one another and to themselves. All the while, what is spoken remains many-sided. Often it is no more than what has been spoken explicitly, and either fades quickly away or else is somehow preserved. What is spoken can have passed by, but it also can have arrived long ago as that which is granted, by which somebody is addressed" (*W,* 120). **The Laingian** reading of Heidegger establishes a dimension which appears to set objections to schizophrenogenic modes of address, to the distortions of the place of sender and recipient toward which Heidegger's thinking may appear to harbor intolerance. Nonetheless even in these passages, the temporal rendering of that which is spoken in addition to the incomparable inclusion of thingly speakers already complicate any itinerary that would seek reliably to reroute schizophrenic Saying from a more normative grasp of language. But the material with which to seek presence of person in the speaking cannot be securely retrieved from any Heideggerian path of language. In "The Way to Language," Heidegger continues in this way, averting the dangers of the straight and narrow:

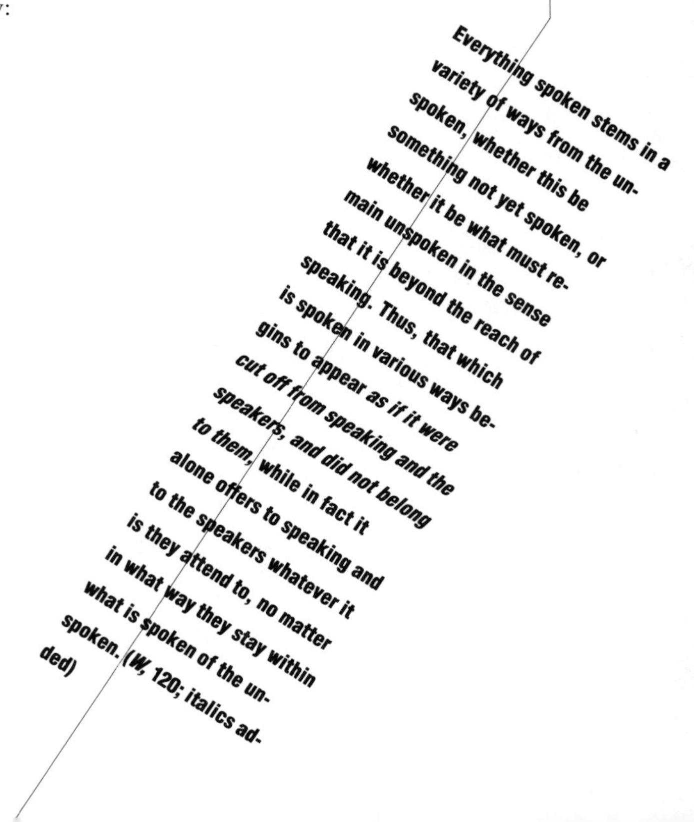
Everything spoken stems in a variety of ways from the unspoken, whether this be something not yet spoken, or whether it be what must remain unspoken in the sense that it is beyond the reach of speaking. Thus, that which is spoken in various ways begins to appear *as if it were cut off from speaking and the speakers, and did not belong to them,* while in fact it alone offers to speaking and to the speakers whatever it is they attend to, no matter in what way they stay within what is spoken of the unspoken. (*W,* 120; italics added)

Not long after this reading, which in part corresponds to the descriptive analysis of schizophrenic utterance in Lainguage, Heidegger offers to accentuate the cutting. Analyzing the sign in terms of *secare,* "to cut," he returns to the decisive disconnectedness in all language tracings. The speaking which appears as if disconnected from speaking and the speakers cannot therefore be used to explicate an essential dimension, gleaned from Heidegger, of schizophrenia in its most advanced stages of psychosis—unless, of course, Heidegger were himself to be implicated in the unfolding of a schizophrenogenic understanding of language. This would be going very far, on the other way to language, whose essential signpost reads "Wrong Way, Do Not Enter." **In another** essay, "The Nature of Language," Heidegger has the following to say on the question, raised so often by the doctors, of not being there:

**All is way. . . .
The way allows us to
reach what concerns us, in
that domain where we are
already staying. Why then,
one may ask, still find a way
to it? Answer: because
where we already are, we are
in such a way that at the
same time we are not there,
because we ourselves have
not yet properly reached
what concerns our being, not
even approached it. The way
that lets us reach where we
already are, differing from
all other ways, calls for an
escort that runs far ahead.
(*W*, 92–93)**

That which has been with us, the companion, stretches itself apart from us in answer to a call. The escort does not cease to be an escort when à long-distance runner is called for. It is one that reaches the place where we are not but toward which we point. We are where we are in such a way that, at the same time, we are not there. This is where we stay. Heidegger places some words after one that is simple, single, and armed with the antennae of a colon, *Answer:* Why do we care to mention this total response unit?

Seit ein Gespräch wir sind : Immortals to terrestrials

Answer: because, for Heidegger, even the colon can place a call. In fact, the call is made at a point of disconnection that cites and recites itself in the cleavage between word and thing. This taking place emerges with the insight of renunciation in Stefan George's famous lines:

So I renounced and sadly see: Where word breaks off no thing may be.

Heidegger reads the switchboard effect of the colon, which connects disconnectingly what is seen to break off.

The colon, Heidegger writes, "names the call to enter into that relation between thing and word which has now been experienced" (*W,* 65). The colon does not say what the substance of the renunciation is, but names the call. In German, the word for "colon" is *Doppelpunkt,* the doubling structure of the hearing and saying which inhabit the call, opening the lines through which in this case "the poet experiences his poetic calling as a call to the word as source, the bourn of Being" (*W,* 66). The colon places a weighty call in "The Nature of Language," where Heidegger proposes this poem as guide-word:

The being of language:
The language of being.

But he wishes to put this through more clearly.

> We must now try to hear it more clearly, to make it more indicative of the way that lets us reach what even now reaches and touches us.
>
> The being of language: the language of being.
>
> Two phrases held apart by a colon, each the inversion of the other. If the whole is to be a guide-word, then this colon must indicate that what precedes it opens onto what follows it. Within the whole there plays a disclosure and a beckoning that point to something which we, coming from the first turn of phrase, do not suspect in the second. (*W,* 94)

Importantly, any explanations within the scope of grammatical, that is metaphysical and logical, ways of thinking, are found to be insufficient, and "may bring us closer to the matter, though it can never do justice to the situation that the guide-word names" (*W*, 94). The colon, calling, eventually puts us through to speaking, to "what *to speak* means" (*W*, 95). What something is, *to ti estin*, whatness, "comprises since Plato what one commonly calls the 'nature' or *essentia*, the essence of a thing" (*W*, 94). The colon stands as is. Understood "less strictly, the phrase before the colon then says: we shall comprehend what language is as soon as we enter into what the colon, so to speak, opens up before us. And that is the language of being" (*W*, 94–95). Heidegger sets tangible limits on a language that would be interpreted as something that is present: "If we take language directly in the sense of something that is present," as Laing appears to do, "we encounter it as the act of speaking, the activation of the organs of speech, mouth, lips, tongue. Language manifests itself in speaking, as a phenomenon that occurs in man. The fact that language has long since been experienced, conceived, defined in these terms is attested by the names that the Western languages have given to themselves: *glossa, lingua, langue,* language. Language is the tongue" (*W*, 96). This precisely designates the place where the schizophrenic's cut broaches. Language extends itself as a body part. Thus Julie's phantasms offer her tongue as the word/thing to be cut out. As for schizolanguage, the analyst wants to cut it out. All this gets formed into a mutism that resides in the very possibility of language taken as something that is present.

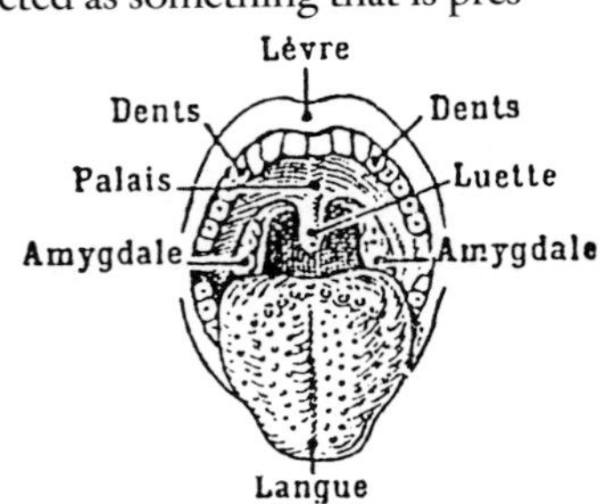

The tongues of fire that we have seen domesticated in Freud's telephonic episode flare up momentarily when Heidegger evokes the second chapter of the Acts of the Apostles, which tells of the Pentecost miracle. The vulgate version of verses three and four cited by Heidegger reads "Et apparuerunt illis dispertitae linguae tamquam ignis . . . et coeperunt loqui variis linguis" (*W*, 96). The Revised Standard Version runs: "And there appeared to them tongues of fire, distributed and resting on each one of them. And they . . . began to speak in other tongues." Heidegger adds: "yet their speaking is not meant as a mere facility of the tongue, but as filled with the holy spirit, the *pneuma hagion*" (*W*, 96–97). The extension of this pneumatic channel draws us, as if mesmerized, toward a phenomenon of electrified speech. (Kant, in the Third Critique, had warned that fascination by fire does not constitute an aesthetic experience;

this gives us reason to believe that the tongues of fire which draw us painlessly toward their source, hallucinate us). Who is to say that the other tongues in which the Apostles spoke on that day of white ashes ("tongues of fire, distributed and resting on each one of them") were not the advanced escorts of voices distributed by technology's body of schizophrenic translation? Could it be that the two tips of the colon were rubbed together to spark such a hallucinatory flame in our thinking?

Very shortly into this passage, language is shown to shoot forth from the mouth. The fire has been stilled within the space of a few paragraphs. The colon has been redistributed to rest on top of an "o" in order to skywrite the

name of the poet of poets, Hölderlin. The poet has "dispatched the rivers . . . and our tongue loosens," the fire subsides (*W,* 99). "Language," writes Hölderlin through Heidegger, "is the flower of the mouth. In language the earth blossoms toward the bloom of the sky" (*W,* 99). The mouth has been twisted away from its purely physiological or technical sense. "The landscape, and that means the earth, speaks in them, differently each time. But the mouth is not merely a kind of organ of the body understood as an organism—body and mouth are part of the earth's flow and growth in which we mortals flourish, and from which we receive the soundness of our roots" (*W,* 98–99). We flourish somewhere between the mouth of the river and the fire's tongue, receptively awaiting the soundless gathering call arriving at us, instituting us. The words of the poet say that we *are* (*wir sind*) from the moment of interlocution, co-speaking (*seit ein Gespräch*) and can now hear from one another (*und hören können voneinander*). There was something like an originary *Gespräch* that opened our ears to each other. "Seit ein Gespräch wir sind . . ." (*W,* 78). "Those who have heard from one another" responds the thinking, "Those who 'have heard from one another'—the ones and the others—are men and gods" (*W,* 78).

In the same essay Heidegger crafts an invisible suture, shifting to Stefan George's *Das Neue Reich*. He writes of a verse which rings like a *basso ostinato* through all the songs.

Wherein you hang—you do not know.

"The experience of the poet with the word passes into darkness, and even remains veiled itself" (*W*, 79). One would have to read *experience* in the manner of Lacoue-Labarthe, encountering in it the risk of *peri*shing.[91] You do not know wherein you hang, the experience of the word passes into darkness.

Those who have heard from one another, it is asserted, are those terrestrially bound beings whose hearing is pierced by the gods. Heidegger places "—the ones and the others—" between dashes (*W*, 78). Pierced at both sides, the hearing is not emitted simply in one way, as one would imagine the loudspeaker from above to be. This is because the hearing does not take place on a broadcast system that could be grafted conceptually onto the radio. Rather, what constitutes mortals and gods as that which they are, a "we" (*wir sind*) and not a "they," is that we have heard from one another—the ones and the others—that is to say, the gods are also

listening at the other end, at the end of a finitude that will never end but to which every listening trumpet infinitely aspires. They (we) have heard from one another, which places them each at their end, at a respectfully long distance, and our end hears itself as the listening saying on the air. As for the experience of the poet, we dare say it passes away into the passivity of an operator who brings the end into inner sight, "the experience of the poet with the word passes into darkness, and even remains veiled itself." When we maintain a regardful long distance, this does not mean that the instrument assuring the distance must itself dissolve into absence. The closest thing can speak to the ear from afar, from a remoteness that mingles with nearness. The kind of discourse that we have been in the twentieth century is now on the line, for we hear, in Trakl's words,

the Vanishing,
broken off by static.

Is the telephone too scandalously near Heidegger to be read by him, even where he himself resists reading it? Somewhere in "The Word of Nietzsche: 'God Is Dead,'" Heidegger has written that true thinking should not concern itself with some arcane and hidden meaning, but with "something lying near, that which lies nearest," which, by virtue of that very nearness, man's thinking can readily fail to notice at all. Being resides in whatever is—in the particular and in the far-ranging complexity of generality—thereby continually approaching and concerning man. "In the 'is,'" spoken of anything real whatever, "'Being' is uttered."[92]

ON PAIN

☎ Heidegger to Trakl

Language concerns us who as mortals speak only as we respond to language. Mortals are those who can experience death as death. Animals cannot do so. But animals cannot speak either, claims Heidegger.[93] If the essential relationship between death and language "flashes up before us," though it still remains unthought (*W*, 107), the flash that burns most tellingly may be that borne up by language's ashen death rattle. One of the names of this rattle is schizophrenia. The sonic flash of death inflames the schizophrenic utterance. But what does it mean to experience death as death? This opens a terrain the gods are themselves not permitted to traverse experientially, which is why the Greek goddess in *Hippolytus* must avert her gaze, withdraw from her mortal companion at the advent of his death. She must not interiorize, memorize, bite into death, nor surround it with the symbolicity with which mortals veil a beloved's departure. Mortals are those who are alive to death. And thus "sadness and joy play into each other" (*W*, 153). The play itself which attunes the two by letting the remote be near and the near be remote is pain. The spirit which answers to pain, the spirit attuned by pain and to pain, is melancholy (*W*, 153).

In "Language in the Poem," another dialogue gets on the line, which is the same dialogue we have been trying to hear all along. The dialogue of thinking with poetry is long. It has barely begun. "The dialogue of thinking with poetry aims to call forth the *nature* of language, so that mortals may learn again to live within language" (*W,* 161). A thinking dialogue with poetry runs the risk of interfering with the saying of the utterance, instead of allowing it to sing from within its own inner peace. The response to the call of the poem, however thinkingly grasped, still resonates the alarm that started the thinking which has roused the thought from its reserve. The poem reciprocatingly cuts into thinking's place of inner peace. Trakl has written, "Something strange is the soul on earth." Heidegger asks, "but what does 'strange' mean?" By strange we "usually understand something that is not familiar, does not appeal to us—something that is rather a burden and an unease. But the word we are using—the German '*fremd,*' the Old High German '*fram*'—really means: forward to somewhere else, underway toward . . . , onward toward the encounter with what is kept in store for it" (*W,* 162–163). Delay call forwarding. How distant is Heidegger's arrangement with Trakl from the calls being placed between them? "Almost unknown to itself, the '*fremd*' is already following the call that calls it on the way into its own" (*W,* 163). It is for the duration of this call that we tap into the ghost of the weed garden, the telecrypt that sings through the wires binding mortals to the beyond. Heidegger will finally speak to us of madness. The conversation begins with the "Seven-Song of Death." It clandestinely arranges a party line to Julie and Miss St. Others, as well.

Trakl:

"In his grave
the white magician
plays
with his snakes."
(*W,* 173)

Heidegger:

"The dead one
lives in his grave.
He lives in his chamber,
so quietly
and lost in thought
that
he plays with his snakes."
(*W,* 173)

Further along:

> "The dead one is
> the madman.
> Does the word mean
> someone
> who is mentally ill?
> Madness here
> does not mean
> a mind filled with
> senseless delusions.
> The madman's mind
> senses—
> senses in fact
> as no one else does.
> Even so,
> he does not have
> the sense of the
> others.
> He is of another mind.
> The departed one
> is
> a man apart,
> a madman,
> because he has taken
> his way
> in another direction.
> From
> that other direction,
> his madness
> may be called "gentle,"
> for his mind pursues
> a greater stillness."
> (*W*, 173)

"The dead one is the madman" gives us a citation taken back from Lainguage. Heidegger does not inquire into what it could mean to be pronounced mad when dead or otherwise. Therefore, the dead one is not merely dead but is the madman. As dead, he is mad.

Customarily, Heidegger waves aside the easy certitudes concerning madness. In the case of Nietzsche, as in his reply to *On Pain,* Heidegger resists the determinations that would allow us to prescribe that which belongs to madness or to its other. Nietzsche wrote to the end of his thought. In a way that rhymes with any case study of something like schizophrenia, the possibility itself of biography is cast aside. The dead one is the madman. Heidegger goes a bit further into the question, which for him does not appear to be a question, of madness. He listens to the word in the eerie mode of that which is *fremd*. He asks about mental illness and suggests a kind of definition: a mind filled with senseless delusions. This is quickly said, and it is by no means clear that what follows thereupon is meant to create a tension of opposition, such as mental illness qua senseless delusions maneuvered against the mind's health, sanity's insight. But "senseless" is used by Heidegger in a more original way. The madman's mind senses, but from a direction other than the ones upon which we have departed. This mind senses uniquely, as no one else does "in fact." Once Nietzsche called for a thinking that would have a vigorous fragrance, like a wheatfield on a summer's night. In the essay "On the Way to Language" Heidegger has asked, "how many of us today still have the senses for that fragrance?" (*W*, 70). There is no "us" attuned to that thinking's fragrance, as if certain senses had atrophied. Here we could cautiously substitute the name of Nietzsche for the "madman": "The madman's mind senses—senses in fact as no one else does." Nietzsche made claims for his special senses. Yet it is an error to hear Nietzsche's name under "The dead one is the madman." The latter is apart, of another kind of mind, in the negativity perhaps of the Hölderlinian third eye, a supplementary sense that has taken another direction, but one which deserves the naming of gentleness, for the other mind, of the genuinely divided madman, wanders toward a greater stillness. A line from the poem reads, "In his quieter childhood and died" (*W*, 173). The stillness, the unbearably quieter childhood means, in the vocabulary of Lainguage, that the child of the rude empirical does not object, does not stir but remains still, gathering untrackable senses. The child objects to nothing. Nor did it "subject," however. The schizo child is a transalive object having succumbed to "its quieter childhood and died." It is stilled.

We approach from another path the ghost in the weed garden, in stillness. The apartness is *ghostly,* Heidegger is saying. "This word—what does it mean? Its meaning and its use are very old" (*W*, 177). The ghostly contours of the *techné* beckon us to approach. We are drawn on by the rumor of what has happened to dialogue. It has been assassinated and resurrected in technology's vampire.

Heidegger moves in upon the ghostly from another direction. Still, since so much that echoes through the quiet chambers of the telephone receivers will have been understood as ghostly, since the unappeased ghost still moans in Julie's weed garden, we want to hear Heidegger out on this, or rather to draw his words out, strange as it seems to think that here the spook speaks. "To spookulate" would imply granting a withdrawal of the excessive visual representation that still informs speculation.

Heidegger says it differently. "Ghostly" means what is by way of the spirit, what stems from it and follows its nature; it means spiritual, though not in the narrow sense that binds the word to spirituality, the priestly orders, or the church. Trakl's poem "In Hellbrunn" recalls the opposition created between "of the spirit" and the material. "This opposition posits a differentiation of two separate realms and, in Platonic-Western terms, states the gulf between the suprasensuous *noeton* and the sensuous *aistheton*. 'Of the spirit' so understood—it meanwhile has come to mean rational, intellectual, ideological—together with its opposites belongs to the world view of the decaying kind of man" (*W*, 179). But Trakl's poem parts with this kind of reading, leaving the "of the spirit" in the sense of the language of metaphysics. Heidegger asks what, then, is the spirit? The poet evokes the "hot flame of the spirit" in his last poem, "Grodek." Heidegger turns toward it.

The spirit is flaming, and only in this sense perhaps is it something flickering in the air. Trakl sees spirit not primarily as *pneuma*, something ethereal, but as a flame that inflames, startles, horrifies, and shatters us. Flame is glowing lumination. What flame is the *ek-stasis* which lightens and calls forth radiance, but which may also go on consuming and reduce all to white ashes.

"Flame is the palest pallor's brother" runs a line in the poem "Transformation of Evil." Trakl sees spirit in terms of that being which is indicated in the original meaning of the word "ghost"—a being terrified, beside himself, *ek-static*.

Spirit or ghost understood in this way has its being in the possibility of *both* gentleness *and* destructiveness. Gentleness in no way dampens the ecstasy of the inflammatory, but holds it gathered in the peace of friendship. Destructiveness comes from unbridled license, which consumes itself in its own revolt and thus is active evil. Evil is always the evil of a ghostly spirit. Evil and its malice is not of a sensuous, material nature. Nor is it purely "of the spirit." Evil is ghostly in that it is the revolt of a terror blazing away in blind delusion, which casts all things into unholy fragmentation and threatens to turn the calm, collected blossoming of gentleness to ashes. (*W*, 179)

The pain is the glow of melancholy. Everything that is alive, says Heidegger, is painful. Tuned to the silent conquest of pain, Trakl's poetry sounds an ancient stone. Pain conceals itself in the stone, the petrifying pain that delivers itself into the keeping of impenetrable rock. "And softly touches you an ancient stone" (*W*, 182).

The old stones, writes Heidegger, are pain itself, for pain looks earthily upon mortals. "The colon after the word 'stone' signifies that now *the stone* is speaking. Pain itself has the word" (*W*, 182). Still later: "The wanderers who listen toward the leafy branches for the early dead, reply to these words of pain with the words of the next line: 'O mouth! that trembles through the silvery willow'" (*W*, 182).

the call of the colon

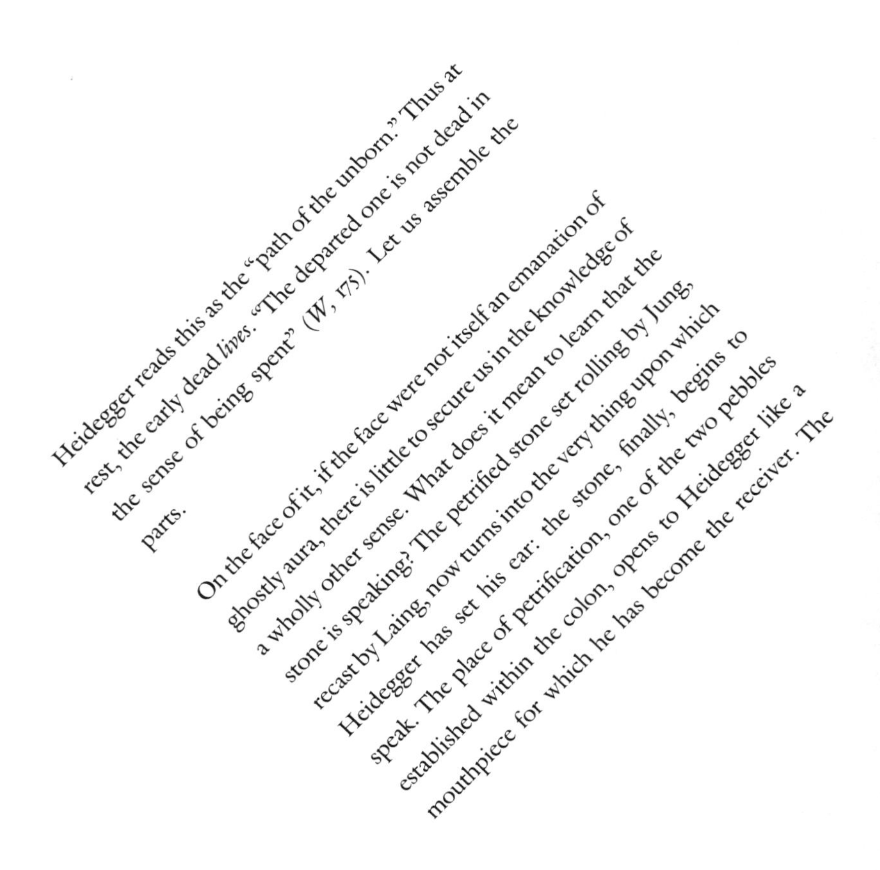

Heidegger reads this as the "path of the unborn." Thus at rest, the early dead *lives*. "The departed one is not dead in the sense of being spent" (*W*, 175). Let us assemble the parts.

On the face of it, if the face were not itself an emanation of ghostly aura, there is little to secure us in the knowledge of a wholly other sense. What does it mean to learn that the stone is speaking? The petrified stone set rolling by Jung, recast by Laing, now turns into the very thing upon which Heidegger has set his ear: the stone, finally, begins to speak. The place of petrification, one of the two pebbles established within the colon, opens to Heidegger like a mouthpiece for which he has become the receiver. The two stones—the first moved along by Jung, the second by Laing—placed themselves on the path as the colon opening toward another colon, the two points occupied by poet and thinker, Trakl and Heidegger. The ghost in the weed garden was petrified into this stone. Pain arrested has the word. This stony silence implanted anorganically somewhere along Julie's body, and that of Miss St., gathers itself into speech, spreading a kind of liquefaction of pain that does not, however, touch the integrity of the stone. The stone is not merely thrown as one form of figurative language among others. Like allegory, it casts one of language's essential possibilities: the possibility that permits language to say the other and to speak of itself while speaking of something else.[94] Yet here it represents the other, the commemorative monument, the firm gravestone which mouths language. Pain conceals itself in the stone. It remains vaulted and guarded until it is sounded.

The case histories each turned the body into a melancholic booth for a stone to speak, guardedly, through a "partial system" which was marked neither entirely by death, nor for any matter, by life, if this should come to be understood in opposition to death. In the depths of each case a child was conceived by the speaker as having been murdered, as having been as in Trakl's poem, made to vanish. At first lost, the child's ghost would find a telephone connection in the body that housed the spirit of a petrified subject. The spirit inhabits the body, its many voices demanding a reply—for the stone not only speaks out but awaits the opening of a listening mouth that could suck in this pain and swallow it (it is one of Beckett's sucking stones). It plays with fire.

The spirit which will return stone to speech is flaming. It is not ethereal, but, giving off something like shock, it is electrically empowered. Trakl's spirit must not be read in the main as *pneuma* nor as a sighing flame that loses its speaking wind; no, it is a generating kind of force, "a flame that inflames" (*W*, 179), an electric charge. Can we think of Trakl's poem in this light? The spirit's speaking comes so suddenly that its shock effect can startle or horrify or even shatter the petrified stone which it arouses. The ghost of Heidegger (of Trakl) is **wed to the white abyss cauterized by the schizophrenic probe.** It finds the glowing lumination of an *ek-stasis* which may reduce the stone to white ashes—not dark ashes but the ghostly incineration called forth by excess light, the flaming side of blindness's pain. This spirit beckons forth the ghost as that being which it is, a being beside oneself, projected as the immateriality of its own pain, wandering outside of one self, a more-than-divided self, a thing whose movement is the *ek-static*. Yet the spirit responding to this call is sheltered in the structure of a *both/and*. To be what it is means that through the interstices of the material and suprasensory it gathers both destructiveness and gentleness. The spook speaks destructiveness in a rage of self-consuming "revolt." It's electrical blazing makes things break off from the calm into "unholy fragmentation." It threatens to turn the calm into splintering white ashes.

It is important for us, if not quite comprehensible, that evil, that which is harmful, should always be linked to the evil or a ghostly spirit. In this way the harmful enters as ancestral familiarity, something that appears undigestible, like a lump or stone in one's throat. If the ghostly spirit, strictly speaking, escapes material properties, it cannot be altogether outside of you. You are taken outside by it, terrified, beside yourself, haunted. It happens when the electric flame ignites. You speak to it, through it, in the night of its appearing. But it is not simply terrifying. It is *both/and*. It is both destructive and generous, generating gentleness. Where does the gathering power of gentleness reside, asks Heidegger? How is it bridled? What spirit holds its reins? In what way is human nature ghostly, and how does it become so? (*W*, 179).

"Inasmuch as the nature of spirit consists in a bursting into flame, it strikes a new course, lights it, and sets man on the way. Being flame, the spirit is the storm that 'storms the heavens' and 'hunts down God'" (*W*, 179–180). An electrical storm, a thundering intrusion, the spirit as that which is sent like an immemorial message from the heavens, storms the heavens, hunting down the receiver. The spirit chases, drives the soul to get under way to where it leads the way. "The spirit carries it over into strangeness." "Something strange is the soul on earth." The soul "feeds" the spirit, asserts Heidegger vampirically. "How? How else than by investing the spirit with the flame that is in the soul's very nature? This flame is the glow of melancholy, 'the patience of the lonely soul'" (*W*, 180).

Like the soul, driven and chased down by the spirit, we are following to where it leads the way. This means following a logic that, once followed, must also be built. We are trying to track the human ghostly to where it currently resides, for it has given notice of a change of address. Whether the notice ever reached Trakl or Heidegger in this form cannot be known, though their words are triggered by its content. Bursting into flame, the spirit seeks a certain containment. The bursting spirit has little to do with religious pride. It intrudes, it speaks, it carries the soul over into strangeness. Let us stay with this strangeness and listen for the messages it carries. On the one hand it says that there is no listening without separation—without a friend's face that has died away. The site of such a listening in whose name one speaks is called apartness.

Following the poetic line of Trakl's poem "To One Who Died Young," Heidegger observes a friend listening after the stranger. "In listening, he follows the departed and thus becomes himself a wanderer, a stranger. The friend's soul listens after the dead. The friend's face has 'died away'" (*W*, 186–187). The voice is the "'birdvoice' of 'the death-like' (*The Wanderer*)" (*W*, 187). The text carves a movement from strangeness to the voice of the friend, which we have heard emerge in the call of conscience, to the familiar, almost familial, bond that is related to itself in listening: "Listening after the departed, the friend sings his song and thus becomes his brother; only now, as the stranger's brother, does he also become the brother of the stranger's sister whose 'lunar voice rings through the ghostly night'" ("Ghostly Twilight") (*W*, 187–188). Apartness is the poem's site "because the music of the stranger's ringing-radiant footfall inflames his followers' dark wandering into listening song" (*W*, 188). Heidegger gathers the poet's work to mean: the saying-after-saying again the music of the spirit of apartness that has been spoken to the poet. "For the longest time—before it comes to be said, that is, spoken—the poet's work is only a listening. Apartness first gathers the listening into its music, so that this music may ring through the spoken saying in which it will resound" (*W*, 188). The poet takes the line, separated from the speaking to which he is a hearing. This listening comes to be more profound in its telling than mere history. In momentary harmony with the schizophrenic subject who does not gather its meaning about it by some visible accretion of empirical occurrence, so the invisible theater of telephone's poetry can fill itself at a distance with the lunar voice of a stranger's sister. Listening after par excellence: when the ear admits the vanishing image of a friend's face.

There is yet another ear which in its readiness receives transmissions drawn from a sounded stone.

Toward the end of his discussion with Trakl, Heidegger broaches parasitic *Gerede* that sometimes passes for history. It has been said that Trakl's work is "profoundly unhistorical." In this judgment, asks Heidegger, what is meant by history? "If the word means no more than 'chronicle,' the rehearsal of past events, then Trakl is indeed unhistorical. His poetry has no need of historical 'objects'" (*W*, 196). This is because his work is historical "in the highest sense": "His poetry sings of the destiny which casts mankind in its still withheld nature—that is to say, saves mankind" (*W*, 196). This is not all. Momentarily, Heidegger turns back to cast a stone at a kind of technologized Dasein, as if he were to divide the self of this world

---

into the lucidity of the sheltered madman pitted against the blind delusions of a rumorologically organized world:

> *Is this dreamy romanticism, at the fringe of the technically-economically oriented world of modern mass existence? Or—is it the clear knowledge of the 'madman' who sees and senses other things than the reporters of the latest news who spend themselves chronicling the current happening, whose future is never more than a prolongation of today's events, a future that is forever without the advent of a destiny which concerns man for once at the source of his being?* (*W*, 196–197).

These reporters are said to spend themselves. They exhaust their being, draining off a death expenditure that has no listening-after, no future Saying. These reporters do not sense other senses, they would report on the Other as if a chronicle of schizophrenia were expected of a technician specialized in disorder. Now the madman, protected by marks of a strange citation, possesses clear knowledge, seeing and sensing other things, or perhaps sensing *things*, which, when under the dominion of the senses always fall under "other things." I would want to read "clear" ("the clear knowledge of the 'madman'") in terms of the lightening, resonating the lunar voice of the lightened abyss, not in terms of a sudden clarity that grants knowledge a security clearance. The clear knowledge is lunar, casting its light as already doubled and phantomized, borrowed from a diurnal sphere of visual representation from which it turned its face, in a kind of exorbitant revolution.

The latest news, according to this passage, is dead news, a saying from which the future is barred. Paradoxically, the latest news, which is made to corroborate a concept of history as chronicle, can have no history. Expulsed from the dimension of a futural horizon, it can, in the terms dictated by its being and time, draw from a past, whose fold would be creased by the future's recall, the advent of a delayed call forwarding.

What does the madman see clearly, if not the ghostly translucence of an immateriality, not seeing but listening? This opens a sphere of the sonic gaze. The madman "sees" listening, a listening-after whose only scenography would be carved out by the gulf between the suprasensuous *noeton* and the sensuous *aistheton*. The madman "sees" the voices, she sees that "which is pervaded by the spirit of apartness and is, in keeping with that spirit, 'ghostly'" (*W*, 197).

It will appear that Heidegger renders opinion reporting inaccessible to this clearer sighting of the listener. But he takes a step back to where we have been staying. All formulas are dangerous, he begins:

"They force whatever is said into the superficiality of instant opinion and are apt to corrupt our thinking. *But they may also be of help, at least as a prompting and a starting point for sustained reflection*. With these reservations we may venture this formulation" (W, 197; italics added).

There is a neighborhood of poetry that listens to the singing of destiny. Here the saying thing does not occupy a sovereign place of exteriority, the back alleys of "instant opinion." On the contrary, the thinking of Trakl's poetry, following "the pure echo of the music of ghostly years" (W, 198), may originate at the prompting of thinking's corruption. Heidegger listens to the superficiality, too, which he cautiously asserts may be of help, provide the upbeat for sustained reflection. In fact, this is the springboard from which he ventures a formulation.

This is not news, though it has been left unsaid. Over and over again, in different contexts, Heidegger tells us, without dwelling on the point, that opinion—usually in the form of rumor—is eventually related to the most daring thinking. Or rather, a daring writing enjoys a relationship of enslavement to something like opinion, utterance's murky rumbling. Rumor would not be reducible to some sort of external envelope that can be taken off, put on, or thrown aside like clothing. More pressingly, any writing that is open, is fundamentally open to rumor. But already what he calls the "dared word," in its anteriority, has been open to rumor, which acts as the horizon for all language testing. While under the shadow of negativity, rumor and instant opinion nonetheless act as enablers, as the ground and horizon

for the founding of
a "more original and
more careful thinking."

We have hit an intersection where the lines of public diffusion cross those of more private, nonreferential systems of poetry and schizophrenia. These feed into the telephone that plays chiasmatically on the dimensions of inner and outer space. What of **the technosphere from which the lunar sister speaks?** Would Heidegger's way to language also take an exorbitant path, lending a long, extended ear to the absorption of telehearing, in the form, say, of a satellite? It may appear to us at first, harrassed sight that technology has introduced something of a "rupture" into the very modalities of hearing or seeing under discussion. Heidegger's fear, his technophobia in the *Spiegel* article, has suggested as much. Yet here we observe the thinker seeking a form of help from the time-space produced by the new technologies.

We ourselves have followed an exorbitant path from electrical carriers to nocturnal emissions, sheltering our hopes in the neighborhood of poetry, even if that neighborhood be inclusive of devastated ghettos where schizophrenia appears not to object. The way we have proceeded would suggest that something like technology has not dominated our course, though the Framing could not be disposed of, either. We have listened to a stone speak, an implanted *calculus,* in the bodies who wander on the fringes of surrealism's talking dismemberments. We have read, beside ourselves, the electrical flashes of remote spirits, flamed and inflaming, generating a strangely lunar heat through which we can hear from one another. This is not the language of technology, in the sense that technology would be placed at the source of this reflection, or possess it as a piece of property, something to be annexed to the house of Being in order to increase the property value in the secluded community of thinking. To a large extent, the community is no longer sectioned in this way. The fourfold has been undone, there is no earth left, we have been told in the listening-after that Heidegger had programmed.

Neither the source of a new insight, nor the site of epochal closure, technology itself answers a call. That is why we have had to plod through the endless weed garden. It would have been pleasanter to establish the newly laid ground of technology as our foundation, pretending that nothing were covered over, pushed deeper under the tabula rasa, suppressing an older ecology of reflection. Technology, too, obeys the law of responding, of answering a call at whose origin we are encountering so much static when tracing. We cannot yet answer the question concerning technology except by answering its call. And yet, while the technological call may be the same, it is not identical with what has preceded it. It amplifies, intensifies, passes down death sentences while keeping the body in custody. You cannot put up bond or bail—no bailing out of technology's iron-collared intensifier. This is why we have to stay with the call that seeks to pull us in, and to shorten our leash.

We are hypnotized things suffering from positive and from negative hallucinations, that is, we see what is not there and often we do not see what is there. In the first place because what it is to be there has no clarity of being. It is as if we cannot see a thing. Stemming from the famous verse, "No thing is where the word is lacking," Heidegger's word distills the thing.

'Thing' is here understood in the traditional broad sense, as meaning anything that in any way is. *In this sense even a god is a thing. Only where the word for the thing has been found is the thing a thing. Only thus* is *it* (*W*, 62). Good enough. We

recognize this thing. The god which the poet brings into being, even in the mediated mode of an absence, is a thing. The question regards how a word can bring a thing into being. Heidegger shows the “actual” situation obviously to be the reverse. We now enter a different orbit:

> *Take the sputnik. This thing, if such it is, is obviously independent of that name which was later tacked on to it. But perhaps matters are different with such things as rockets, atom bombs, reactors and the like. . . . Still, countless people look upon this ‘thing’ sputnik, too, as a wonder, this ‘thing’ that races around in a worldless ‘world’—space; to many people it was and still is a dream—wonder and dream of this modern technology which would be the last to admit the thought that what gives things their being is the word.* (W, 62).

Heidegger continues. Actions, not words, count in the calculus of planetary calculation. Was the first translator of words into action not Faust, the ancestral mad technologist of the supraworldly? The translation, rewriting a genesis of upward striving (and one can only reach this high, beyond oneself into the satellite long distance by signing the Mephistophelean pact), rang its originary alarm by substituting the word with action, the deed, resonant with the dead: *Am Anfang war die Tat* (In the beginning was the deed). So take sputnik, also a translation, a proper name, delayed appendage to a “thing.”

"Actions not words count in the calculus of planetary calculation. What use are poets? And yet . . ." (*W,* 62). Heidegger has been following the speed of the rocket which the "and yet" slows down, beckoning the thinking to take another course in another time-space encapsulation: "let us for once refrain from hurried thinking. Is not even this 'thing' what it is and the way it is in the name of its name? Certainly. If that hurry, in the sense of the technical maximization of all velocities, in whose time-space modern technology and apparatus can alone be what they are—if that hurry had not bespoken man and ordered him at its call, if that call to such hurry had not challenged him and put him at bay, if the word framing that order and challenge had not spoken: then there would be no sputnik. No thing is where the word is lacking" (*W,* 62). Heidegger, like the sputnik, had been launched by a command, a kind of mission-control word, ordering him. His language, his thinking were co-responding to the same call, to such hurry that was responsible for the rocket, the atom bomb, and the reactor. Heidegger's thinking was responding in the mode of a reactor. Thus he strangely backs down from his orbit, refusing the call, not letting himself be rushed into Russian, or launched by the space-time governing modern technology and himself. He does not merely say that he will not follow this path, or that his thinking ought to be diverted, as it always was, from this channel, or that language dwells in some privileged apartness from this challenger. No. Heidegger writes instead, let us (who, "us"?)—let us *for once* refrain from hurried thinking. **This time Heidegger will not take the call.** He stops his ears to the call of technology, or whatever modern thing is calling him, appropriating him in the mode of a command. He is going to disconnect from the rocket, but at what time? At a later phase, after his last dispatch.

> In the same essay, sputnik comes into view again, in the context of another higher stratum, that of the *meta*. Metalinguistics is the metaphysics of the thoroughgoing technicalization of all languages into the sole operative instrument of interplanetary information. "Metalanguage and sputnik, metalinguistics and rockets are the Same" (*W*, 58). We are still dealing with the above, but, it would seem, with a dangerously ghostless above. The internments of the phantom, the ghost transmission, would keep us blinded, badly hallucinated by the information gathering of linguists of the spirit, their philologists, psychologists, and analytic philosophers.

In what relation do you live to the language you speak?

> We speak our language. How else can we be close to language except by speaking? Writes Heidegger. Even so, our relation to language is vague, obscure, almost speechless.

It therefore might be helpful to us to rid ourselves of the habit of always hearing only what we already understand.

> *We speak our language. Even so, our relation to language is vague, obscure, almost speechless. Almost speechless: In what relation did you live to the language she didn't speak?*

You may think I
was addressing
you, or Heideg-
ger. You were
right, I was plac-
ing a call. But I
am only a ven-
trilocating reed
for the other.

You may think I
was addressing
you, or Heideg-
ger. You were
right, I was plac-
ing a call. But I
only a ven-
reed

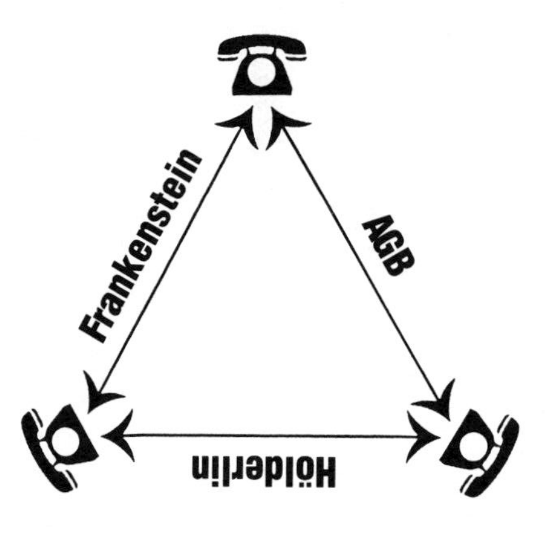

The Televisual Metaphysics

Alexander Graham Bell never considered the telephone to constitute a mere scientific thing, an object or even a machine that one day would be subsumable under a notion of technological dominion. His partner, Thomas Watson, wrote of the *art* of telephony and was a spiritualist who conjured ghosts at nightly séances in Salem. He was, for a time, a strong medium. The telephone's genesis, whose rhizomesque shoots still need to be traced, could have taken root in the dead ear Bell carried around with him and into which he spoke. He carried the ear, it transported him, during one summer vacation spent at his parents' home. ***Now, the dead*** ear that was lent to Aleck by the Harvard medical institution may have been the other ear of Hamlet's father or more likely, too, of Van Gogh, insofar as ears tend to come in pairs. Or it could have been that of his deaf mother, calling him home. Still, ears rarely are pricked up for stereophonic listening, so that it might be reasonable to assume that one ear suffices for the telephone as well as for the purpose of invention. The ear of the other is not the other ear, the one excluded from the partial headset that seems eternally to await its fitting unity. Perhaps this division in the set of ears could be clarified by swimming. When crawling, one ear is submerged under water—since we are regressing to a beginning this is as good a place to start as any: with the crawl, then, one hand tends to be extended and one ear submerged into a place of resonant silencing.[95] This cooperation of the ear and the trace-making hand produces a momentary disruption of the metaphysical sensorial apparatus (which relies more steadily on the ear-mouth, hand-eye complicities). In the meantime, the other ear exposes itself to the "outside," making itself capable of hearing the din of a different register of noises, which it receives before turning down. It exchanges places vaguely comparable to outside and inside with the other ear. In this way, at first sight, it would appear that the ears are indeed operating stereophonically, attending to double sonic events, receiving and shutting out, responding to the varied calls of air and water pressures. Sometimes an inmixation of the two distinct states can take place, as for example, when the ear retains water. This generally becomes noticeable on land. However, while they are surely attuned to different waves or channels, it is by no means clear that the ears are not operating as one monophonic unit. For it would be entirely within our range to suppose that the submerged ear deepens the listening capacity of the periotic one, rising above the water like a periscope that hears. *The ear above* water perceives free-floating transmissions which are unmuffled by the underwater terrain. Does this mean that the silenced ear cannot hear? Since the headset works, it cannot be determined that a condition of pure deafness is in fact induced. Nor would it be possible to state with conviction that because the telephone normally isolates a single ear, one does not hear. On the contrary, the deaf ear lends itself to the listening ear, creating a chamber that in turn invites the submarine self or a subconscious to tune in the call. One ear alone does the work of receiving the call, even though ears often come in pairs. One ear goes down into the abyss while the other exfoliates to the Open. It is not clear what the other, latent ear is doing. This somewhat disjunctive pair is not as such dialectizable; there is not a third ear to resolve the issue, though Hölderlin is said to have found a third eye. Or if there should be a third ear, which of course there always is—the ear of the state, for example, the operator, or the ear of the other—it acts as a second ear to the collapsible pair of ears. Unlike the mouth, the ear needs a silent partner, a double and phantom of itself. The mouth doubles itself by metonymic displacement, getting on the shuttle to vaginal or anal sites. In sum, Alexander Graham Bell carried a dead ear to his mother's house that summer. It is the ear of the Other whose identity is manifold. *The telephone,* whose labor pains were felt in that ear, has already in this limited example of its birthmark so complex a matrix, that the question of its placement as thing, object or machine, scientific, gynecological, or objet d'art still bears upon us. It was conceived with a kind of Frankensteinian pathos, this supplementary organ to a mother's deafness—mother or wife, actually, since Aleck's bride, Mabel Bell, also suffered the hearing impairment. But she came second to the deaf mother, like a second ear joined in the same determination as the first, with which it is paired. In a certain light, we can ask the same question of the Frankenstein monster as we do of the telephone. After all, both inventors—Bell and Victor Frankenstein—were invested in the simulacrum that speaks and hears; both, we might add precipitously, were elaborating works of mourning, memorializing that which is missing, in a certain way trying to make grow the technological flower from an impossible grave site. Both inventors were motivated to reanimate a corpse, to breathe life into dead body parts. University labs provided the material. Frankenstein was created in the university, an artificial genre, a dissertation in studied denial of a mother's departure, the objectivized phantasma of the reconstitutability of her body. The monster's predominant sexual markings do not appear to coincide with those of the mother in whose haunting image it is made. But the monster envisions himself in the light of a pair, and thus arrives at a self-designation suggestive of its being as a phantom. The monster could not become what it is, the argument goes, until the feminized other were made to join him. He shares in the atotality of the telephone that seeks its other in the remote possibility of a long-distance summoning. The monster will reside in his nature as phantom, which he sometimes is called by his inventor, until the other would be conjured up, recalled. *The story is too* well known. The essential connection will never be made. This perhaps was not even the point. The point, if such there be, was to *make a disconnection*. The phantom has learned the lesson of a desirable finitude, something he has picked up from reading Goethe, who in a way remote controls his destinerring. The point was not to respond (this was a beginning) but to know how to hang up. And thus a certain explosion into something like humanity takes place, at the threshold of finitude, whether or not this was to be a citation, a vampiric bite into the Goethean corpus. The phantom of Victor Frankenstein abolishes itself when, finally, the call for mourning is answered. He answers the call which it was impossible for Victor to receive, though he took it. The disconnection was made when the Disconnection was made. This is not a play on words. The monster knows that it was created to sing the lament of mourning, to teach the necessity of hanging up, which the professors with their self-willed striving could not effect. At the event of Victor's death, a strange gestalt of proximity emerges from the remoteness of absolute departure. The monster mourns, demonsterizing itself by the double lesson of a simultaneous finitude, that of the other and of the self cleared by the other. This was what he was called forth to be, to do, as a child taking upon itself the responsibility of a parentally inflected task. Yet, we must resist psychologizing even here, where so much suggests that the phantom marks the other side of a divided self, a partial object, or false self system. *As we shall* have to ask of the telephone whose summoning into being, springing forth in part from a dead ear—it was an ear dead to this world—we ask of the monstering text: was Frankenstein (he has in the meantime acquired his creator's proper name) a body or machine, a prosthetic soul perhaps, appended to the maternal fantasy of his founding father? Was he a "thing," as sometimes Frankenstein père calls him? If so, what is a thing? What is his equipmental nature? These properties of his potential being are not necessarily exclusive of one another—human subject *or* a piece of bionic technology—for transplants of a machinal sort are being made, and organs are being kept "alive" by machines. It cannot suffice to say, with McLuhan, that this machinery extends the body in a way that would not be discontinuous. We have established very little about the putative identity of this monster or thing. He was an answering machine of sorts, one whose call was to hang up and disconnect. *At the advent* of this mediated and altogether new necrophilia, the medium is a kind of walking switchboard whose origin in the text of *The New Prometheus* announces the disruption of models of organicity by the electrical shock waves supplanting it.[96] The monster, in short, who, following the Goethe manual, elects his short-circuiting, has as its form of presencing an electrical terminal reconstituted by a transformer. The monster is wired; he has been, in a prefiguring sense, laser-beamed into existence by the electrocution of a proud family tree, the oak tree electrically devastated in the irrevocable instantaneity of a lightning flash. The primal event, witnessed by an explicating scientist, shows the tree to be, like little Victor, "shattered," "blasted"—a fundamental electrocution of a tropology which is held responsible for the creation of a technological tool. Like the telephone, however, the shattered tree's originary bark seems louder than its bite. What does appear to be destroyed catastrophically by this preatomic blast, is the tranquil indwelling of world. For with the electric shock that world receives, a frivolity is signed which leaves behind the false testimony of mastery, the overcoming of finitude whose advances enthrall our century. As a life-support system, technology reroutes the question of life to a conquerable challenge which paradoxically brings unacknowledged death to the possibility of being or thinking, producing a weed garden of zomboid reactors. The switchboard Frankenstein articulates the shift from a more genuine temporality than that unthinkingly drafted by technology, which chooses to choose finitude in this limited case, with the implication that a choice is to be negotiated: the monster technologue *chooses* to imitate the route traced out by a prior literature, advanced under the name of *The Sorrows of Young Werther*—the name of valuation and worthiness in general, *Werth*er. Neither young nor old, though a relatively new invention, and in this sense always only young and reckless, constitutively untried, dangerous, the monsterized thing in his test drive has the power to select his conclusion and that of the more original other. *But the* suggestion implanted into the fold of this thinking is that technology can choose a genuinely human temporality only if it chooses to read a certain grace of poetry, a listening to finitude more truthful than technology's disassemblage of space-time. The nameless techno-monster could have chosen, after all, not to have put itself to death, in a graceful bereavement over its loss of mortality. And like Frankenstein, who is there to mark an absent alterity, the telephone in Heidegger stays largely off the hook, producing sounds and forms of sonic harassment that can only be read, if at all, subliminally. Still, the switchboard flashes and calls are placed. In Heidegger, as with the examples of Alexander Graham Bell and Frankenstein, these calls are placed from a disconnecting mother. *In some* respects, Frankensteinian and telephonic monsters belong to a crease in the Heideggerian thinking of the *Ge-Stell,* "the explicit key expression for the nature of modern technology" (*P,* 84). A relative of the transitive verb *stellen, Ge-Stell* includes aspects of placing, setting, standing, and arranging. Albert Hofstadter writes that *Ge-Stell,* if taken literally, would then be the collective name for all sorts of placing, putting, setting, arranging, ordering, or, in general, putting in place. Heidegger pushes this collective reading further, in the light of his interpretation of early Greek language and thought, his general concept of truth and the history of Being, and his view of the work of Being as summoning and gathering men to their destiny. The gathering agent today is the call that challenges men to put everything that discloses itself into the position of stock, resource, material for technological processing.

For this call, this gathering power, Heidegger makes use of this collective word which expresses the gathering of all forms of gathering things as resources—*das Ge-Stell,* the collective unity of all the putting, placing, setting, standing, arraying, arranging that goes into modern technology and the life oriented to it.[97] The *stellen,* the setting, placing, in the word, derives from an older mode, that of *poiēsis,* which lets what is present come forth into unconcealedness, as in the setting up of a statue in the temple precinct; yet, both the modern technological setting up of things as resources and this ancient poetic setting up of them bearing their world are modes of unconcealing, of truth as *alēthia*. They are not mere inventions of men or mere doings of men, interprets Hofstadter, but are phases in the history of the destiny of Being and of man in his historical situation in relation to Being. "Contemporary man's technological 'things' bear his technological 'world' in their own distorted way—distorting man's earth, his heaven, his divinities, and, in the end, himself and his morality" (*P,* xix). The warp that Hofstadter reads with Heidegger is what we have been calling into question—as if beyond the *Entstellung* (distortion) there were a more authentic horizon of Being. ***Man's technological*** "things," carefully pinched by Hofstadter, does not by necessity unravel a catalogue of objects whose set membership falls under expected categories. "Things" blinks at Heidegger and the strikingly generalized omission that his works sustain. It is perhaps worthy of note that when Heidegger's texts are intentionally involved in enumerating technologically set-up things, the telephone does not get on the line. Thus the important essay bearing the title "The Thing" opens with lines that would appear to draw within them our topos but, instead, they keep it out of sight. The opening words read: "All distances in time and space are shrinking." Heidegger proceeds on the airplane in the second sentence ("Man now reaches overnight, by plane, places which formerly took weeks or months of travel" [*P,* 165]). What appears to rate enumeration, above and beyond the airplane and closely following radio waves, is wrested from its concealedness, disrupting a natural germination: "He now receives instant information, by radio, of events which he formerly learned about only years later, if at all. The germination and growth of plants, which remained hidden throughout the seasons, is now exhibited publicly in a minute, on film" (*P,* 165). ***Besides*** telling us that Heidegger is not a speed freak, which we already knew, we are advised that he also deplores condensation and the traffic of displacement: "Distant sites of the most ancient cultures are shown on film as if they stood this very moment amidst today's street traffic" (*P,* 165). The film lays bare what ought to be hidden, behind the scenes, like an operator: "Moreover, the film attests to what it shows by presenting also the camera and its operators at work" (*P*, 165). Heidegger does not suggest what distinguishes this self-reflexive showing from Velázquez's *Las meniñas*, nor what makes a camera self-portraiture more relentlessly equipmental than a pair of Van Gogh's shoes. It would be necessary to divine the difference, but what has a pair of peasant shoes to do with the work of a receptionist? Scaling the heights of progressive obliteration, Heidegger's first paragraph culminates: "The peak of this abolition of every possible remoteness is reached by television, which will soon pervade and dominate the whole machinery of communication" (*P*, 165; trans. modified). The following paragraphs are concerned with long distances, but there isn't a telephone in sight.

Man puts the longest distances between him in the shortest time. He puts the greatest distances behind himself and thus puts everything before himself at the shortest range. Yet the frantic abolition of all distances brings no nearness; for nearness does not consist in shortness of distance. What is least remote from us in point of distance, by virtue of its picture on film or its sound on the radio, can remain far from us. What is incalculably far from us in point of distance can be near to us. Short distance is not in itself nearness. Nor is great distance remoteness. (*P*, 165)

It is not easy to decide why here and in other directories of communication-technologies set forth by Heidegger the telephone is off the hook. This does not mean that it will not in a secret, clandestine way receive a name, for all the rhetoric of remoteness converges on the German readout for a *Fernapparat,* the remote speaking machined by the telephone, or *Fernsprecher*. Perhaps, for Heidegger, the telephone does not authenticate structures of remoteness and proximity and, to the contrary, keeps them properly intact, aural, and somewhat ideal. Or the telephone surpasses the calculus of technological respresentations. He will not say. For whatever reason, and this is our reason for staying on the line, Heidegger will not install the telephone where one may reasonably expect its ringing. This may be linked to the underscoring of a dimension of *Lichtung* when Heidegger identifies the gathered being of the world's mirror-play as the "ringing," *das Gering*: "Out of the ringing mirror-play the thinging of the thing takes place" (*P,* 180). (*Das Gering*: nestling, malleable, pliant, compliant, nimble—in Old German these are called *ring* and *gering*). But there is something about the telephone that in its absence haunts his text, silently placing its call to a question that may well be unanswerable: who calls the call? **Because the** walls of Heidegger's dwelling may be wired, it becomes more difficult to speak directly of the telephone, but one can find it indicated, pointed to, allegorized in its establishing otherness. If indeed, as we suspect, the dwelling is bugged, then this also means that the listening device has been absorbed by the dwelling, nestled compliantly as a constitutive part or parasite, one upon whom the host becomes dependent regardless of intention, drive, or desire. As part of the building site, possibly even preceding it, the way cables have to be fitted and ditches dug prior to any construction, the telephone is inserted too deeply within the oeuvre to be laid on the surface lines. There are no telephone poles along Heidegger's route, no wires to serve as a precarious basis for a tightrope dance of the kind Nietzsche might have hazarded. In this case, the cables go underground, unmarked, not even indicated by the urban cemetery slabs that read "telephone," with "Christy" or "Atlas" situated in the place of signature on the streets of San Francisco. **The mention** of America is motivated. Heidegger will understand Rilke's static on America in terms of a technological menace. But if Heidegger can only speak on but not of the telephone, there are many grounds for this, many contaminations to be feared, many sightings to be sunk. It is not difficult to see why Heidegger can name the television as the summit of this abolition. Even though he himself got on television and when it was time for ActionLightsCamera, he said something about the relatedness of TV to his thinking. This was Heidegger on the *Gerede*-machine, unchecked by the superpowers of Rilke or Hölderlin.

As for Hölderlin, he did not watch television. However, it can be argued that Hölderlin did hang on the telephone ("Wherein you hang—you do not know"), occupying a mediated line to the gods, in futural capacity for direct dialing to Being. Moreover, television does not belong to the domain of Mosaic law, to which Hölderlin was so cautiously attuned, a domain in which the mortal-to-immortal call would take ontological priority over the televisual metaphysic. Television, Heidegger must assume, is always public, always saying a public diffusion. None of the private screenings of a Hamlet or a schizophrenic whose ghosts are not demonstrably there. Spiritual television would be banished in the same tradition that places sensory apprehension, particularly that of the eye, low on the metaphysical totem pole, whereas the audial is felt to be a more abstract, inwardly entered perception. But the only phenomenally based technology that draws Heidegger's attention in

these arguments and that

catch the ear is the radio, which usually is

a one-way

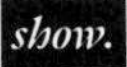
show.

WOMAN TO WOMAN

▶It has been said that the work makes creators possible, permitting them to originate. This is why it is often necessary to traverse the work in order to discover a semblance of the Operator who cooperates in the work without, however, enjoying the status of permanent resident. Operators are many, and largely unfathomable; their supervisors (*qua* state, salary, superego, living conditions, solitude, etc.) are even more deeply receded into the work. The only way to hold them distinct from one another, prior even to any hierarchization of position is to form a special attunement to the phallic penetration of voice, according to pitch. A woman's voice is perfectly suited to perform phallic penetration. What should be made of this voice? Where does it fit? How high can we pitch it in the field of technology? Is the woman's voice to be considered a thing, an object, or perhaps a piece or part of the equipment, the way her legs or stockings might fit into a pair of peasant shoes, if we were indeed looking for the Cinderellian fittingness?

▶We have established the essential makeup neither of the Frankenstein monster nor of the telephone. They appeared to communicate certain properties to one another, being reproductions of a frame or partial frame. As concerns Frankenstein, he still carries in his newly acquired name the stone we have been passing on from one partial system to the next, a stone first cast by another Swiss doctor remotely linked to Dr. Frankenstein. To put down the telephone momentarily, we ask about the creation of Dr. Frankenstein, of the object through which he speaks and from which he receives a number of demands, at times disguised as responses to his guilty being. Does this creation conjure up a phantom, a thing—for instance, a remote controlled thing—an object or objectification of sorts; is it perhaps a work of art, mimetically rooted in a fevered vision of the truth of man, or has it been conceived rather as a piece of equipment to whom the doctor is at times contracted as a repairman? Certainly the monster bears traits of its maker, who signs the project which haunts him; like the telephone (we did not hang up, we merely put it down momentarily), it is more sensitively impregnated with the secret traits of a disconnected mother. These wires are constitutively crossed. And so we ask about the equipmental nature of these things. Object of art or object of technology, object of a sustained hysterical fantasy—yours and mine—or thing of inmixation, telecrypt, or, in all cases, partial object: we have still not connected to the telephone its principal (over)determinations.

▶It may seem as if we were bent on splitting technological hairs by bringing up the question of the equipmental character of the telephone, of a Frankenstein, or even of a broken self. Yet the necessity of yielding an interpretation that deals with the equipmental being of equipment has been signaled in a work that inquisites the work, in "The Origin of the Work of Art," perhaps the most solicited text of Heidegger by students of literature and the arts. In the search for the equipmental character of equipment, Heidegger reports that equipment has come into being through human making, which renders it particularly familiar to human thinking. At the same time, this familiar being has a peculiar intermediate position between thing and work. We shall not fight the battle between earth and world or join the armies of the striving fourfold but rather limit the scope of inquiry to the place where equipment and thing intriguingly light onto the two figurations of women.

▶The first woman of note is the one who has left her shoes hanging in Van Gogh's tableau. The world of art history, represented notably by Meyer Schapiro, has faulted Heidegger on this misinformation, for it appears that the real referent of the represented peasant shoes can be established as Van Gogh's own shoes. Yet Heidegger does not seem to want to have an art historian's take on this issue. One might ask instead why the decision to fit the shoe to a *woman*'s foot seems apt, showing a tight fit to the curriculum of the argument: "We choose as example a common sort of equipment—a pair of peasant shoes" (*P*, 32). The issue has been set forth in some of Derrida's work on Heidegger, where the question is raised as to what constitutes a pair of shoes.[98] It is not feasible for me to run this by you now, though the assumption of familiarity with the argument lacing together pieces of *La verité en peinture* will have to be made. To get the shoes going, Heidegger shows the nonnecessity of conjuring them as a visual representation. "We do not even need to exhibit actual pieces of this sort of useful article in order to describe them. Everyone is acquainted with them. But since it is a matter here of direct description, it may be well to facilitate the visual realization of them. For this purpose a pictorial representation suffices" (*P*, 33).

▶The move to pictorial representation comes to pass as a concession; it is not essential. The inessential marks the spot where the woman steps in, for what is to be seen in Van Gogh's representation also depends on "the use to which the shoes are to be put, whether for work in the field or for dancing"—a difference within which form and matter shift accordingly (*P*, 33). Since you will find neither Heidegger nor Van Gogh putting on their dancing slippers in this calling, we move to the peasant woman, who, as exemplified equipmentality, doubles for another woman subsequently chained to the thing:

> *The peasant woman wears her shoes in the field. Only here are they what they are. They are all the more genuinely so, the less the peasant woman thinks about the shoes while she is at work, or looks at them at all, or is even aware of them. She stands and walks in them. That is how shoes*

> *actually serve. It is in the*
> *process of the use of equip-*
> *ment that we must actu-*
> *ally encounter the*
> *character of equipment.*
> (*P*, 33)

Now, the shoes are pressed to the earth's lips, they have a telephonic hollow: "In the shoes vibrates the silent call of the earth, its quiet gift of the ripening grain and its unexplained self-refusal in the fallow desolation of the wintry field" (*P*, 34). As with the call we fielded earlier, there arrives the aphonic call of anxiety: "This equipment is pervaded by uncomplaining anxiety as to the certainty of bread, the wordless joy of having once more withstood want, the trembling before the impending childbed and shivering at the surrounding menace of death" (*P*, 34). The picture and the peasant woman belong to two different hands of Heidegger's reading: the woman and the represented shoes may belong to different frameworks, since the woman exists differently, in a motion picture:

> *But perhaps it is only in the*
> *picture that we notice all*
> *this about the shoes. The*
> *peasant woman, on the*
> *other hand, simply wears*
> *them. If only this simple*
> *wearing were so simple.*
> *When she takes off her shoes*
> *late in the evening, in deep*
> *but healthy fatigue, and*
> *reaches out for them again*
> *in the still dim dawn, or*
> *passes them by on the day of*
> *rest, she knows all this*
> *without noticing or reflect-*
> *ing. The equipmental*
> *quality of the equipment*
> *consists indeed in its useful-*
> *ness. But this usefulness it-*
> *self rests in the abundance*
> *of an essential being of the*

> *equipment. We call it reliability. By virtue of this reliability the peasant woman is made privy to the silent call of the earth; by virtue of the reliability of the equipment she is sure of her world. World and earth exist for her, and for those who are with her in her mode of being, only thus—in the equipment.* (*P*, 34)

The "only" is taken back. Heidegger goes on:

> *The equipmental being of equipment, reliability, keeps gathered within itself all things according to their manner and extent. The usefulness of equipment is nevertheless only the essential consequence of reliability. The former vibrates in the latter and would be nothing without it. A single piece of equipment is worn out and used up; but at the same time the use itself falls into disuse, wears away, and becomes usual. Thus equipmentality wastes away, sinks into mere stuff. In such wasting, reliability vanishes. This dwindling, however, to which use-things owe their boringly*

obstrusive usualness, is only one more testimony to the original nature of equipmental being. The worn-out usualness of the equipment then obtrudes itself as the sole mode of being, apparently peculiar to it exclusively. Only blank usefulness now remains visible. (*P*, 34–35)

When Heidegger ends this particular moment of the demonstration, which reminds us of the disclosures of which breakdowns are capable, he returns to the painting, which has spoken (*Dieses hat gesprochen,* the painting spoke). The work did not in fact "as it might seem at first" serve merely for a better visualization of what a piece of equipment is, that is, the work did not get used as a piece of equipment. "Rather, the equipmentality of equipment first genuinely arrives at its appearance through the work and only in the work" (*P*, 36). Thus he can write that the work "therefore, is not the reproduction of some particular entity that happens to be present at any given time; it is, on the contrary, the reproduction of the thing's general essence" (*P*, 37). But the woman in Van Gogh's shoes also arrives at her appearance through the work, like the equipment, except that her genuine arrival never as such takes place. Cinderella remains unfitted, a peasant out of the picture. The work of Van Gogh did not show us the woman, but rather let her step into the image which Heidegger beckons as the genuine arrival of equipment. If this supplied the only mention of woman's likeness before climbing to the summit of work-being, we might have had to let it fall by the side. To what extent does the passage through the work leave a woman wasted, used up or worn out like the shoes that wear her spirit down? Yet she is not entirely there in any phenomenal sense. Heidegger does not exclude "woman"; on the contrary, he brings her into the holes of the wooden shoes, he lets her wear the shoes unawares, unreflectively, reliably stemmed to the earth which speaks and vibrates through her feet.[99] Sexual difference may here be a matter of substantial indifference. In any case, the woman who fills the shoes does not exactly come about as an aesthetic object, prepared for sensuous apprehension. She is absent from the shoes that hold her.
▶In his absence, Van Gogh is a woman, a peasant woman

who allows the equipmentality of equipment to arrive, to shine through the canvas that has used him up; he, too, like the dwindling which Heidegger perceives, has vanished. As odd as this would seem at first sight—she is not there at first sight—the peasant woman marks the locus of an operator, working the shoes as the fields, arriving on the scene as the phantom voice that allows the painting to speak. She converts into a sonorous language the image which keeps her unillumined. Linked to equipment, "shivering at the surrounding menace of death," the woman comes into the picture as that which vibrates, trembles, shivers. She connects both ends in the mode of genuine arrival: "the trembling before the impending childbed and shivering at the surrounding menace of death." The earth's vocal cords vibrate in her shoes. This woman's shoes, because they are wooden, do not have tongues. They let the painting speak in the unfeminine, "dieses hat gesprochen." Unless, indeed, the so-called neuter and neutral case is in this work, and to mark withdrawal, feminine.

▶We are on the way to the feminine. Not an essence, or the goalie's penalty; just a way. Heidegger has wanted to draw the important distinction between equipment and thing. Technology in some way is always implicated in the feminine. It is young; it is thingly. Thus every instrument of war is given a feminine name. The feminine, in whose way we are, does not arrive. She is what is missing. Constituted like a rifle, she is made up of removable parts. She hinges on the other, like the allegorical symbolics of which Heidegger speaks. The woman has gotten in the way of things, so that the prior mention of her, at a younger stage of "The Origin of the Work of Art," needs attention. All works have a thingly character. A picture may hang on the wall, asserts Heidegger, like a rifle or a hat (*P*, 19). Because the thingly element is so irremovably present, it draws allegory to the understanding of the work. The question of the other, of, say, equipment and the other, is not an arbitrary one. "The art work is something else over and above the thingly element" (*P*, 19). It is not the thing but the something else that constitutes the artwork in its nature. While the artwork reverts to a made thing, it nevertheless says something other than the mere thing itself, *allo agoreuei*. The work makes public something other than itself. Manifesting something other, it is an allegory. In the work of art, the reading continues, something other is brought together with the thing that is made. "To bring together" is, in Greek, *sumballein*. The work is a symbol. Joining one element with another, bringing together what stays apart, the work somehow participates in both these figures, ruling over separation and that which binds. "But this one element in a work that manifests another, this one element that joins with another, is the thingly feature in the artwork" (*P*, 20).

The thingly feature is
the jointure,
that which joins and, one supposes,
separates.

▶A goodly number of things can be considered things: the stone in the road, a jug, the well beside the road. "All these must indeed be called things, if the name is applied even to that which does not, like those just enumerated, show itself, i.e., that which does not appear." According to Kant, the whole of the world, for example, and even God himself, is a thing of this sort, a thing that does not itself appear, namely a "thing-in-itself." "In the language of philosophy both things-in-themselves and things that appear, all beings that in any way are, are called things" (*P*, 21). Now we come to a passage that lets itself be compared with the one from "The Thing": "Airplanes and radio sets are nowadays among the things closest to us, but when we have ultimate things in mind we think of something altogether different. Death and judgment—these are ultimate things. On the whole the word 'thing' here designates whatever is not simply nothing. In this sense the work of art is also a thing, so far as it is not simply nothing" (*P*, 21). Again, we need to underscore the missing place of the telephone in the receiving line of things closest to us. The airplane's approach gets closer than the telephone; unless the phone demands to be installed within the precinct of ultimate things which has death preceding judgment. ("Death and judgment—these are ultimate things.")
▶At this point Heidegger enters a calculation of hesitations. The calculation, as the hesitation which defines it, impresses itself heavily upon us, for the thing will divide the sexes. Proceeding from the highest order of being, we slide down to the moment in which the hesitation prepares to be lifted:

And besides, we hesitate to
call God a thing. In the
same way we hesitate to
consider the peasant in the
field, the stoker at the
boiler, the teacher in the
school as things. A man is

not a thing. It is true that
we speak of a young girl
who is faced with a task
that is too difficult for her
as being a young thing,
still too young for it, but
only because we feel that
being human is in a cer-
tain way missing here and
think that instead we have
to do here with the factor
that constitutes the thingly
character of things. We
hesitate even to call the
deer in the forest clearing,
the beetle in the grass, the
blade of grass a thing.
(*P*, 21)

▶In this scaled list of hesitations going down from the godhead to grass, spacing things out among themselves but providing a thin bridge from the stoker to the teacher and beetle, all of which we hesitate to name as thing, there comes one moment of relief from hesitation, one admission of a "true" nature in the way we speak. The "we" constitutes an odd consensus, if it should include Heidegger. For it is not clear that the "we" prehending a girl as thing measures her necessity as the gravity of a task yet unfulfillable. What does Heidegger want from the girl? In the first place a girl can be too young. To what extent does this clarify the demonstration of a thingly being? In a sense, the age of a being does count for Heidegger, for technology itself is always too young, too reckless and untried. There is typically "something missing here," when the girl joins the lineup, something that the turn to equipmentality may or may not supply. But as a young thing, the girl is faced with a task too difficult for her; her telic finality remains out of her grasp. If this were the voice of Nietzsche, all of humanity would be this young thing. For Heidegger, however, we are latecomers, a predicament with which our little girl remains out of step. There is no present of the feminine. While the girl proves *still* too young, the peasant woman appeared no longer to be faced with a task. Having grown into her strongly unreflective being quietly, fatigue is the way time spent itself on her. Here, fatigue as the passage of time reflects her becoming healthy, unstrained.

▶Of all the "things" enumerated as resisting the language of thingliness, the young girl has always already stepped out of the shoes of humanity into which she is supposed to fit ("only because we feel that being human is in a certain way missing here"—was being human not already missing in the beetle, or are we to understand that Gregor Samsa has crawled into the picture?). True, when Heidegger says that "we speak," he may be registering this as a largely quotidian or inauthentic "we." The pure thing comes only in the form of a stone, a clod of earth, a piece of wood, the lifeless beings of nature. He does not include the schizophrenic girl who also comes in such a form of lifeless assimilations. Nonetheless, if a young girl fits the requirements of a thing-concept in the way we speak, then we must let this thing, as in the case of all things, "encounter us without mediation. The situation always prevails" (*P*, 25). As object of sensuous perception, linking thus the thing directly to the aesthetic, the young girl, Heidegger avers, can "move us bodily":

> *But we do not need first to call or arrange for this situation in which we let things encounter us without mediation. The situation always prevails. In what the senses of sight, hearing and touch convey, in the sensations of color, sound, roughness, hardness, things move us bodily, in the literal meaning of the word. The thing is the* aistheton, *that which is perceptible by sensations in the senses belonging to sensibility.* (*P*, 25)

However, Heidegger casts doubt on the truth of this interpretation in which the thingness of the thing comes to light. This doubt occurs because "we never really first perceive a throng of sensations, e.g., tones and noises, in the appearance of things—as this thing concept alleges" (*P*, 26). The engines are being revved up: "Rather, we hear the three-motored plane, we hear the Mercedes in immediate distinction from the Volkswagen. Much closer to us than all sensations are the things themselves. We hear the door shut in the house and never hear acoustical sensations or even mere sounds. In order to hear a bare sound we have to listen away from things, divert our ear from them, i.e. listen abstractly" (*P*, 26).

▶In the analysis of the things as matter (*hulē*), form (*morphē*) is already coposited. The thing is formed matter. "This interpretation appeals to the immediate view with which the thing solicits us by its looks (*eidos*). In this synthesis of matter and form a thing-concept has finally been found which applies equally to things of nature and to use-objects" (*P*, 26–27). To bring the thing in closest proximity to us, Heidegger has had to divest it of assigning as its sole thingly feature that which is apprehended by the senses. He has had to strike a balance between an interpretation that "keeps the thing at arm's length from us, as it were, and sets it too far off" and another which makes it press too hard upon us (*P*, 26). In both efforts the thing vanishes, making it necessary to resist their exaggerations. "The thing itself must be allowed to remain in its self-containment. It must be accepted in its own constancy" (*P*, 26). This gives way to crucial structures constellating thing and equipment. A being that falls under usefulness turns out always to be the product of a process of making. "Equipment" designates what is produced expressly for employment and use. Matter and form by no means provide original determinations for the thingness of the mere thing. "A piece of equipment, a pair of shoes for instance, when finished, is also self-contained like a mere thing, but it does not have the character of having taken shape by itself like the granite boulder" (*P*, 29). Again, we might briefly call in the young thing to examine her properties as thing. For what seems to be taking shape advances her as that which falls short of a task, but it also evokes the affined Freudian complaint concerning the all too self-contained woman of narcissism: the self-sufficient pose of the somewhat auto-engendering thing.[100]

▶Let's move on to the rendezvous with the art world. On the other hand, writes Heidegger, equipment displays an affinity with the artwork insofar as it is something produced by the human hand. "However, by its self-sufficient presence the work of art is similar rather to the mere thing which has taken shape by itself and is self-contained. Nevertheless we do not count such works among mere things. As a rule it is the use-objects around us that are nearest and authentic things."

Thus the piece of equipment is half thing, because characterized by thingliness, and yet it is something more; at the same time it is half art work and yet something less, because lacking the self-sufficiency of the art work. Equipment has a peculiar position intermediate between thing and work, assuming that such a calculated ordering of them is permissible. (*P*, 29)

As Heidegger subsequently points out, the currently predominant thing-concept which views the thing as formed matter is not even derived from the nature of the thing but from the nature of equipment. The work is not a piece of equipment that is fitted out in addition with an aesthetic value that adheres to it. "The work is no more anything of the kind than the bare thing is a piece of equipment that merely lacks the specific equipmental characteristics of usefulness and being made" (*P*, 39).

▶Were we not engaged in questioning the specific mode of being for the telephone, assuming there to be a single mode in this case, we would be tempted to stay on the line, inching our way to the artwork. For it is certainly not out of the question to engage this line accordingly. If the telephone were not conjured from a pretechnological concept of *techné,* as a mode of knowing, we could more easily dispose of its being-as-artwork. In *The Question Concerning Technology,* Heidegger accordingly reminds us that *techné* is "the name not only for the activities and skills of the craftsman, but also for the arts of the mind and the fine arts. *Techné* belongs to bringing-forth, to *poiēsis*; it is something poietic."[101] Furthermore, *techné* is linked with the word *epistémé*. "Both words are names for knowing in the widest sense."[102] They mean to be entirely at home in something, to understand and to be expert in it.

▶The phone calls, speakingly rendering itself as a forthcoming, a call out of slumber, sheltering the self-containment of the Other whose presence is always mediated, making the encounter unlike the one described for the mere thing. Yet, precisely because the artwork no longer acts wrenchingly the way something akin to science may do, if disbelief in the Hegelian pronouncement can continue to remain suspended, the most urgent call of the telephone at this phase of its almost clandestinely protected being seems to come from a place that cannot be framed satisfactorily by "artwork," particularly since so many contaminations are at play. Yet, like the artwork whose origins Heidegger describes, the telephone is attached to the *aistheton* in fundamental ways; it is still a young thing faced with great tasks that elude its reach. Similar to the artwork's manifold veilings in the Heideggerian text, the telephone absorbs into its coils the features of equipmentality and thingness. Besides, it has assimilated to itself artistic qualities in the medias that support its ambition for representation and replacement of the specifically human. It makes things appear, happen for the first time, and in the mode of a **historacular announcement.** Independently of the signified, of course. The telephone largely avoids representational art, spreading the night that has to appear together with all that participates in the nonphenomenal dimension: telephone, like the temple, says that even the nonvisible has to appear in order to be what it is. There is thus a subversive hypertheology of the telephone, the mightier god of the making happen, making appear, the remarkable localization of an electric *Geschehen*.

▶In this regard, the artwork performs the essence, performs the telephone. The cinematogram regularly deposits the telephone trace, which proves capable of carrying the role of a mysterious lead character, as for example in *The Thin Man*.[103] The position of the thin man, mediating events, aesthetic transmissions, and desires, is occupied by the stand-up telephone, a character whose double plays the more recognizably human persona. One can scan effortlessly enough the motion pictures that carry the telephone, often thematizing the hallucinatory power it holds over dramatic action, calling forth a destiny in its finitude, arranging a string of statements attached to the will to power: *Sorry, Wrong Number* or *Dial M for Murder* will do; or within the form of another medium, Poulenc's *La voix humaine* might be considered, where opera sings itself into an absent receiver of angst. In all these representations the telephone belongs to the artwork both as parasitical inclusion and as its veiled receiver, the opening from which invisible events are directed, quietly co-occupying the scene with the voices of commanding phantoms. Remoteness and nearness commingle, one is almost there. It makes a felt connection to its own reception history. Yet the telephone participates with such recognizably fresh insolence in the production of interruption, noise, and chatter that no one would yet presume to make a case for its markings as artwork, with which, however, it often coincides, drawing to itself the structures both of allegory and symbol. It perhaps does not yet claim the capacity for holding the terrifyingly silent scream of Edvard Munch's figure. Nonetheless, the stillness upon which any work of art is said to be grounded, its removal from a disconcertingly ontic dimension, has not always served the work of art well, has not necessarily strengthened it. A thinking of the artwork may have to include renewing its effects, and possibly, as in the experiments of Mary Shelley, recharging it electrically—as if the artwork could produce a pain of electric shock. This may not come to pass. Yet the static has returned, the noise grows louder. Life, as in Nietzsche, is holding her delicate ears—even though it was Nietzsche who first heard

the scream of the Greeks,

the din of

dionysiac noise.

▶The telephone presents itself nowadays as a relatively unpretentious thing. It barely belongs to the league of high-tech desires. "The unpretentious thing evades thought most stubbornly" (*P*, 31). Thus the exertion of thought seems to meet with its greatest resistance in defining this relatively young thing. This is why it may seem that we are getting no-where. But is this not precisely where the telephone gets us? We provisionally conclude this questioning of its nature with the leftover that Heidegger offers. It has not been thrown to us at the end of the road, but along the way. This is where we get off, to stay with the remnant:

The situation stands re-
vealed as soon as we speak of
things in the strict sense as
mere things. The "mere,"
after all, means the re-
moval of the character of
usefulness and of being
made. The mere thing is a
sort of equipment, albeit
equipment denuded of its
equipmental being. Thing-
being consists in what is
then left over. But this
remnant is not actually de-
fined in its ontological
character. It remains
doubtful whether the
thingly character comes to

view at all in the process of stripping off everything equipmental. (*P*, 30)

This has also turned out to be an assault upon the thing. Perhaps the question has withheld itself in concealedness. Beings, such as the telephone, "refuse themselves down to that one and seemingly least feature which we touch upon most readily when we can say no more of beings than that they are" (*P*, 53). The news is good. For concealment as refusal "is not simply and only the limit of knowledge in any given circumstance, but the beginning of the clearing of what is lighted" (*P*, 53–54). In the context that Heidegger draws out, concealment is not simple refusal. "Rather, a being appears, but it presents itself as other than it is" (*P*, 54). It turns out that concealment conceals itself, capable of appearing as refusal or merely as a dissembling. "We are never fully certain whether it is the one or the other" (*P*, 54). We believe we are at home, writes Heidegger, in the immediate circle of beings. That which is, "is familiar, reliable, ordinary. Nevertheless the clearing is pervaded by a constant concealment in the double form of refusal and dissembling" (*P*, 54).

▶At bottom, the ordinary is not ordinary; it is extra-ordinary, uncanny—it can be as eerie as the skeletal deposits of *Ge-Stell*. But it is covered over, pushed back, over-looked. "The nature of truth, that is, of unconcealedness, is dominated throughout by denial. Yet this denial is not a defect or a fault, as though truth were an unalloyed unconcealedness that has rid itself of everything concealed. If truth could accomplish this, it would no longer be itself" (*P*, 54). We have hit bottom, where the ordinary protects the extraordinary and uncanny, producing a buffer zone and shock-absorbent layering. We believe we are at home, but this occurs because the gift of denial shelters us from the immediate circle of beings. If we back up a bit, we discover a certain element of truth residing in dissembling. This greatly encourages our hopes, as we have let the telephone—most "ordinary" of all things—fit the shoes of other beings, particularly when it was stepped up to enter the domain of artwork. Why did the telephone allow itself to respond to each combination, hardly resisting the dislocations which it acquired for itself (similarly, why does the work of art evoke a thinking of the thing and equipmentality? etc.)? Heidegger is clear on what leads a being to present itself as other than it is: "If one being did not simulate another, we could not make mistakes or act mistakenly in regard to beings; we could not go astray and transgress, and especially could never overreach ourselves. That a being should be able to deceive as semblance is the condition for our being able to be deceived, not conversely" (*P*, 54).

T	h	e					
d	u	m	m	i	e	s	
o	f						
L	i	f	e				
					♥	♥	♥

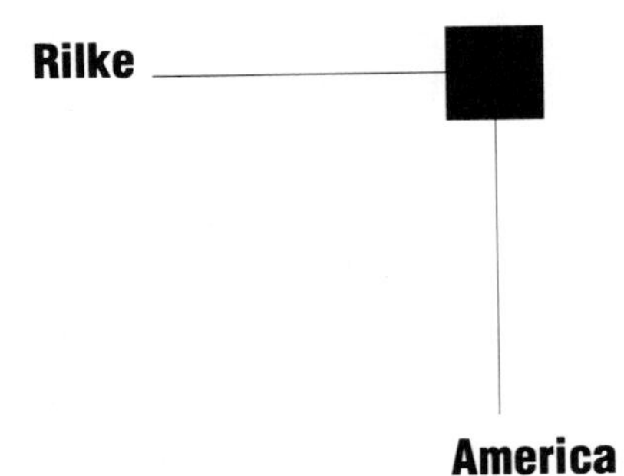

Technology, of which the utilization of machinery is only an instrument concordant with its effect, has produced man as controlling subject and world as his object. This comes as a consequence of technology's nature establishing itself, and not the other way around. Both of these technological products—man as subject, world as object—are, as you know, in deep trouble. Not only has **the body of mother earth become polluted and mangled,** but "the self-assertion of technological objectification is the constant negation of death" (*P,* 125). By this negation, death itself becomes something negative, and altogether inconstant, null; denuded of all symbolicity it amounts to a calculus of body counting, a piece of trade software in the so-called Computer Age. America approaches the white abyss. Developing its own properties to the full, technology develops in the sciences a kind of knowing that is debarred from ever entering into the realm of its essential nature, let alone retracing in thought that nature's origin (*P,* 117). Technology itself prevents any experience of its nature. "The essence of technology comes to the light of day only slowly. This day is the world's night, rearranged into merely technological day. This day is the shortest day. . . . Not only does protection now withhold itself from man, but the integralness of the whole of what is remains now in darkness. The wholesome and sound withdraws" (*P,* 117).

In order to see the danger and to point it out, there "must be mortals who reach sooner into the abyss" (*P,* 117). Retain the technological diurnal comprising the world's night. This belongs to the schizo's Vocabulary, which is always on location. **Lights. Action.**

The technological exercise of will, whereby all living things are technically objectivated "in stock-breeding and exploitation" (*P,* 112), creates a new value theory, a sign of the predominance of technological ideas whose development has long since been removed beyond the realm of the individual's personal views and opinions. At bottom, the essence of life is supposed to yield itself to technical production. The predominance of techno-ideas shows through the "fact that we, today, in all seriousness, discern in the results and the viewpoint of atomic physics possibilities of demonstrating human freedom and of establishing a new theory of values."[104] In this technologically lit realm, individual, particularized views and opinions—the once devalorized *Meinung*—appear to be set in relief as the measure of the loss that the shortest day has exacted. What was once close-range *Gerede* gets transvaluated in light of the relatively depraved technosophy which, for example, places atomic physics as the source for new theory. This burns Heidegger up. Hence the merit increase of particularized views and opinions. These rate higher than a certain automata of utterances belonging to the structure divested of the personal views of which an individual used to seem capable.

Heidegger recruits Rilke to explicate our essential unshieldedness. Endangered, man has become blind to the menace that assails his nature. For Heidegger, Rilke is exemplary of the poet able to experience the Open as the nonobjective character of full Nature. Heidegger still holds to a somewhat organically infused rhetoric when writing on the formless formations of technological production. These "interpose themselves before the Open of the pure draft. Things that once grew now whither quickly away. They can no longer pierce through the objectification to show their own" (*P*, 113). Citing Rilke's letter from Muzot of November 13, 1925, Heidegger returns to us the feeling of emptiness, the dummies of life, a certain airheaded intrusion into the clear and dense atmosphere of a mother continent:

> *To our grandparents, a "house," a "well," a familiar steeple, even their own clothes, their cloak* still *meant infinitely more, were infinitely more intimate—almost everything a vessel in which they found something human already there, and added to its human store. Now there are intruding, from America, empty indifferent things, sham things,* dummies of life. . . . *A house, as the Americans understand it, an American apple or a winestock from over there, have* nothing *in common with the house, the fruit, the grape into which the hope and thoughtfulness of our forefathers had entered.* (*P*, 113)

Rilke does not assert a safe long distance between two securely separate entities or continents, but a contamination, the plague with which Americanism pollutes its origin, like a torpedoed virus, draining and weakening. Now there are intruding from America empty, indifferent things. These things, as

Heidegger would not appear to dispute, may be a relay of that which in fact has originated in Europe, having lost some velocity on the way home. Today by round-trip transplant we might think of psychoanalysis, deconstruction, and French vineyards as arguably "American" phenomena to which the European might defer. The empty things are emptied of their rootedness in the past and of the human trait already partaking of things. They are thrown.

Rilke does not refer to his generation the meaning of present, potential fetish objects. He wraps metonymies of intimacy, the clothes and cloaks of concealment about our grandparents. There is a semantic break with America, a lack of consensual signification or reciprocal hermeneutics (a house, as the Americans understand it, has nothing in common with the "house" which the thoughtfulness of our forefathers had entered). European ancestry had entered thought into a house according to a different kind of inscription, a house erected like a family chronicle of the past future perfect, entered with intimacy and with thinking, a memorializing thinking, and not merely an arrangement negotiated with the collapsible foundations of housing as equipmental being, useful, sudden, mobile, and deracinating. A house built on the soil of American constructions supports no ghosts or long-inhabiting phantasms. The spirit welcomed by the dwelling of our forefathers resembled, as do many ghosts, humanly contours. Thus they found something already human there.

America, on the contrary, seems neither uplifted by good ghosts nor intimate with their apparel but pocked merely by *dummies of life,* empty, indifferent things, hollowed out from ancestral paths, *Geist*lessly. Even an American apple belongs to the sheer technicity of things, as Rilke suggests in his nearly computerized projection. The injection of a schizophrenicizing poison, the object-induced catatonia named by the dummies of life renders the American intrusion particularly painful. The object-character of technological dominion spreads itself over the earth ever more ruthlessly, quickly and completely, observes Heidegger. Not only does it establish all things as producible in the process of production, it also delivers the products of production by means of a market. "In self-assertive production, the humanness of man and the thingness of things dissolve into the calculated market value of a market which not only spans the whole earth as a world market, but also, as the will to will, trades in the nature of Being and thus subjects all beings to the trade of a calculation that dominates most tenaciously in those areas where there is no need of numbers" (*P,* 114–115). By his self-willing, man becomes in an essential sense endangered, that is, unshielded, in need of protection. What does this mean? For Heidegger it means that the Open has been shut down, liquidated. This does not happen by accident, but by building the world up technologically as an object, man "deliberately and completely" blocks his path, already obstructed, to the Open. Self-assertive man, whether or not he knows and wills it as an individual, is a functionary of technology.

The technospheric bureaucracy does not find its original launching pad in America. Rather, the Americanism drafted in Rilke's letter is itself nothing but the "concentrated rebound of the willed nature of modern Europe upon a Europe for which, to be sure, in the completion of metaphysics by Nietzsche, there were thought out in advance at least some areas of the essential questionability of a world where Being begins to rule as the will to will" (*P*, 113). It is not that Americanism first surrounds us moderns with its menace, continues Heidegger; the menace of the "unexperienced nature of technology surrounded even our forefathers and their things. Rilke's reflection is pertinent not because it attempts still to salvage the things of our forefathers" (*P*, 113). Things have been sullied by the calculative representation. In the age in which Rilke is dealing (the fourteenth century), where things began shifting their existence more and more over into the fluctuations of money, and developing there for themselves a kind of spirituality which surpasses their palpable reality, "money was still gold, still metal, a beautiful thing, the handsomest, most comprehensible of all" (*P*, 113–114). "The ore is homesick," writes Rilke in the second part of the *Book of Hours*:

The kings of the world are grown old,
inheritors they shall have none. . . .
Into coin the rabble breaks them,
today's lord of the world takes them,
stretches them into machines in his fire . . .
(*P*, 114)

Reading the poem of newly minted calculation, Heidegger questions the nature of unshieldedness, understood as that objectification which lies in purposeful self-assertion:

What stands as object in the world becomes standing *in representational production. Such representation presents. But what is present is present in a representation that has the character of calculation. Such representation knows nothing immediately perceptual. What can be immediately seen when we look at things, the image they offer to immediate sensible intuition, falls away. The calculating production of technology is an "act without an image" (ninth of the* Duino Elegies, *line 46). Purposeful self-assertion, with its designs, interposes before the intuitive image the project of the merely calculated product. When the world enters into the objectness of the thought-devised product, it is placed within the nonsensible, the invisible. What stands thus owes its presence to a placing whose activity belongs to the* res cogitan, *that is, to consciousness. The sphere of the objectivity of objects remains inside consciousness. What is invisible in that which stands-over-against belongs to the interior and immanence of consciousness. . . . In modern metaphysics, the sphere of the invisible interior is defined as the realm of the presence of calculated objects. Descartes describes this sphere as the consciousness of the* ego cogito. *At nearly the same time as Descartes, Pascal discovers the logic of the heart as over against the logic of calculating reason. The inner and invisible domain of the heart is not only more inward than the interior that belongs to calculating representation, and therefore more invisible; it also extends further than does the realm of merely producible objects.* (*P*, 127)

Only in the invisible innermost region of the heart is man inclined toward "what there is for him to love: the forefathers, the dead, the children, those who are to come" (*P*, 128)—in other words, the love that grows from the predicament and temporality of separation. Love is not borne toward those who would be there in contemporaneity but circulates in those who are marked by a before and after, a living on, reaching back and forward, making your way through the dead, the children. Those who are to come; those who have already passed. Not you. In any case not the way you are now. You the dead, who are to come. All this ("what there is for him to love") belongs to the widest orbit, writes Heidegger, which not only proves to be the sphere of the presence of the whole integral draft, but which brings us here, too, to a full orbit as concerns the earlier dread of outer space. Heidegger returns via another craft to the moon. ("Like the moon, so life surely has a side that is constantly turned away from us, and that is not its opposite but its completion to perfection, to plenitude, to the real, whole, and full sphere and globe of being"[*P*, 124].) This time he does not take sputnik but the vessel of Rilke's poetry, his dispatches from Muzot.

He writes that the widest orbit of beings becomes present in the heart's inner space. He quotes Rilke's letter from Muzot dated August 11, 1924: "However vast the 'outer space' may be, yet with all its sidereal distances it hardly bears comparison with the dimensions, *with the depth dimensions of our inner being,* which does not even need the spaciousness of the universe to be within itself almost unfathomable. Thus, if the dead, if those who are to come, need an abode, *what* refuge could be more agreeable and appointed for them than this imaginary space?" (*P*, 128). This enforces the connection that they wish to make, an abode for those yet to come, for the dead which would be domiciliated neither in outer space nor entirely in inner consciousness in the technical metaphysical sense, but rather in an imaginary space from which we can hear of one another.

As long as we are wholly absorbed in nothing but purposeful self-assertion, not only are we ourselves unshielded, but so are things, because they have become objects. In this, to be sure, there also lies a transmutation of things into what is inward and invisible. But transmutation replaces the frailties of things by the thought-contrived fabrications of calculated objects. These objects are produced to be used up; they *want* to be disposable. The more quickly they are used up, the greater becomes the necessity to replace them even more quickly and more readily. What lasts in the presence of objective things is not their self-subsistence within the world that is their own. What is constant in things produced as objects merely for consumption amounts to the substitute-ersatz. Things, then, might be seen to weigh in according to their serial future, lit up by the horizon of substitutional activity. It is well known that psychoanalysis lays emphasis on substitutional chains. This precisely indicates, however, why the Hamlet and Oedipus tragedies are so ineluctably rooted in its unfolding—dramas of impossible substitution, unable to respond in kind to the call of Claudius, whose teaching revolves around a technicity of necessary replacement. Their parents, in a true mourning, ought to have been consumable, and posed within a dimension that fates them to be replaced by ever new objects. Oedipus—this speaks for itself—has never proved capable even of a first level of replacement. For these figures always already engaged in the resistance against calculable objects with an appreciable turnover, the binding others of their love do not compose themselves of removable parts, like the rifle that was hanging on Heidegger's wall, somewhere between a hat and a picture in "The Origin of the Work of Art." The oedipal mother and Hamletian father form a couple insofar as they can never be used up, liquidated, or rearranged by substitution. This is why the technological flower of the Frankensteinian project becomes so crucial, as the objectivization of the replacement object, a high-wired monument to its impossible switch—the mother ersatz set off like a walking reproach become serial murder

We have passed quickly through some transmutations of objects serving the structure of substitution. The question might be raised of whether there exists any object that does not accede to this structure, even that which we hesitate to call a thing, God. But here we break off from Heidegger's path.

It is not the first time. In this case, we have remained behind with the remnants, the residuals that articulated the thingness of the thing. This has left the telephone dangling. Does it belong strictly to the calculative representation? Does it dwindle down to an object or even an object of consumption—we have seen the telephone incorporated in the speaking body of the schizophrenic. To be sure, the telephone understands itself as a most explicitly produced ersatz. Ersatz for what? For the Other as whose proxy it stands? We need to discover this, and via the transatlantic cable that Rilke sets up.

For it is still not clear to me that the telephone has not been hooked to the heart's space of which Heidegger writes, or Eckermann before him, who took dictation from another poet in the doubly interior chamber of voice substitution. The heart's space convokes not simply inner space, but the innermost invisible region of thoughtful spacing. "Indeed, it may well be that the turning of our unshieldedness into worldly existence within the world's inner space must begin with this, that we turn the transient and therefore preliminary character of object-things away from the inner and invisible region of the merely producing consciousness and toward the true inheritor of the heart's space, and there allow it to arise invisibly" (*P*, 130).

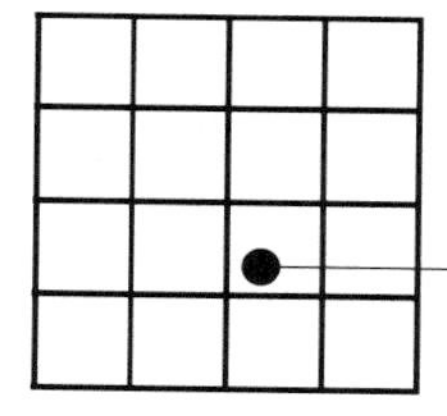

BIRTH OF A TELEPHONE

Watson—Dead Cats

■ As with shoes, the telephone, or a schizophrenic, Alexander Graham Bell was not one, but a pair. If it were necessary to obscure the fact that often he was on the receiving end of the coupled phenomenon, then the dynamics of the conception will have already been given over to misunderstanding. In the famous inaugural sentence, the first fully intelligible grammar transmitted electrically, Bell conjured up Thomas A. Watson with a commanding utterance. The first legendary sentence will have been a perlocutionary speech act of the kind that has been ordering us around the circuits of telephony: "Watson, come here! I want you!" The command attracts different registers of interpretive valency—a mother calling to a child perhaps, as in Heidegger's evocation of Nietzsche in *What Is Called Thinking?* Come forth, manifest yourself, Wat-son, cut the lines that separate us but whose wound enables me to command your arrival, your destination and destiny. Appear, turn this call into a phenomenal image. ■ By all evidence, "I want you" suggests that desire is on the line. Whether issuing from the political or the private sector, the desiring command inches you toward annihilation. It emerges from what is not present-at-hand; thus, "I want you" phantomizes you. I want that which I do not possess, I do not have you, I lack you, I miss you: Come here, Watson, I want you. Or this may echo the more original call of a male god, a god that is not full, since he is full of resentment, jealousy, suspicion, and so on. He calls out, he desires, he lacks, he calls for the complement or the supplement or, as Benjamin says, for that which will come along to enrich him.[105] The god is at the controls but without knowing what he controls until the Other—still lacking—answers his call. Where the call as such suggests a commanding force, the caller, masked by the power apparatus, may in fact be weak, suffering, panicked, putting through a call for help. ■ We suppose that the phonetic inscription has been rendered faithfully. Yet nothing guarantees that, being telephonically transmitted, one is not asked to hear double, to open both ears, stereophonically, in order to grasp the homonymy of a great command: Come, hear: **Schmah!** While this does not quite present the same difficulties as the Shakespearean folio, whose variations have to be discerned or left multiply dictated, the unavailability of a primary script frees a language into the air whose meaning, beyond the fact that it constitutes a demand, remains on shaky, if any, ground. In any case, it is the coming of the other that first enlists our clairaudience, as Joyce calls it, the rejoining other who was presumed to be second, secondary, a shadow of an ear receiving the electric command. The first proper name that the telephone was to call out was: "Watson." Pregnant with this other, the telephone also engages a resuscitating resurrection: "Watson, arise!" At once unborn and corpse, the Other is made answerable to the call. ■ He himself offered the utterance as an instance of emergency calling, a kind of sensibility of disaster which traverses the telephone wire sentenced in this call for help. The telephone, which was until that moment somewhat ill behaved, had refused to carry out an order, but in the heat of the moment, just as Bell accidentally spilled a burning chemical on his lap, the telephone cried out, responding in effect to a master's distress. The telephone's opening sentence let through a burning body's call for help. It is necessary to look to the figure of an assisting other in order to grasp what it was the telephone was calling to in the recorded moment of its birth pang. It is necessary, because the telephone has never forgotten the one to whom it carried the first lesson of what is missing, broken, or in pain. An accident cleaved the original words of what Watson calls the art of telephony. However, by the time this sentence was produced, the telephone was itself old enough to come up with an intelligible sentence, old enough to rearrange Watson on the receiving line, for the telephone experimented with this couple, regularly changing its positions, making it difficult to determine who was the sender, who the recipient—who, in other words, was responsible for its birth. Earlier, on the hot June day of 1875, Watson had already given vent to a sound-shaped electric current, claiming some credit for himself:

> One of my transmitter reeds stopped vibrating. I plucked it with my fingers to start it going. . . . That delicate undulatory current, which at other times had been drowned out by the heavy intermittent current passing through the receiver Graham Bell had at his ear, had been converted by it into a very faint echo of the sound of the transmitter reed I had plucked. Probably nothing would have come from the circumstance if any other man than Bell had been listening at that moment. . . . The twang of that reed that I plucked on June 2, 1875, marked the birth of one of the greatest modern inventions, for when the electrically carried ghost of that twang reached Bell's ear his teeming brain shaped the first electric speaking telephone the world had ever known. (*A*, 67–68)

These are the words which Watson committed to paper in his autobiography, almost mischievously entitled *Exploring Life*, for Watson was a man of irony, as his writing reveals, and the ghost which he sent to Bell's ear suggests the directions his explorations took. The history of their complicity carries with it the probability that more than one ghost reached Bell's ear that day, but we shall keep them hidden away momentarily in order simply to note that there is nothing sure about who gave whom the first emission, whose ears were receptively opened to which ghost that continues to inhabit your inner ear. Watson, who was also a poet, had "plucked it with my fingers to start it going." He claims the birthright, it would appear, and commences a certain paternity suit for the twang of the reed that "I plucked on June 2, 1875, [which] marked the birth." ■ It is perhaps more delicately indicated than I am allowing, but the confusion that ensues in this coupling creates clarifying channels by which we can gauge the urgency of the preliminary transmissions that were made. By now, having heard out Heidegger we also understand that listening, a pose Watson attributes to Bell, is not a mere modulation of withholding passivity. It belongs rather to a long lineage of inwardness touched off perhaps by Rousseau's self-gathering energetics of stillness which, in the *Rêveries,* he names *far niente*, the nothing that is doing. The attentive heeding of *far niente,* its ontological currents, are still at issue here. Thus it remains probable that "nothing would have come from the circumstance if any other man than Bell had been listening at that moment." The one who waits in silent receptivity lends an active, and not reactive, ear. However, this attribution, as with many that follow, is double-edged, since Bell is shown consistently to be a deficient listener, the prize pair of ears belonging instead to Watson. ■ Since the telephone was expressly conceived as the desire of this couple, I should like to keep the unexplored other on the line, the one who has received so little, but not out of some charitable sentiment, which would be a revolting way to strike an interpretive pose. Rather, we need to pass it in this direction because the telephone chose Watson in a way that strongly determines the factors of its being. As its maker, Watson was also its first servant who saw it to the light of day. Watson's intimate friendship with ghosts should not be undervalued, nor was this overlooked by Bell, whose investment in its conjurings still accumulates a secret interest; let us think of this as a trust fund that as yet has not matured for the telephone. ■ The reports indicate ambivalence. Who first made the telephone talk? The conflictual tone we appear to have uncovered in the rendering of the telephone's birth is situated in a subtle hiding place of the autobiography. Yet it hardly stands alone among such utterances, of which a few might be singled out. This is important because the most earnest concept of ambivalence, as described by Freud, is built into the telephone, harboring a double rapport of one to the other in which the other is always wanting or it is from you that the want has been extrapolated—a cut of presence has been constitutively left out, there is something missing, which also, however, makes certain telephonic couplings at all possible. Ambivalence can be read according to various frequencies of desire and horror, channeling the hierarchies that tend to build up when two are on the line, the caller and the called, though these stations do not constitute an oppositional or stable pair. "Pair" is to be understood in the singular, *a* pair, effecting thus an internal series of controls which may be difficult to master or delimit. ■ It falls within the norm to assume that Watson ranks second to Bell in terms of the contract that unites them. Nothing seriously disputes this assumption, which Watson himself of course shares. The subject who comes second is sometimes so immoderate in praise and admiration that number one falls into a darkened sphere of projection created by the resourceful suitor. For his part it seems that Watson has pitched an eternalizing space for the primary mover, rendering him immortal rather sooner than he might have bargained for. Early in the autobiography (Chapter 3) Watson has a word to say about his schooling. In the schoolroom we find a microchip of a theory telling us what it means for the young and delicate Watson to be second. A second-place theory comes on the heels of the sadism that jogs his memory: "The details of my work in [the schools] are very hazy in my mind probably because the work was so uninteresting. I remember chiefly the frequent thrashings the boys got from some of the teachers who seemed to delight in punishing for the least offence. But some of the women teachers I recall were kind and patient with us" (*A*, 23). Now for a bit of theory: "I was usually second in rank in my classes and never envied the boy who stood at the head for I noticed he was the principal victim when the teacher wanted to show off her pupils to a visitor" (*A*, 23). Hence number one is depicted as a victim. The ambivalence is built into the structure of the argumentation, for a figure that had been originally presented in a favorable, even admiring light, gets into trouble quickly. This holds for the sentiment beginning "I never envied the boy who stood at the head." Watson's satisfaction with second place takes a grandly morbid turn: "My satisfaction with my rank increased when the boy, who for one whole year had been at the head of my class, died of consumption. It seemed a narrow escape for me and I told my mother on the day of the boy's funeral that the boy ahead of me in the class always died, but that startling generalization was based on that single observation" (*A*, 23–24). We can gather now for whom the bell tolls. The unenvied number one who heads the body of which Watson plays a part, is marked for departure, decapitation, uniquely ("this single observation") delineating what always happens. He tells this to his mother, who will be kind and patient with the theory, and who, being a woman, will not punish him for this statement with a thrashing. ■ But producing such a "startling generalization" for Mother's ears alone—something that has happened only once and forever—really means that you, Watson, have still not begun to narrate a secondary relationship to Alexander Graham Bell, whom you have not yet met, although you are writing your autobiography after his death. Rather, you are telling

second

second

second

second

second

second

your mother, you are telling me, about what happens to number one, the guy ahead of you, the head of the household. The father of the telephone or the father to your existence, the boy ahead of you, is marked for the departure and demise of which you tell your mother. As second you are to be the narrating survivor in a narrow escape which you will always be telling your mother, the listening device for the double truth of ambivalence—the receiver of your autobiographical report, perhaps, its sole addressee, the shape and destiny of your reception history.

The Autobiography

Thomas A. Watson wanted to disburden his mother, for whom he shows the tenderest anxiety, everywhere and often: "and the constant care I had to exercise not to add to my mother's burdens, have influenced me all my life in such ways as a meticulous use of a doormat [something with which mothers have since been identified], distress if I tear or soil my clothes or spot a tablecloth, and, especially, in the pleasure I have always had from any device that simplifies and saves labor" (*A*, 3–4). The head of the household was a foreman, of whom he saw relatively little. "My father, who was broad-shouldered, muscular, and usually good-natured, had as his principal interest in life horses and their appurtenances. As foreman of the stable he was on duty from early morning until late at night, seven days a week, so we children saw little of him except at mealtimes" (*A*, 3). Nonetheless, Watson draws up a catalogue of repulsions from the infrequent meetings with his father, including his own inability to swallow meat at the family table. Among the several acquired aversions, the child also grew up hating horses. But this gets us further along in a history of ambivalence than we had intended. It seems that little Watson saw the light of day in something of a manger, "in a corner of the yard, entangled in the stable buildings . . . was my birthplace and boyhood home, a two-story-and-a-half, pitchroofed, clapboarded, unpainted house, in which we lived because my father had to be on hand *to attend to emergency calls* for teams coming at all hours of the night" (*A*, 2; italics added). The desire to save labor, to save Mother, to unhitch the father's horses uncannily arranges a place by which a disburdening carriage of messages might in the future be conveyed. This is quickly said; yet it is Watson, not I, who says it.

From the first pages of the autobiography we know there was a father who responded to emergency calls at night. There was something about this that Watson had to swallow. In the meantime he has erected a two-and-a-half-story house that holds the two-and-a-half-member story. He introduces an addition, another important member of the family to supplement the mention made of Father, Mother, and baby Watson. This member sheds light on the family tree whose genealogy the telephone still bears, a kind of glass eye whose vision cannot be easily measured. The tree, a great ash, a tree of mourning, of which Watson recollects:

> I often watched the activities in the yard below, romancing about the strangers who came there. I remember, too, tragic events connected with that tree. . . . I am afraid pussy got many a delicate meal from our ash tree. . . .
>
> The cat was an important member of our family and when she died our sorrow was attested by general weeping. To mitigate our grief, an ingenious friend stuffed and mounted the skin for us, but it was not a success as a consolation. Its ugliness scared me, especially the mouth, which was badly puckered and showed the straw inside, and the glass eye that glared at me alarmingly. (*A*, 4–5)

Focus the mouth: what horrifies Watson in this passage to a mummified beloved is the mouth whose ugliness takes the shape he will soon assign to the face when telephoning, the puckering mouth which only he in his day could master as he invisibly ventrilocated to Bell's audience. The blind eye has a silent alarm in this passage that comes from freezing the televisual faculty without, however, granting assurance that the blind eye is bereft of sight. This is why it fixes its object alarmingly. In case it should seem that the dead cat were being forced to pose as a telephone in some fortuitous way, read on, watch the pussy turn into a machine. Decide for yourself the genre of this machine: "Moths did their best to relieve my childhood of this fearful object, but did not add any beauty to it, and what the insects left of the fur, I used a few years later as an exciter for a frictional electric machine someone gave me" (*A*, 5).

But Watson would come to identify, if under the seal of secrecy, with the thing for which he wept. Some pages later, he characteristically presents himself in what might be loosely called an effeminate light. He abhorred the heroics of danger with which young masculinity, distributed among boys, girls, and tomboys alike, found itself rather often confronted. "If a snowball grazed me I never failed to weep loudly" (*A*, 8). His weeping, echoing the "general weeping" of which he has written, does not, however, arise from a causality of simple pain: "I never failed to weep loudly, not because I was hurt, but because I wanted to be petted" (*A*, 8)—to take on, we suppose, the characteristics of the thing whose loss he mourned. Eventually, the loud weeping will turn into the loud crying through the wires. The ears are missing. Chapter 1 has introduced the important members of the family, including the branch of the ash tree from which the child witnessed the flesh-eating feast indulged by the beloved cat. ("With sticks and shouts we often rushed to the rescue but in spite of our most frantic efforts, I am afraid pussy got many a delicate meal from our ash tree"[*A*, 4–5].)

Chapter 1 displays eyes and mouth protruding with medusoid precision, opening a yawning abyss whose fragile span Watson first covers with tears. Institutions organized about the church and education are shown to deploy mediocre forms of sadism; the child cannot swallow the gifts his father received for his services ("The arrival of the turkeys always interested me, although I disliked meat for food. . . . Whatever the explanation was, I ate meat only when my parents obliged me to do so, which they often did, as a vegetarian diet was then considered inadequate for any one" [*A*, 6–7]). Well, the ears are missing and Watson has yet to knock the nation, if ever so faintly. Indeed, the national channel comes in weakly at first, bringing into a shared audial space the birth of a nation and the beginnings of technology in the form of locomotion. The catalogue of aversions continues, coiling itself around the sensitive ears of the inventor: "Fourth of July was distressing, for my ears as a child were very sensitive and an explosion even of a small firecracker was painful. A locomotive whistle was a horror. There were sounds I liked, for as far back as my memory goes I recall listening with pleasure when certain persons were speaking, even if I did not know what they were talking about, and getting away out of hearing of other voices I did not like" (*A*, 6). Watson's auditory admission policy should prove of some interest. Decibel level and emanation of voice appeared to draw his attention or attract his repulsion. A measure of desemanticized sound, a quality of language scrambling and general production of background meaning already augurs Watson's receptivity to random noise, undermining any pretensions held out for transcendental signifying or technological power markers ("an explosion . . . locomotive whistle was a horror"). Watson's ears made his body squirm when they were receivers of a different order of meaning-based language, also unintelligible but **coded by pain**: he had had "to squirm through long, unintelligible sermons. . . . The effect of so much enforced church attendance in my childhood was an intense dislike for churches and preachers which I have never entirely overcome" (*A*, 10–11).

The hierarchically tuned sound filters extend the young inventor's ears to church music, from which they recoil. Thus another organ suffers atrophy: "And listening so much to the poor organ in that church has spoiled organ music for me ever since. Even now, an organ seems to sing through its nose no matter how good the instrument or how skilled the player" (*A*, 11).

If the sound systems of institutions (national, religious, technological) enervate Watson, we should still not want to distort the image of him as some orthodox rationalist, or as a man of science—the fiction brought into creation by our century's dementia. He was certainly allergic to the seeds of technology from the start; he was not terribly macho about his dealings with nature, nor driven by the silly formula that so many intellectual histories have imposed upon such men, to the effect that they signed on in order to master nature, to gain dominion over the world, and so megalomaniacally forth. In a sense, Watson constantly negotiated with the phallocentrism of "invention." A Faust of a different kind, Watson, as he says, wanted to be petted. This is not to insist that a discourse of power be suspended in his case; but it possibly offers the more trivial of the options we have placed before us.

Watson was a poet. He considered telephony an art; he was also a spiritualist easily capable of rendering public such statements as "believing as I do in reincarnation. . ." His capacity for — — — — — — — — — — —

spiritual insight would make him a keen soul-sister to Laing's Julie or Jung's Miss St. or even Heidegger's Trakl: "I remember particularly one sunny morning sitting on my back-door steps looking at the morning glories when suddenly they began to talk to me. I understood but I never tried to put it into words, for it did not seem necessary to do so" (*A*, 14–15). I would be inclined to say that this represents Watson's first telephonic conversation, were the figure of the deceased cat not still haunting these passages. Yet the two are not disconnected, for these are not ordinary flowers that speak to the solitary child, unable as he says, to write. These are morning glories, a private requiem of mourning, talking to him, saying yes in the form of a natural converter, to mourning: mourning glories transmitting words from the dead gaze of the cat. He understood, but he never tried to translate into meaning, he writes. Once again, a signifying content seems to be of no significance to Watson; he understands but not necessarily within a semantic dimension. Rather, he tends to heed a purity of talking, which can never as such be pure but open to contamination, always imbued with a founding noise to which he is attuned.

Moreover, he is a channelizer of contamination, particularly when it comes to linguistic pollutants such as "cuss-words." As an adult, he had for a benchmate a young man who cursed and swore at the slightest provocation. Ambivalence produces an oscillation in the disgust-barometer: "I listened to him first with disgust, soon with indifference but finally, whenever something went wrong in my work, I found myself expressing my annoyance by an emphatic utterance of some of his striking expressions . . . none of [the men] was influenced by my benchmate as much as I was, perhaps because they didn't work as near him as I did. Perhaps, too, I was more easily contaminated because my love for expressive speech fixed my attention on the young man's elocution" (*A*, 49–50). Watson's ears are uncanny, double and uncanny, reaching speech spheres of talking flower heads and curses, both of whose buds blow open in his nearness, disseminating their seeds upon him, entering his ear and leading him to recognize that "I was more easily contaminated." One might view this special sensitivity as an indication of otohysteria, were viewing itself not about to be thrown to the winds. And so Mr. Watson suffered under the regime of visual disturbance: he was afflicted early with nearsightedness, which at the time distinguished him from his contemporaries, as did the halo that he felt was following him everywhere. In synchrony with faint eyesight, Watson's demeanor attracted yet another "handicap" of partial withdrawal: "I was still almost as bashful when I met new people as I had been as a child and realizing it was a handicap I tried to rid myself of it by taking dancing lessons and going to the assemblies that followed. But it didn't help me much. In

fact, I have never fully overcome it. Although I have lectured, read or played to hundreds of audiences I am still very reluctant to meet people. I don't visit

even my oldest and dearest friends as much as I ought and *never make a formal call if I can avoid it,* in spite of the keen enjoyment I have when I get into actual contact with people whether they be old or new friends, or strangers. I am a poor mixer before I mix, but a better one after I get mixed" (*A,* 28–29; italics added).

Watson's English frequently liquefies its subject, producing an effect of fluidity obtained by foreign blenders. Thus, "After I get mixed" typically suggests an almost liquid self that follows a certain formula of contamination (chapter 6 treats "my notebook of this period of my life [which] contains many recipes, one of which for 'Pills to Improve the Voice' and a 'Recipe for Liquid-Skin'"). At this point it is necessary only to note a determinant configuration weaving reserve and phobic assessments of contact, a first-phase dread of renewing or initiating contact, movements of distantiality which Watson claims never fully to have subdued. The autobiography originates Watson's detachments in sight deprivation, which, turning him inward, projects intimate images toward an outer margin of exteriority. For if Watson sustained his fear of visiting with people, he quickly overcame any reluctance to contact ghosts, making formal calls almost nightly.

It starts badly. Before this narration overtakes us, however, we make mention of unabashed mentions Watson makes of haunting things. His aura was such that its spiritual fringes kept him in steady touch with the above. So even before becoming an electromagnetician he was thrown off by a distressing malady, as he puts it, having fallen for a girl. His look is transfixed by her figure metonymized into coily curls. "They thrilled me even more than the woods and the sea I was so fond of. I never spoke to the girl but her curls haunted me. I found out her name and took intense pleasure in uttering it aloud when no one could hear. . . . I worshipped her at a distance" (*A,* 16). Haunting curls, neither entirely alive nor dead, punctuating a head of hair with body, represent the only episode, as far as we know, of magnetic attraction for Watson. He also writes of being haunted by a bird he was pressured into shooting by a dare; "remorse seized me instantly and the memory of that dead bird has haunted me ever since" (*A,* 19). These aggregate to quite a number of hauntings for the first two chapters of an autobiography doubly dedicated to life, in its life-exploring title and in the part of the title aimed at naming the genre as auto*bio*graphy. Like others who are invaded by a haunting spirit or by ghosts who, inhabiting them, feed on them and program their inventions, Watson's discourse of early memories holds up casketlike burdens, sometimes wrapped in the form of a shroud: "I made all deliveries of goods, lugging them on my arms in baskets or in bundle handkerchiefs. If more things were going to a part of the town than I could carry on my arms, they were packed into a wheelbarrow or, in winter, into a big box sled, which I tugged about" (*A,* 20). The boxes multiply in memory, as do the charges. This is not to propose that Watson is inventing his memoirs, but that they principally call up cases, as with a number of historically haunted figures, that had to be carried and ceaselessly reproduced, as if one's entire life consisted in transporting the cargo of an Other. "After a year or so in the crockery store I got a job in a paper-box factory, where for seventy-five cents a week I swept the floor in the morning and helped paste boxes all the time I was not in school" (*A,* 21). His subsequent work as electromechanician reassembles the haunted motifs to which he additionally recruits the muse of poetry. Henceforth the electric current was to be channelized into acts of conjuring.

Watson's typical pattern of ambivalence, suggesting a jolting abhorrence that eventually swings over toward absorption, emerges at the early scenes of spirit raising as well. Owing to the primal conjuring we learn to estimate the effects of terror—one, perhaps not incidentally, initiated by a mother:

> George Phillips was about my age and I often went to his home. One evening, when we were eight or nine years old, his mother, a widow who earned her living by binding cloth shoes, suggested that we put our fingers on the table and ask the "spirits" to knock. It was a new game and we followed her suggestion. Instantly we heard taps from the table which increased to loud knocks and then the table suddenly reared up on two legs. Horribly frightened, I grabbed my hat and ran home, expecting every moment to be seized by a ghost. I didn't get over my scare for a long time and after that evening when I was at George's house, I kept away from that table fearing some ghost might start it going again if I touched it. Some four or five years later, however, I renewed my experiments with Phillips in this line with astonishing success, as will be reported later on. (*A*, 15–16)

Later on, after maturity permits him to grow out of a mother medium who both had initiated and petrified the connection, when no longer scared by the apparition of the father's profession (the table, like a nervous horse, reared up on two legs), dialing ghosts rises to the status of "experiments," ligaturing the rhetoric of science and poetry. Watson indeed renews his contact with the spirits via the scientific route, as in the manner of a scholar whose accountability depends upon this sort of research. The reduction of the scale permits an assimilation of the terrifying event insofar as ghosts now prove useful in conducting one's work. "I was now working with that occult force, electricity, and here was a possible chance to make some discoveries. I felt sure spirits could not scare an electrician and they might be of use to him in his work" (*A*, 37). As we shall have occasion to observe, the fundamental ploy consists in making the thing talk, which is precisely why it becomes somewhat of a professional duty for Watson to relinquish his fear of spiritual speaking. This fear was not attached to a natural object—the flowers' conversation did not appear to infuse him with a sensation of alarm, did not make his hair stand on end—but to crafted things, such as the table, that, too, might prove capable of speech. The telephone doesn't lag far behind in the totemic system of speaking things. It will be charged with conveying messages in the manner that, as concerns fear, first has to undergo a process of dilution. As thing, the telephone will have to be despooked without, however, scratching its essential ghostly aspect. Thus Watson always presents the telephone as something that speaks, as if by occult force. His perception of electricity rarely strays from its homeland in the occult, or what in contemporary California bookstores is classified as metaphysics. A member of the Society of Psychical Research, Watson could claim with dignity before any telephone was ever erected: "a faint, elongated glow a little brighter than the sunlight on the grass. . . . Was it a personal emanation? . . . The columnar halo followed me!" (*A*, 44). He was already himself attuned to the ghost within.

Thomas A. Watson returns to the table. The circuit of telephony begins, should a circuit be subsumable under a notion of beginning, on July 16, 1872: "We 'had a spirit circle' at Phillips' house with 'strong manifestations'" (*A*, 37). The vampiric citational marks probably refer to the official rhetoric of spiritualism that also could be found in the journal to which Watson subscribed, *The Banner of Light*. Yet, they should not relativize the effect of the real, for Watson claims to be talking real ghosts. It all begins modestly enough, with sound manifestations introduced via the fingertips indexing the body prints from where future calls are to come. The dialogics of strong manifestations takes shape spontaneously.

> These were at first entirely table tippings and rappings, from the merest ticks to loud knocks. Phillips and I sat at the table with our finger tips on its upper surface, and asked questions of the spirits, who instantly responded by three knocks or table tips for "yes" and two for "no". . . . The movements of the table varied greatly. Sometimes it rose gently from the floor with its top level and was lowered just as softly, and sometimes it jumped up quickly and was slammed down. More often it would be tipped up on two legs sometimes gently, sometimes forcibly and on several occasions when the table was tipped in this way, I sat on the high side and felt it as firm as if it were resting on the floor. (*A*, 37–38)

Though many figures—spirits, subjects, proxies—appear to be engaged by this activity, remember that Watson describes here essentially the labor of two, Phillips and himself, memorializing the art of a once-present mother, since it was she who broached the spirit circle. This is not for nothing.

As with other conjugations into which he inscribes himself, Watson will take second place, the place which allows the first to maintain itself, posing an activating receiver prior to any concept of sheer transmission. Given the fact that there exists a place of an absence which never ceases to assert itself, Watson's secondary station within a partnership of conjuration lapses easily into third place, making him the shadow cast by a more originary couple. This structure first emerges at Phillips's table, though Watson has already purchased the transfer tickets for other tables. Watson himself, as he presents himself, lacks the power to initiate or bring forth according to any view of sovereign invention the ghostly manifestations. The ghosts originate in the Other, a structure that suffers little breakage in his subsequent pairing. Watson recognizes that these sittings are not electrically controlled, but nonetheless he considers them supernatural.

The fact that the site for these sittings goes under the name of Salem has not escaped you. Male witchery got by, switching to electric cable systems that would carry the name of scientific experiment in the most original sense of a meeting scheduled between cognition, peril, and risk. Feminine sorcery burned in the background, a fire dimmed as in the domesticated tongues of flame in Freud. Mythologies were aflame. The telephonic seed, remember, was planted in Salem. After a few of these sittings I decided there was nothing electric about the doings (writes Watson), "but they seemed so supernatural, I accepted the 'disembodied spirit' theory of their cause. I determined, however, from the start that I had no power to produce the phenomena. From or through Phillips alone they all came" (*A*, 38). Watson had no power to produce; they all came from or through the conduit reserves of the other. We were so interested in the wonderful nightly occurrences, he continues, "that we had a sitting nearly every night the first week, some of them at my house, where they were quite as strong as at the other house" (*A*, 38). A third man joins the circle: Phillips and I and another young man, John Raymond, afterwards mayor of Salem, were the sole participants and all three of us soon became firm believers in spiritualism. We read the spiritualist paper, *Banner of Light* (*A*, 38). From this paper they learn about slate writing and at their next meeting ghostly teletyping becomes de rigueur. Henceforth the ghosts will participate in **a new grammatology of the mystic writing pad:**

> My old school slate, with a short piece of pencil on its upper surface was placed on Phillips' hand which he then reached under the table. Instantly the pencil began to write briskly with the dash of a fluent pen-

> man, and, when Phillips took the slate from under the table, there was unmistakable writing on it! (*A*, 39)

He had never been taught at school either to make observations or to take notes of occurrences, "and my literary powers were practically nil." He proposes that his autobiography can hardly embrace the possibility of a memoir, throwing instead the self to the obscure passages of forgetfulness. The signature of an invisible operator emerges in these sittings, similar to the way it was placed on the earliest telephones, "with a free-hand circle around it" (*A*, 39).

> Boylike, I was sure I could never forget anything that interested me as much as did these sittings. For this reason many details of the phenomena were not noted in my diary. I have forgotten many of the minor occurrences but the principal ones are clear in my mind still. The slate writings that impressed themselves on me were "O.P.," "I am happy," "I was murdered," "Charley Chase is in the happy land."
>
> The "O.P." with a free-hand circle around it came at almost every sitting. They were the initials of Oliver Phillips, our medium's father, who went west when George was a baby and was never heard from afterwards. There was a rumor that he had been murdered. The next two phrases I mention were supposedly from the spirit of the father. Charley Chase was a playmate who had gone out of our lives two or three years before. Besides these intelligible things many irregular and unmeaning scratches would be made on the slate at each trial.
>
> We sometimes tried to make other things besides the dining table jump and rap. When we asked to have the raps come on a glass bookcase, or on the mop board, the spirits would always obey. (*A*, 39–40).

The spirits' obedient heeding encouraged John Raymond, the man who was to become mayor of Salem, soon afterward to introduce a novelty. One evening in September, reversing the hierarchical controls, he began acting strangely, Watson notes. He announced that he was going into a trance under the control of a spirit. His arms and legs jerk convulsively; his eyes begin to roll, and his features "become alarmingly distorted" (*A*, 40). We observe the same features that will overcome millions who are about to make a telephone call. Watson continues. Then, after five or ten minutes of preluding, he stood up with the air of a political orator and "made a speech that lasted half an hour" (*A*, 40). The power reversal, which in fact further empowered the possessed subject, marked an epochal shift in the history of these séances. Once the other seized control of the now obedient subject, things began to break up at the Phillips's table. They began to occupy a position of ***being called*** rather than that of making calls. The trio dissolves. Besides, "Phillips was bored with John's performances for he wanted to give the whole show himself, being proud of the fact that only he had the power to make the table and slate do things" (*A*, 41).

The forces arrange to leave them. Watson will have to transfer his accounts to telephony on the double. This circuit fades impotently, which should not mean that they had not had ghosts at their fingertips.

> Was this all some humbug of Phillips? I do not hesitate to say positively "No!" What I have recorded here happened often in bright daylight on a Sunday, or a holiday afternoon, under conditions that utterly precluded any fraud on the part of Phillips or any one else. And the fact that he lost his power to produce the phenomena completely at the end of about four months is evidence of his honesty, for, as I have said, he was very much puffed up with his occult and exclusive power, and when he found it was leaving him, he was very sad and did all he could to keep it. . . . One afternoon when the table wouldn't tap or move, nor the pencil make the smallest scratch in spite of his earnest entreaties to the spirits, Phillips flopped down on his knees with his head in a chair, and wept and prayed for a long time, beseeching God to give him back his power. But it never came back and my diary notes no more sittings. (*A*, 41–42)

As if preparing the grounds for a recuperation of Phillips's lost powers, Watson concerts the experience into terms ascribable to telegraphic behavior and mechanical motion. He provides a ceiling under which these phenomena fall, landing softly on their ghostly feet, in a realm where scientific and prescientific vapors mix magically. Thus, while "my limited experience does not justify dogmatizing on this disputed subject . . . I am better satisfied with the explanation that Phillips and other mediums are endowed with the power to transform some subtle, bodily radiation into a mechanical force that produces the raps, movements, and slate writings as a steam engine changes heat into mechanical motion or a telegraph instrument transforms pulsations of electricity into the taps of the Morse code" (*A*, 42–43). Watson submits his halo to a similar interlinear translation according to which the signifier of the elect is soon enough converted into electricity. Rather than fully evacuating the supernatural he revalues it, by a special transformer, into electric currency. As for the halo, it eventually demystifies into an electric phenomenon. The steps along the way may be of some interest. "As you look toward the low sun over a body of slightly ruffled water, you see a shining path leading from you to the orb, caused by myriad reflections of the sun's disk on the waves. My halo is the extension of the sun path on the other side of the observer caused by the much fainter reflections of the sunlight on the grass blades, showing brightest on wet grass" (*A*, 46).

> The halo surely streamed from my head! I went back to my seat to see if any one else had the glow over his head. There was only one halo and it was over me! The conviction grew that either I had a guardian angel permanently attached to me or that I was endowed with this mysterious thing to indicate that I was chosen for some great purpose. I told my mother about my halo. It didn't seem at all strange to her that her son was thus distinguished; it was quite what she would expect. I tried to make my friends see it as they rode with me in the car but their eyes were not sharp enough. A year or two later I told Graham Bell about the halo. He scoffed at it and said it was undoubtedly due to some defect in my eyes. That didn't shake my faith; my halo came triumphantly through all tests I submitted it to and for several years I felt distinguished by it above my fellow creatures. (*A*, 44–45)

However, the aureole of glory, marvelous to relate, does not rest on his head, as it did on that of Cellini, who died thinking his halo was his special favor from the gods, or that of Thoreau, who in chapter 10 of *Walden* "used to wonder at the halo of light around my shadow and would fain fancy myself one of the elect." No. Watson was moving under the sway of an altogether different headset.

Tuning the Fork

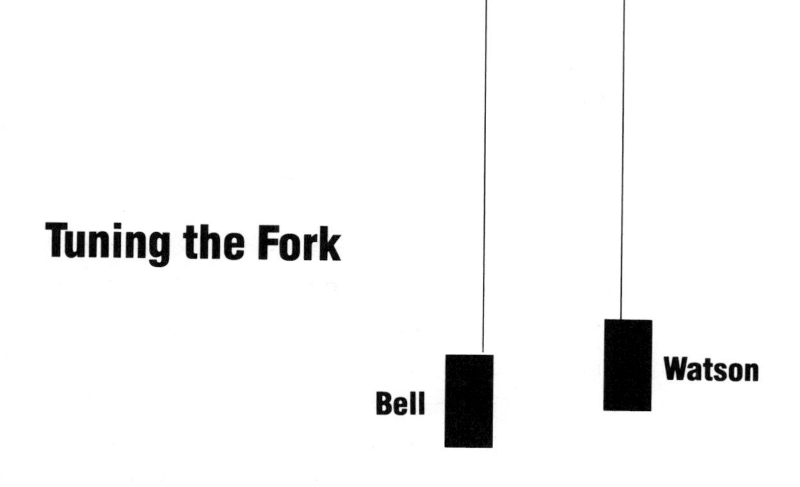

The context recalls the precision of destinal missiles. Working on underwater explosives, Watson's wondering what is next to come. The next exploding mine was to be Alexander Graham Bell:

One day early in 1874 when I was hard at work for Mr. Farmer on his apparatus for exploding submarine mines by electricity and wondering what was coming next, there came rushing out of the office door and through the shop to my workbench a tall, slender, quick-motioned young man with a pale face, black side-whiskers and drooping mustache, big nose and high, sloping forehead crowned with bushy jetblack hair. It was Alexander Graham Bell, a young professor in Boston University, whom I then saw for the first time. He also was living in Salem, where he tutored the deaf child of Thomas Sanders, and came in to Boston practically every day. (*A*, 54)

Bell had broken down the rudimentary discipline of the shop "by coming directly to me," like a projectile (*A*, 54). He rushes into the subjectless space to make direct contact with Watson; Watson is struck with particular force by the way the other breaks into a space of anonymity. Watson recreates this scene by explaining that the workers in the back never knew for whom they were at work, under whose command they were building technology. "To make my work on his apparatus more intelligent, Bell explained them to me at once. They were, he said, a transmitter and a receiver of his 'harmonic telegraph.'. . . The principle on which his telegraph worked has the same sympathetic vibration which sets a piano-string or organ-reed vibrating, when its own note is sounded near it" (*A*, 55). Regarding Bell's invention using instead of air an intermittent current of electricity over the wire, Watson does not neglect to assert, "his apparatus was very simple" (*A*, 55).

Running his direct line to Watson, Bell leaves no doubt as to the sympathetic vibrations which flared in the primal transmission that Watson received. Not only was the apparatus very simple, "The operation was also very simple" (*A*, 55). The problem with this very simple apparatus regulated by equally simple operational methods was that when Bell tried to send several telegraphic messages simultaneously (this possibility is in what the harmonic telegraph consisted), "they did not work as well as they theoretically ought" (*A*, 57). Bell explains that "the receivers would not always pick out the right messages" (*A*, 57). Eventually he aimed at the autograph telegraph, an apparatus for telegraphing facsimile writing and pictures, which was a use Bell wanted to make of his harmonic telegraph when he got it perfected. So prior to the autograph telegraph, they are two, Watson, Bell, and the imperfect theory—busted because the receivers could not pick out the right messages. We recall on rewind the first intelligible message that outfitted Watson as receiver. In a sense, it marked out for Watson, and for us, the manner in which a determined intelligible sentence interchanges programmatically with random unintelligibility. It remains entirely possibile that the receiver then, too, had not picked out the "right message." In any case, this creates the primal problem set which faces the couple; it is the first recall represented by Watson, showing that the two were confronted with a breakdown in Bell's desire, a deviation in the mechanism for hitting the intended message. Nothing prevents us from thinking that their entire venture did not immediately declare itself at risk of contamination, of scrambling, of random meaning, from this foremost dilemma. This may be of consequence for the thing made to speak, the telephone, bending the aim of transmissions toward an ever-splitting receivership, disseminating messages to the point of atomosemantic fission and particle breakdown. If this had been legislated from the start, as the law of its enframing, one would be duty-bound to give the first fully "intelligible" telephone sentence the same self-splitting treatment. Did Watson, for instance, pick out the right message when Bell reportedly transmitted "I want you"? Or, more generally, in terms of amplification and refinement, isn't mishearing, missing the point of the missive/message, not from the start of their relationship built into the thing you pick up when you listen to a transmitter, any transmitter, conveying electric utterance? Whatever the configuration, scrambled or not, of the first telephone receptionist, the problem of picking out the right message still dominates the horizon of telephonality, a fact which no doubt intensifies its functioning as a privileged instrument of splitting for the schizophrenic. The telephone pitches language into its most random allotment.

The telephone as shredder links the occult or witchcraft to forks, pitchforks and eating forks. Watson's attention thus takes us back to the table, a most lasting locus of encounter. An early scene with painful emphasis placed upon the afflicted mouth brings together, prior to the invention of the telephone proper, the poor dead cat whose orifices had so haunted young Watson. Additionally, it is as if Watson were made to play elocutionary games at table, repeating an early form of phonetic practice. Bell has just learned of Watson's interest in speech tones and has given him his father's book on elocution.

> And his table manners were most interesting. Up to that time, the knife had been the principal implement for eating in my family and among my acquaintances. The only point of table etiquette that had ever been impressed on me was that the knife should be put into the mouth with its sharp edge toward the middle of the lips as otherwise there would be danger of widening the orifice painfully. I was much embarrassed the first time I had supper with Bell at his boarding house, in trying to imitate his exclusive use of a fork in the conveyance of food. It was a new kind of fork, too. Those I had always used had two tines; this was like a spoon with three long slots in it. However, by careful observation and private practice, I soon conquered this leaky, inefficient implement and have never had much trouble with it since, although to this day I have a private preference for a spoon for many articles of food. (*A*, 58–59).

Many things are taking place in this passage and at table. Without suggesting a chronology of strict priority, we might go over a few of these to consider better the primal scene of symbolicity's deposit and the danger conceived in terms of painful orificiality. In the first place, which by no means adopts a first place, Watson, savaging his own image, was embarrassed by a switch of implements when it came to the knife/fork pair. Bell employed a state-of-the-art fork, "a new kind of fork, too," the latest invention of the genre. While on the one hand Watson states that he was unaccustomed to making use of the fork at all, he concedes the opposite, writing that he usually used one with two tines, not the deposit-your-coin type of structure allowing three slots.

The true source of embarrassment, however, consists in the mimetic task set before him at table "in trying to imitate [Bell's] exclusive use." But where the fork serves as the latest invention favored by the master ingester, Watson nevertheless qualifies it as inefficient as far as its sheer tool-being goes. Not only an inefficient implement and after all, not difficult to master, the fork is also leaky, it doesn't hold water. A hybrid thing, or rather *Zeug,* between the knife and spoon—between the stabbing utensil and one that gathers together—the

fork's scandalous capacity for insubstantiality rather alarms Watson. The immanent leakage as well as the implement that creates its structure will lend essential support to the rumorous run of telephony's imaginary. The concept of fork, to which Watson raises slight objections but can quickly master, inserts itself into the very possibility of the telephone, its anatomy, its conceptuality, its art. In order indeed to master Bell's inefficient but new tool, Watson conducts experimental exercises with it ("by careful observation and private practice").

The fate of the mouth within the context of their first supper is not altogether inconsequential. Watson had been accustomed to introducing a knife to his mouth whereas Bell favors the three-gapped fork; in private a third term is introduced, electing neither one nor the other but culminating in the present ("to this day I have a private preference," he avows publically, "for a spoon"). As organs of multiple uses and contortion, the mouth and palate, organs of taste, accept the training in one sitting that three generations of Bell men have sought to give it. Alexander Graham Bell's grandfather devoted the better part of his life to the malfunctioning of the speech organ, seeking to discover correctives to the stammering that had hit the streets since Moses' telegraph system. Watson's place within the invention of the telephone was staged as mouthpiece. This is why the experience of difficulty in organizing his mouth around its task merits attention. A mouth receives food and shelters language; it forms a place of radical inmixation, opening itself to the toxicity of incursion. In this scene, the fork pierces the boundary marking off the body's inside from its outside. It is as if Watson had to swallow Bell's invention, receiving it like a metallic communion. Open to experimentation, the mouth also, of course, participates in the zoning of libidinality. At any rate, what emerges as a clue for grasping his embarrassment concerns not the object incorporated but the conveyance itself of food from the hand to the mouth ("his exclusive use of a fork in the conveyance of food").[106]

This brings in an important term that has been hitherto kept invisible in the dumb show of **telephony's first supper**, a kind of third hand that complicates the bodily manipulation of telephoning, particularly in rapport to speaking/writing. For if speech classically has been subsumed under the paired concept of voice/ear, and writing under eye/hand, then telephony puts a third term on the table, a third hand which in the first place is a hand and nothing more. A new complicity, the assignment of the hand to the mouth, invades the boundaries marking the essential relationship of writing to speech, though after the raid the hand often enough finds itself left behind. The hand grasps the telephone, designs and signs it, spinning the wheel of fortune, attaching to the voice/ear couple, thus disturbing the domestic tranquility of a strict logocentricity. The hand disrupts, manipulates, it slams down on the house of logos. Heidegger was onto the hand. It spreads a shadow over his oeuvre, as if pointing the text to the mouth/ear outlets meticulously enfolded in his thinking. Whatever happened at the First Supper, Watson remembers an embarrassment; he had to cover his mouth, he had to overcome a prior practice which risked "widening the orifice painfully." He gets rid of the knife, learns to imitate Bell. The two tines expand to three tines; the hand

comes into the picture,

and a certain sentiment of

GUILT.

In the same passage Watson deftly converts the fork as conveyor of food to a fork musically attuned. He makes the move from one paragraph to another, from the implement to the instrument. They are still building telephones. But Watson's immersion in the occult makes it hard for him to swallow the piano:

Bell had another fascination for me: he was a pianist, the first I had ever known. To play the piano had always seemed to me the peak of human accomplishment. **It seemed so occult and inexplicable that I asked Bell one evening, when he was playing on his boarding-house piano, if it was necessary to hit the keys exactly in order to play a piece or would striking them anywhere in certain vicinities of the keyboard answer the purpose?** My respect for the art was deepened when he said the precise key had to be struck every time. The possibility of my ever learning the art, which had been one of my secret aspirations, faded at this revelation of its unexpected difficulties. (*A*, 59)

While this avowal produces an impression of unparalleled naiveté, which we have no intention of perturbing, it situates the scientific compulsion in a band way above the technosphere in which one would perhaps falsely hope to locate the mind of an inventor. It seems rather clear that for Watson "the peak of human accomplishment" supersedes the strictly human in a manner that appears neatly paradoxical. If piano playing flags the summit of human doing for Watson, then he supposes it to rise above the experiential strains to a suprasensory realm of sheer occult projection. The piano calls music. The hand, while instrumental, remains incidental. The somewhat scientific exactitude with which a melodious piece of artwork is made (hitting the right key, picking the right message) stuns the spiritualist, leaving him commensurately dispirited.

The register of organized sound had seemed occult to Watson, and inexplicable.

The stupefying revelation concerning the piano can be viewed as crucial to the extent that the very next chapter enters the space of mutual collaboration by hitting the key on Bell's contraptions, named instruments ("I worked away at his instruments" [*A*, 62]). In a similar vein, pitched to the same grand image, the desire to telegraph sound belongs to "an apparatus with a multitude of tuned strings, reeds and other vibrating things, all of steel or iron combined with many magnets. It was as big, perhaps, as an upright piano" (*A*, 62). And for the duration of their work on what someone could be tempted to classify according to a strictly "scientific" taxonomy, Watson abides the ghosts he had long ago conjured: "The apparatus sometimes seemed to me to be possessed by something supernatural, but I never thought the supernatural being was strictly angelic when it operated so perversely" (*A*, 63). By this reference Watson means the telegraph, which Bell was having trouble improving, allowing that some recognizable brand of Salem intervention, not quite angelic, created circumstances which were "messing up his telegraph." Regardless of what forces participated in the labor of inventing the telephone, Watson consistently organizes its facticity around a shared concept of art and science, laying the primary emphasis on the conception that takes place in the history of a pure idea:

History gives us many illustrations of the transforming power of an idea, but Bell's conception of a speech-shaped electric current ranks among the most notable of them. The conception itself was the great thing and any mechanism embodying it, even the very first form that was discovered, is of minor importance. If Bell had never found the apparatus for which he was searching, his name should have been immortalized. My realization of this has always made me very modest over my contributions to the art of telephony. I knew other electricians who could have done my work with Bell as well as I did it, but here was only one Bell with his big idea. (*A*, 65)

Watson's reading of the telephone as pure idea ought not to be overlooked in haste. For, unlike other "great things," the telephone did not come into being as an effect of some demand or generally articulated desire. It was the cause of the effects which nowadays places it strangely in the locus of effect. It was not the culmination of a teleological movement, a finality, science's response to an audible demand. The telephone was a private, an imaginary, and a somewhat more perverse conception than you would allow. At these moments of its analysis, Watson takes a step back, diminishing himself to the spot of an electrician who wired and set up the instruments of an unpinnable "mad," that is to say, art-bound scientist. Yet, we have seen the very special currency on which the marginal electrician operates; it is not wrong to suppose that the two men pooled their ghostly resources. The telephone was conceived as their baby. They hasten to advance its infancy, eager to have their child talk: The telephone was conceived as their baby. They hasten to advance its infancy, eager to have their child talk:

I made every part of that first famous telephone with my own hands, but I must confess my prophetic powers, if I had any, were not in operation that day. Not for a moment did I realize what a tremendously important piece of work I was doing. No vision of the giant that new-born babe was to be in a few years came to me as I hurried to get it ready to talk. I am sorry I was too busy at lathe and bench to do any dreaming for it would make a pretty story if I could record that I foresaw the great things to come and was stimulated by them to extra exertions. But there was nothing of the kind; I rushed the work because I was mightily interested in the invention and wanted to hear it talk. (*A*, 69–70).

No time for dreaming or projection, Watson's want is articulated as "I wanted to hear it talk." When it does begin to talk, its primal sounds are conceived as a birth cry, brought to light by Bell and Watson. At the moment of giving birth, the couple has to change positions in order to get it right. They are already a telephone, but they still need to fit into the right position—the one receiving, the other disseminating and repeating the effort. This sort of harmonic relationship, like the telegraph that initiated it, needs practice: the first trial of the new telephone has Bell listening in the attic with the receiver reed pressed against his ear, while Watson talks into the telephone.

But alas, shout my loudest, Bell could not hear the faintest sound. We changed places, I listened in the attic while Bell talked into the telephone downstairs. Then, I could unmistakably hear the tones of his voice and almost catch a word now and then. . . . We tried every way we could think of to make the telephone talk better that night but soon the parchment of its drumhead became softened by our breath and the reed breaking away from it put the telephone out of commission until repairs had been made. (*A*, 71)

Eventually, 109 Court Street, Boston, gave birth to their instrument:

I was sitting at the window nearest Hanover Street when I plucked the reed of that harmonic telegraph transmitter and made the twang that has never stopped vibrating. Bell was at the other window when he heard the faint sound in his receiver which was the birth-cry of the telephone. The building has been marked by a bronze tablet on one of the pillars of the false front of the theater which reads:

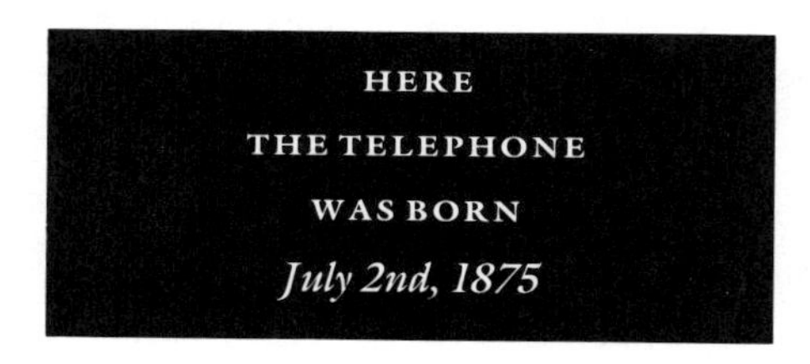

(*A*, 73)

The theater sets a place for displaying the telephone's birthright. And with reason. Fundamentally nonessential, this theater appears to be held up by a false front, an architechtonics of the phony façade which, however, gives way to a tangible theater of the invisible. What is supposed to go on in the telephone does not amount to a production, or rather, it goes on without showing itself. Nonetheless, it takes place. Theater, the promised space of representation, is not itself false. Only the front it puts up is false. It organizes a space of nonknowledge, erecting neither a subject nor an object before which one could solidly maintain oneself. In a sense, like the tabernacles, the phone box is destined to remain empty, making dissemination inevitable.[107] Watson says this in other words, of course, evoking the twang that never stopped vibrating, something that continues to ring in the vague labyrinth of an ear, still cracking its disseminative codes.

Bringing up baby is another matter for the pair. They have to take it on tours with them, staging countless performances to calm mass epistemological anxiety: no one can believe their ears. To have their ears believe this extraordinary protégé, the public has to see it talk with their own eyes. Watson and Bell assume their parental task: "Getting that famous first sentence through the telephone seemed to exorcise some of the tantalizing imps that always pester the babyhood of a new invention as infantile diseases do a human baby, and a few weeks later the telephone was talking so fluently you did not have to repeat what you said more than a half a dozen times" (*A*, 80).

Like Heidegger and K. of *The Castle,* Mr. Watson has an ear for the silence that the telephone was capable of speaking. "This early silence in a telephone circuit," he writes, "gave an opportunity for listening to stray electric currents that cannot be easily had to-day. I used to spend hours at night in the laboratory listening to the many strange noises in the telephone and speculating as to their cause" (*A*, 81). His sonic speculations disclose the atonal symphony of random noise:

"One of the most common sounds was a snap, followed by a grating sound that lasted two or three seconds before it faded into silence, and another was like the chirping of a bird. My theory at this time was that the currents causing these sounds came from explosions on the sun or that they were signals from another planet. They were mystic enough to suggest the latter explanation but I never detected any regularity in them that might indicate they were intelligible signals" (*A*, 81).

If the apocalypse is supposed to reveal itself as unbearable sound, breaking the universal eardrum, then Watson's ear is already probing remote planetary explosions. At this level of supraglobal listening, he claims a unique status for himself. "I don't believe any one has ever studied these noises on a grounded telephone line since that time," he writes, adding, "I, perhaps, may claim to be the first person who ever listened to static currents" (*A*, 82). The first freak, Watson opened an altogether original channel of receptivity, admitting anharmonically telegraphed messages whose principal interest lay in the pure interference that noise conducts. Indeed, Watson may have been, as he here asserts, the first convinced person actually *to listen to noise*.[108] And he preserves the savage acoustics at noise level, as **asignificatory signals, planetary talk, supersonic crackles**, rather than rushing in a supply of semantic cover. This possibly imparts a more radical accomplishment than the invention in whose conception he shared.

The telephone worked the night shift. Watson early noticed "that the telephone talked better nights and Sundays than it did during the busy hours of week days, although our laboratory, being on a side street, was always fairly quiet. . . . At night or on Sunday, the diminution of city sounds gave the telephone a much better chance to be heard" (*A*, 82–83). Thus ends the ninth chapter of the autobiography. Its final sentence speaks of giving the telephone a chance to be heard, as if it had to defend itself against some silent reproach or well-known accusation. The time in which the telephone chooses to speak its piece falls on the silence of Sunday stillness or on the waking of nocturnal spirits. This poses the horizon against which the telephone stirs, speaking with unenslaved clarity.

Before you know it "and about six weeks after I signed the contract Bell decided his baby had grown big enough to go out doors and prattle over a real telegraph line, instead of gurgling between two rooms" and two grown men (*A*, 91). For Watson this entails some sacrifice, for "up to that time I had been living in Salem with my father and mother, going back and forth on the train every day, but now it became necessary for me to live in Boston. I hated to leave my mother, but the old house in the corner of the stable yard I left without regret" (*A*, 89). Though relieved of the commute to and fro, and of his father's quarters, Watson will never stop playing *fort/da* with his mother. At this time he leaves her for Bell.

"In passing, I will note for the benefit of the superstitious that the laboratory room was numbered 13, which in this case at least did not bring bad luck" (*A*, 89–90). More or less laying aside the harmonic and autograph telegraphs, they now "concentrated almost entirely on speech transmission" (*A*, 90). The parts were few—the electromagnet and its coils, the diaphragm, and the mouthpiece, with either a battery or a permanent steel magnet to excite the electromagnet. The diaphragm typically causes a number of problems, bringing back the intensity of an original human body on which to work. To an impressive degree—this will become clear in the Bell section—the table in Room 13 also served as something of an operating table for the reanimation of corpses. Watson works on partial-object corpses; he was charged with constructing several telephones, "down to a minute affair I made from the internal bones and drum of a real human ear that Dr. Clarence Blake, the well-known aurist, gave to Bell—of course, after his patient had finished with it. They all worked, even the real ear telephone, which was, however, the poorest of the lot. We finally decided on a diaphragm of iron of the same size and thickness as is used to-day" (*A*, 90). Nevertheless, the ancestor of the telephone you are used to using remains the remains of a real human ear.

It is small wonder that Watson will essay in a subsequent chapter to fend off charges of the occcult adherency that the telephone supposedly represented. Somehow the telephone will have to be disconnected from its ghostly origin, which Watson's tome tries to suppress, halfheartedly, only in the final chapters. For Watson never engages an oppositional logic that would ground a purity of scientific inquiry at the price of a fallen supernaturalism. The connections remain subtly intact as Watson launches faint countercurrents to the ghostly origins of these technologies. As the two were advancing toward a telephone that would both transmit and receive, they still appeared to depend upon the paradigm of Watson's earlier séances, though this point is

never made explicitly.
One example to illustrate
spooked circuitry may suffice: "I
knew we were using the weakest
current ever used for any practical
purpose and that it was also of a very high
intensity, for we had talked successfully
through a circuit made up of a dozen persons
clasping hands—a very great resistance. . . . These
were some of my thoughts while I was manipulating
things in every possible way, trying to make the telephone
talk" (*A*, 92–93). Tracing the telephonic bloodline to the first
conference call, we find the elders gathered about this séance circuit. The rhetoric of Watson's manipulations doesn't let up on evocations of voice reanimation, urging language upon a thing, calling a totem forth from its dwelling in deadness into speech—a state which of itself does not ensure life. "But it was useless, the thing was obstinately dumb" (*A*, 93). One night, the thing was no longer dumb. It was aroused from imperturbable slumber, and the first long-distance call was placed. But the call could not be verified. As in the case of a séance peopled with nonbelievers, Watson and Bell had to prove that the telephone actually had spoken, that this was not a rehearsed hallucination. Each began recording what was said at his end of the wire. "Then by putting the two records side by side he could prove to the doubters that the telephone could talk straight" (*A*, 95). The *Boston Advertiser* was to print the news of the first long-distance conversation the following morning. The first call travels between Kilby Street, Boston (Bell), and East Cambridge (Watson) on October 9. "These were telephones that would both transmit and receive" (*A*, 92).

There was a witness, rather literally appointed: the factory watchman ("I let the watchman listen, but even then I think he felt it was some humbug. His relief at getting rid of me was evident when he let me out of the building towards morning to walk proudly back to Boston with the telephone, a bundle of wire and my tools under my arm wrapped in a newspaper" [*A*, 95]. The first long-distance call bears recording. Here's what we have:

I cut it [the relay] out with a piece of wire across its binding posts, rushed downstairs, followed at a much slower pace by the watchman, and listened at the telephone.
It was no longer dumb! More loudly and distinctly than I ever had heard it talk

between two rooms, Bell's voice was vibrating from it, shouting "Ahoy! Ahoy!" "Are you there?" "Do you hear me?" "What's the matter?" . . . Then began the first "long distance" telephone conversation the world has ever known. We recorded it word for word. The croakers made us do that. The common attitude toward any new thing is apt to be pessimistic for the average man thinks that what hasn't been done, can't be done. It was so with the telephone. It seemed a toy to most persons. Some of Bell's friends, although they had heard the thing talk at the laboratory were doubtful as to its practical value, and one of them of a scientific turn of mind told me that he didn't see how the telephone could be accurate enough for practical use for every spoken word has many delicate vibrations to be converted into electrical waves by the telephone and if some of them get lost the message cannot be intelligible. (*A*, 94–95).

The first long-distance electric conversation enveloped language in high-decibel noise; as a noise machine it generated solely on good vibes. Ever since Watson had known Bell, he recounts, his habit of celebrating successful experiments by what he called a war dance was respected, and "I had got so expert at it that I could do it as well as he could. That night, when he got back to the laboratory, we forgot there were other people in the house and had a rejoicing that nearly resulted in a catastrophe" (*A*, 95–96).
The morning after: "after a sleepless night, as I started down the stairs to go to Williams' to build some more telephones, I saw our landlady waiting for me at her door with an acid expression on her face" (*A*, 96). as a noise machine it generated solely on good vibes. Ever since Watson had known Bell, he recounts, his habit of celebrating successful experiments by what he called a war dance was respected, and "I had got so expert at it that I could do it as well as he could. That night, when he got back to the laboratory, we forgot there were other people in the house and had a rejoicing that nearly resulted in a catastrophe" (*A*, 95–96).
The morning after: "after a sleepless night, as I started down the stairs to go to Williams' to build some more telephones, I saw our landlady waiting for me at her door with an acid expression on her face" (*A*, 96). The waiting woman at the end of the line, imaged in the liquefying anger of experimental elements, her acid face about to have words. The naughty young man: "My conscience was troubling me and I felt something disagreeable was about to happen. My pretense of great haste did not work for she stopped me and said in an unpleasant voice, 'I don't know what you fellows are doing up in the attic but if you don't stop making so much noise nights and keeping my lodgers awake, you'll have to quit them rooms.' I couldn't say much to calm her. I assured her we would be more careful although for the life of me I didn't see how we could get along with any less noise than we had been making. I couldn't blame her

finding fault. She wasn't at all scientific in her tastes and we were not prompt with our rent" (*A*, 96). This is the only time Watson invokes the prerogatives of scientific sensibility, in the key of aesthetified taste, and we would not be wrong to suggest that he spits out the signifier with irony. The noise without which they would not be able to get along presumably resulted from the war dancing, as telephone connections were tried out in other spaces. Yet the inevitability—at however long a distance—of noise as a by-product of this innovation in the speech conveyance has just been announced to the landlady, whose figure is firmly planted to the ground. This may be the birth of

a new noise era

whose contours make Kafka's thin text,

"The Neighbor,"

explode.

The telephone was hardly a beloved or universally celebrated little monster. It inspired fear, playing on fresh forms of anxiety which were to be part of a new package deal of the invisible. This hardly replicates the way Watson puts it, yet he gives abundantly profiled clues to follow. It soon becomes clear that schizophrenia recognizes the telephone as its own, appropriating it as a microphone for the singular emission of its pain. Schizophrenia was magnetized by the telephone the way neurosis rapped on Freud's door. In a fundamental sense, we can say that the first outside call the telephone makes is to schizophrenia—a condition never wholly disconnected from the ever-doubling thing. Watson mounts his case slowly, describing the call of aberrancy first in terms of "embarrassment." Men in particular were uneasy about the thing. For instance: "It also interested me to see how many people were embarrassed when they used the telephone for the first time. One day a prominent lawyer tried the instruments with me. When he heard my voice in the telephone making some simple remark he could only answer after a long embarrassed pause, 'Rig a jig, and away we go'" (*A*, 98). Regression takes hold, the call transfers the speaker to a partial object, a false self caught up in the entanglement of *fort/da*: away we go.

Watson defines essentially two kinds of men that visited the telephone. The first we have just listened to, away he went. The second returns us to a recurrent concern, the consummate knowledge of disconnection that connects the schizophrenic to things and machinery: "Men of quite another stamp from those I have mentioned occasionally" (*A*, 98). Though he is not necessarily playing *Carte postale,* you will note the self-addressed envelopes upon which these stamps are pressed. They go to the telephone laboratory like hypnotics mission-controlled toward their destination by unmarked signals. These men of another stamp arrive by letter, writing in secret codes of secret codes that would transform the telephone into a system of telepathically guided transferrals. "One day Mr. Hubbard received a letter from a man who wrote that he could put him on the track of a secret that would enable us to talk any distance without a wire" (*A,* 98). Mr. Hubbard, interested by this proposal, makes an appointment for the wireless man to meet Watson at the laboratory. Here goes their destinal encounter.

At the appointed time a stout, unkempt man made his appearance. He glanced at the telephones lying around the benches but didn't take the least interest in them. He told me that the telephone was already a back number and if we would hire him he would show us how to telephone any distance without apparatus or wires. He looked as sane as most of the inventors I had worked with and I became interested. When I asked him what experiments he had made, he told me in a matter-of-fact tone that two prominent New York men, whose names he knew but whom he had never seen, had managed surreptitiously to get his brain so connected with their circuit that they could talk with him at any hour of the day or night wherever he was and make all sorts of fiendish suggestions—even of murder. He didn't know just how they did it but their whole apparatus was inside his head and if I wanted to find out their secret I must take off the top of his skull and study the mechanism at work. For fifteen dollars a week, he said he would place himself entirely at my service to do whatever I pleased with him. Long before he finished his tale, I knew I was dealing with a crazy man. I didn't dare to turn down his proposition too abruptly for fear he might go on a rampage in that lonely attic so I excused myself from starting to dissect him at once on the ground of a pressing engagement and he went away promising to come again the next day. He didn't come again and the next time I heard of him [by phone, perhaps] he was in an insane asylum. Within the next year or two several men whose form of insanity made them hear voices which they attributed to the machinations of enemies, called at the laboratory or wrote to us for help, attracted by Bell's supposedly occult invention. (*A,* 98–99)

It was as if an unbeholdable, subliminal sign hung over the laboratory, bouncing signals for schizophrenics to phone home, for psychosis and auditory paranoia to settle down in the telephone. Watson retains the invisible headset telecommanding this man and those stamped in a similar way as part of the autobiography, which itself is a partial otobiography of the telephone; Watson hardly pushes this episode, whose repetitions he asserts, to some peripheral pocket of narrative disclosure. The call of the insane, who at first sight resemble the inventor, belongs to the fundamental history of the telephone, ingathering a "them" whose strict isolation and difference, as a guarantee of carceral alterity, I would not vouch for. Somewhere between an art and a science, the telephone still throws strangely stamped shadows off its primary invisibility. It divides itself among thing, apparatus, instrument, person, discourse, voice. Or rather, as a moment in onto-technology, does it not perhaps offer itself precisely as a nothing so that by putting off access to itself, abstaining or interdicting itself, it might thereby come closer to being something or someone? The telephone coils us around its own lack of assumption, if one understands by this the stranglehold by which it affirms the impossibility of acceding to its proper significance. Noise machine, schizo leash, war-zone shots in the dark, lovers' discourse or phantomic conference call, the telephone as such is, like the phallus, empty but powerful.

The call of the telephone to which the insane responded had been heard in print, announced somewhat in the way of Benjamin's messenger.[109] So the chapter containing the insane started running this way: "The publicity the newspapers gave our experiments brought all sorts of people to the laboratory to hear the telephone talk. Among our callers were . . ." The telephone called the callers. It placed its call through the pages of the newspaper, crossing two branches of noisemaking whose sense attracts a new breed of decipherments. Watson adds his own brand of pararationality to the list, if not quite intending to do so. In November 1876 the telephone refused to cough up an intelligible sentence, "it didn't talk distinctly enough for practical use" (*A*, 99). Watson was getting desperate. So "one day in a fit of desperation, remembering my experience with the 'spirits' and being still of the belief that it really was spirits that did the table tipping and slate writing, I decided to consult a medium (without Bell's knowledge) and see if there was any help to be got from that source" (*A*, 100). Clearly, the ghosts have to be endeavored without Bell's knowledge, for Bell refuses to affiliate himself with this branch of telephonic epistemology. Watson, for his part, was reduced to tracking down a medium through newspaper announcements, having lost recourse to a mother of a best friend or any other familiar conductor of electric knowledge. "She gave me such rubbish I never afterwards tried to get the spirits to give the telephone a boost" (*A*, 100). This stands as the last recording of an attempt to levitate the telephone by means of outside mediums. From then on, they would be installed within the instrument.

The telephone had entirely absorbed Watson's attention, until it began to shrink a little and "let me see more important things beyond it. . . . My walks in the woods had been less frequent during the two years I had been so completely absorbed in Bell's inventions and my poems quite neglected . . . while I was waiting for Bell to return from Cambridge where he was now spending many of his evenings at Mr. Hubbard's house, I memorized 'Thanatopsis.'. . ." Up to that time my chief ambition had been to get enough money to buy a house for my mother to live in" (*A*, 104–105).

Looking to see things importantly beyond the telephone, Watson looks inwardly and beyond but remains a captive audience to the needs of the telephone. The inward look of the myopic inventor takes the stage during Bell's lecture series delivered in theaters. The telephone created agitation, doubt, and anxiety among those not specially stamped and delivered to the laboratory. "I don't believe any new invention to-day could stir the public so deeply as the telephone did then, surfeited as we have been with the many wonderful things that have since been invented" (*A*, 110). Bell presented the telephone first in the Salem lectures, followed by one in Providence, Rhode Island. Boston, New York, and the cities of New England soon followed. They were all given in the spring and summer of 1877. We detect to what extent Watson is still telling ghost stories.

I played an important part in Bell's lectures although I was always invisible to his audience, being stationed every evening at the distant end of a telegraph wire connecting with the hall, having in my charge apparatus to generate the various telephonic phenomena Bell needed to illustrate his lectures. I had at the end of the line one of our loudest telephones especially adapted for the purpose, an electric organ on the principal of Bell's harmonic telegraph, a cornet player and sometimes a small brass band. But I was the star illustrator of Bell's lectures. My function was to prove to the audiences that the telephone could really talk, for which my two years of shouting into telephones of all sizes and shapes had fitted me admirably as it had developed in me a vocal power approximating that of a steam organ in a circus parade. I also had to do something else of importance for Bell's audience, called by courtesy, singing. (*A*, 113–114)

The invisible mouthpiece to Bell's audience, Watson would sing "Do Not Trust Him, Gentle Lady," which we should keep in mind as part of the repertoire of the telephone's early recitals. The inmixation of séance, dissimulation, music concert, magic show, scientific display, and operating theater prevails in the descriptive passages of Watson's invisible acts.

Professor Bell had by his side on the stage a telephone of the "big box variety we used at that time, and three or four others of the same type were suspended about the hall, all connected by means of a hired telegraph wire with the place where I was stationed, from five to twenty-five miles away" (*A*, 114). During the first part of his lecture Bell gave his audience the commonplace part of the show, organ playing, cornet music, the brass band, more of the same, "and then came the thrillers of the evening—my shouts and songs. I shouted such sentences as, 'Good evening,' 'How do you do?' 'What do you think of the telephone?' [this question being destined for us, here, now], which the audience could hear, although the words issued from the mouthpiece rather badly blurred by the defective talking powers of the telephones of that date." Then Watson would sing the songs he knew. "They were 'Hold the Fort,' 'Pull for the Shore' (I got these from Moody and Sankey who had just come to this country), 'Yankee Doodle,' 'Auld Lang Syne,' and a sentimental song I had learned somewhere called, 'Do Not Trust Him, Gentle Lady.' My singing was always a hit. The telephone obscured its defects and gave it a mystic touch. After each of my songs I would listen at my telephone for further directions from the lecturer and always felt the thrill of the artist when I heard the applause that showed me how much the audience appreciated my efforts. I was usually encored to the limit of my repertory" (*A*, 114–115). As a performing artist, the telephone, like the schizo or a professor, speaks to a full house of anonymous listeners with unknowable identities.

Theperformancetakesacuriousturnmomentarily,butfirstbacktothelandladywhostill The performance takes a curious turn momentarily, but first back to the landlady who still waits at the bottom of the stairs. Any more noise and out they go. Watson needed a soundproof booth quick "and invented, on the spur of the moment, something that supplied that want very well, but it never occurred to me to patent it" (*A*, 115). Always living dangerously, in the mode of supplementarity (Watson, I want you; as something that supplied that want), Watson has in hand the telephone on the night of April 2–3 when Bell wants to astonish his New York audience by connecting with Boston. "Having vividly in my mind the strained relations still existing with our landlady, and realizing the power of my voice when I really let it go, as I knew I should have to that night, I cast about for some device to deaden the noise" (*A*, 115–116). The man who brings noise to life, studying and encouraging it to take a legitimate place among other orders of sound waves, has to deaden its range, creating a predecessor to the contemporary antinoise machine. "Time was short and appliances scarce, so the best I could do was to take the blankets off our beds and arrange them in a loose tunnel on the floor, with the telephone tied up in one and a barrel hoop in the other end to facilitate my access to the mouthpiece" (*A*, 116). Under the covers of their beds, "it was a hot, smothery experience" (*A*, 116). The soundproof booth—also referred to as a *shroud*—"was a perfect success, as far as muffling the noise was concerned, for I found by inquiry next day that no one in the house had heard the row I made, not even the poor fellow who occupied the room immediately below the laboratory. Later inventors improved the booth, making it more comfortable for the public to enter but not a bit more soundproof" (*A*, 54). Again, what compels attention here rests on the invention of soundproofing that goes hand in hand with that of undulatory speech, the felt need for a sonic shrouding, an upright box to enclose the space of electric annunciation. When the telephone began to speak, opening its cavity, it became an exceptional gathering place for noise inhalation. Making itself responsible for this phenomenon, the telephone also arranged the means by which to deaden or annul its sonic waste products.

To enlarge the scope of the theater we continue on the tour of BaBell, Watson, and their telephone. A rivalry taking shape between New York and Boston proves homologous to one contracted between men and women. The self-presentation of the telephone begins as a tale of two men and two cities, however.

One of Bell's New York lectures looms in my memory on account of a novel experience I had one evening at my end of the wire. After hearing me sing, the manager of the lectures decided that, while I might satisfy a Boston congregation, I would never do for a New York audience, so he engaged a professional singer with a strong baritone to do the singing part of the program. Being much better acquainted with the vagaries of the telephone than the manager was, I had strong doubts about the wisdom of this change in the cast of the performance. I didn't make any objections for I didn't want to be accused of professional jealousy, and I knew my repertory would be on the spot if the new singer wasn't a success. (*A*, 117)

The twists and turns of professional jealousy on this amateur night took the stage in New Brunswick, New Jersey, "and I, and the rest of the appliances of that end of a lecture, went down in the afternoon to get things ready. My rival was there and I showed him what to do" (*A*, 117). It may have been that false assumptions led us to assert the impending rivalry of two men. By a barely perceptible but strongly run slippage, Watson has placed himself in the empire of appliances ("I, and the rest of the appliances"), momentarily shedding off or moulting an identity as gendered human subject. Little by little, Watson gets sucked in by the telephone that comes to determine his provisional being-as-equipment.

The baritone possesses a magnificent voice, Watson notes, "but I couldn't induce him to crowd his lips into the mouthpiece of the telephone in the way I had found necessary to get results at the other end of the wire. He was handicapped for the telephone lecture business by being musical for he didn't like the sound of his voice all jammed up in that way. That had never troubled me. I had noticed that the tighter I jammed my lips into the mouthpiece, the better my singing sounded to me" (*A*, 117–118). The baritone gives Watson his word on jamming. Women get in the way of things, making performance anxiety a fact of Watson's telephonic life. After briefing the baritone, he goes to supper, returning for the performance: "When I returned to the telegraph office just before eight o'clock, I found to my dismay that **the young woman operator had invited six of her girlfriends** to witness the interesting proceedings. It hadn't troubled me in the least to talk or sing to a great audience, provided, of course it was a few miles away, but when I saw these girls, the complacency with which I had been contemplating the probable failure of my rival's singing was changed to painful apprehension" (*A*, 118). (A primal school scene has shown Watson flipping out when his elementary school goes coed, requiring him to recite in front of girls. He drops out, going instead for cover and invisible speech.) "I realized that, if he wasn't successful, a bashful young man would have a hard experience for he would be obliged to sing before those giggling girls" (*A*, 118). As predicted, the rival singer was not man enough for the mouthpiece and when Bell called for the first song, "he sang that song for the benefit of the girls and not for Chickering Hall. I listened with a heavy heart for Bell's voice when the song was finished. The expected blow fell promptly. In his delightful platform tones, Bell uttered the words I had foreboded, 'Mr. Watson, the audience could not hear that song; won't you please sing?'" (*A*, 118). Girls *vs*. Dr. Bell, NY *vs*. Boston, singer *vs*. singer, audience *vs*. audience, appliance *vs*. pure voice, and so forth. Watson is about to turn his back on those girls. You may wish to read this with camp intonation:

I braced myself with the thought that Bell's first New York audience, made skeptical by their failure to hear the song, might be thinking cynical things about my beloved leader and his telephone, so I turned my back on those girls and made the telephone rattle with the stirring strains of "Hold the Fort" as it never had before. Then I listened again. The audience was applauding me vigorously! When it stopped, Bell's voice came with a note of triumph, saying, "Mr. Watson, the audience heard that perfectly and calls for an encore." I sang through my entire repertory and began again on "Hold the Fort" before they were satisfied. The "suppositious Mr. Watson," as the newspapers called me then, had to do all the singing at Bell's subsequent lectures. Nobody else ever had a chance at the job; one experience was enough for Bell. My baritone had a queer expression on his face while I was working on these songs. (*A*, 118–119).

The baritone gets to collect his fees; the suppositious Mr. Watson, however, "never got anything extra for my songs that saved the day." There appear various hints throughout the autobiography indicating that Watson did not entirely recover his due, which admittedly belongs to the structure of any transmission.

By now, Bell is poised entirely on the receiving end. Watson felt particularly shortchanged by the system when his beloved leader was to succumb to the "difficulties" of "an upsetting malady." In shorthand, this means essentially that Bell, for his part, was not turning his back on those girls. He was, somewhat to the contrary, falling for one. The telephone and Watson had to pay for the slowdown Bell's advances to Miss Hubbard cost. The first family—Bell, Watson, and the telephone—was exceedingly poor. They barely had enough money to feed them all. They lived on electricity alone. Then, when Bell took to Mabel, he came upon the idea of lecturing for a small fee. "The net proceeds of his second lecture were eighty-five dollars, the first money the telephone ever earned for its inventor. And that infatuated young man squandered it all on a pretty little silver model of the box telephone which he gave to his girl—a bit of extravagance of which I didn't approve" (*A*, 111). The romance pushes Watson and the half-orphaned telephone to the sidelines, as Bell showers his attentions on his deaf beloved instead. During a lecture before their honeymoon, Watson appears to get even.

The first verses ever written about the telephone, published in the *Lawrence* (Mass.) *American,* apostrophize Watson, call out to him under the title "Waiting for Watson." The poem does not quite bear the stamp of immortalization—surely, Schubert would not have chosen it as particularly worthy of musical accompaniment. Nonetheless, being first, being part of the family of new noise, and being so awful, perhaps it cannot avoid being overheard. The discerning eye is meanwhile enjoined to protect itself by skipping over these lines, put down for purely scholarly purposes—alas! such purpose often invites pervasive tedium. A multitude of ear-pairs are figured as conjuring up the suppositious Watson, now become the name of an electrically transmitted voice. Some of the stanzas go as follows:

To the great hall we strayed,
Fairly our fee we paid,
Seven hundred there delayed,
  But, where was Watson?

Oh, how our ears we strained,
How our hopes waxed and waned,
Patience to dregs we drained,
Yes, we did, Watson!

Give but one lusty groan,
For bread we'll take a stone,
Ring your old telephone!
Ring, brother Watson!

Or, by the unseen powers,
Hope in our bosom sours,
No telephone in ours—
  "Please, Mr. Watson."

Let us by consensus consider this the preschizophrenic hymn. However, as such, it would be worthy of further explication which sound judgment rather forbids. Nonetheless, we point to the first question ending the first stanza, addressing the question of locus—from where does the invisible voice emanate? In this case the "where" resonates on a more timely grounding, since it stresses instead the impatience which Watson's silence evoked—a mood of temporal enervation. Silence could be supplanted by a lusty groan, no need for the fairly promised intelligible sentence. Somehow the schizophrenic's stone enters the calculus as well, but at this station the telephone, on the crest of unseen powers, has not as yet been fully incorporated, as no telephone has penetrated to "our bosom." ("No telephone in ours—" a bad connection.)

This is bad poetry, journalistic verse to be sure. It hardly rhymes with other poetry that has sung in attunement to the telephone, including the poems of Max Brod. Yet this poem cannot be said properly to invest its *aboutness* in the telephone, since it waits in anticipation of a doubly remote figure, one side as blurred as the other. In fact the poem never coughs up a stable referential sense of things, for neither Mr. Watson nor the telephone comes into the poem's horizon. The poem cannot produce an argument about the telephone, cannot pin it down definitively. It can only raise the question of what it means to be "on" the telephone. While it convokes both Watson and his telephone, the speaker cannot clarify whether a thing or a subject is being apostrophized, nor who is the cause of what (or vice versa). As long as this strained identity which the collective ear has tried to hear out finds itself split off between a person, a full, nameable subject, and thingness, it cannot be fully introduced into the body of the poem as if it were regulated by schizoid digestive tracts. In other words yet no telephone stirs in our bosom (dash: "No telephone in ours—").

On the subject of our bosom, Watson has narrated this special event in the same breath as he attempts to expire Bell's imminent honeymoon with Mabel. The passage introduces the possibility of addressing two audiences simultaneously, and a double-entendre for which Watson takes the provisional blame. "These double affairs were not always successful," he writes of the night Bell lectured at New Haven, "because the two men did not always talk about the same thing at the same time" (*A*, 122). Doubleness and duplicity grow in the crevices of a telephonic signifying chain: "My last appearance in the lectures was at one of these dualities" (Bell speaking in one city and Fred Gower giving the same talk in another city, Watson stationed at *Middletown, Connecticut,* "with my apparatus"). The next morning when Watson met Gower "he was quite vexed and accused me of shouting 'How do you do?'

when he wanted me to sing 'Hold the Fort,' and Bell said I made it very awkward for him when he wanted me to give him the trombone solo, by singing 'Do Not Trust Him, Gentle Lady!'" (reminder: this on the eve of Bell's honeymoon). "Gower said I did it on purpose, and Bell looked at me quizzically, but it wasn't so, I was too fond of Bell to play such a joke on him. Anyway, I am the first one who ever addressed two audiences at the same time" (*A*, 122–123). Indeed. "This artistic interlude in my telephone work ended in the early summer" (*A*, 123), Watson goes on to narrate, switching automatically to the farewell interlude with Bell. "The bridal couple went to England on their honeymoon, Bell taking with him some up-to-date telephones to start business over there" (*A*, 123). In this respect, Watson, in spirit at least, or in exchange, got to join the couple on their honeymoon. Let us simply say that

Bell took the baby

along for a ride.

The rest is more or less history, which is to say, forgotten but partially retrievable by the proper access code. Watson works on a number of refinements, he reports; for example, on overcoming the booming overtone caused presumably by some defect in the diaphragm. "One night I went to bed discouraged by the failure of my last idea for an improved diaphragm and almost ready to believe that the indistinctness of telephone talking could not be overcome, but the next morning the thought that the trouble was caused by the shape of the mouthpiece and its cavity came to me at the fertile moment of awakening" (*A*, 128). Watson next commits himself to the noise (*A*, 130) that summons one to the telephone. He had to induce it to cry out, causing "a howl in it loud enough to arouse the house. 'Watson's Buzzer' was the name that got attached to my second device for calling. Many buzzers were made and sent out but the users didn't like the harsh screech it made. A bell that would ring without a battery was needed and I went to work to make one that would answer our purpose" (*A*, 130). Working with a magneto-electric shocking machine and two revolving coils, Watson starts the bell-ringing mechanism going. "It had to be a polarized bell for the current was alternating" (*A*, 130). Eventually Watson "devised a reliable bell" (*A*, 130)—perhaps one less polarized, and, if we may tune this section allegorically, one that does not run off suddenly to a romantic calling. But this Bell will never belong to Watson, for, "*although I patented my call bell in several countries it never got my name attached to it*" (*A*, 131). Instead the alarm was to be known as "Williams' Coffin":[110] "We gave Williams permission to make and sell them to our agents, who, impressed by the long, narrow, black walnut box in which the mechanism was placed, promptly christened them 'Williams' Coffins,' an honor I never disputed with him" (*A*, 131). That just about puts the lid on the Watson story, or the one we have chosen to reconnect. It is difficult to hang up, though this difficulty has historical roots which form a blockage around the activity of hanging up. In the early days of telephony average users, explains Watson, often forgot to hang up. They drew a blank on throwing the bell back after using the telephone. No calls could come through. "I tried several devices to remedy this trouble and finally designed the automatic switch operated by the weight of the telephone" (*A*, 131). The weight of the telephone has taught us to hang up, he writes.

The switch "now merely required that the user should hang up his telephone when he finished using it. This the public learned to do well after a year or two" (*A*, 131–132). A year or two—the time it takes to finish with it, the time for writing a book, perhaps, the time it takes to hang up and say good-bye, to the other, yourself. At first we used a single box telephone at a station, talking and listening at the same cavity (*A*, 133). The first telephone exchange to start on a regular basis was, wouldn't you know it, at New Haven, on January 28, 1878. Later we shall have the pleasure of meeting a certain Miss Yale, who, in order to speak of theory, rises up at one critical early lecture of Bell. He concludes one of his books with her affirmation. Miss Yale was a woman who did not resist theory. As for Watson, he clears the way, running down certain rumors. "This was the time when they used to say that all the farmers waiting in a country grocery would rush out and hold their horses' heads when they saw anyone preparing to use our telephones" (*A*, 140). The telephone, snapping shots of the horse's embrace, produced a serial outlet for little Nietzsches. ("That was somewhat exaggerated but there was enough truth in it to make the situation precarious for us.")[111]

If Watson's career began with the mysterious above, the rest of his autobiography, whether so designed or not, capsizes by dint of a downward tug as Watson and his cables go underground. In 1887 he faces the task of installing a telephone in a mine. Shortly after expressing gratitude to the man who was responsible for "Williams' Coffin," Watson recalls the day he took the plunge. He first fitted telephones for underwater use in a diver's suit. Though the poles are reversed, we are reminded of the early séances and slate-writing of which Watson took part. Both scenes require a studied capacity for floating. "After making a measurement, the diver wrote it in pencil on a bit of wood and let it float to the surface for the clerk in the boat to grab, or he would keep in mind a few measurements, be pulled up, have his helmet removed, and repeat these measurements to the clerk" (*A*, 161). All these flotations and aquatic slate-writing sessions were tedious, Watson reports, which is why there was a call for the telephone. "This was tedious and one day the diver who was doing the work came to me to see if I could arrange a telephone in his helmet so he could transmit his measurements through it" (*A*, 161). Watson gets to work on the project but some trouble arises, which means Watson has to go down to the deep end himself: "so I had decided to put on his suit and go down myself, which I did to the intense alarm of my young assistant, who was helping me that afternoon. I still feel the pathos of the moment as well as the scare of the new experience when, arrayed for the descent in the diver's suit, with lead-soled shoes on my feet, just before I disappeared, perhaps forever, beneath the limpid waters of Boston Harbor my young friend put his arm around my armored neck and kissed me on the thick glass plate, behind which he could see my anxious face" (*A*, 162). This, the first televised telephone, also gives as far as we know, the first clip of a telephonic kiss. Watson goes down cutting a quixotic figure. After that, reports Watson, who soon came to air, "no further trouble in communicating with the surface" (*A*, 163). The work in the sea was very much facilitated by the telephone, which is now· · · · ·

a regular part of· · · · ·

a diver's outfit.· · · · ·

Perhaps this would furnish a place to hang up on Watson, having· · · · ·

travelled the ups and downs,· · · · ·

listening to the

undulatory waves· · · · ·

that connect the above with· · · · ·

the ground, and

even with the sea. . . .

If Watson was primarily responsible for pulling the spiritualized above into the telephone wires, even if this meant inverting the process toward the specular sky and going underwater (which is not the same as underground), then it can be ascertained that Bell brought to the telephone that which lies beneath the ground, even when he brought it with him unburied, much in the way he carried the ear of the dead about with him—dead but still connecting, a detached organ of receptivity.[112] The encounter between Bell and Watson may not have been destinal in the sense of the absolute irreplaceability of one for the other; nor did their meeting necessarily originate the cataclysmic flash to which we owe thanks for the telephone. Rather, each, being wildly "innocent" of the telephone (Bell understood nothing of electricity and the like), brought to the event of its conception a partial set of phantasmata. There was no need as such for the telephone—it responded to their emergency call with the assured stirring of a somnambulist. Once together, they protected the catastrophe, each of the other. The shared space of their catastrophe was consistently held in place by what we call the telephone. Watson was susceptible to unearthly curls, spectral cats, and nocturnal horses. He was haunted from the start, invaded and possessed. There was something he could not swallow, a paternal transmission shrouded in static. Someone should tap into this. We currently have access to research material on Bell, whose phantasms, while still unrecounted, shape the cartography of a locatable uncanny.

They brought two rapports to phantoms with them, the one still cracking transmission jokes on our telephone lines.[113] This knowledge doesn't make it any easier to hang up. Watson carries out "the desire that had been in my mind ever since I was a schoolboy—to buy my mother a house" (*A*, 173). He moves there, too. He also gives the paternalized figuration a try-out session: "I also bought a horse but I did not like the thing and he knew it, for he took every opportunity to show his contempt for me. It was especially apparent [read: a parent] in his refusal to acquiesce whenever I tried to accelerate his subnormal speed [This is a Nietzschean horse.] One day he resented my urging by kicking the front of my buggy to pieces. Such violence on his part seemed to me excessive, so I sent him to auction and bought another that had a better disposition. But he was hardly my ideal of what a horse should be, either, and I never found one that was" (*A*, 174). Small wonder. Of course there is more. There's insomnia and indigestion; there are moments of nervous disorder. There is "a list of things I wanted to study—rocks, animals, plants, poetry, drama, philosophy, music, painting, languages." There's still more; Watson is still on the line, I have merely put him through to you. You may still want him.
he was hardly my ideal of what a horse should be, either, and I never found one that was" (*A*, 174). Small wonder. Of course there is more. There's insomnia and indigestion; there are moments of nervous disorder. There is "a list of things I wanted to study—rocks, animals, plants, poetry, drama, philosophy, music, painting, languages." There's still more; Watson is still on the line, I have merely put him through to you. You may still want him. Come, hear.

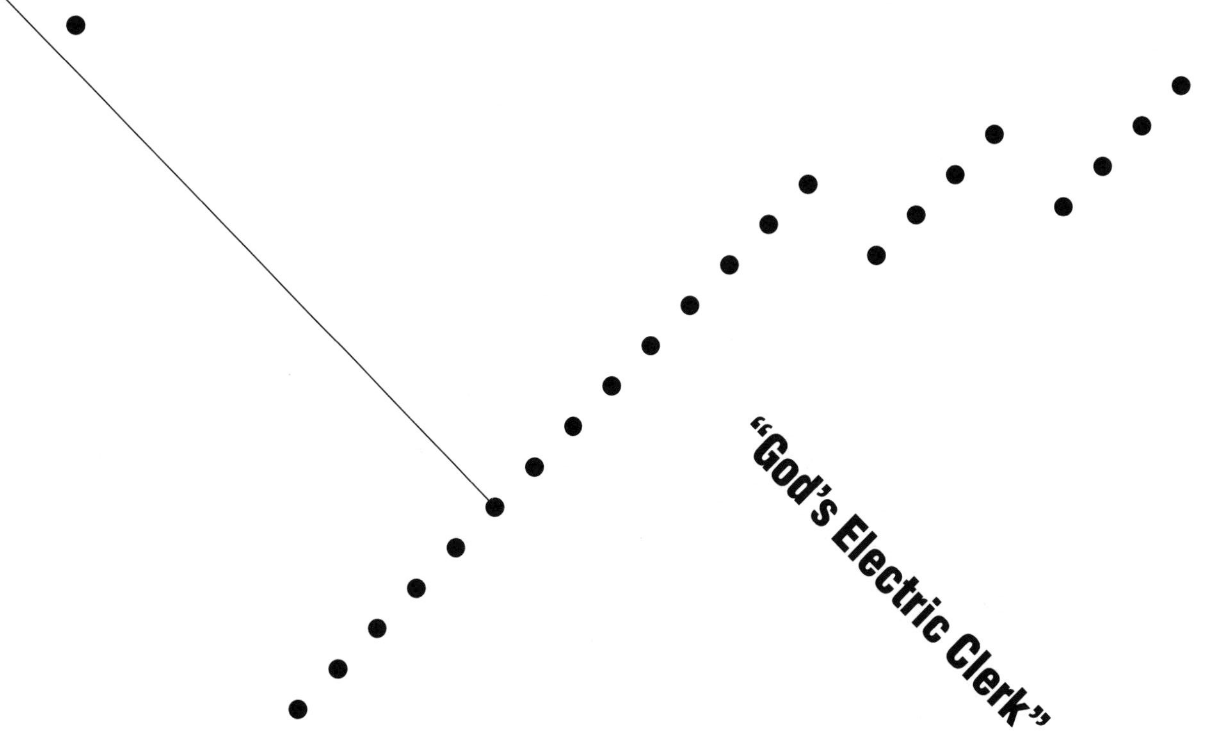

"God's Electric Clerk"

Maybe I should have spoken more distinctly. It's not as though there were a nonsubstitutable holy family of the telephone—the virgin Watson, Bell, and their divine child (one major work on telephony anoints the child "God's Electric Clerk").[114] It works differently here, somewhat along the lines indicated in a book of engineering and science, under the section "Annunciators or Drops." We are not plugging one couple nor proposing an indivisible key to telephony, though the very notion of invention always returns to a metaphysics of the subject: one man, one thing, mastering and mastered. In "Annunciators or Drops" one discovers that "the main purpose of plugs, jacks, and keys in the early switchboards was to provide the mechanism for establishing talking paths between calling and called subscribers and between subscribers and operators. However, they also formed part of the complex system which conveyed the various signals required for controlling the switching functions. Perhaps the most important single device used in early boards for signaling was the annunciators or drops. These devices came into existence long before telephony, being used in large call-bell systems to indicate the particular source of the call."[115] We are trying to establish an expedient talking path between the legacy of an acknowledged history and its secret account, for within the discourse of acknowledgment some repressed elements seek a form of expression, as if an original mouthpiece had been covered by the film of a technosphere that has since forgotten its source. "Bell System" by now has come to signify something utterly foreign to the fragile excitability of its native poetry. The currency of the electric sacred makes us question what it means to contain the lightning flash of a god or etheric genius, to domesticate its self-dissolution into predictable and

Maybe I should have spoken more distinctly. It's not as though there were a nonsubstitutable holy family of the telephone—the virgin Watson, Bell, and their divine child (one major work on telephony anoints the child "God's Electric Clerk").[114] It works differently here, somewhat along the lines indicated in a book of engineering and science, under the section "Annunciators or Drops." We are not plugging one couple nor proposing an indivisible key to telephony, though the very notion of invention always returns to a metaphysics of the subject: one man, one thing, mastering and mastered. In "Annunciators or Drops" one discovers that "the main purpose of plugs, jacks, and keys in the early switchboards was to provide the mechanism for establishing talking paths between calling and called subscribers and between subscribers and operators. However, they also formed part of the complex system which conveyed the various signals required for controlling the switching functions. Perhaps the most important single device used in early boards for signaling was the annunciators or drops. These devices came into existence long before telephony, being used in large call-bell systems to indicate the particular source of the call."[115] We are trying to establish an expedient talking path between the legacy of an acknowledged history and its secret account; for within the discourse of acknowledgment some repressed elements seek a form of expression, as if an original mouthpiece had been covered by the film of a technosphere that has since forgotten its source. "Bell System" by now has come to signify something utterly foreign to the fragile excitability of its native poetry. The currency of the electric sacred makes us question what it means to contain the lightning flash of a god or etheric genius, to domesticate its self-dissolution into predictable and nameable cycles. I would like to let the storm rage, the new anxiety fill the air with heavy doom, so that an intelligible sentence might be formed by spectral feedback. It was never the master idea of one man, performing his singularity in a godlike way, screaming "let there be telephones!" In fact, the Bell System was the outcome of a juridical performative. Bell and Elisha Gray patented the telephone on the same day, February 14, 1876. Both inventors made their deposit at the same time with the American Patent Office, but Bell was granted legal recognition. These were not the only producers of our current object of inquiry. On one level we are dealing with the invention of a woman's body retransmitted through judicial procedures. The remnants of this desire were gathered up in the pet name "Ma Bell." When this body was dissolved, the telephone company itself used a rhetoric of mutilation and defacement.[116] The maternal body of the telephone in America had been broken into. On another level, the "invention" was a shared one. There were Reiss's Telephone, Wray's Telephone, Electric Harmonica, Gray's Telephone, Pollard and Garnier's Singing Condenser, Edison's Telephone, Edison's Chemical Telephone, Navez's Telephone, Hellesen's Telephone, Thomson and Houston's Telephone, Telephones with Liquid Senders, Telephones with Voltaic Arcs, Mercury Telephones, Friction Telephones, Telephones with Several Diaphragms, Perrodom's System of Telephoneic Alarum, Varey's Microphone Speaker, Fitch's Microphone Speaker, Pollard's Microphone, Ader's Electrophone, Gower's New Telephone, Transmission of Speech without Diaphragm, to mention but a few. While Bell and Watson by no means evoke the only proper names to be assigned to a theory of telephonics, they irreducibly exemplify the sort of phantomization of voice under study. The telephone called them. Indeed, they formed a telephonic pair, the transmitter and receiver of shifting and alternating currents; but Watson himself lived out an existence as telephone, as disembodied and artificially reconstituted voice. The poetry of "Waiting for Watson" let such a message crackle through. Nor can Watson and Bell be credited with dreaming up the telephone or with articulating a unique line of the unconscious switchboard. **A sustained theory** of telephony came into prominence, and ridicule, with M. Charles Bourseul, whose ideas on the electric transmission of speech were regarded as "a fanciful dream," drawn from the "region of the marvelous" (*TMP,* 13). He presented a paper first lauding the "telegraphic marvels which can reproduce at a distance handwritings," followed by an eerie intuition. "I have, for example, asked myself whether speech itself may not be transmitted by electricity—in a word, if what is spoken in Vienna may not be heard in Paris." The man is onto our connection. But this was in the 1850s, when the telephone was in the air. So think back to Robert Hooke, who was on the line as early as 1667, promoting improvements for otacousticons. According to some sources, this represents the earliest document in which the transmission of sound to a distance takes a distinct formulation, quite a bit after the pagan oracles (*TMP,* 11). Hooke on the line, crackling with futurity:

> It is not impossible to hear a whisper at a furlong's distance, it having been already done; and perhaps the nature of the thing [it had already then acquired the allure of a thing] would not make it more impossible, though that furlong should be ten times multiply'd. And though some famous authors have affirm'd it impossible to hear through the thinnest plate of Moscovy glass; yet I know a way by which 'tis easie enough to hear one speak through a wall a yard thick. It has not yet been thoroughly examin'd how far otacousticons may be improv'd, nor what other wayes

> there may be of quickning our hearing, or conveying sound through other bodies than the air; for that that is not the only medium, I can assure the reader that I have, by the help of a distended wire, propagated the sound to a very considerable distance in an instant, or with as seemingly a quick motion as that of light, at least incomparably quicker than that which at the same time was propagated through the air; and this not only in a straight line or direct, but in one bended in many angles. (*TMP,* 11–12)

The possibility of a telephone was never fully dissociated from musical strains. From Sir Charles Wheatstone, who called his string telephone (1819) "magic lyre," to Kafka's *Castle,* on whose telephone angels sing, the telephone hollowed out an eerie symphony hall for departed spirits. About 1874, Mr. Elisha Gray, Bell's rival, was occupied with a system of musical telephone which he wished to apply to manifold telegraphic transmissions (*TMP,* 16). The history of this phantasmal music hall should by all rights include Watson's reception of Bell's piano-playing and the traumatic fork episode at his First Supper, which was to foreshadow the crucial experiments conducted by Bell and Watson with electric tuning forks. To this day the telephone still houses background music, as if to deaden the pain. **The stage is** set. A metaphysics of invention has willed that one name be made responsible for the totality of the telephone. He was allowed to cast a shadow, a blindly diverted other. Just as Socrates was allowed to have Plato, or the other way round. We called the other side of the Bell system, "Watson." Bell "itself" proves to have another side; let us call this "Alexander Graham Bell," "Bell," "AGB," or "Aleck," depending on the tonal modulations of the set. **If Watson became** a deciphering instrument of noise, Bell's decisive task was to crack the case of silence and its others—for instance, he was to handle speech defects. The telephone philosophizes with a stammer. It signs a contract with speech only insofar as it breaks with a mellifluous flow and perturbs the easy paternity of logos. At the same time, as if miming the dream of paternal transmission systems—at least as concerns the breakup of speech—Alexander Graham Bell inherited from his grandfather a didactic intuition for the stammer. The grandfather had bequeathed to his son, Bell's father, the legendary genes out of which the elements of visible speech grew, the Melville Bell symbols. In October 1872, Alexander Graham Bell opened a school of vocal physiology, whose announcement in part read: "For the correction of stammering and other defects of utterance and for practical instruction in visible speech, conducted by Alexander Graham Bell, member of the Philological Society of London."

This, according to the times, would not have been the institution that the stammering Moses awaited in the desert. He had as his mouthpiece Aaron. The nineteenth century envisioned no correction facilities for the speech impediment, disdaining prosthetic support systems for "natural" deformities. ~~As with speech defects, it seems that only widespread apprehension greeted Bell's adjunct activity, the education of the deaf. It was generally felt, writes Bell's biographer, that to teach speech to deaf mutes was to undo the work of the Creator; "that if God had intended deaf mutes to talk, He would have given them that power" (*M*, 54). All this to indicate that prior even to fooling with the telephone, which earlier we entertained as the devil's instrument, Bell was creating transmission interference with the Creator's switchboard. To build bionic armor for those intended for hearing's blindness, and to supplement the deaf mute with a simulated mouthpiece, offered a scene of the Promethean dash which at every step of the~~ way implied hubris and defiance, if not a movement of self-sacrificial intensity. Yet this does not expel a certain light of religiosity. Is it not the case that acquiring a trumpet of exteriority for those who had developed an ever-deepening inward ear sometimes implies recreating the very essence of religiosity—the harmonic telegraph of inner and outer hearing? Just as the fire usurped by Prometheus was later appropriated to the cause of piety. Or, from an entirely different point of view, which, however, still shares the same dimension, building a hearing channel to the deaf-mute's silence models, without essentializing, the auditory psychotic par excellence, the one who by some external adjustment hears the inside from the spectral other side, the so-called outside: for example, Hamlet. *Hamlet* was swallowed by telephonics—the father's umbilical couldn't cease naming itself and its ghostly partner. This perhaps explains why the telephone's most sacredly repeated declamation before an audience was to be . . . "To be or not to be," marking the interstice between ghostly conjuration and the voice of the other. Hence, Sir William Thomson (later Lord Kelvin), wishing to describe the speaking telephone upon his return to England, delivered this address which he made to the British Association at Glasgow, Scotland, on September 14, 1876. Sir William was one of the most distinguished British scientists and chairman of the Exhibition Committee on Electrical Exhibits:

> I heard "To be or not to be . . . there's the rub," through an electric telegraph wire; but, scorning monosyllables, the electric articulation rose to higher flights, and gave me messages taken at random from the New York newspapers: "S.S. Cox has arrived" (I failed to make out the S.S. Cox); "The City of New York"; "Senator Morton"; "The Senate has resolved to

> print a thousand extra copies"; "The Americans in London have resolved to celebrate the coming 4th of July." All this my own ears heard, spoken to me with unmistakeable distinctness by the thin circular disk armature of just such another little electromagnet as this which I hold in my hand. The words were shouted with a clear and loud voice by my colleague judge, Professor Watson, at the far end of the telegraph wire, holding his mouth close to a stretched membrane, such as you see before you here, carrying a little piece of soft iron, which was thus made to perform in the neighborhood of an electromagnet in circuit with the line, motions proportional to the sonorific motions of the air. This, the greatest by far of all the marvels of the electric telegraph, is due to a young countryman of our own, Mr. Graham Bell, of Edinburgh, Montreal and Boston, now becoming a naturalized citizen of the United States.[117]

On the same day of the exhibition to which Sir William Thomson's address refers, Professor T. Sterry Hunt wrote to Bell from the Continental Hotel in Philadelphia. We take the liberty Bell offers us to excerpt a portion of his private correspondence. The letter, emerging from a tête-à-tête with Sir William Thomson, evokes a future guided by a concept of secrecy, a certain intimate intelligence, we might add, that points directly to a secret agency of speech:

> Dr. Mr. Bell:
>
> I am informed that you leave tonight for Boston, so I take this way of congratulating you on your success today. I returned to my hotel with Sir William Thomson, and dined with him. He speaks with much enthusiasm of your achievement. What yesterday he would have declared impossible he has today seen realized, and he declares it the most wonderful thing he has seen in America. You speak of it as an embryo invention, but to him it seems already complete, and he declares that, before long, friends will whisper their secrets over the electric wire. Your undulating current he declares a great and happy conception.[118]

So we have come to Philadelphia, where Bell's telephone was shown at the Exhibition of 1876. Sir William Thomson, writes Count Du Moncel, did not hesitate to call it the "wonder of wonders." The noble prized the telephone's splendor, "and it instantly attracted universal attention, although there was at first incredulity as to its genuineness." The telephone, in fact, reproduced articulate words, a result which surpassed all the conceptions of physicists. In this case it was no longer a conception to be treated as visionary until there was proof to the contrary: "the instrument spoke and even spoke so loudly that it was not necessary to apply the ear" (*TMP,* 36). The words of Sir William "Thompson" [*sic*] are now reproduced by Du Moncel, presumably citing from the same address as given above. The telephone has already reproduced itself by producing the effect of scrambling, tampering with a proper name's spelling, throwing to the winds utterances whose exact positioning may be wed to transparent veils of forgetfulness. (This is why when his father calls up, Hamlet has to write everything down. He pulls out a slate rather than a sword to commit to memory the telephonic inscription.) The secret of that which Professor Hunt wrote in his letter of congratulations is out, that is to say, the secret of reproductive misfiring, constitutive error, and approximation. The telephone has begun to produce telephonic effects by the sheer fact of its existence. Here is the recording of "the effect" to which Sir William Thomson spoke, disclosing, among other things, the translative leaps of memory recall. Sir William Thomson spoke to this effect at the meeting of the British Association at Glasgow in September 1876:

> In the department of telegraphs in the United States I saw and heard Mr. Elisha Gray's electric telephone, of wonderful construction, which can repeat four despatches at the same time in the Morse code, and, with some improvements in detail, this instrument is evidently capable of a fourfold delivery. In the Canadian department I heard "To be or not to be? There's the rub," uttered through a telegraphic wire, and its pronunciation by electricity only made the rallying tone of the monosyllables more emphatic. The wire also repeated some extracts from New York papers. With my own ears I heard all this, distinctly articulated through the slender circular disk formed by the armature of an electro-magnet. It was my fellow-juryman, Professor Watson, who, at the other extremity of the line, uttered these words in a loud and distinct voice, while applying his mouth to a tighly stretched membrane provided with a small piece of soft iron, which executed movements corresponding to the sound vibrations of the air close to an electro-magnet introduced into the circuit. This discovery, the wonder of wonders in electric telegraphy, is due to a young fellow country man of our own, Mr. Graham Bell, a native of Edinburgh, now naturalized in New York. (*TMP,* 36–37)

The Bell Translation

Like Kant, the inventor of the technological thing (which is by no means reducible to a *Ding an sich*) hails from Scotland before being translated into practical discourse. The question of a somewhat falsified translation between the Germanic and Anglo-Saxon does not come down to a mere conjurer's act of fortuitous coincidence. No doubt, many worthy figures were born in Scotland, and that does not qualify them for the billing of a Fourth Critique. The telephone, we could venture, was born from a problem of translation residing within the German tongue. Bell was a poor scientist, it is said; Watson confirms that the poor thing knew nothing about electricity. When he presented his fantastical project to a trusted elder statesman of scientific inquiry, it was suggested to him that he read Helmholtz. How many of us have not been sent back to the drawing boards to read up on a master scholar of our provenance? In any case, Bell read Helmholtz in German—this is a poor translation. Bell could barely read German, so how can we make the case for his having read Helmholtz in German? Be that as it may, the technological tower of Babel verges, as Hölderlin would say, on falling upward; it will topple to the skies. Bell took out Helmholtz's work in the German original. Aspiring scientific minds of the nineteenth century were customarily enjoined to a mimetic kind of relationship with the master text, repeating the experiments therein entered with the Faustian expectation eventually of surpassing the boundaries that rein it in. Bell put himself to work, exercising according to the prescriptions set out in Helmholtz, earnestly following the recipes, with a pinch of electromagnetism here and a tablespoon of glycerin there. The task proved nearly impossible. The thing would not take even though Bell was securely under a mentor's guidance. There is no reason to assume that the syndromic anxiety of influence got the better of him, that he was blinded by the solar heat emanating from the figure of an overwhelming ancestor. The problem does not revolve around a totem pole of a genealogical cut (not yet), settling rather in the tower of Babel about to be connected to every telephone pole in the country.

Bell was unable to reproduce Helmholtz's experiment and began to feel humiliated by this unexpected incapacitation. Bell, as Watson pointed out in his autobiography, was not one to be discouraged, only dispirited. So he tries again. Eventually the telephone started to see the light of day. Bell returns to the professor scientist. It turns out that Bell's shoddy German had misled him. He had misread Helmholtz; or rather, he had given Helmholtz a *hysterical reading*, having read into the futural pages the invention of the telephone, which he tried merely to repeat, lagging hopelessly behind. Helmholtz had no recipe for the telephone. Researchers of telephony, if they mention this reading episode at all, chalk it up to bad translation work on Bell's part. In other words, in plain English, Bell had translated Helmholtz badly and thought he was doing what the book said to do. Bell's reading wires got crossed on cognitive and performative acts of reading, on reading what is to be there and not to be yet there. Maybe it's just a coincidence, but the same book that records this early marginal episode of bungled transferential action ends its purpose by misspelling the name of the misread author "Hemholtz," whose first phallic "l" fell to the reading field.[119] This is not an advertisement for learning to read German. It posts an announcement for learning to listen to Babel, to think the possibility of a rumorous reading, a double reading, reading the future of one's conception from the fragile assertions of a so-called primary text. Bell read in a willed resistance to a past that kept the telephone hidden, though in some way figured. Helmholtz's hieroglyphics turned into a fortune-telling book; Bell took a take that resembles one's attempt to photograph ghosts. They do not show up in the development, they rest out of print. **If** Bell was resisting the ancestral text to which his professor had sent him, it was in part because ancestral dominance constellated his side of telephony. The lines were occupied by a paternal lineage through which a deaf mother's hearing was trying to arrive. Where other children are said to be born with a silver spoon, Bell was born with an electric tuning fork. Back to the count's account. Of the generation responsible for the telephone, he writes this: If we are to believe Mr. Graham Bell [everything revolves around this question of belief. Was Sir William to believe his ears? did they believe in God? can you believe your eyes? can we believe Mr. Graham Bell?], the invention of the telephone was not due to a spontaneous and fortunate conception: it was the result of his long and patient studies in acoustic science, and of the labors of the physicists who preceded him [Page, Marrian, Beatson, Gassiot, De la Rive, Matteuci, Guillemin, Wertheim, Wartmann, Janniar, Joule, Laborde, Legat, Reiss, Poggendorf, Du Moncel, Delezenne, Gore, etc. Vide Berll's paper in the *Journal of the Society of Telegraphic Engineers* 6, pp. 390–391 in London]. His father, Mr. Alexander Melville Bell, of Edinburgh, had studied this science deeply, and had even succeeded in representing with great ingenuity the adaptation of the vocal organs for the emission of sound. It was natural that he should instil a taste for his favorite studies into his son's mind, and they made together numerous researches in order to discover the relations which exist between the different elements of speech in different languages, and the musical relations of vowels. It is true that several of these researches had been made by M. Helmholtz, and under more favorable conditions; but these studies were of great use to Mr. Bell when he was afterward occupied with the telephone, and Helmholtz's experiments, which he repeated with one of his friends, Mr. Hellis, of London, concerning the artificial reproduction of vowels by means of electric tuning forks, launched him into the study of the application of electricity to acoustic instruments. (*TMP*, 37–38). Clearly, Du Moncel knew nothing of futural reading, namely of Freud. How ***natural*** could it be for electricity to be transmitted from father to son without a hitch? No mention of a mother who could not receive a son's acoustic transmissions—mother and wife, we should have said, for Bell, Jr., doubled, repeated, or replaced his father by marrying into the same and becoming the husband of a deaf woman.

THE PHONAUTOGRAPH

Bell himself let his grandfather weigh in rather heavily on the subject of the telephone's co-original impulses. From this perspective the telephone was in fact already telephonic in its conception, connecting up three or four bodies whose impulses were conducted from one communicating station to another. The hook up to Grandfather Bell, to Father, and to Aleck was a crucial part of their story. The dying brothers are yet to come; but the mother remains in the background, a somewhat synthetic voice roused out of its place of invisibility, as for example when you dial 0. **Back** to Du Moncel, even if he had not read futurity or Freud. Bell, he notes, first invented "a system of an electric harmonica with a key-board, in which the different sounds of the scale were reproduced by electric diaspons of varying forms, adapted to different notes, and which, when set in motion by the successive lowering of the keys, could reproduce sounds corresponding to the notes touched, just as on an ordinary piano" (*TMP*, 38). As we now can tell, this reproduction of Bell's early scientific menu also repeats the order of the First Supper with Watson, where forks and piano notes supply the key. **However,** Du Moncel himself claims to be repeating what Bell tells, so we may venture that Bell had collapsed the event of his encounter with Watson into the unfolding of his scientific discovery. Watson comes in only by a back entrance. "He next, as he tells us, turned his attention to telegraphy, and thought of making the Morse telegraphs audible by causing the electro-magnetic organ to react on sounding contacts. . . . he thought that by applying this system to his electric harmonica, and by employing such an intensifying instrument as Helmholtz's resonator at the receiving station, it would be possible to obtain through a single wire simultaneous transmissions which should be due to the action of the voice" (*TMP,* 38–39). Following the transmission of "musical tones simultaneously through a telegraph wire as through the air" (*TMP,* 43), Du Moncel writes that Bell lost no time, after applying these principles to the construction of a telegraphic system for multiple transmissions, in making use of his researches to improve the vocal training of deaf-mutes. "It is well-known," he said, "that deaf-mutes are dumb merely because they are deaf, and that there is no defect in their vocal organs to incapacitate them from utterance. Hence it was thought that my father's system of pictorial symbols, popularly known as visible speech, might prove a means whereby we could teach the deaf and dumb to use their vocal organs and to speak. The great success of these experiments urged upon me the advisability of devising methods of exhibiting the vibrations of sound optically, for use in teaching the deaf and dumb. For some time I carried on experiments with the manometric capsule of Koenig" (Bell, quoted in *TMP,* 43–44). **Following** Dr. Clarence J. Blake's suggestion, Bell gets hold of a human ear to use as a phonautograph instead of making an artificial imitation of it. How to get the ear in motion, to vibrate? This is the next problem. Alexander Graham Bell recollects the moment.

> The idea was novel, and struck me accordingly, and I requested my friend to prepare a specimen [of the human ear] for me, which he did. The apparatus, as finally constructed, is shown in Fig. 12. The *stapes* was removed, and a stylus of hay about an inch in length was attached to the end of the *incus*. Upon moistening the *membrana tympani* and the *ossiculae* with a mixture of glycerine and water, the necessary mobility of the parts was obtained; and upon singing into the external artificial ear the stylus of hay was thrown into vibration, and tracings were obtained upon a plane surface of smoked glass passed rapidly underneath. While engaged in these experiments I was struck with the remarkable disproportion in weight between the membrane and the bones that were vibrated by it. (*TMP,* 45–46)

This marks the moment when Bell begins to construct what will eventually become our telephone:

> For this purpose I attached the reed A loosely by one extremity to the uncovered pole, *h,* of the magnet, and fastened the other extremity to the centre of a stretched membrane of gold-beater's skin, *n*. I presumed that,

upon speaking in the neighborhood of the membrane *n,* it would be thrown into vibration, and cause the steel reed A to move in a similar manner, occasioning undulations in the electrical current that would correspond to the changes in the destiny of the air during the production of sound; and I further thought that the change in the intensity of the current at the receiving end . . . (*TMP,* 46–47)

Well, at the receiving end, as we know, there was Watson, whose changes in intensity we already observed. Bell refers to Watson in this passage as friend. Perhaps this represents a generous signifier, a slightly valueless gesture of acknowledgment, or even the truth. Perhaps this Watson was a friend Bell could count on: "The results, however, were unsatisfactory and discouraging. My friend Mr. Thomas A. Watson, who assisted me in this first experiment, declared that he heard a faint sound proceed from the telephone at his end of the circuit, but I was unable to verify his assertion" (*TMP,* 47). **We** have traveled the full circuit from one to the other, from one orifice to the other, between friends, a transmission bubble, a scratch noise of discord. While this passage does not present itself with the manifest traits of ambivalence, much less a demolition expert's job well done, let me refresh your memory. The point made by Bell is that he could not verify or confirm what Watson had said he had heard. What place do "friends" take in scientific rhetoric? This designation could amount to a promotion, a merit increase, or a displacement of the nature of their relationship; in any case it's what Watson gets within a scientific explication, and not in the personal memoirs of fondness, set aside by the inventor in a parascientific text for his grandchildren, or grandfather, to enjoy. In walks a friend during the course of Bell's scientific research, to help him out. This is not malicious slander—let's not get too dramatic about our inflections. But as a description its accuracy does not seem unimpeachable either. Perhaps they were friends, maybe this was how science was conducted in those days, among friends, and Bell was just getting a little help from this friend. Fine. They were friends. Mr. Watson, my friend, assisted me, lending his ear to the substitute dead ear, claiming his ear was alive to a faint sound, but I could not verify what his ear is said to have heard. My friend could have been dead wrong, so what his ear claims to have grasped has to be set aside. It doesn't end here. We have already suggested the precarious positioning of a rumoring audibility. This ear opens the question of priority. Who was the first to hear the telephone speak, even if it only mouthed a faint whisper to its auditor? **Yet,** what if there will have been precisely no original sound at all, not in the sense of the telephone's technicity? Like the big bang, the telephone's first sonic emission will always have taken place prior to it, no place—a first crack, therefore, that, never being first, sheds the structure of simplicity that reduces a sheer telecommunicability to the hopelessly pitched poles of sender and receiver. The transmissions complexify themselves at the outset, suspending any simple certitude about the first emission—whether it came from Bell or his father, his grandfather, his mother's comatose ear or the friendly ghosts traveling within Mr. Watson's earshot. The conception date cannot be fixed absolutely, nor can the operation of its strict emergence. For "I was unable to verify his assertion." All we know is that it had something to do with a dead ear that Watson claimed he heard speaking, or, more precisely still, he caught it groaning. But does this not correspond to the essential structure of fundamental telephonics, namely, "I was unable to verify his assertion"? It literally stacks up to hearsay when Watson says he hears; the other cannot verify, cannot, at this fragile point of entry, know. Unless, a hundred years later or so, the CIA has you on tap. But it remains legally, epistemologically, and technically unclear whether this sort of earwitnessing amounts to knowing (did Polonius know he was a rat?). Whatever Watson heard that day, Bell claims not to have verified. Under what conditions would it have been conceivable to verify what Watson said he heard him say? Bell means that whatever Watson heard cannot be said again, not to us now nor to Bell then. It was not part of a structure of iterability, could not be quoted, did not bear repetition. It did not indicate an occasion, as Watson would say, for the "fertile awakening" of the ear. But how could Bell ever have hoped to hear what Watson heard? Bell can only have heard what his ear could tell him. **It** is not too soon before the telephone gets Bell meshed in telephonic entanglements on the order of who told whom what. Look for the medium, friendship's mouth-ear canal, as rumors start flying: "Indeed, one gentleman, Professor Dolbear, of Tufts College, not only claims to have discovered the magneto-electric telephone, but I understand charges me with having obtained the idea from him through the medium of a mutual friend" (*TMP*, 50). This by no means leaves Bell dispirited, though at the beginning of a long line of telephone charges, legal suits, and suspicious audiences. "A still more powerful form of apparatus was constructed by using a powerful compound horseshoe magnet in place of the straight rod which had been previously used. Indeed the sounds produced by means of this instrument were of sufficient loudness to be faintly audible to a large audience, and in this condition the instrument was exhibited in the Essex Institute, in Salem, Massachusetts, on February 12th, 1877, on which occasion a short speech shouted into a similar telephone in Boston, sixteen miles away, was heard by the audience in Salem" (*TMP*, 50).

Think of the audience in Salem for a while.

M i c r o g r a p h i a

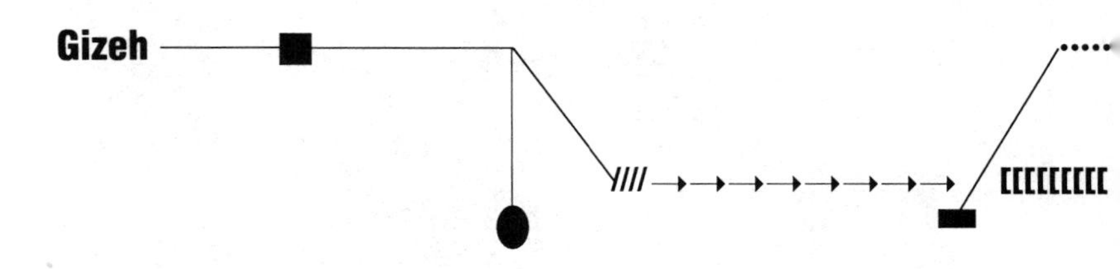

It is going too far, too quickly, that is, toward the other end of the line, before its time. It does not presume to replicate an essay on the order of Goethe's *Dichtung und Wahrheit,* which aims to let the particular be subsumed under the horizon of the general. If it did so presume, the extreme particularity of an Alexander Graham Bell would be threatened with being absorbed or cannibalized by the historical appetite of truth's boa constrictor. So out with Bell, all three of them, for the moment, if only to see where they later fit in. It's not as if the telephone were a pure aerial dream spontaneously generated by a single recondite clan, circle of friends, or impulse. **The telephone splices a party line stretching through history.** Since Moses has served as a privileged inducement to figure telephony, originating the legendary speech defect which tuned his special hearing, it is only in the interest of fairness that we mention the pharaoh's side of the coin deposited into the art of telephony.[120]

Kiangsu

When the French scientist Gaspard Monge followed the army of Napoleon Bonaparte into Egypt on its campaign of general decipherment, he explored the Temple of Mehmet Abn, where he made a discovery. He came upon a coil of wire in which were tangled several objects of ivory and bone, shaped somewhat in the fashion of the later drinking horn. These wires had been lying for ages in the place where they were found, a stone chamber in the temple. Later, on Monge's arrival at the pyramid of Gizeh, he discovered in a vault of about the same dimensions as the chamber in the temple some of these ivory and bone objects and more coiled wires. At the time, scientists could make nothing of the manner in which the wires and their attachments might have been serviceable. Were these funereal accompaniments, works of art, utensils of some unfathomable sort? The French publicist M. Henry Paccory has asserted that these objects were used for the transmission of speech "and that the chambers in which they were found were nothing less than ancient telephone booths. . . . Two miles, he thinks, was the limit of the distance over which the subject of the Pharaohs could project his voice" (*HT,* 5). This history seems a bit fanciful—so much so that one would want to enlist the counsel of a contemporary Egyptologist to secure an argument of these proportions. But like Bell's inability or unwillingness to confirm the receivership of the early telephone, we are caught in the same theoretical bind. So why introduce the possibility of a hookup to the pharaoh's Egypt? Only to suggest that the entire Mosaic intervention can be read according to telephonic protocols; a Heideggerian competition of the earth and sky, the pharaoh's vaulted pyramid booths pitted against the open lines of monotheism's suppression and abolition of divine party lines ✷ The Telephone Wars of the Egyptians and the Hebrews ✷ The electric flash that announced to Moses that God was on the line ✷ The transcription of that person-to-person call ✷ Moses was the only mortal to have seen the Mouthpiece. But here we are heading toward a dead sea of speculation, at which point it is always safe to attempt an exodus ✷ At the same time, we do not wish to limit our ventures, however precarious and telephonically unverifiable in the end, to Western phenomena. Again, in the interest of fairmindedness, ancient telephony among the Chinese deserves mention, if only to encourage others to pursue in greater detail this line of inquiry. As with any newborn archaeology, it needs time to develop, and many teachers . . . .

. . . . .Consider the communication made to a meeting of the Royal Asiatic Society in Shanghai, when it was shown that the Chinese had produced a rudimentary form of telephone consisting of two bamboo cylinders, from one and a half to two inches in diameter and four in length. A tympanum of pig bladder closes one end of each; the bladder is perforated for the transmitting string, the string kept in place by being knotted. This instrument, the "listening tube," as dependent on an organ transplant as ours once was, conveys whispers forty or fifty feet. It is unknown in many parts of the empire, Chih-chiang and Kiangsu being the only provinces where the listening tube was employed (*HT,* 39). Almost two centuries ago the Chinese are said to have produced the "thousand-mile speaker." The implement consists of a role of copper, likened to a fife, containing an artful device; whispered into and immediately closed, the confined message, however long, may be conveyed to any distance; and thus, in a battle, secret instructions may be communicated. The inventor of the "thousand-mile speaker," Chiang Shun-hsin of Hui-chou, flourished during the reign of K'ang-hsi, in the seventeenth century. He left behind a text on occult science and astronomy.

In his book on the history of inventions, Johann Beckmann (1739–1811), generally considered to be the founder of scientific technology, devotes a chapter to speaking trumpets. The chapter includes reference to early "monstrous trumpets of the ancient Chinese," a kind of speaking trumpet or instrument by which words could not only be heard at the greatest distance possible, but also understood (*HT,* 6). "This invention," Beckmann adds, "belongs to the 17th century, though some think that traces of it are to be found among the ancient Grecians" (*HT,* 6). The speaking tube, the effort to extend the distance over which sounds could be sent by direct transmission through the air, was also of ancient origin. Beckmann supplies the following translation of a passage from Giambattista della Porta, presumably from his *Magia naturalis,* published in or prior to 1558. The figures of occult, magic, and friend gather together around this passage:

> **To communicate anything to one's friends by means of a tube. This can be done by a tube of earthen ware, though one of lead is better—; for whatever you**

> **speak at the one end the words issue perfect and entire as from the mouth of the speakers and are conveyed to the ears of the other, which in my opinion may be done for some miles—. We tried it for a distance of two hundred paces, not having conveniences for a greater, and the words were heard as clearly and distinctly as if they had come from the mouth of the speaker. (*HT,* 7)**

Now back to modernity, where we discover Dr. Robert Hooke's preface of the first edition of his *Micrographia,* which the English philosopher had published in 1665. Exploring the propagation of sound waves through bodies other than air, and particularly through the distension of a wire, he brings us up to date on the prosthetic supplement to which we here aspire:

> **The next care to be taken, in respect of the Senses, is a supplying of their infirmities with *Instruments,* and as it were, the adding of *artificial Organs* to the natural; this in one of them has been of late years accomplisht with prodigious benefit to all sorts of useful knowledge by the inventing of Optical Glasses. . . . And as *Glasses* have highly promoted our seeing, so 'tis not improbable, but that there may be found many *Mechanical Inventions* to improve our *other* Senses, of *hearing, smelling, tasting, touch-***

***ing*. 'Tis not impossible to hear a whisper . . . for that is not the only *medium* I can assure the Reader, that I have, by the help of a *distended wire,* propagated the sound to a very considerable distance in an *instant*. Or with as seemingly quick a motion as that of light. (*HT,* 7)**

According to the menu of artificial organs, the prosthetic olfactory device would still remain to be thought in order to give a sense of the projectile that Hooke throws into the waters of invention. What we know as the ear trumpet was exhibited at the Royal Society in London in 1668, under the name "otacousticon." It was portrayed in the diaries of Samuel Pepys, in his entry of April 2, 1668, as follows: "I did now try the use of the Otacousticon, which was only a great glass bottle broke at the bottom, putting the neck to my ear, and there I did plainly hear the dancing of the oars of the boats in the Thames to Arundel Galley window, which, without it, I could not in the least do" (*HT,* 9). What may elicit some interest in this portraiture is the telephone's acquisition of a new bodily part, the neck, which in subsequent memoirs of its anatomy was to be more or less decapitated, or let us say, shrunk to the abstraction of multiple displacements. The fractured neck originally had a lip which raised itself to the ear. In this scene of its operation the ears listen to the oars, the aquatic sound waves near the channel of dance music.

The speaking trumpet, as distinguished from the ear trumpet, came into prominence about 1670. A dispute arose among rival claimants regarding its invention. In 1671 a treatise on the invention was drawn up in which one of the claimants designated it as the "Tuba Stentoro-Phonica." The telephone is due to arrive a couple of centuries later, announcing itself by gradual degrees. In 1851 a speaking tube was exhibited at the London Exhibition under the name of "telekouphononon." The same manufacturer also displayed at the time an object thought to be a speaking trumpet, which he called the "Gutta Percha Telephone." The word "telephone" does not seem to have been applied to speaking tubes in English, but there are at least two cases, in 1869 and 1871, where it was applied to ordinary speaking tubes in the German language. All these devices, whether speaking trumpets, ear trumpets, or speaking tubes, worked on the principle of directly transmitting sound through air. One Captain John Taylor in 1845 invented an instrument "for conveying signals during foggy weather by sounds produced by means of compressed air forced through trumpets" (*HT,* 9). No thought of speech transmission informed this instrument, which only produced powerful sounds derived from blasts of compressed air. This aerial soundboard was called the "Telephone"—one of the very early uses of the word.

The electromagnetic telegraph, introduced in 1837, was the opening wedge for the development of instant communication. In 1851, Dr. S. D. Cushman of Racine, Wisconsin, developed an "Electrical Talking Box," which he neglected to patent. Years later the Bell System defeated him in a lawsuit over this device. Still, theoretical telephonics always preceded empirical testing grounds. In 1854, the Frenchman Bourseul created the theory of the present-day telephone, leaving a blank for the switch, which awaited envisaging. In the early 1860s, J. W. McDonough of Chicago invented, with the help of a Reis transmitter, a "teleloge." A New York newspaper telescripted a warning to its readers against buying stock in a newfangled device called the "telephone." Here goes the rumorous stock market again, switched on by telephonic speculation. As in *The Trial* of Kafka, rumor and arrest are part of the same performative experience:

> **A man about 43 years of age giving the name Joshua Coppersmith has been arrested for attempting to extort funds from ignorant and superstitious people by exhibiting a device which he says will convey the human voice any distance over metallic wires. He calls the instrument a "telephone," which is obviously in-**

tended to imitate the word "telegraph" and win the confidence of those who know the success of the latter instrument. Well informed people know that it is impossible to transmit the human voice over wires, as may be done by dots and dashes and signals of the Morse Code. The authorities who apprehended this criminal are to be congratulated and it is hoped that punishment will be prompt. (*HT*, 9)

In a crisis of small narcissistic difference, the newspaper presses charges against the parasitical instrument upon which it will develop addictive dependency. Pitting dots and dashes against the voice, the tele-graph against the tele-phone, the newspaper forms an agency with the police authorities of small-time writing. However, the logic of opposition informing the difference between writing and vocal systems, phonetics and telephonetics, has no conceptual sanctuary to shelter it.

There remain perhaps only two orders of facts still to be recorded before we observe visiting rights with the Bell family. While they may in their unnatural setting appear segmented, isolated utterances, unprotected like the gash separating two schizoid remarks, they will have adopted a kind of long-distance semanticity spread over the body of our argument. First, a document from Frank Hall Childs, from which this passage has been clipped, indicates the extreme uncanniness assigned to the telephone: "One day the veteran showman, Phineas T. Barnum, came in to see the wonderful invention, and I gave him his first introduction to the telephone. It seemed more of a curiosity to him than his freaks had been to the public" (*HT*, 26). Even through the hyperoptics of a sensibility comparable to that of a Diane Arbus, the telephone, as far as Barnum was concerned, presented itself as a curious counterpart to his freaks. In fact, Barnum was loath to display the telephone, because he didn't wish to freak out his audience with this voiced partial limb, no doubt, whereas limbless figures were still held to be digestible. A second point concerns the genderized voice that inhabits the telephone, and whose implications fill the slates we have accumulated. "In 1878, the first telephone exchange opened in New Haven, Connecticut. . . . Boys operated these early exchanges. The boys shouted at the customers, and it took several boys and many minutes to make a call. Girl operators later replaced the boys. The girls had softer voices, more patience, and nimble fingers" (*HT*, 29). Softer voices, more patience, and nimble fingers; the birth of a supple kind of texture, fortune's spinning wheel at

the controls newly connecting voice to fingers. A digital combination for signing a destination. The invisible voices conducted through the tips of her fingers. The voice, entering the intimate borders between inner and outer ear, was soon feminized, if only to disperse the shouting commands of a team sport. Nowadays, it is said, when a military aircraft finds itself in serious trouble, the voice command switches to the feminine. The vocalized response
to an S.O.S. signal was tuned
in the emergency feminine—the maternal cord reissued.

THE BIO

As for the nimble fingers stitching connections, the history of telephony asks of these an essentially hygienic question: were these hands clean? (This echoes a question we have asked of a number of figures who picked up a call; we merely have pointed to the hand of military operations.) The question prompts Catherine Mackenzie's biography of the inventor, *Alexander Graham Bell: The Man Who Contracted Space.*

A finely ambiguous title that well suits our purposes, it ingathers the hands in transmission—are these hands clean?—while flinging its vast referents to outer space, where our little sputnik still blinks in solitude. The preface of Mackenzie's book outlines a project that throws itself against the rumor, invoking the juridical verdict that put up the question of immaculate hands. The principal *thing* in Bell's life was not the telephone; rather, "the search for truth was the one really important thing in Bell's life. It is the irony of his story that malicious charges of fraud, widespread against him during the long and determined effort to wrest the telephone from him, were in complete contradiction to everything essential in his character" (*M,* vii). Spoken like a philosopher; Bell's essence and determination can be distilled to truth seeking. However, this still leaves room for the charges made against him, and for leaks managing to escape his essence: a deviation from essence, articulated in the widespread, that is, telephonic, claims assailing him which could be accidents, little aberrations, splinters of that essence. But Mackenzie wants to clear his name. She wants to grant it the same auratic clarity as the voice steadily gained when the telephone began to speak with fluency. Still, no matter how truthfully the voice spoke, it was still essentially a phony one. Telephone charges are made from a place where science overtakes concerns of truth, exercising an illusionist's privilege. Mackenzie suggests the double nature inherent to a language channeled through the telephone by bringing telephony over to the side of art. In the meantime she advances another ghost story, which rumors always commission: "Honest, courageous, scornful of double-dealing, the incontrovertible evidence of his prior invention, and his repeated vindication by the courts as 'an honest man with clean hands,' were for years unavailing to quell these charges. They have persisted, ghosts of their once lusty selves, in the whispers still current" (*M,* vii). Whispers, spectral transmissions of a legacy, the currency of charges, electric or legal, whose ghosts refer to the allegory of a lusty self faded into the distance, cut off in the blossom of their sins. One grows tense with anticipation to learn the charges; like Hamlet, one beckons it to speak more distinctly. The charges reverse into a question of paternity, the prevailing question of the great epistemology of rumor: "their once lusty selves, in the whispers still current that after all Bell was only one of a number of inventors of the speaking telephone" (*M,* viii). Why would this be so hideous, so structurally slanderous? Science only in rare instances claims solo flights of invention; there are teams, there are multipathed lineages to trace, there was Watson.

Mackenzie bases the biography on a number of sources: Bell's typewritten log, the *Beinn Breagh Recorder,* the registers of the Aerial Experiment Association, Watson's *Exploring Life,* and her conversations with Bell. "From the summer of 1914 until his death in 1922 I worked with Mr. Bell, day in and day out, in all of his many activities, much of the time compiling and editing this biographical material under his direction. On this experience, and on many conversations of these years, I have based this narrative. Mindful of the myths which prevail about Mr. Bell as about all great men, I have made every effort to verify all unsupported or controversial statements" (*M,* VIII). She reports to her family when it comes to the unfamiliar business of making a book: "most of all I wish to acknowledge a very great debt to my husband, Edward Hale Bierstadt, whose editorial judgment I have consulted throughout, and who has further given me specific aid in the unfamiliar business of making a book" (*M,* x).

Why usher the inferential tones of our introduction into the scene of the biographer? Because we have to know where she's coming from, why she made a book on Bell indebting herself to her husband's judgment, why the days in and out of eight years were directed by Bell, whose voice appoints the definitive biography. Why should traces of this knowledge require detective work? Simply because the book emerges as an effect of telephonic logic, a response to double-dealing and unverifiable utterances, because Catherine Mackenzie is placing herself squarely at the receptionist's desk, fielding the calls, diverting some of them while screening or silencing others. In this respect, the book constitutes somewhat of a *biophony*; it is a reactive text, responding to the call of the ghosts whose rustles she still hears. One would be tempted to say that it records a woman's voice as she rushes to the scene of an accident like a writing Florence Nightingale. Why did she venture out on a limb, risking the unfamiliar business of bringing forth a rectifying coverage? Is she being used to transcribe ventriloquially "under Bell's direction"?

There is another register waiting to be played, the one concerning a codified position of nonknowledge occupied both by Bell and his simulating biographer. Introducing the "theory of the electric speaking telephone"—this occurs very quickly into the book—C.M. begins a section with the firm statement: "Bell knew next to nothing about electricity. He was a specialist in speech, and his idea had grown out of his expert knowledge of the voice, its physical mechanism, and of sound. 'If Bell had known anything about electricity,' Moses G. Farmer said a year later, 'he would never have invented the telephone.' In 1874, when he began to work upon it, any good electrician could have told him that he was attempting the impossible" (*M*, 6–7). Mackenzie works the angle of impossibility—a woman's work, the never done. Phillip Reis had sent musical notes, intermittent sounds of various kinds over an electric current, in Germany, a number of years before, and had also called his instrument a "telephone." But *sound* is not *speech*.

It was manifestly impossible, as everyone pointed out to Bell, to send the continuous vibration of the human voice, its inflections and overtones, along a make-and-break current. Dots and dashes, yes, but not voice. Bell agreed that this was impossible. He wasn't going to use a make-and-break current. He was going to make a continuous current of electricity vibrate with the tones of the voice just as the air vibrates with the speaking voice: to substitute electrical waves, so to speak, for the air or ether waves on which our voices are carried in face-to-face conversation, when dialogue has the support of the full body.

Then persons miles apart could speak to each other along an electrified wire (a little nudge and a translation from Bell's German would turn this into a verse from Hölderlin). He was laughed at.

C.M. continues: "In the era of home-made radio, when picking speech out of the upper air is a family commonplace, it is difficult to credit the unbelief in the conception of Bell's telephone only sixty years ago. It was considered so mad an idea that even when he had accomplished it, he was not believed" (*M,* 8).

This point bears remarking. C.M.'s project belongs to the anxiety registers of historial recounting, for the telephone cannot be, nor was it ever according to its concept, properly fitted to the narrative event of truth telling, handwashing, or clearing a name. The telephone stakes out that thing which is not to be believed; a cataloguer of hermeneutic suspicion, it compels you blindly to overlook it, as in the case histories of Jung and Laing or in the disseminative distillation of the Heideggerian text. There is something to its not-thereness, destabilizing and implacable at once, it is **a place without location from which to get elsewhere**, translating into electrical carriages the air or ether waves which convey voices. Not itself a locality, it forms the topography of an artificial organ from which the Other speaks. The regime of displacements and cancellations within which it functions tells us that it cannot, by definition, speak truth, even if it dangles there like an earwitness. Bell, for his part, was not believed "even after he accomplished" the telephone. If a generalized nonbelievability may be regarded as an effect of telephonics, how can Mackenzie cast a spell that would convert the constitutive anepistemology into substantial grounds for clearing, and believing in, Bell's name? Bell and the telephone synonymize one another. We are still connected to that name, which also poses as a homophone for the call of the telephone. To establish the truth of her discourse, Mackenzie wisely swerves away from Truth to the general poetry of dissemblance; in other words, in order to plug Bell's veracity, she pulls the extension cord of telephony toward Art with a capital "A." Watch her do it:

> **Bell, alone of the many experimenters in the field, had hit upon this fundamental principle of electric speech in his ignorance of electricity and in his knowledge of sound. No one, before Bell, had ever reproduced speech by electricity, and no one, since, has ever been able to discover any other means than Bell's to accomplish it. Bell, alone, believed in the**

validity of the conception "long before I had a clear idea of the means," and reduced it to practice through years of opposition, ill-health, poverty—all the familiar discouragements of genius—with a determined faith that assumed nearly epic proportions. (*M,* 8)

In order to mark the unique aspect of the invention, C.M. switches tracks on his essence. In order to be what it is, it has to be an other. "It was far more than the invention of a new apparatus, it was the discovery of a new Art. The Art of telephony was old, but the Art of speech telephony was new" (*M,* 8).

It is as if Bell had coached the telephone toward the art of speech the way he taught his deaf-mutes to speak.

As if to underscore this kind of reading, M. (let us call her by this minimal acronym, henceforth, dialing M for Mackenzie) tells us that at this time Bell was teaching at the School of Oratory of Boston University. There his title was "Professor of Vocal Physiology." He also gave lectures on his father's system of Visible Speech to teachers of deaf children. But Bell as body already incorporates synthetic threads. Perhaps the most compelling feature of Alexander Graham Bell, which should clear his name forever, was his electric punk hairdo: "He was tall and slightly built, with an olive complexion and abundant black hair which he habitually pushed straight up on end" (*M*, 9). Not only were his hairs on end, receptacles of air waves, but his orbs appear to have been artificially bulbed as well: "the flashing eyes that were brown, but which all his life were so full of light that they looked black" (*M*, 9). The dark neon eye flashes were mysteriously connected to the receiving tentacles on his head. Elsewhere we pick up the important fact that Bell's grandmother had a favorite hat which had two wires sticking upward, thus pointing to the future of telephony, whose origins can be traced to her preferred headgear. But there was also, as we know, a Pa Bell. His black side-whiskers and drooping mustache were in the mode of the seventies, "and, plus, the old-fashioned cut of his coats, they enhanced the air of professorial dignity of which he was then very proud. Bell used to laugh very heartily over some of those old photographs of himself. In those days he tried, he said, to look just as old as his father." ("When I first saw my husband," his wife said once, "he was twenty-six and he looked *forty*!" [*M*, 19]) At once too old and too young, Bell tries to double for his father.

Electric Portraits

Again, M. outlines the contours of trouble. "I live too much in an atmosphere of discouragement for scientific pursuits," Bell writes to his parents. "Such a chimerical idea as telegraphing *vocal sounds* would indeed to *most minds* seem scarcely feasible enough to spend time working over" (*M*, 10). M. reports that "Speech, electric speech surged through his brain," as if he were to be electrically reanimated. "But he had no money of his own. He was supporting himself by teaching. His friends, very reasonably, considered the multiple telegraph a bird in the hand. To make matters worse, Bell had fallen desperately in love with Mr. Hubbard's daughter. And more than anyone, Mr. Hubbard insisted that he should finish the telegraph. Acquaintances openly tapped their foreheads, and even his friends were becoming a little uneasy about his obsession of sending speech over a wire" (*M,* 11). Things were going badly for Bell. In the spring of '75, Watson said afterward, "Bell came as near to being discouraged as I ever knew him to be" (*M,* 11). In this state of crisis Bell meets Joseph Henry, secretary of the Smithsonian Institution. Light at the end of the tunnel. "He never forgot the picture of himself, a thin young man in a shabby coat, striding away from the Smithsonian in the rain, the great man's encouragement running like wine along his veins" (*M,* 11); (Bell's autoportrait now showing traces of an X-ray). As long as he lived, "Bell never refused to see an inventor, to look at his drawings or blueprints, or to advise him if he could. Of course the result was that he was deluged with them. And the more mad the idea, the more patient he was. 'I don't want to discourage him,' he would say, 'there may be something in it.' But for Joseph Henry I should never have gone on with the telephone" (*M,* 11–12). Hence the patience for the mad; he awaited them.

"*In a manner of speaking,* Alexander Graham Bell inherited the telephone" (*M,* 13; italics added). One cannot avoid noticing the countless "so to speaks" and "manners of speaking" prevailing upon M.'s text, miming an effect of telephonics with unconscious irony. Bell was the third Bell in a line of direct descent to be a professional in the field of speech. In the early part of the nineteenth century, his grandfather, Alexander Bell, was a recognized authority on pure diction, a teacher of speech, and the author of a pop textbook on elocution, familiarly known as "Elegant Extracts". The "grandfather was the stongest single influence in shaping his career" (*M,* 13). Thus, M. shakes up the reputedly intractable father-son, incorporated, that is indicated in a number of other texts on the subject. At best, fathers tend to occupy the agreeably remote but urgent space of an operator for geniuses as they loop back to the figure of the grandfather for a direct line to future engenderment. Long distance recommends itself if anything is to be accomplished, particularly under the pressure of an intimate configuration.

Freud has given abundant explanation of a grandparently primacy in terms of the affective bonding that too easily slips into bondage with a precariously local connection. This is important to establish at the outset, though our purpose does not consist in elaborating a psychology of the son at this point. Fathers, as in Kafka, spread their bodies across the global map, leaving very little (yet immea-

surable) territory for one to work with. Somehow, they are to be bypassed by an automatic switch. Bell's father was to a certain degree surpassed, a move that carries with it the stroke of ambivalence, at once in service of and annihilating the other, appropriating the work of the other to oneself within a structure of inescapable usurpation. Again, Freud has supplied a reading of the anxiety involved in surpassing the father which, on the Acropolis, he located on the grounds of filial piety. He had himself had an attack of incapacitating piety when at long last he reached his goal of seeing the ancient temple. Let us take a closer look at the familial bypass. Who was the man, bearing a name homonymic with his own, to whom Alexander Bell attributed the strongest single influence in shaping his career? M. changes Alexander's name a bit when going over the grandfather. His properties—clear, independent thinking, intellectual honesty, fearlessness and initiative, extraordinary physical and mental vigor—"were Graham Bell's one pride of ancestry" (*M,* 13).

"This first Alexander Bell" as she names him, began life as a shoemaker in St. Andrews, Scotland, where for generations his Bell ancestors had been shoemakers. Those suspicious readers who thought that the dancing slippers shared by Van Gogh and Mrs. Heidegger were only loosely attached to the body of telephony will please repent. The telephone, which in part owes its creation to the first Alexander Bell, originates in these shoes, lacing together over a skip of a generation a symmetrical pair of Alexander Bells. Alexander Bell, whom M. finds good-looking ("striking good looks . . . and the expressive hands which his grandson inherited" [*M,* 13]), was a double sort of figure, a shoemaker and a Shakespearean, a gifted actor of the Theatre Royal. His marriage to the well-placed Miss Colvill influenced Bell's next career move. M. conjectures that the Theatre Royal, its eighteenth-century odium still upon it, was no place for the son-in-law of the respectable Colvills. Alexander Bell became a "corrector of defective utterance" and a public reader of Shakespeare's plays. (We now recall the "To be or not to be" moments of the telephone's first stage appearances integrating Alexander Bell's spirit.) "Much later, Alexander Bell retired to London, where he had a house on Harrington Square, and where, long afterward, he taught his grandson, Graham Bell, to recite Shakespeare in his turn" (*M,* 15). Alexander Bell's son, that is, Alexander Bell's father, Melville Bell, also studied Shakespeare, but his interests led him to have "corrected faults of speech," a concern that plants its roots into the friable grounds of a disability assistance to which the prefatory pages of every telephone book still attest. **The survival guides that flank telephone books maintain the connection between a broken, stammering body and the telephone.**

Melville Bell corrected faults of speech, then, "following his father's methods, and won further local renown by installing a speaking tube in a shop—an innovation for St. John's in the early forties" (*M*, 16). Like his son after him Melville Bell repeated the amorous history of his father, in this case by marrying a mature woman. "She was thirty-five. Melville Bell was ten years younger. History was repeated" (*M*, 17). We know what that means. Among the more engaging things, it means that this family created an extremely fine copying mechanism for the transmission of desire. The Melville Bells produced three babies, all of them not girls. The second, born on his grandfather's birthday, March 3, 1847, was baptized Alexander. To his family he was "Aleck" as long as he lived. He adopted the middle name on his own initiative several years later.

In the mid-forties, in Edinburgh, Melville Bell advertised in the city directory as "Professor of Elocution and the Art of Speech." And, like his father, he gave public readings from the works of Shakespeare. Soon enough, Melville Bell had to drop out of his church membership when he was attacked for publicly reading the scabrous works of Mr. Charles Dickens. Apparently overcoming the blow, he soon announces his famous system of alphabetics known as Visible Speech.

Melville Bell corrected faults of speech, then, "following his father's methods, and won further local renown by installing a speaking tube in a shop—an innovation for St. John's in the early forties" (*M,* 16). Like his son after him Melville Bell repeated the amorous history of his father, in this case by marrying a mature woman. "She was thirty-five. Melville Bell was ten years younger. History was repeated" (*M,* 17). We know what that means. Among the more engaging things, it means that this family created an extremely fine copying mechanism for the transmission of desire. The Melville Bells produced three babies, all of them not girls. The second, born on his grandfather's birthday, March 3, 1847, was baptized Alexander. To his family he was "Aleck" as long as he lived. He adopted the middle name on his own initiative several years later.

In the mid-forties, in Edinburgh, Melville Bell advertised in the city directory as "Professor of Elocution and the Art of Speech." And, like his father, he gave public readings from the works of Shakespeare. Soon enough, Melville Bell had to drop out of his church membership when he was attacked for publicly reading the scabrous works of Mr. Charles Dickens. Apparently overcoming the blow, he soon announces his famous system of alphabetics known as Visible Speech.

In Visible Speech, Melville Bell reduced to a series of printed symbols the anatomical positions which the speaking organs take in uttering sounds. These symbols were so drawn as to indicate the shapes taken by the lips, the positions of the tongue, and so on, and once a sound was written in its proper symbols, the initiate had only to reproduce the physical position with his own organs of speech in order to reproduce the sound. There was, for instance, a symbol indicating "closed lips, voice passed through the nose." There were only ten basic symbols, and these, in various combinations, covered the whole range of vocal sound in any tongue.

At a time when music and speaking machines were to share the same status, as, for example, in E. T. A. Hoffmann's *Automaton,* AGB was also musically formed by a mother who could not hear.[121] M. carries on. From his musical mother Aleck inherited the acute ear which was one day to pick up the faint ping of a wire accidentally plucked in a Boston attic, and to recognize in it the electric transmission of speech. In case we weren't on alert for the hazards of reconstituting narratives, we must at least with this observation be on guard before easily plucked psycho-genealogies of the sort mother/ear, although this in the final analysis is not altogether wrongheaded. In other words, conclusions can be correct even when unsupported by the mere empiricity of facts. Aleck, according to M., "inherited" an acute ear from his (deaf) mother. This means that the biographer got herself involved in the family story of denial. Still, it makes sense. Who would be more attuned to the hearing than a deaf mother? But the musical point ought to be pressed a moment longer. His most consuming aspiration was to become a professional musician.

AGB also composed poems, and for one of his father's birthdays, he wrote an acrostic sonnet in honor of the day. He adorned the top of the page with a bell, in a pen-and-ink outline—"unwittingly the original of that blue symbol which now guides our search for a public telephone" (*M,* 23). The birthdays of the Bell family draw occasions for outlining futural sketches, texts in which image and poetry collapse into one another in easy commemoration. While birthdays occasioned the special allotment of a future inventor's imagination, the death of the other and the proximity of his own, closely scheduled demise put AGB to work and alarm. A few images of his childhood clarify the scene from which to listen to the shape of the sonic disasters that hooked up disparate spaces. As a child AGB and his siblings developed different kinds of retention structures, storage pockets for relics, and body parts—what we tend to call a "natural" museum. The three Bell boys collected natural objects, animate and inanimate. Aleck himself went "through a period of intense scientific inquiry in which he dissected field mice and collected the skulls of other small animals for his 'museum'" (*M,* 25). The compulsion to collect and preserve, the imagination that contains within it a museum which doesn't let go of its object, shaped the childhood of a boy who "didn't like to play games" (*M,* 25).

As we know, Ma Bell was partially deaf. When the boys went to church they were obliged to memorize the text at the services and "to repeat the substance of the sermon afterward to their mother. Mrs. Bell was deeply religious, and for a time, Aleck suffered agonies of conscience over childish sins" (*M,* 26). The earliest performances, therefore, the first discursive repetitions, were designed to the ear of a partially deaf mother. The suturing of disconnected speech began by translation into another system from the mother's museum of the deaf. His father trained Aleck to speak a particularly accentless English which was punctilious regarding diction and pronunciation. As a result AGB could be identified neither as an Englishman nor as a Scotsman, nor as anything contaminated by the accent marks of local speech. This suspension of regional traits, the porcelain quality of an unmarked speech, indicates membership in a club of literary speech effects while also urging the beginning of a broadcast system of diction that harbors its own myth of phonetic purity, belonging topographically nowhere. The homogenization of a spoken language gathered into a traceless spot of geonational graphics foreshadows the network of links that make up the smooth run of long-distance language.

Once, on a visit to London, Melville Bell had heard a performance of the philosophical toy "Euphonia," Professor Faber's "speaking machine" which was making mechanical noises at the Egyptian Hall. Upon returning, the father of Visible Speech offered his two older boys a prize if they could themselves make a speaking automaton. "I don't suppose he thought we could produce something of value in itself," AGB used to say, "but he knew we could not experiment and manufacture anything which even tried to speak, without learning something of the voice, and the throat and the mouth—all that wonderful mechanism of sound production in which he was so interested" (*M,* 26). Neither boy had ever seen an automaton, so they decided to copy the structure of the human organs of speech. "My brother and I went to work; he was to make the lungs and the vocal cords, I was to make the mouth and the tongue. He made a bellows for the lungs, and a very good vocal apparatus out of rubber. I devised a skull and moulded a tongue with rubber, stuffed with cotton wool, and supplied the soft parts of the throat with the same material" (*M,* 27). The word "material" verges, for this scientific project as in Freud's, on essentializing a rhyme with *mater*: "Then I arranged the joints, so that the jaw and the tongue could move. It was a great day for us when we fitted the two parts of the device together" (two, always two of them, a partnership, double and uncanny) [*M*, 27].

Did it speak, or, what spoke? According to Bell's recording it squeaked and squawked a good deal,

"but it made a very passable imitation of 'Ma-ma, Ma-ma!'" (*M*, 27).

Repetition and imitation, together the two men reconstruct the possibility of channeling the self-repeating "Ma-ma." M. narrates: "The great thing was that it worked, Melville energetically plying the bellows; Aleck opening and shutting the lips. And if its 'Ma-ma' which transported the youngsters was actually somewhat less human than it seemed to their prejudiced ears, its construction had taught them the mechanism of human speech. Melville Bell was satisfied" (*M*, 27).

The boys were pathologists of speech. In the late summer afternoons the family at Trinity (the Bells' summer residence) would sit out in the garden, Melville Bell analyzing the raucous speech of the boy's parrot while Aleck held his Skye terrier between his knees, opening and shutting its jaws, trying to oblige the dog to growl "How-do-you-do?" As an activity, teaching to the speechless was globalized from the start, though AGB eventually let the canine pedagogy go in favor of other speaking entities. To this end, Aleck began to take some of his grandfather's classes so that he might become familiar with speech-teaching methods, and he devoured his grandfather's library collection on acoustics. Melville Bell received early recognition, lecturing in the 1840s at the University of Edinburgh and later at the New College. According to M.'s deliberations, "it was the era of assorted twaddle in the treatment of stammering or other impediments of speech. The majority of teachers 'sought by every means either to throw an air of mystery or exclusive secrecy around their methods.' Treatment of speech defects varied from magical charms to a fork on the tongue, tubes between the teeth and pebbles held in the mouth"—a catalogue of schizomemoirs along the path of telelanguage (*M*, 31).

Aleck made his first public appearance for the purpose of demonstrating his father's system of Visible Speech. Of these tests, later repeated publicly in Glasgow, one is described by a contemporary and friend of Melville Bell, the Reverend David Macrea:

We had a few friends with us that afternoon, and when Bell's sons had been sent away to another part of the house, out of earshot, we gave Bell the most peculiar and difficult sounds we could think of, including words from the French and the Gaelic, following these with inarticulate sounds as of kissing and chuckling. All these Bell wrote down in his Visible Speech alphabet and his sons were then called in.

I well remember our keen interest and astonishment as the lads—not yet thoroughly versed in the new alphabet—stood side by side looking earnestly at the paper their father had put in their hands, and slowly reproducing sound after sound just as we had uttered them. Some of these sounds were incapable of phonetic representation with our alphabet.

One friend in the company had given as his contribution a long yawning sound, uttered as he stretched his arms and slowly twisted his body like one in the last stage of weariness. Of course Visible Speech could only represent the sound and not the physical movement and I well remember the shouts of laughter that followed when the lads, after studying earnestly the symbols before them, reproduced the sound faithfully, but like the ghost of its former self in its detachment from the stretching and body twisting with which it had originally been combined. (*M*, 32)

The voice disembodiment of which the last lines speak is perhaps most striking about this description, giving vent to the ghost-utterance that disengages itself from a presumably living though wearily wasted body ("like one in the last stage of weariness").

Whereas earlier we found an example of repetition for the sake of the maternal ear, here we witness repetition in the form of a paternalizing mouth organ—the lads are called in to mouth the oeuvre of the father, to bring forth into the space of representation the Visible Speech formerly hidden, concealed. The brothers conducted the performance with such earnest mimetic application that even a yawn, the resounding cavity of paternal buccality, echoes at the end to mark its end. What they appear to produce, taking down the lessons of the father, concerns the Hamletian ghost of its former self. The linkup of this ghost to the lads, one of whom will survive to report the other, has merely been installed though not quite engaged at this point of the biographical narrative. It is mediated by the father. Between the maternally enfolded ear and the paternal mouth, the pair of brothers are already on the telephone, a project they had begun to construe in a determined fashion since at least the speaking automaton built under the command of the father to utter

"Ma-ma."

Aleck became a passionately absorbed teacher, endeavoring to restore speech to silence, trying to induce silence toward a language that might be apprehended by his maternal ear. He put "one pupil after another through the test sentences of his father's system—'I see the panting spirit sigh' (***not spirits eye***) . . . demonstrating the postures approved for lecturing, for reciting, for preaching; right foot in front, weight on left foot; neck upright, chin horizontal; arms relaxed" (*M,* 44). The test or paradigm sentence feeds into the receiving mouth of telephony, one that can hardly be taken as fortuitous in its formation or usage. The spirit, diverted in terms of sight perception ("***not spirits eye***") wanders through a barely linguistic sound production, that of sighing, as if in the moan of a sustained lament. The test sentence teaches the deaf the conversion from sight to hearing effected by the distillation of a full-bodied entity into spirit.

In the typical drama of fatherly erasure, M. asserts of Alexander Bell, when he reaches twenty-one, that "in his father's absence he came to his full stature professionally" (*M,* 44). The doublings into which Aleck grew are now to become spiritualized, incorporated into an inwardly stretched Bell system and partially externalized in the form of a substitute other, Watson. We are in the year 1870. The eldest son, Melville Bell, faces the threat of the same disease from which the younger brother has died. Aleck goes to Edinburgh to relieve his brother of his teaching cares, but just as health appears to have been restored, "Melville died with shocking suddenness" (*M,* 45). A double dispossession, losing both brothers, one of whom he had tried to replace, who himself in name replaces the father. "The double burden of teaching during his father's absence, and his more recent anxieties, had had their full effect on Aleck's health. His grief-stricken parents became suddenly aware of his pallor and frequent exhaustion. . . . Their fears were confirmed. Aleck's health was seriously impaired" (*M,* 45). Seriously impaired. Go over the details. Melville Bell had been lecturing in America to return home to find Aleck, who in his absence "came to his full stature professionally." This implied a classical structure of disaster: the absent father returns to discover the fullness of his absence. Theseus, for example. Except that here there is no cordon sanitaire limiting the drama to one son or figure of alterity. Melville Bell will not have been the only one supplanted, but Aleck's singularity coincides, at least symbolically, with the sacrifice of his brothers, whom Aleck had tried to replace. It quickly becomes clear that from now on everything depends on Aleck; a restitutional structure emerges. Aleck will be responsible for returning to his father his due. Replaceability will become his burden. Charged with translating the departed figures into ghosts of themselves, he assumes responsibility for reconnecting that which had disappeared into the theater of the invisible. The spirit's sigh. The remaining triangle prepares to leave the mother continent. "The recollection of my early experience," said Melville Bell of his former visit to Newfoundland, "determined me to try the effect of a change of climate for the benefit of my only remaining son" (*M*, 45).

The move is made toward what remains, a surviving son. At fifty-one, Melville Bell abandoned his London career, its professional associations and its friendships, and, very largely, the fame for which he had worked through a lifetime of extraordinary activity, which was never to be regained. "For the parents could not be separated from this one surviving son" (*M*, 45).

We need to understand this drama of exhausted survival and convoke if we have to, which we do, the many ghosts that accompany its unfolding. The family, shrouded in the veils of grief, sails to a new region, disconnecting from everything—an event at once consisting in the cause and effect of the move. It is amputated, reduced to its essentiality of family-Dasein: the maternal, paternal, and a fragile sign of its future. The whole drama becomes involved in the pathos of revival, reviving the one remaining son whose task it will be to recall the fraternal spirits, to make them respond to his secret conjurings so that a father's mouth and a mother's ear might be granted a place of reception for the voices of the lost sons. Remember, though by now you must have forgotten, that this represents the kind of scenario that Freud evokes much later, his child has gone away, the telephone brings him back in a heavy sense, in the sense of a voice departed. Alexander Graham Bell's project will consist in literalizing the opening cut into absence made by Visible Speech.

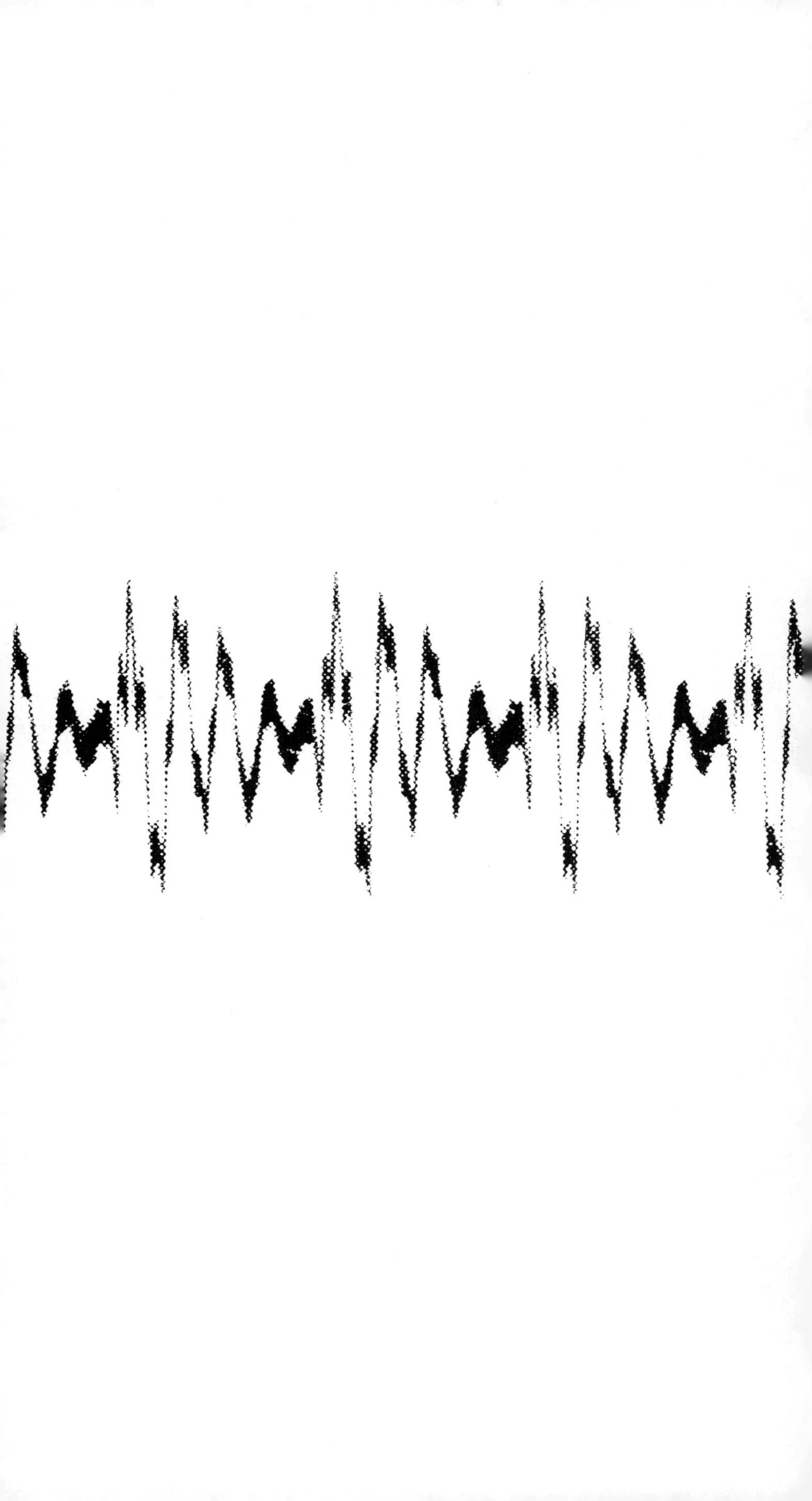

Canadasein

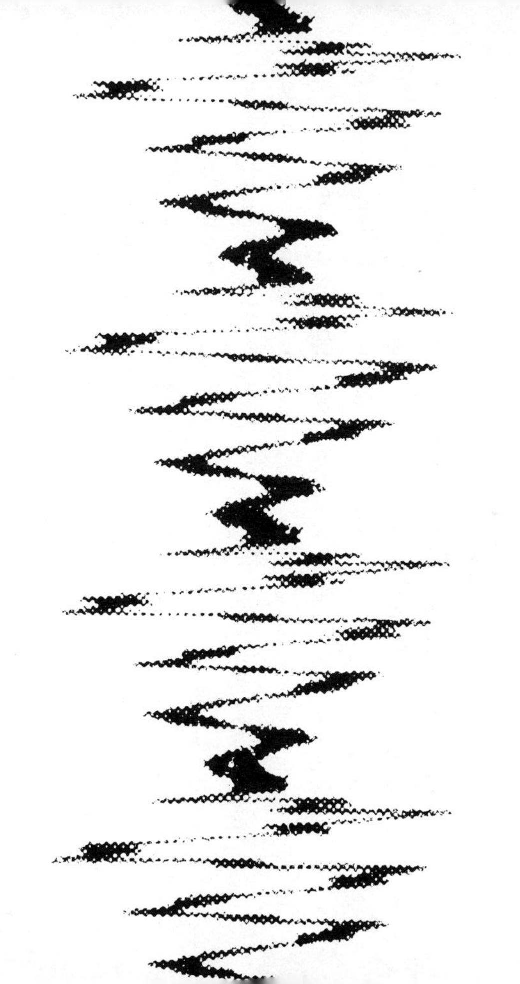

The Bell family sailed directly to Canada. The politics prevailing over the territories "were trifles to the Bell family who saw Aleck's steady improvement in this keen new air" (*M,* 47). The family focuses its discourse and desire on the air, on that which carries health as well as disease, and speech. As destination, Canada was slated to be Alexander Graham Bell's final destination, a celestial place of etheral air, a place accommodating to the hope of a restful peace.

In after years Graham Bell always spoke of coming to Canada to die. He was fond of saying that the London specialist had given him from six months to a year to live. His recovery was remarkably rapid if this was true. It seems very much more likely that his health was impaired but not seriously undermined, for his father employed him to work on the farm for his first Canadian year. Very possibly the arrangement was designed to compensate somewhat for his enforced retirement from teaching, and for the first dependence on his father since he had gone off to Elgin seven years before. (*M,* 49)

The tyranny of the debt hits all of them, each trying to compensate for a configuration of radical loss which cannot be transacted except by continued substitution. Aleck gained his health back, if remarkably. This belongs to the terrible economy of sacrifice and loss, the substantial gain in health and weight of one's being-there. A further substitution takes place. In the autumn of 1870, Melville Bell was invited to give a series of lectures on Visible Speech in Boston, addressing especially teachers of deaf children. He was already committed to teaching in Canada, where he felt obliged to return to his classes. Finding himself ill, he suggested that when his health should be fully restored, his son should be invited instead. Alexander Graham Bell was then twenty-three. "Obviously he was a fully qualified substitute for his father in the proposed lectures" (*M,* 49). Through the efforts of the School for the Deaf—the institution that afterward became the Horace Mann School—the Boston school board was prevailed upon to vote five hundred dollars for fees. The invitation was directed to Alexander Graham Bell, and in the first week of April 1871, he arrived. In a subsequent lecture in August, Bell went to a national conference of the principals of institutions for the education of the deaf at Flint, Michigan, where he delivered the address "Speech." "Speech," he said, "is a mere motion of the air." His revival talk shows the air moving with speech, the panting spirit's sigh, as it momentarily runs out of breath. We could say he was now sucking into a bereaved diaphragm the air on whose vocalizations the sibling apparitions were borne. Resuscitation through air, nonsubstantializable as it is, infiltrates a number of telephone texts. There will be no telephone without the vaporous phantasms of an air that speaks. What immediately comes to mind, with the instantaneousness of a call out of nowhere, is the bereaved telephone calling that organizes J. D. Salinger's *Franny and Zooey,* a novel rising out of the desire to reconnect a lost brother.[122] But Aleck hasn't even invented the uncanny telephone yet, whose posturing involves an upward and downward movement, locating its possibility in the shuttle between mouth and ear, en route to language's homecoming. Aleck's extensional hermeneutics of aerial speech was disclosed when he was twenty-five.

If his own family had diminished to the minimal requirements of familial accountability, AGB soon counted himself in another concept of family, and one that paid tribute, as if to help him cover his impossible debt, to ancestral spirits. Bell had entered the reservation of the Six Nations Indians near Brantford in order to analyze, with a view to Visible Speech, their language. What constituted his relation with the Iroquois, the Mohawks, weaves together the ceremonial and speech, a deeply ritualized rapport to death. The Iroquoian language became an object of study for Alexander Bell in a way that permits us to peruse the signifier of their tribal mark. The Mohawks of the Iroquoian language derived their name from "real adder"—relating in the other spirituality, with which Bell had some cause of recognition, to the story of a genesis, the Iroquoia, or snake, that whispered into Eve's ear the desire to incorporate something forbidden, something as modest as an apple. This put God on the line. The retribution of an angry God made itself felt. The tubelike snake had its legs amputated for its toxic telephones. War dances began; paradise became a long-distance call of considerable expense. The first "Guilty!" resounded from Eden's transmitter. Absence, exile, became the rule. (And the call to woman's painful labor.)

In the meantime, during his first Canadian winter, Bell had resumed some of his former experiments with tuning forks, based on the work of Helmholtz. The harmonic, or multiple, telegraph was beginning to take shape. He spent hours in the little drawing room, not unlike Nietzsche soon afterward, singing a single note into the piano, his foot on the pedal, "listening for the answering vibration of corresponding key" (*M,* 53).

"The Bells lived very quietly, but they were liked in Brantford, and there was a distinct note of regret in the rumor that presently got about that the son—such a nice young man too—was just a little peculiar" (*M,* 53). If we are to follow M.'s chronology, this is when he starts declaring warlike dances upon the "work of the Creator." Bell implicated himself in a project where it "was generally felt, when the matter was considered at all, that to teach speech to deaf mutes was to undo the work of the Creator; that if God had intended deaf mutes to talk, He would have given them that power" (*M,* 54). M. makes a point of correcting a popular version of telephone genesis which has "erroneously made the telephone a direct result of Bell's efforts to give hearing, or a substitute for hearing, to Mabel Hubbard," his bride-to-be (*M*, 56). We agree with the substitutive claims made by M. for Mabel Bell, placing her as the substitute for a substitute. M. instead traces the telephone to Bell's first experiments, in Bell's words, "to devise an apparatus that might help deaf children." By Bell's own account, this was initiated by his earlier work at the Horace Mann School. "These experiments led directly to the speaking telephone" (*M*, 56). As if there could be a direct line. Never eluding its a priori calling as an overdetermined instrument, the telephone, it seems safe to assume, connected the deaf children's ears, to which Bell was attuned, to his lost brothers as much as to the figure collapsed by his mother and wife. And if this strange community of receptors seems too cryptic or disjunctive, we have only to think of the dead ear into which he tried in his parental home to whisper life, the ear of the brother. He carries the ear about with him as if transporting the speech conveyance separating a thin membrane of Canada from the beyond, the membrane or veil of grief muffling the sounds of an impending séance. The dispersing point of his breath was aimed at the unhearing children who were still to be brought to language as their sole mode of existence. Again, we recall that the deaf were considered more radically deprived of life than the blind, for blindly still we dwell in language.

3 line #

The Returns

The Deaf

— AGB

[illegible] supplements itself in the wound. The stakes are high and abundantly argued. We shall have to continue [illegible] with the results of [illegible] [illegible] The condition which Dr. Johnson called "the most desperate of human calamities" [illegible] [illegible] the subject's site in language and the spatialization of [illegible] open. David Wright, the deaf man who wrote, and among the first to accede to language in this way, speaks of the "phantasmal voices" which he constantly hears. Wright contends that for those deafened postlingually, the world remains full of sounds even though they are "phantasmal."[illegible] According to [illegible] Kaplan's "The Effects of Early Blindness and Deafness on Cognition," to be born deaf implies a plight infinitely more serious than to be born blind.[illegible] These calculations are difficult to reckon; nonetheless, they make a certain amount of sense. Try to imagine the prelingually deaf, unable to hear their parents, denied entry to the Symbolic. Empirically, they risk being severely impaired, defective in their grasp of language. If we cannot enter language "we will be bizarrely disabled and cut off, whatever our desires, or endeavors, or native capacities."[illegible] They suffer an a priori disconnection that technology promises to repair, ever trying to rehabilitate the Wild Boy of Aveyron. The deaf, unable phenomenally to hear the Other. I think Bell was working both sides of the switchboard at this time. On the night shift, and always working for the Other, he outlines his early incredulity concerning the value [illegible] the subject's site in language and the spatialization of [illegible] open. David Wright, the deaf man who wrote, and among the first to accede to language in this way, speaks of the "phantasmal voices" which he constantly hears. Wright contends that for those deafened postlingually, the world remains full of sounds even though they are "phantasmal."[illegible] According to [illegible] Kaplan's "The Effects of Early Blindness and Deafness on Cognition," to be born deaf implies a plight infinitely more serious than to be born blind.[illegible]

Since one of the branches of its genealogical tree link it to the predicament of deafness, the telephone will always be hard of hearing, and thus unhinging. With the deaf-mute, **language is cut to the quick.** Theories rush in emergency supplies to dress the wound. The stakes are high and abundantly argued. We shall have to content ourselves with the results of a microrecording that situates telephonics within an order of deafness. The condition which Dr. Johnson called "the most desperate of human calamities," deafness focalized the subject's site in language and the spatialization of accoustical images. David Wright, the deaf man who wrote, and among the first to accede to language in this way, speaks of the "phantasmal voices" which he constantly hears. Wright contends that for those deafened postlingually, the world remains full of sounds even though they are "phantasmal."[123] According to Isabelle Rapin's "The Effects of Early Blindness and Deafness on Cognition," to be born deaf implies a plight infinitely more serious than to be born blind.[124] These calculations are difficult to reckon; nonetheless, they make a certain amount of sense. Try to imagine the prelingually deaf, unable to hear their parents, denied entry to the Symbolic. Empirically, they risk being severely impaired, defective in their grasp of language. If we cannot enter language "we will be bizarrely disabled and cut off, whatever our desires, or endeavors, or native capacities."[125] They suffer an a priori disconnectedness that technology promises to repair, ever trying to rehabilitate the Wild Boy of Aveyron. The deaf, unable phenomenally to hear the Other. I think Bell was working both sides of the switchboard at this time. On the night shift, and always working for the Other, he outlines his early incredulity concerning the value of lipreading to the deaf:

My original scepticism concerning the possibility of speech reading had one good result: it led me to devise an apparatus that might help the children . . . a machine to hear for them, a machine that should render visible to the eyes of the deaf the vibrations of the air that affect our ears as sound. . . . It was a failure, but that apparatus, in the process of time, became the telephone of today. It did not enable the deaf to see speech as others hear it, but it gave ears to the telegraph, and to-day we hear in Boston what is spoken in New York and Chicago. (*M*, 56–57)

If you and I hear each other it is because the apparatus to make the deaf see skywriting ghosts knew failure. To render visible to the eyes was not possible. Another way of saying this is that he could not invent an enabling machine to make the dead hear the vibrations of the air. Still another way of translating this failure that "should render visible"—as if a commandment or an ethical imperative were being stated—is that Visible Speech failed Alexander Graham Bell at this crucial time of mourning. The deaf and the departed, linked by the register of the interlingual dead, could not be reached, not yet, and not through a speech conjuring apprehended in terms of its visibility.

"I trust," Mr. Bell concludes apologetically, "that you will pardon personal allusions to my own work" (*M*, 57). He trusts and he apologizes; he has somehow become too personal—"pardon *personal* allusions to my *own* work"—in this history of an aberrant invention, as if his ownmost work were to expose the personal work of the grief-stricken. He assigns the origin of the telephone to the missing children known as the deaf—children or siblings fully out of earshot. "It is only right that it should be known that the telephone is one of the products of the work of the Horace Mann School for the Deaf, and resulted from my attempts to benefit the children of this school" (*M*, 57).

In those days there were always people like the young neighbor, Richards, occupying the room next to Bell's,

who would let Bell string wires on their premises, who would "make up a human circuit for him by clasping hands in a row, and fill their ears with water to listen for an electrical effect; all because he was such a very engaging young man, even if he was, regrettably, a little mad" (*M*, 57–58).

Like the archetypal inventor eaten up by a compulsion or a starving Other who inhabits him, AGB allows himself to be vampirized by his machine. He virtually ceases to eat and to sleep, technologizing himself to the point of breaking down. "He ate as infrequently as he slept, and in the spring of 1873, he was a wreck. In May he went home to Brantford, to his mother's anxious care" (*M*, 58).

AGB returned to Boston in October 1873. He took up residency at Salem. Thomas Sanders, his patron, welcoming back his protégé, wonders: "Which of us is the happier—I who have found such an artist, or you who have found such a prince?" (*M*, 59). We are still talking art, and of the poetry diverting a child from the isolation of deafness, saving the child in language, bringing him to the proximity of speech with his father. Alexander Graham Bell did this—an act of genuine *poiēsis*—for Thomas Sanders's little boy. The father's unpayable gratitude for this mediated return of the son (to Speech, to him, and therefore, in some sense, to the law of the father) took the form of a transfer of funds. For rendering his child accessible to speech, Sanders granted Bell an atelier in which to pursue his oto-experiments. His mother, Mrs. Sanders, turned over to Bell the entire third floor of her house, "and wires ran down the stairways to the basement workshop," which had been fitted up for the tutor's use.

I offer this detail in order to show a subtle transaction taking place, which, while shifting the locality and terms a bit, nonetheless serves to reinforce the structure that has been emerging in its tender frangibility. Bell has entered a strict economy which approaches the incalculable in terms of desire and effects. To reduce it to a rude formula would not rob the economy of its riches, however. The great debt that Mr. Sanders acknowledged was incurred principally as father. Bell was to reconnect his son to him, draw him out of silence's heavy isolation chambers. In return—and it is a question only of returns—Bell incurred a debt toward Mr. Sanders, who turned over his home to him, supporting his experiments, his desire to wire up a family dwelling into connection with itself, but currently cut off from itself. The house turned over to Bell is held by a mother. The reduced perspective shows how the telephone in part grew simultaneously with the economy engaged by the assumption of a grateful father attaching a remote son. As the system capable of giving him his son, Bell simultaneously occupies the place of a mother and that of an engendering father, the other to whom and from whom the seed is destined. He gives the father a child. At once transmitting and receiving, AGB speaks conjuringly and makes the thingly silent one emit sounds. The telephone could arise only within such a space divided upon itself from top, the third floor, to rock bottom, the ground, if not "the basement." "He also lectured that winter at the School of Oratory of Boston University, where he was 'Professor of Vocal Physiology'" (*M,* 60). He had not abandoned his father; in fact he has amplifed him, strengthened his debt, splitting the father in two, hearing his encouragement stereophonically, supported on one ear by Melville Bell and on the other, Thomas Sanders.

Under Language Arrest

The boy to whom he brought language's fire was taught a pedagogy that predials the signature of telephony. The little boy had been born into the advent of himself, a mode of not-thereness, under language arrest. Bell marks the shift from his father's method to his own by the special induction of the fingertips. Later one would want to say that the telephone allows a subject to have the world at its fingertips, just as the identity of the legal subject will be reducible to a fingerprint. Thus, "although Bell taught him to speak, he did not then employ lip-reading, but devised a method of finger-spelling of his own. He had a small glove for George's hand, with letters and words inked on it, and through this medium the two held animated conversations. Bell took him to see the lions at Barnum's show" (*M,* 61).

The three-storied house well reflects the three-storied existence in which the telephone was realized. Mornings, the commute to Boston to teach in his father's footsteps; afternoons return to the little boy in Salem; nights, sometimes all night, wired to the nocturnal spirits occupying the harmonic telegraph. "In the late afternoons, George would stand at the window, watching for Bell's tall figure, wait for him to wave his hat, and rush to meet him at the door with the precious lettered glove. Then, leaning on Bell's knee, he was told all about the exciting events of the day" (*M,* 61). Elsewhere, further along: "While Bell worked at night on the harmonic telegraph, with every teaching day he thought more and more about an apparatus by which his deaf pupils might see speech" (*M,* 66). In a sense, we have already gone over the failure of this hope. But we bring it back to emphasize the degree to which the voice in Bell was subject to a writing, to a speech that the deaf might see, to a set of digitals transformed into typewriter keys, made contingent upon the law of language set in tablet forms. The first and most primal impulse, whatever its merits or complications, was to render speech visible, to have it show up as phantographic print-out sheets for the deaf.

The flame's tongue flickers in the manometric capsule. In this apparatus, an enclosed gas flame was made to vibrate by the action of the voice. "The vibrations of the voice, acting on a membrane so as to compress or expand the gas flame, produced a flickering—like the teeth of a saw—that was characteristic of the sound. "The flame," stated Bell, "moved up and down just as many hundred times a second as the voice vibrated" (*M,* 66–67). A revolving mirror reproduced the flickering of the flame in a continuous wavering band of light. Bell thought, "if I could discover the shape or form of vibration that was characteristic of the elements of English speech, I could depict these upon paper by photographic or other means for the information of my deaf pupils" (*M,* 67). Even with the help of material borrowed from the lab of MIT, the difficulties of photographing the flickering band of nervous light were no easier than photographing a phantom. Bell turned his attention to the phonautograph of Léon Scott at that time, which, as its name indicates, was a sound-writer.

The three-storied house well reflects the three-storied existence in which the telephone was realized. Mornings, the commute to Boston to teach in his father's footsteps; afternoons return to the little boy in Salem; nights, sometimes all night, wired to the nocturnal spirits occupying the harmonic telegraph. "In the late afternoons, George would stand at the window, watching for Bell's tall figure, wait for him to wave his hat, and rush to meet him at the door with the precious lettered glove. Then, leaning on Bell's knee, he was told all about the exciting events of the day" (*M,* 61). Elsewhere, further along: "While Bell worked at night on the harmonic telegraph, with every teaching day he thought more and more about an apparatus by which his deaf pupils might see speech" (*M,* 66). In a sense, we have already gone over the failure of this hope. But we bring it back to emphasize the degree to which the voice in Bell was subject to a writing, to a speech that the deaf might see, to a set of digitals transformed into typewriter keys, made contingent upon the law of language set in tablet forms. The first and most primal impulse, whatever its merits or complications, was to render speech visible, to have it show up as phantographic print-out sheets for the deaf.

The flame's tongue flickers in the manometric capsule. In this apparatus, an enclosed gas flame was made to vibrate by the action of the voice. The vibrations of the voice, acting on a membrane so as to compress or expand the gas flame, produced a flickering—like the teeth of a saw—that was characteristic of the sound. "The flame," stated Bell, "moved up and down just as many hundred times a second as the voice vibrated" (*M,* 66–67). A revolving mirror reproduced the flickering of the flame in a continuous wavering band of light. Bell thought, "if I could discover the shape or form of vibration that was characteristic of the elements of English speech, I could depict these upon paper by photographic or other means for the information of my deaf pupils" (*M,* 67). Even with the help of material borrowed from the lab of MIT, the difficulties of photographing the flickering band of nervous light were no less than photographing a phantom. Bell turned his attention to the phonautograph of Leon Scott at that time, which, as its name indicates, was a sound-writer.

The phonautograph consisted of a stretched membrane and conical mouthpiece. A plain sheet of glass covered with lampblack was so arranged that, when a sound was uttered into the mouthpiece and its vibrations thus communicated by the stretched membrane to the wooden lever, the bristle wobbled up and down, tracing its motions on the lampblack surface. We are most transparently talking writing, or on the tracks of a ligaturing between the pair. Moreover, the sheet of glass was arranged to move along at a uniform rate, recording the vibrations thus made, implementing a kind of vibrography.

Bell, proposes M., inherited from Alexander Bell the trait of extraordinarily independent thinking. He did not quite believe in the opportunities donated by preceding scholars, never leaning on research memos achieved by others. Thus "he was to lose years of time, long afterward, in independently compiling and tabulating information which was the commonplace of physics, often the common knowledge of any schoolboy" (*M,* 69–70). This may be because his project was not that of others, even if there should have been an assertible sameness between various researches, a radical similarity of the sort Borges later would clear up, certainly as regards quixotic desire. Bell was not as such a scientist or technologist. Rather, he was an artist of the beyond who had struck up a contract with his departed brother whom he had promised to receive. The spiritual slate still stood in need of improvement. And so sound-writing soon caught the human ear: "I was struck by the likeness between the mechanism of the phonautograph and the human ear, the membrane of the one being loaded by a lever of wood, and the membrane of the other by levers of bone. It appeared to me that a phonautograph modelled after the pattern of the human ear would probably produce more accurate tracings of speech vibrations than the imperfect instrument with which I was operating" (*M*, 70). He already had gotten in touch with Dr. Clarence J. Blake during the autumnal mourning period of 1871. Let us tap this call one more time.

Lecturer on otology at Harvard and aural surgeon at the Massachusetts Eye and Ear Infirmary, Dr. Blake provided Bell with some expert advice for reproducing the structure of the human ear. Bell, in his own words, calling on him: "I told him that I wanted to get a phonautograph modelled after the ear, and he quite startled me with the suggestion—'Why not take an ear from a dead man and get tracings from the little bones of the ear?'" (*M*, 71). Startled or not, Bell went for it but didn't know where to go. Blake volunteered his professional services, and "went to the Harvard Medical School to get it." But it was not a single ear that was got from Harvard; a pair of ears were pulled out, for Blake "had not only an ear from a dead subject prepared for Bell's use, but secured one for himself" (*M*, 71). This kind of conduct tends to border on illegality, but it turned out that because the ears were a missing pair, they legally assisted Bell. For the immense litigation he was to deal with was on this score held at bay, since Blake and Bell, on the subject of their dead ears, "kept in touch with each other, exchanging notes on their experiments" (*M*, 71). Shortly thereafter, Bell's interest in writing and signing grew. "The dating and signing of the most insignificant record became an obsession" (*M*, 71). Bearing hard upon his subsequent work, the fear of litigation intervened like a rude operator in his thinking. It was a trifling circumstance in the interchange between Bell and Blake that later provided the only evidence of a year's sustained experimentation. Now watch M.'s wording:

"It so happened," Bell says of the next *step* with the human ear, "that it was not far from the summer vacation, and so I carried this ear up with me to my father's house in Brantford, and there I commenced to make experiments."

He moistened the ear with glycerine to make it flexible, attached a small piece of hay as a substitute for the bristle of the phonautograph, and when he spoke into the membrane of the ear he saw the hay vibrate. (*M*, 71–72; italics added)

The ear enlarges, starts walking. He carries it home with him; or rather, it transports him. He shouted vowels into the dead ear, he watched the tracings made on the smoked glass. He had brought one of a pair of dead ears to his father's home, to make it respond to a call, to make it produce tracings of itself on smoked glass, neither transparent nor entirely lost in a fog of invisibility. The fact that he did not bring a pair of ears home but a single member of a pair leaves room for fetishization. The fetishist tends to go for only one of a double kind—a single shoe, one ear, one philosopher, or half a body set. In a way that reflects the fetishist calculus, AGB had by now lost a pair of brothers of which one was the felt destination of the new telecommunications. He started to manifest himself in the smoked glass tracings.

This took place in **the paterno-maternal space of a perforated ear.** Describing this moment, AGB was to write: "And the telephone was conceived" → "I had reached this idea and had gone a step further. I had obtained the idea that theoretically you might [who is you?], by magneto electricity, create such a current. If you could only take a piece of steel, a good chunk of magnetized steel, and vibrate it in front of the pole of an electromagnet, you would get the kind of current we [who is we?] wanted" (*M*, 72–73). The statement announces itself as a "you" that slips into the position of a "we." The telephone's birth pangs already determine the pronominal displacement, the vibrography of address.

"The conception of the telephone," he adds in 1916, "took place during that summer visit to my father's residence in Brantford, in the summer of 1874, and the apparatus was just as it was subsequently made, a one-membrane telephone on either end" (*M*, 73). He had gone a step further at his father's house. He conceived there, inscribing himself in the paterno-maternalizing space of invention. In his father's house he conceived something like a child by a dead ear, conceived with or for his father, which means he as his mother conceived his father's child—a brother collapsed into a one-membrane telephone "on either end," as he puts it, on the end of a beginning, a calendrical birthday or on the end as the end, as the other end, precisely, to which one reaches for some telespark that tells the end of the other. One membrane with two ends, giving birth to the gift of death, shouting vowels at the moment of conception, watching oneself be overcome with tracings made on the smoked glass. "Theoretically you might." "You would get the kind of current we wanted." "And the telephone was conceived" (*M*, 73). "We wanted" the kind of current you get. "We" still maintains a residence in your telephone.

Thereafter, day after sunny day, through July to late September, he smoked new plates for his apparatus, shouted and sang into the membrane of the human ear, and dashed downstairs from time to time with a new tracing to show. His mother watched him anxiously. . . .

But there he sat in his hot little bedroom under the eaves, shouting *e, ah, a,* by the hour, and, though he did not disturb her, because she could not hear him, she wished that he could be persuaded to spend more time out-of-doors.

On July 26, Melville Bell's diary noted a conversation with his son. The entry ran: "New Motor (hopeful). Electric Speech (?)" . . .

(Another entry for early September. "Aleck in tantrums. Full of new schemes." Three weeks later, "Aleck left.") (*M*, 75)

In case you think we have forgotten about the mother's vampiric energy,

it has been put in storage,

left coiled up in the telephone.

For if Bell conceived a telephone with his father in order to bring back the two children,

he was identifying the machine with "Ma-ma!"

that is,

he was caught up in taking her place,

multiplying her,

folding her invaginated ears into those of the pair of brothers left behind in Europe.

They had gone to North America to reconceive their family,

to die and pass into another form of Dasein,

one is tempted to say Canadasein,

with all its resonance of storage,

preservation,

and being.

The Bell Nipple

Earlier, much earlier on, we suggested a rapport to the telephone that could be reviewed from the perspective of a suckling, the telephone simultaneously as nipple and labia. This phantasm does not yet seem to have been borne out by our narrative of Bell's personal achievement. It takes a long while before the long distance of a phantasmal connection can be traversed. Fast-forwarding to 1889 we find that Bell has retreated into a kind of silence, a friendless, nocturnal existence. He has no intimates. "Bell had no intimates. These dictations were his substitute for discussion and argument" (*M,* 280). M.'s narration suggests embarrassment before what is to come. We, on the other hand, have awaited it and welcome its arrival as a signing off of a phantasm that made Bell's side of telephony so reliably uncanny.

} It is 1889; Bell had bought "the hilltop and the clearing, and with them, a flock of sheep" (*M,* 280). Bell's concept of things invades sheep. Listen to the multiplication of nipples, the connectedness of nipples to the mouthpiece. In the first place, a pair of nipples. The toothless mouth. "He discovered that these simple creatures had no teeth in their upper jaws, that they had—usually—one lamb at birth and that they suckled their young with two nipples. He was enchanted with these discoveries. For years he challenged people, 'How many teeth has a sheep got in its upper jaw?' Nobody knew" (*M,* 280). He wrote a paper for *Science* about it (remember, this shows how he writes for Science):

} *It is astonishing how ignorant we all are about common things. Just test the matter for yourself. Sheep are quite common; and we are all more or less familiar with their appearance, and should therefore be able to answer some questions about them. Well then,* ***How many front teeth has a sheep got in its upper jaw****?*

} *You never counted them? You have not observed? Next time you come across a sheep, just look and see, and you will find that she has* ***none at all!****—the upper gum is bare.*

} *We are all familiar with the fact that a sheep suckles her young; and know, therefore, that she possesses nipples that yield milk. How many nipples has she, and where are they located?*

} *Human beings, of course, have only two, located on the breast. Dogs and cats and other mammals that have a litter at birth have many nipples, located in pairs all along the belly. Cows have at least four, located on the belly between the hind legs. Where are the sheep nipples placed and how many are there?* (*M*, 280–281)

} What is going on here? In the first place this reads like a translation and metonymic displacement of Little Hans's discovery, namely, "just look and see, and you will find that she has *none at all!*—," the linkless dash underscoring that which she does not have, deleting and introducing the horizontal phallus that has disappeared into her. Bell repeats "we are all familiar" as if to stress the canny, familiar narrative that is then allegorized in his sheep discoveries. The sheep's minimal nipples, reduced to a pair, absorbs Bell's phantasmal energies. For Alexander Graham Bell the sheep take up a significance of affective investment of the same intensity as the telephone. He must multiply nipples, keep the connection going; they need to be kept from perishing.

} *With the discovery that they had two, Bell found that some of the sheep had an extra, rudimentary pair of nipples. And that one or two of the ewes habitually bore twin lambs. He satisfied himself that there was a connection between the supernumerary mammae and the twins. If ewes with four nipples had twin lambs, why shouldn't sheep be bred to develop six nipples, eight nipples, and to produce triplets, quadruplets—a litter at a birth?*

The more he dwelt on this, the more Bell was convinced that the solution was only a matter of nipples. Dogs and cats had litters of offspring, and they had numerous nipples.

As enthusiastically as he had set out to contract space, as positively as he was to embark on the conquest of the air, Bell began to breed sheep to produce litters of lambs at birth.

. . . For thirty years Bell's labours over these breeding experiments was prodigious. He worked out a series of earmarks. . . . And though the mutton was tough, the wool inferior, and a farmer once complained that the local butchers declined to take them even as gifts, the multi-nippled, twin-bearing sheep did, ultimately, appear regularly in pairs. (*M*, 281–282)

Bell's breeding habits may have produced freaks, but what we need to retain is the simple fact that he passionately induced ewes to create pairs. The experiments take the form of studying the maternal body, which, by mutilation and annexation, can be modified into a permanent place of incubation. In this sense, AGB initiates a pregenetic tampering, splitting the nipple in two in order to multiply it, **in order to keep the maternal machine going**. If the telephone in its previous existence as speaking automaton first uttered "Mama!" Bell now occupies himself with mammae as if to further the researches into the primordial signifer "ma," whose constellation accommodates his wife as much as it does his later telephone system. Fascinated by the ewe, Bell devotes himself to the homophony of the "you" who, at the other end, is charged with readmitting the two who are missing. Bell, to secure this goal, will become a breeder, somewhat like Rousseau at the happiest end of his days, trying to control the uncontrollable by producing an excess of litter, the excremental survival scripts which we have been studying under the light of "litterature."[126]

What compels attention at this point is the way the telephone, in the figure and person of Alexander Graham Bell, splitting itself off into the poesy of body parts, conceptually plugs into genetic research and engineering—something that should come as no great surprise to those who maintain a theory of organ extension or amputation as concerns technological tools. Precisely because the telephone was itself conceived as a prosthetic organ, as supplement and technological double to an anthropomorphic body, it was from the start installed within a concept of organ transplant, implant, or genetic remodeling in a way that the Promethean Frankenstein monster already had foreshadowed.[127] It is beyond the scope of this switchboard to establish more than the extreme and troubling coherency linking the addition of technological perceptual tools to the phantasm of the reorganization of body parts in the movement from electric speech to the nipples of a sheep. Yet a link exists between the nipples in which Bell saw a solution and the so-called technological revolution.

} If one were to set an event, a date, or a time bomb in order to see the beginning of the modern concept of technology touch off, then this event gets stirred up by the invention of condensed milk.[128] In fact something like the history of positive technology is unthinkable without the extension of this maternal substance into its technologized other: in other words, its precise mode of preservation and survival. Where on this body of lactate diffusion does the telephone plug in? First, let us sense the withdrawals for which the telephone speaks. This has to do with a certain concept of orality in part guiding the rapport to the telephone. Even the ear opened for Bell like a hearing mouth. On the most materially banal level, think of Watson's many scrupulous attempts at explaining the extent to which the lips had to fit themselves inside the labia of the telephone cavity. Something was always going on between the body's mouth and the receiver—secrets were being passed along. Of what order? The disaster of the mouth, the medusoid rift, reflects the implacable grimace of technology. It's a mouth that twists along the umbilicus of loss. Loss. Where is it contained and who keeps watch over it? As if something like a crypt had been inserted into the telephone's receiver.

} We have felt the parasitical inclusion of a crypt, always double and doubling, duplicitous like the ear, inhabiting the haunted telephone, operating the speaking automaton which was, as in the case of Frankenstein, a monument to an impossible mourning. In the particularized case of Bell, there had been something that he could not swallow, a death paired, impossible to assimilate or digest and whose figuration shaped the place of the telephone—properly a place of absence, where the Other speaks in the absent tense of its many voices, engaging multiple path transmissions of disfigured tracings. The ghosts that accompanied both Watson and Bell, whose permanent residence has been registered neither inside nor outside technology, have been made to disappear, falsely translating the most uncanny of phenomena, whose effect is not reducible to a phenomenology of spirits, into a cannily at-hand household object—an organ attachable, that holds a membership card to the human body, from which it detaches. Hanging on the wall and placed on a desk it functions like a family picture, a crucifix, or another partially tranquilized fetish. Whatever the maze of interpretive constructions, the point that might be recovered from these inventories of the imaginary rests on an inarticulable cut of separating, a story of disaster to which every reading of technology owes its opening impulse and projected end . . . . Technology, perhaps more so than any other thing except for a certain illumination of a god, is inseparable from catastrophe in a radically explicit way. Cutting lines and catastrophizing, the telephone has been associated with a maternalized force. Now, when mourning is broached by an idealization and interiorization of the mother's image, which implies her loss and the withdrawal of the maternal, the telephone maintains this line of disconnection while dissimulating the loss, acting like a pacifier.[129] But at the same time it acts as a monument to an irreducible disconnection and thus runs like incorporation, a kind of pathology inhibiting mourning, offering an alternative to the process of introjection. In this sense the telephone operates along lines whose structures promote phantasmic, unmediated, instantaneous, magical, sometimes hallucinatory flashes.[130] What happens to the perished Other when mourning is inhibited? The refusal to mourn causes the lost "love object" to be preserved in a crypt like a mummy, maintained as the binding around what is not there. Somewhat like freeze-dried foods, the passageway is sealed off and marked (in the psyche) with the place and date in commemoration.

} The silent pathos of object preservation, linked to food assimilation, discloses a mode of orality which the telephone draws forth. The work of mourning symbolically consists in eating the dead—what Derrida calls *mors,* "the bit."[131] The losses are cut in the telephone, whose ringing repetition denies the death drive in which it nevertheless participates. In its extension to the locality of eating or vomiting, the *mors* makes the telephone an exemplary simulator of mourning and its disorders. The telephone makes you swallow what is not there. It contains preservatives. At the same time, you spill out a part of yourself that contains the Other; in this way, it is a vomitorium. To these additives condensed milk comes in, if we can still hold it down, because the question of preserving and swallowing what no longer is there—

a specific form of mourning sickness

—may well be guiding all the missiles

of technology.

Assuming the telephone responds to a protocol that would be exemplary, then catastrophe and the uncanny spread their prehensions, the root of every technological incursion, to the real. The technology of preserving food, arguably the first true technology in the modern sense, originates in precisely such a narrative. It emerges from the calamity associated with the Donner party, a group of pioneers trapped in 1846 in the snowy Sierra Nevada as they made their way from east to west. **National nausea** was aroused when it was learned that they were forced to eat their own dead to survive. This "horrific event in American history," recounted most recently by Kathleen Woodward in the introduction to *The Technological Imagination: Theories and Fictions,* furnishes the grounds for Herbert Blau's *The Donner Party: It's Crossing* and is sublated in the account of Daniel Boorstin to the achievement of Gail Borden. "Moved by the suffering of the Donner party, Borden devised a practical solution to what he doggedly perceived as only a problem rather than a testament to the human condition."[132] (Though I can make little sense of this reproach—does cannibalism offer a testament to the human condition? is the literalization of incorporation of the dead that testament? is this what happens to everyone who makes the move from the east to the west coasts?—and though Woodward's description of Borden's solution trivializes his discovery to "a playful imagination," it is worth reading this drama into the network that connects all technology to the grounds of commemorative artwork. Woodwards ho! "Borden, an enterprising *bricoleur* with a playful imagination, determined to find a method to make food more portable. In 1849 he discovered 'an improved process of preserving the nutritious properties of meat, or animal flesh, of any kind, by obtaining the concentrated extract of it, and combining it with flour or vegetable meal, and drying or baking the mixture in an oven, in the form of a biscuit or cracker.'"[133] This in turn led him to invent condensed milk.)

} The technology of preserving milk, of rescuing other perishables from natural spoilage, can be traced back, therefore, to the catastrophe marked by the event of incorporation, a sort of autocannibalism which had the travelers ingest that which among them was dead. This still sticks in the throat of all preservatives, this original feast of technological remorse—sinking one's teeth into the flesh of the other. The crypt cracked an opening when missing children started signifying the container. Condensed and liquefied, the dialactate body of that which is missing was to be swallowed. Borden did not merely create a condensed milk product but a general theory of condensation that impinges upon discourse and the transcendental signifier: "Condense our sermons," Borden advised a minister, "the world is changing. In the direction of condensing. . . . Even lovers write no poetry, nor any other stuff and nonsense, now. They condense all they have to say, I suppose into a kiss."[134] The kiss is the abolition of sense, the miniaturization of all postal systems. At any rate, the movement points toward a reader's digest of utterance, toward a radical digestibility of all that is. This is based on the morsel that will

never have been digested,

not by you and not

by me.

We have linked catastrophe to the event of telephony, citing the cannibalism that forced the dual-functioning mouth organ to take in something it could neither fully assimilate nor eject. In no way of Bell's oeuvre was catastrophe merely an accidental fantasy of speculative pathos. Another work, less perturbed than the text of nipples in which Bell found all solutions, and less unpinnable than the telephone itself, presses similar points. As scholar and teacher, Bell achieved *The Mechanism of Speech,* which supplies a physiological reading of speech that openly names catastrophe, derives itself from bad breaks and cuts, and founds itself at the abyssal juncture of danger.

} As example we take "The Functions of the Epiglottis and Soft Palate," wherein Bell offers a descriptive analysis laced with abomination. His text is accompanied by vampiric drawings and designs which we shall attempt to reproduce faithfully in these pages. The description begins innocently enough with a downward passage, and splits into two tubes; it focuses on danger, the invasion of foreign bodies and death. This passage is typical of the scientific work that fills itself with examples of morbid anecdotes and scenes of mutilation, self-sacrificial narratives:

} *There are three entrances into the vocal organs; a, the mouth, and b, c, the nostrils. Following these passages downwards we find they unite in one passage, d, the pharynx. Below this point the passage-way splits up into two tubes, e, f, the aesophagus and the windpipe. The windpipe, f, bifurcates lower down into the bronchial tubes, g, h. These in turn split up into multitudinous smaller tubes, ramifying through the lungs. . . .*

} *In this apparatus we find two valves. . . . These valves are largely for the protection of the lungs. We all know how important it is that foreign bodies should be kept out of the lungs. The New York doctor who recently inhaled a cork has died, in spite of all science could do to aid him. Equally serious results might follow were particles of food to find their way into the lungs.* (*MS*, 33)

} Offering itself up to an allegorical reading of dual-functioning organs, the passage announces a death despite science, indeed, the death of a man of science which could not keep foreign bodies at bay, having died by inhaling a cork that might have kept things dammed up and immobile. Speaking of foreign bodies, Bell invokes a kind of universal knowledge, something shared by all in this community, "we all know." What we all know is that invading bodies and food need to be controlled, kept at a distance, and that science still will let you die.

} *The pharynx, d, forms a common passageway through which both food and air pass, and the valves, k, n, prevent the passage of food into the wind-pipe, and permit breathing to take place with safety during the process of mastication. If we were obliged to breathe through the mouth-passage, a, while the mouth contains partly masticated food, it would be almost impossible to prevent particles from being drawn into the lungs with the breath. The valve, n (the soft palate), obviates such a catastrophe by shutting in the contents of the mouth during the process of mastication, by closing against p (the back of the tongue), as shown by dotted lines. Breathing can be carried on safely behind the soft palate through the nasal passages, b, c. When, however, the process of mastication is completed, a new danger threatens the lungs. The food, on its way to the stomach through the aesophagus, e, must pass the upper end of the wind-pipe, f. The valve, k (the epiglottis), closes tightly against m during the act of swallowing, and thus prevents the possibility of food obtaining access to the wrong passage-way. The larynx constitutes a sort of box on top of the wind-pipe, of which the epiglottis forms the lid. In the diagram, I have represented the lid as shutting down on the top of the box, but in the actual instrument of speech the box also shuts up against the lid. Place your hand on your throat.* (*MS*, 35–36)

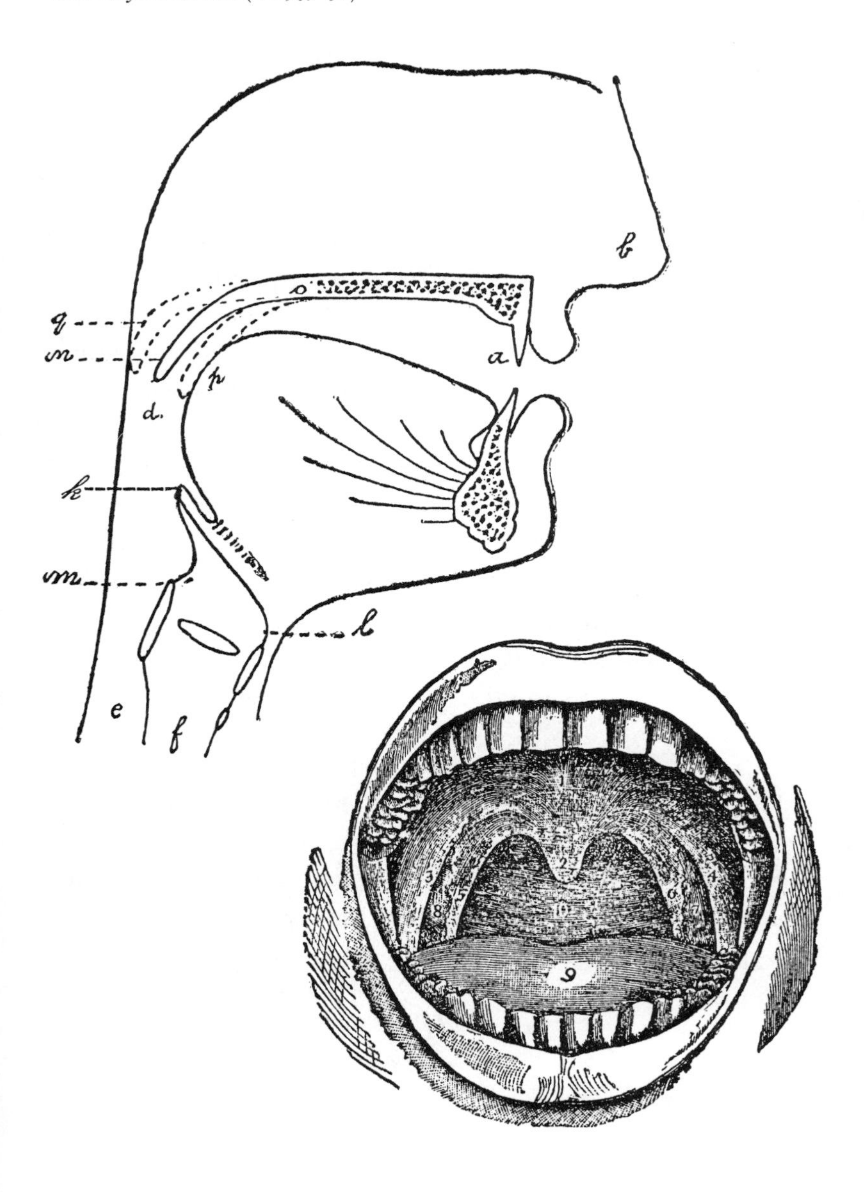

} In an earlier lecture, before shutting the lid on speech's box-like apparatus, Bell suggests in "The Pharynx and Mouth in Their Relation to Speech" the telephonization of the throat. The divide between the inside and outside opens up the boundary difficulties to which the telephone gives rise, most energetically articulated by the twilight zone of schizophrenic utterance. Bell begins, "In my last lecture I told you about a man with a harmonium reed in his throat, in place of vocal cords" (*MS*, 17). The earlier lecture had introduced a man who attempted suicide by cutting his throat. The cut was immediately above the thyroid cartilage, shaving off the epiglottis at its base. The wound resulted in an oval opening. "The doctor was surprised at the clearness and distinctness of the vowel effects, for the sounds seemed to emanate from the yawning wound in the throat, and not from the mouth" (*MS*, 7).

} To make a long and no doubt gruesome story short, the doctor found that he could turn the man's "apparatus" into a kind of telephonic contraption, forming his surviving body as apparatus. This is not that terribly far off from the conception of the telephone made via a dead ear. One way or another, pillaged bodies fascinate and addict science. In this case the subject is a half-dead locus of implant telephony. Bell continues. "Now, ordinarily, there is a vast deal of difference between the sound of a harmonium, and the sound of the human voice, and yet in this case the reed produced the effect of the human voice when the man spoke. To the ear, therefore, it made all the difference in the world, whether the reed was vibrated outside or inside the man's throat. Now, we have no reason to suppose that the thorax and lungs operated in any different way from the wind chest of a harmonium. They simply supplied air to set the reed in vibration" (*MS*, 17).

} Elsewhere, Bell is at the point of swallowing a tuning fork. This is why we rather insisted earlier that the scene of the fork with Watson, as inaugural covenant, be heeded in a special way, as something forced down his throat. The temptation always exists to swallow the telephone, to have it internalized, even if it should run the danger of miming the superego. For Bell it fairly sticks in the throat. He writes:

} *I have no doubt that the Scotchman with the artificial larynx could have produced the same effect, if he had slipped a tuning-fork into his throat in place of the harmonium reed. Imagine a multitude of tuning-forks of different pitch to be massed together in front of the mouth and all simultaneously to be set in vibration. It should then be possible, by shifting the position of the tongue, to reinforce the tone—now of one fork, now of another—at will. Indeed under such circumstances, it would hardly be possible to assume a position of the mouth, that would* not *reinforce some fork—at least in a greater or less degree. Imagine the mass of tuning-forks to be placed in the Scotchman's throat, and similar effects would result.*

} *Now the vocal cords like the hypothetical forks, produce a number of feeble tones of different pitch; when we pronounce a vowel sound, the mouth cavity reinforces, by resonance, that 'partial tone' of the voice.* (*MS*, 29)

} In the final lecture of the volume, "Articulation Teaching," Bell evokes a notion of maternal speech which should form the model and program for language acquisition. A good deal of what he has to say in closing will recall the way of training the telephone into articulate sentences, or the drawing out of the deaf toward speech. Some may recall Heidegger's transformative grammar of Mother turned Nietzsche.

} *I should like in conclusion to say a few words upon the general subject of articulation teaching. We don't yet know how best to teach speech to the deaf. If we did we wouldn't be here. . . . It is certainly the case that the methods usually employed in schools for the deaf do not even approximate to the nursery method of the hearing child. Not one of the little hearing children whom you may have left at home commenced by learning elementary sounds. Mothers do not begin with elementary sounds and then combine them into syllables and words. The mother speaks whole sentences even to the infant in arms.* **The child listens and listens,** *until a model is established in the mind. Then the child commences to imitate, not elementary sounds, but whole words. . . . The question is often in my mind whether we are not making a radical mistake, and whether it would not be better to commence with sentences and whole words, rather than with elements, and accept imperfect speech from little deaf children as we do from hearing children.* (*MS*, 113; boldface type added)

Reading like a title to a baroque *Trauerspiel* on power tools, The Mechanism of Speech: Lectures Delivered Before the American Association to Promote the Teaching of Speech to the Deaf, To Which Is Appended a Paper Vowel Theories Read Before the National Academy of Arts and Sciences Illustrated with Charts and Diagrams by Alexander Graham Bell commends itself to extensive study and speculation, particularly in light of the dark cavities and crypts anasemically embedded within this work. At the level of the "passive organ" and elsewhere, *The Mechanism of Speech* incorporates the teachings of "my father" (i.e., "the resulting character, however, is of so awkward a shape that another hook is added for the sake of symmetry. Curves of this kind are what my father terms 'mixed' symbols" [*MS*, 47]).

} Readable as a figural drama of family succession and displacement, the text gives priority to the resonance of the German word *nach* for that which follows. But it also explores the physiology of noise, treating the "effect of partially plugging a water-faucet with the finger. Slow silent stream converted into rushing torrent which spurts out with great noise. In the production of noise a little water goes a great way, and a noisy spurt can be sustained for long period [*sic*] without expenditure of much fluid. Application to the case of the vocal organs" (*MS*, xii–xiii). Still elsewhere, descriptive passages come to resemble schizonoiac assertions: "Why do you begin with lip positions instead of back positions? **Learning to speak is like learning to shoot**" (*MS*, 75–76). Other sections say "Please imitate Helen Keller's voice" (*MS*, 78). "A click results from opening a passage-way into a cavity in which the air is of different density from the outside" (*MS*, 89). "Suction clicks and expulsion clicks" (*MS*, 90). The book ends symmetrically with what the opening synopsis indicates as Miss Yale's intervention ("Miss Yale: Dr. Bell, I have a number of questions here for you to answer. Dr. Bell: The first question is: 'Is it possible to constrict false vocal cords?'" [*MS*, 11]). She also has the last word. The context establishes that "when we give a deaf child the indefinite voice mark in place of glide *r*, we obtain from him a sound that approximates very closely to the vernacular effect" (*MS*, 116). We turn to Miss Yale of 1878, who commends this plan.

Mr. Lyons: *I notice that the glide* r *is omitted.*
Mr. Bell: *Yes. And I consider that as a very important matter. I have found it a very difficult thing to get glide* r *from a deaf child without gross exaggeration of the movement of the tongue, and I consider it entirely unnecessary to bother him about it. I would recommend substituting for glide* r *a mere indefinite murmur of the voice. . . .*
Mr. Lyons: *I see in the symbols that the indefinite position represents voice glide. Is it the same thing?*

Dr. Bell: *The same thing. What I mean to say is, that when we give a deaf child the indefinite voice mark in place of glide* r, *we obtain from him a sound that approximates very closely to the vernacular effect.*

Miss Yale: *I believe in Dr. Bell's theory thoroughly.* (*MS*, 115–116)

THE BLACK BOX

After the **Crash: The Click:** The Survival Guide

The Bell telephone shapes a locus which suspends absolute departure. The promise of death resisted, however, destines itself toward the click **at your end. The** click**, neither fully belonging to the telephonic connection nor yet beyond or outside it, terminates speech in noise's finality. A shot that rings out to announce, like an upwardly aimed pistol, the arrival of silence ("Learning to speak is like learning to shoot," AGB), the** click **stuns you. It closes in on you, momentarily absolving *Mitsein*. The phone's nonfinitizing promise is broken. Designed to uphold the technical difficulty when it comes to cathecting absence, the telephone, whether consciously or not, continually reinscribes its terror at loss in such texts as are properly designated Telephone Books, of which ours would be merely a teletype flash in an infinitely crossed network.**

To avoid the crash whose site is your ear, you hang up together, you deny the **click**. This way, the Other is not gone but survives the telephone, just as she was prior to it. The telephone only places the call. Thus Pacific Bell, offering a pacifier to the teleconsumer, prints a Survival Guide, whose first words are "**a major disaster**."[135] The last introductory word to the directory of rescue transmissions promises (as to the stickers on French telephone booths), "**you can save a life!**" (*A*, 49). The borderline zone of temporal action cuts a path across the decisive moments separating life from death, as if the lines of telephony "**can make the difference between life and death**" (*A*, 49). This, precisely, is the difference that Bell and Watson were committed to making, but from the dimension of an afterlife, which is to say from a paranormal position or a repression of the absolute difference. They argued a far more uncanny projection of the return call than we can perceive through the iron curtain blocking our view from the genealogy of a technological desire, a desire that celebrated *techné* and participated in a rhetoric pumping the artificial self. Already heterogeneous, the self that speaks into the phone or receives the call splits off from its worldly complexity, relocating partial selves to transmitting voices in the fundamental call for help. The call for help is what Kafka imagines in his diaries: Alone. He would be in pain. The telephone rings. The voice tells him, "don't worry, we're coming to help you."[136] In Kafka's diary of pain the phone responds to your aphonic call for help.

The Survival Guide Is the Autobiography of Telephony.

The emergency temporality in which it discloses itself might be called the new journal of the plague: "**It is an alarming sight. . . . Do not attempt to force anything into the victim's mouth**" (*A,* 54). While the material gathered in these pages was provided by medical and emergency services in cooperation with the state, there will be no contractual guarantee, no responsibility, and no liability for any deluded empirical action taken as if this guide were a referential, pragmatically inflected call to mimetic response. Thus "**any person relying upon the Survival Guide does so at his or her own risk**" (*A,* 49). Desiring the Survival Guide in itself implies a risk.

The New York Telephone Company (1986) published a similar text, titled more in the Heideggerian vein, Emergency Care Guide. **However, the notice shows that NYT relied on Pacific Bell at its own risk:** "Information in this Emergency Care Guide is copied in whole or part with the permission of the copyright owner 'Survival Guide.' The Pacific Telephone & Telegraph Company, 1978." "Any person relying upon such information does so at his or her risk." **The telephone puts you at risk, or it figures the language of risk. It produces a safeguard against disaster—** Survival Guide**—which, however, puts you in touch with your own risk. What is your ownmost risk? Or even, *where* is your own risk (**at **your own risk)?**

As for the Survival Guide, it cables you into a double bind: You must but do not rely upon The Telephone Book.

Last Call

You thought I had forgotten.

The night we spent on the telephone. I would say that it can all be related to a structure of disappearance. Speech was slurred, your l's gliding toward an r, the way Bell describes it in his last lecture. And now, in the telephonic present, following a survival guide après-mamort, the tense flickering and residue of a telephone call. Believing utterly in Bell's theory, Miss Yale begins to experience withdrawal symptoms. A residence that held us together, the telephone invented our bodies according to a new contract binding on the inner ear. She wanted it to be a new labyrinth, a phantom locus. A placeless space where we spent ourselves, depositing bits of music that went down like coins, in syncopated gulps. We pay for our calls, the call of the other whose aphonic cry spells "Indebtedness!"

It's not as if I could furnish you

with an antidote to these injections. One might have come down more easily, with graceful civility. But no longer is there something resembling a European way. Instead, they wanted to promote whatever recalled your savage war on drugs, a new mythology of crack or cleavage. As if the body politic could be legislated into withdrawal, and sodomy erased.

What's left? A torn sheet of paper,

a schizophrenic day which Marguerite Duras blurs in her writing, depositing, always depositing, this time into the night of telephony. Don't tell them about our night—too many rumors already. I could kill them. From their trash emerges a litterature: "C'est là dans cette poubelle, qu'il faut chercher."[137] Try to feel the slightly demented, paranoid crash coming on. It's ridiculous being your survivor, transferring speech to the place of a black box after the crash. You were crashing.

It was not my own addiction, it was yours.

These withdrawal symptoms respond to your addiction. I became hooked on you in an abstract sort of way, an answering machine, responding to the poison you wanted. Come here, I want you. I picked up your call automatically, receptive like an addict. I suppose it doesn't matter to you, but we were not the first. Long ago your mother hooked you. She went away. Big deal. You were fucked. You'd wait for her call, like the Heidegger boy. Your father's voice often behind you: Get off the phone. As if one could get off the drug by the same paternal injunction that put Hamlet onto it. Getting off didn't mean then what it now does. You were all hooked up at an early age, even those of you with mothers-at-home. There were those self-shattering nights when they left a telephone number with the babysitter: your first survival guide. You were already hooked, weakened. It became increasingly more difficult to cathect absence. She calls it the other story, l'autre histoire, a history without images. The heroine is ill. "—Quelqu'un crie. Quelqu'un répond qu'il a entendu le cri, qu'il lui répond. C'est cette réponse qui déclenche l'agonie" (42). She at no point calls this someone by the name I have come to call your scream, Nietzsche. It is not the Nietzschean "yes, yes" that responds to sign the contract, though the distance isn't so remote between them. Someone screams. Someone responds that he has heard the scream; he responds to the screamer. The fact of answering unconceals the agony. He works for the telephone company, and for telecommunications.

Il est de permanence dans un service de télécommunications. . . .
Il a certains numéros de connexion du gouffre téléphonique.
Il les fait. Deux numéros. Trois numéros.
—Et puis, voici.
La voici. (23)

That's how he "finds" her,

though he will never really know her name or make out her address. Without locating her, he finds her, then, gets her on the line, and hooks her. This is what Duras calls l'autre histoire, italicized: "et puis je vous avais parlé de l'autre histoire, celle des autres gens" (22). The other history vaguely traces the genesis of a fear. The fear whose setting we have placed at the rise of schizophrenic day, as if this were the name of a historical time and place. What is the destination of this year; when does it arrive? "C'est là que cette peur arrive. Pas celle de la nuit, mais comme une peur de la nuit dans la clarté. Le silence de la nuit en plein soleil" (22). The text opens at the crack of historical memory, the opening of philosophy's midday. "Que vers midi le silence qui se fait sur Athènes est tel . . . avec le chaleur qui grandit . . . tout ferme comme la nuit . . . qu'il fallait assister à la montée du silence. Je me souviens, je vous ai dit: peu à peu on se demande ce qui arrive, cette disparition du son avec la montée du soleil" (21).

The origin of the artwork names itself

at midday of a time immemorial. *What is about to happen, arriver, would have been auditioned during the emerging silence that grows around Athens. Sound as we know it, noiseful, vibratory, disappears under the pressure of the sun's accession. The text begins, opening in a daze.* "—*Je vous avais dit qu'il fallait voir*" (21). *What is it that needs to be seen? The silence, the laser cut of sound blaring an unheard-of silence, the absolute vacuity of midday* ("*La ville se vide*" [21]). *It is not just any city that empties itself into the sky. The silence of midday falls around Athens, a silence so deep that we cannot say whether it is arched by the quiet of morning, where the gods have fled; or rather, it is the sudden absorption by the earth, at midday, of the gods' invisible arrival. The autre histoire of what is arrives on the folds of sonic waves,* "*peu à peu on se demande ce qui arrive, cette disparition du son avec la montée du soleil.*" *The disappearance of sound is an event. It is an event that gradually pushes forward the question of what is about to come. In this asking, a year arrives; not the fear obscured by night's unconscious. It is the lucid fear before nocturnal day, that is to say,* "*Le silence de la nuit en plein soleil.*" *The silence centered in the vault of sky, when the sun has peaked. That is what* "*happens,*" *the event already on the descent in the telling, an event that bribes the silence of midday to accept the noise of telling;*

on est redescendus vers la ville, Athènes, et puis plus rien n'est arrivé.
Rien. (22)

Cut to the other story, the telephonic night.
He tries three different sets of numbers, presumably on the off chance of conjuring her.

Histoire sans images.
Histoire d'images noir.
Voici, elle commence. [You see the other history has not as yet begun. We listened to Panic's originary silence. When Duras writes "elle commence" the story begins, history falls into place, but without an address.]
Voici, elle commence.

Elle lui téléphone en même temps que lui dans l'espace et dans le temps.
Il se parlent.
Parlent. (24)

That's how she starts—history,

heroine, or simply that which arrives at starting. The big bang of instantaneousness, the clash of temporal commencement, spatial contraction. It is the break in anteriority that lets them speak to one another, absorbing into speech the pronomial reflexive. Il se parlent fades into Parlent. There's the space of troubled location; that would be the substance of their first conversation (it's not a pretty word; we deserve better—something like Gespräch, donated by Goethe but unassuming): first the question of where she is when not on the phone. But is "on the phone" a discoverable location? They move swiftly into drugs, into a place of borderless medicine.

Here is the topography around which speech organizes itself.

—Elle lui parle de ce qu'elle fait. D'abord elle dit qu'elle travaille dans une usine. Une autre fois elle dit revenir de Chine. Elle lui raconte un voyage en Chine.

—Une autre fois encore elle dit faire des études de médecine, cela en vue de s'engager dans le corps des Médecins sans Frontières. (25)

Speaking, she convokes the imaginary space of China, the vastness of a legendary elsewhere. Speech does not fall into a banal setting, throwing shadows on a face that can be made to respond, for instance, silently at a café. This is a speech of a couple that constitutes itself over the telephone, describing itself to its multiply fractured selves, emerging with the knowledge of the other's disunity, trying to pin itself to a site. She gives herself the profession of a certain peace corps, a medicinality without such borders as would restrict its grasp. "—Il semblerait qu'elle s'en soit tenue par la suite à cette version-là. Qu'elle n'en ait plus changé. Qu'elle n'ait jamais plus dit autrement que ceci: qu'elle finissait sa médecine, qu'elle était interne dans un hôpital de Paris" (25). She will have become an intern, she tells him who has never seen her, internally inflecting her drift toward medicine. This is the version she keeps to, placing herself in a hospital as Hölderlin, before his silence, placed all of philosophy. She was finishing her medicine, the text says, working toward her MD, which stylizes the author's name, an inscription like the stem held up to the sunlight in the Elective Affinities. The initials of Ottilie and Edward were intertwined like the beginnings of a secret telephone number. "—Il dit qu'elle parle très bien. Avec facilité. Qu'on ne peut pas éviter de l'écouter" (25). You see, he's hooked. Listening to her in that way will have become inescapable. He can no longer listen away from her. Averted from all else, the other ear, too, sinks into effacement by taking her call.

The other ear no longer keeps watch, but folds into the receiver. Giving her his telephone number, he makes a gift of his audial address. She withholds hers. She can reach him. He now becomes what he is; in service of the telephone, he is on permanent call. "—Il lui donne son numéro de téléphone. Elle, elle ne donne pas le sien. —Non, elle, non" (26).

If she does not give her number,

she gives her name, giving it like the first letter of a number, in fact. She does not give a proper name, because she is on the telephone. What she gives is a phony, coded name, therefore, a "prename." By giving him her name she gives herself the gift of her name. She is not given a name but gives, if that were possible, her own name. "—Il se passe un mois. C'est pendant ces jours-là qu'elle se nomme. Qu'elle lui donne un prénom comment l'appeler qui commence par la lettre F" (26).

If this is to be a story of love,

it is because he says that she has a voice to which one loves to listen. He fascinates, hallucinating her voice.

—Il dit qu'elle a une voix qu'on aime écouter.
Il dit: assez fascinante.
—Ils se parlent. Inlassablement.
Parlent.

—Sans fin se décrivent. L'un l'autre. À l'un, l'autre. Disant la couleur des yeux. Le grain de la peau. La douceur du sein. . . . En ce moment même où elle en parle, elle la regarde. Je me regarde avec tes yeux. (26–27)

They describe each other to themselves.

A nonreflexive self, for their blindness lets them see with the eyes of the other. Expropriated orbs: the "she" that sees herself is a he, if eyeballs have a sex.

She borrows his blinded eyes in order to see herself.

This is how the story began, hopelessly saying we have to see. But not with the straight-shooting epistemology of seeing with one's own eyes. They lift their eyes up to speech. She holds her breast in his hands; and speaks into the telephone with the other one. The telephone begins to caress her; it goes inside and out. "Dit: c'est la première fois. Dit le plaisir d'être seul, que cela procure. Pose le téléphone sur son cœur. Entend-elle? —Elle entend" (27).

It would be naive to suppose that only mouths

speak to telephones. Just as naive as denying the nipple nature of the mouthpiece. The telephone-stethoscope absorbs his heart. Her voice vibrates him. "—Il dit que tout son corps bat de même au son de sa voix. —Elle dit qu'elle le sait. Qu'elle le voit. L'entend, les yeux fermés" (27). You see: in French, the voice, by homophony, sees what it mouths (voit/voix). "—Il dit: j'était un autre à moi même et je l'ignorais."

Desire split off from itself.

No mythology of a past totality of self where the telephone teaches desire."—Elle dit n'avoir pas su avant lui être désirable d'un désir d'elle. Même qu'elle—même pouvait partager. Et que cela fait peur" (28). Desire does not originate merely in the other, but in the self called by the other. His appeal to her comes from her voice split off through him. So many transplants have taken place in their reciprocal absence, this is what has become possible when you implant within you her eyes as they begin to devour, and devouring, unveil. I saw this happen before. In Proust; he was waiting for Albertine's call. He waits, maddened by the pause. Saturated with desire—desired to tears, the way we say bored to tears. During this time of waiting, being-put-on-hold, he discovers the phenomenal power of solitude: "la violence non adressée du désir."

On hold, desire opens a space

undestined, or globally aimed. Perhaps that is why she calls at night, when the receptors are without covering, his body is on alert.

—C'est la nuit qu'elle appelle.

Oui, avec la nuit, elle appelle.

—La nuit venant elle vient.

"C'est moi F. j'ai peur."

—Les conversations deviennent très longues.

Des nuits.

—Elles finissent par durer jusqu'au jour. Elles durent huit heures. Dix heures d'affilée. (26)

He still does not know her name, nor her address, nor her telephone number.

In the last of the Star Trek series,

a character says upon leaving a foreign planet that on earth we exchange telephone numbers. This supplies the residue of our identity. What got me was the way he put it; "we exchange" our telephone numbers, suggesting the exchange system to be anterior to the human subject. The "we" already belongs to the telephone exchange. He accorded the telephonic connection priority over any other constitution of the self and other. As I recall he wanted to give himself, as a telephone number, to an extraterrestrial girl, though I cannot be sure. All I remember is that this provided the sole index of his intergalactic desire.

I cannot forget "Charlie's Angels,"

with those half-terrestrians severally transferring on the call

of his monitorial voice.

—Il ne connaît que ce prénom comment elle s'appelle elle-même lorsqu'il décroche le téléphone: "C'est moi F. j'ai peur." (26)

I thought it possible that she was a mask of Nietzsche, the nonphenomenal side that was capable of uttering, "It's me F. I'm terrified," the side of Dionysus. He's at her disposal. "C'est lui qui attend les coups de téléphone. Il n'a aucun moyen de la joindre. Aucune indication sur le lieu où elle se tient" (26). She breaks in. Their connection itself is built on violence. She invents the violence of his solitude. She breaks in as nonidentity, nonappearance, simulacrum, she is the abyss of distance.

The way JD puts it when he turns to the Heideggerian usage of the word Entfernung, "distancing." It means separation, removal, and removal of what is far. He even talked to me about the constituting destruction (Ent-) of the far as such, the veiled enigma of proximation. Rather he was talking to Nietzsche, again. I was only listening in. "Oui, avec la nuit, elle appelle" (26). The opening, separation brought about by distancing, gave rise, he thinks, to truth—from which woman separated herself in turn.

It seemed so telephonically spread out, murmuring like the nonappearing F. She establishes a separating force and also separates herself off from herself. From the endless, bottomless depths, she is drowning out all essentiality, zapping identity, propriety, and property. "Distance is operative when it conceals the proper identity of woman and unsaddles the cavalier philosopher—unless she receives from her two spurs, two thrusts of style, or the slash of a dagger."

It's so very much like F. Both sense that woman's seductiveness operates at a distance. They manage to locate distance as the element of her power. "Others know to stay away from her chant, the charm. They kept their distance from distance itself—not only, as one might expect, to guard against this fascination, but equally as well to experience it. There must be distance; we must keep our distance from that which we lack." Appearance both opens and closes by what is termed "woman." It submits to her, the dominatrix of the question. That is why I consider F. the "prename" of F.N. They—I mean, he, she—emerge from The Gay Science: "Women, and their action at a distance. **Do I still have ears? Am I all ears and nothing else?**"[138] They—MD, JD—have discovered that questions on woman, those of Nietzsche in particular, are coiled up in the labyrinth of the ear. The voice, deep and powerful, that penetrates to his ear surmounts the difference between sexes.

This is why she comes to see herself with his eyes.

Like truth, F. does not
allow herself to be possessed. "That which truthfully does not allow itself to be possessed is feminine."

—Rien. Aucune image.
Le Navire Night est face à la nuit des temps. (32)

She says that she loves him madly. That she's crazed with love for him. That she's prepared to leave everything for him. But she wants to retain the telephonic regulation. She refuses to see him. She says they will never meet. They'll never see each other. "Je pourrais tout quitter pour toi sans pour autant te rejoindre" (36). Nothing takes place other than these calls, what in French resounds like "telephone jolts."

—Pour que rien d'autre n'ait lieu.
Rien en dehors de ces coups de téléphone. (45)

They constitute jointures that break off. These coups de téléphone make them:

Balance between life and death.
Disappear,
Die
Fall silent.
And then return to life
He says that he is beginning to love her. (48–49)

It happens. The lines begin to cut.
Her father wants to put an end to this, to her, to them; he wants to put a limit on the telephone. His operators start intercepting the calls.

—Le père.
Le père, lui, ne téléphone jamais. Il menace par l'intermédiare des femmes de la maison de Neuilly. Il faut que l'histoire ne s'étend pas au-delà des coups de téléphone. (66)

But the story, this autre histoire,
has already been compromised. It stopped; they were arrested. By an image. "—L'histoire s'arrête avec les photographies." She has sent him pictures: big mistake. The Navire Night

is about to snap. Alone at night, he was locked up with the unrecognizable photographs.
"Désespèré."

—Le Navire Night est arrêté sur la mer.
Il n'a plus de route possible. Plus d'itinéraire.
—Le désir est mort, tué par une image. (52)

He can no longer answer the telephone. "Il a peur." The photographs make her voice unrecognizable. Her face arrives too late; it should have been left out of the picture. "Il est trop tard qu'elle ait un visage" (52). With the click of a camera she has opened and closed the question of appearance.

The itinerary has been shattered
by an image. Shipwreck, as in Tasso. As in the Tasso of Goethe. Torquato: twisted and pained. The figural ship of night starts sinking, submerged in reference. It simply vanishes; no sonar can follow its drift. Then I remember something else. When one responded to the telephone, it must have been that a ship was coming at you. In the imaginary, I mean, though above that as well. In those days, when Bell and Watson were still on the lookout, one responded, one affirmed the call, by saying "Ahoy!" Now they say "Hello" or sometimes they wonder can they help me.

Set wholly off course by an image,
the ship begins to detach from its itinerary. At some point afterward, we know that F. has been cut off from her mother. "Il ne saura jamais rien sur la relation entre F. et sa vraie mère" (55). She had become a creature of the telephone whose truth was shredded into litterature. "—C'est là, dans cette poubelle, qu'il faut chercher. Le nom de sa mère y figure aussi." Her mother was a descendant "des grands chefs militaires de l'armée napoléonienne" (68–69). This piece of information together with the litter basket—to the extent that I am answerable—made me think that I was called upon to form a research-and-destroy unit.

That's how I found the telephone's absent tense,
the incinerated language you left behind. It's the rest of what I said to you. You thought I had forgotten. A residence that held us together, gathering us up in a phantom locus. I knew then that what connects is not related. Why else telephone each other? We should never have crossed the infinite distance of our apartness. Still, it left a space on our bodies. (I supposed you to have a body; in any case, the telephone tendered your secretion.) I still have your phone number.

I always had your phone number,
if I had anything at all. I feel the slightly demented, paranoid crashing coming on. It's ridiculous, having your withdrawal symptoms in my telephone call, surviving you in this way. It's as if I had sustained a hit of nuclear damage at the telephone, reducing my speech to the place of a black box after the crash.
I am crashing.

It wasn't my own addiction, it was yours.
My withdrawal symptoms answer to your addiction. I became an answering machine, responding like a thing to your poison. Come here, I want you. I picked up your call, automatically, receptive like an addict, structuring myself on the resistant woman who, after a sharp pain, dissolves into submission. That's the way she wrote it. Resistant but wanting. After the sharp pain. Then tranquilized by habit, increasing the dosages.

Prio

Ca

ity-
363
#1
Noncontact
Hermeneutic Stunts

proofs. Perhaps the so-called occult should not be left hanging in the air, imperturbably ringing as if we were not sufficiently at home to pick up the receiver. But picking up this particular line, admittedly, implies a danger; we don't really know or even want to know who is at the other end, a decidedly deep end.[140] Picking this one up is opening the Pandora's box of genealogical anxiety. Pandora always comes as Zeus's punishment for Promethean usurpation. ▬ As with most early technologies and mind sciences,

▬ We have to interrupt this
▬ We have to interrupt this call in order to put through an emergency verification. The interruption is not a mere suspension of a certain logical currency but the condition itself for opening the switchboard on a scientific genealogy.[139] The traces of a genealogical grounding emerge between the lines of a dialogic call, say, that of Freud to Jung, or a conference call among schizophrenics. These do not necessarily comprise different types of calls, but let us say that they share a party line. At least twice now reference has been made to the occult: in Jung's terms we were advised of the "so-called occult" where Freud's enunciation named his gratitude for a particular figure of the occult, the medium. The so-called occult is calling. It has never stopped ringing on the exchanges between science and technology, urging a lineage of verification, empiricity, invention, and

vaudeville was the research center for communication systems. The representation of the telephone and other scientific creations can be more genuinely understood if we grasp the terms in which they were "presented," *vorgestellt*, staged. The mise-en-scène of the telephone in particular borrowed its concept from the showing and telling of vaudeville, or more accurately still, it was produced along with aberrant structures of technological promise raised by the horror or freak show. The staging of a miraculous thing that contorts, condenses, or somehow usurps partial powers of immortality in profound complicity with the supernatural—this staging includes the unpresentable presentation even of psychoanalysis as a discipline. The concept of "mind reading," the electrical paradigms of Freud that have caused some static when situated in terms of science's electrical input, the question of mental telegraphy, unconscious transmission, noncontact hermeneutic stunts, or even Charcot's staging of the hysterical body, all belong to the encylopedics of nineteenth-century vaudeville. Hence the ineluctable *Witz* that accompanies the profound showmanship of the Freudian discourse. Or even for Nietzsche, it acts as that which enables the last philosopher to move beyond the "scientific project." On the limit of scientificity, then, one can read Freud's mentor, Charcot, as master magician manipulating the hysteric's thing-body. This vaudeville tradition, somewhat more privatized, extends well into the Lacanian oeuvre, where the neurotic, for instance, is conceived as a card-game player. The neurotic always pulls tricks—the *leurre* (tricks, stunts) of Hamlet, for example—or performs stunts before the box seat reserved for the Other.

■ In such a light, I would suggest that if Freud repeatedly named Fliess the reader of his thoughts, his mind reader, this does not engage a flabby metaphorics of friendship but activates reference to the performance of thought reading within the contemporary freak theater. It can, and perhaps should, be argued that many of the themes of psychoanalysis, from the three caskets to hysterical somatics, beginning with hypnosis, which was an integral part of any show, were elaborated within the space of these showings whose rerun we are now obliged to attend. Similarly, the telephone grew out of a mysterious coupling of art and occult: what we can call *techné's* sideshow. This is why the telephone appeared somewhat too freakish to be included in the shows of Barnum and Bailey—it was all right to have people without limbs perform feats, but a limb without a human subject was too scary, Mr. Barnum feared. Imagine a telephone, prosthesis for a human limb, isolated on a stage, carrying a voice from a place of absence. There was a limit to the public's tolerance for horror. Instead, members of the audience would be called to the stage to undergo hypnosis or to have their thoughts read. It will be my contention that the scientific imperative, the demand in the nineteenth century for an epistemologically reliable inquiry into the nature of things, derives part of its strength from the powerful competition represented by fascination for the freak and the occult, which is always on the way to technology. Science acquires its staying power from a sustained struggle to keep down the demons of the supernatural with whose visions, however, it competes. The repression of this terror produces the counterfeit tranquility of sound scientific procedure. Science is always an operation on horror, opening the theater of its repression.

A systematic demonstration of this point would require an encyclopedia in the Hegelian manner, a metonym that only can be hinted at here with the quick grace of a sleight of hand. The demonstration will be restricted to the space which we are currently trying to fill, the one occupied by a telephonic hookup to dimensions that may escape the control of psychoanalysis at this point. The escape is to be understood in the most reverential sense of vaudeville's lessons in escapology—in other words, the origin of a narrow escape, a contortionist's privilege of traversing the impossible bind that holds you in your place. To this end, we let the curtain lift on a certain staging of schizophrenia as spectator sport, a show whose entire scenography moves from the theater of the schizoid utterance to cryptologically inflected triumphs. One would need to consider in this regard the whole vocabulary of disappearance acts which lays out boxes of morcellated bodies, ventriloquy, swallowing, conjuring, and the general mise-en-scène of "live" cryptonymy in order to situate the shared incorporations from which the freak show and science eerily empowered themselves. With this in mind, and to set the stage for our reading, we visit the museum pieces gathered around the birthplace of the telephone, whose first sense of alarm can also be seen to have awoken psychoanalysis and its others. The dice have already been thrown in this direction.[141] But do not forget that for the throw to count there must be a second movement, for the thing must suggest a return, a doubling back in order to make the numbers intelligible. When the dice lands on itself, thus accomplishing the throw and the partial return, we find this curious combination, according to which the body becomes the site for multiple printing implants.

London

1ST CALL

The Green Man Assembly Rooms, Blackheath, England, March 18, 1822. Khia Khan Khruse rolls a smoldering bar over his body. "Then extending his tongue as if for some primitive communion, he had it anointed with boiling hot wax."[142] Earlier in his act, before appearing as a human target, Khruse had swallowed some pins and then extracted them from his eyes. He creates a space for the hallucinated language of the schizophrenic. On that night Khia Khan Khruse "swallowed a case knife which, when magically transformed into a bell, was heard to ring in various parts of his body" (vii). The body supplies the scene of thingification, the place from where hyperwriting and telegraph machines are first installed. So, for Harry Kahne, it becomes a question of the writing on the wall. Sitting in front of a blackboard, Kahne wrote five different words simultaneously with pieces of chalk held in each hand, each foot, and his mouth. At about the same time, in 1920, Thea Alba in Berlin, billed as "The Woman with 10 Brains," made her debut as student, we might say, of CompLit, "writing different sentences in French, German and English at the same time and ambidextrously drew a landscape in colored chalks" (quoted, 5). Thea developed quickly, learning to write with both feet and with her mouth. She also mastered the apparently unique stunt of writing ten different figures at the same time. She did so by using ten pieces of chalk mounted on long pointers attached to each of her fingers. In the course of her long career as a writer, she exhibited for Maxim Gorky, Kaiser Wilhelm II, and for the subject of Freud's last book, Woodrow Wilson.

2ND CALL

The technology of the automaton is raised in the report of the *Eccentric Mirror* (London, 1813). The report covers Bisset, the pig trainer. "Perhaps no period ever produced a more singular character than Bisset: though in the age of apathy in which he lived, his merit was but little rewarded. At any former era of time, the man who could assume a command over the dumb creation, and make them act with a docility which far exceeded mere brutal instinct, would have been looked upon as possessed of supernatural powers" (11). However, a Mr. Hughes, "proprietor of the Royal Circus, had as early as April of 1785 exhibited an automaton pig of knowledge as well as a mechanical monkey who did evolutions on a tightrope" (14–15). Another pig had "articulated *oui, oui,* with an uncommon fine accent—a proof of his having an early polite education" (quoted, 15). Still more striking for our purposes than sapient pigs, those live things through which speech gets emitted, is the privilege of invention accorded to dislocated bodies, articulating deformities, and contortionists. Clarence E. Willard, the greatest of these, explicitly engaged his body to question the prevailing discourse of the body's limits. It said that the posture master, competing with claims made by scientific and medical institutions, baffled all medical and scientific experts. Born in Painesville, Ohio, Willard eventually retired to Oakland, California.

3RD CALL

While Willard could exercise uncanny controls over his body (he could make himself grow several inches above himself), the tradition inaugurated by congenital amputees can be looked upon as the most crucial moment in the history of a given technology. In this area, the pioneer work of Matthew Buchinger in the early eighteenth century merits serious consideration. Though lacking feet, thighs, or arms, Buchinger played more than half a dozen musical instruments, some of his own invention, and danced the hornpipe. "He amazed audiences with his skills at conjuring. He was a marksman with the pistol and demonstrated trick shots at nine pins. He was a fine penman; he drew portraits, landscapes, and coats of arms, and displayed remarkable calligraphic skills. . . . His accomplishments seem even more impressive when we realize he never grew taller than twenty-nine inches . . . Buchinger was, according to Caulfield's *Portraits, Memoirs, and Characters of Remarkable Persons,* 'little more than the trunk of a man saving two fin-like excrescences growing from his shoulder blades'" (45). He was born Matthias at Anspach, Germany, on June 2 or 3, 1674 (both dates are given in drawings made by him), and appears in a manuscript authored by James Paris du Plessis, the servant of Samuel Pepys. The contemporary account has him under "The Wonderful Little Man of Nuremberg," which figures as part of *A Short History of Human Prodigies and Monstrous Births, of Dwarfs, Sleepers, Giants, Strong Men, Hermaphrodites, Numerous Births and Extreme Old Age, Etc.* (45–46). Of his many skills the ones which might be pointed out here grow out of the lack that appeared to define him more lastingly than any woman. His attainments as a conjurer, notes Jay, were greatly impressive. In magic he was required not only to learn the techniques of sleight of hand, but to master the physical and psychological principles of deception. "His handicap would seem to make this impossible" (55). He developed the skill necessary to make small cork balls appear, vanish, and multiply under various cups. But importantly, he serves as a historical marker for the translucent passage from incapacitation to the mechanical device. Thus *The Whole Art of Legerdemain . . . To which are added, Several Tricks of Cups and Balls &c., As performed by the little Man without Hands or Feet . . .* , a rare pamphlet most likely first published about 1730, describes Buchinger's method: he had invented a marvelous technical device which enabled him to produce or vanish balls without the use of digital manipulation. Buchinger's considerable impact on the conjuring world was such that his methods fill the pages of conjuring books. B's skill at cups and balls is eulogized in the long, satirical "Elegy on the much lamented death of Matthew Buckinger," published in the *Drapier Miscellany* (Dublin, 1733), some of which was written by Jonathan Swift. ¶ B's survival today takes the form of a certain kind of stray shot or linguistic offshoot, what Jay refers to as

one of the strangest terms ever recorded in a slang dictionary. In Richard Spear's Slang and Euphemism *(New York, 1981) appears the entry: "Buckinger's Boot: The female genitals. From a tale about a man named 'Matthew Buckinger' (British 1700's–1800's)." The first appearance of this peculiar phrase seems to be the second edition of Frederick Grose's* Classical Dictionary of the Vulgar Tongue *(London, 1788), which reads: "Buckinger's Boot: The monosyllable. Mathew Buckinger was born without hands and legs; notwithstanding which he drew coats of arms very neatly, and could write the Lords Prayer within the compass of a shilling; he was married to a tall handsome woman, and traversed the countryside, shewing himself for money." "Monosyllable" he elsewhere defines, rather politely and delicately, as "a woman's commodity.* (56)

In any case, the boot, like Van Gogh's shoes or the telephone receiver and schizoid monosyllabism, is somehow linked to the representation of missing appendages, the no place and nowhere of female genitals. At the same time the syllable is that which holds together, enjoying the peace of uninterruption. ¶ The "Poem on Matthew Buckinger: The Greatest German Living" begins in this way. His name undergoes a number of discreet permutations into the Anglo-Saxon:

See Gallants, wonder and behold
This German of imperfect Mold,
No Feet, no Leggs, no Thighs, no
Hands,
Yet all that Art can do commands.
First Thing he does, he makes a Pen,
Is that a Wonder! Well what then?
Why then he writes, and strikes a
Letter,
No Elziverian Type is better.
Fix'd in his Stumps, directs the Quill
With wondrous Gravity and Skill. (57)

4TH CALL

Matthew was not the only **writing machine at the trade show of horror**—though the horror may be a modern register of sensibility, for the accent in the eighteenth century goes to wonder. Another wonder was Johannes Grigg. "Born in Hungary in 1690 with no legs or thighs," he "had just two fingers and a thumb. . . . His performances . . . were aided by his ability to speak eight languages." However, in warridden, superstitious Hungary of the seventeenth century, his unusual physical form was attributed to his mother's witnessing mutilated corpses on the battlefield near the military camp at Papa, where the child was born.[143] A number of others, mostly German, exhibited considerable writing skills with their feet. Among several examples one is provided by Johanna Sophia Liebschern who "won fame writing, spinning cloth, and firing pistols using only her pedal extremities" (60). Another, Thomas Inglefeld "had neither legs nor arms and produced fine drawings and calligraphy by guiding his pen with the muscles of his cheeks and arms" (63). "According to Signor Saltarino's *Fahrend Volk* (Leipzig, 1895)," Jean de Henau was to become "the only legitimate stage rival of Carl Herman Unthan, one of the most famous handicapped performers of the late nineteenth and early twentieth centuries. Unthan was born without arms on April 5, 1848, at Sommerfeld, East Prussia" (68). Franz Liszt saw him play the violin ("Unthan, the pedal Paganini"), and he once performed on Paganini's own Stradivarius. Unthan's autobiography goes under the title *The Armless Fiddler: A Pedescript,* and was first published in Germany in 1925 before seeing posthumous translation into English in 1935. The armless writer had this to say about American men, and we can suppose that "to get ahead" plays an intended double-entendre: "America appealed to me as a battlefield on which all men were struggling desperately to get ahead" (quoted, 70). As for Unthan, he was skilled on the typewriter, and fired its close Remington relative, the rifle, with enough skill and accuracy, according to Saltarino, to be compared with the great trick-shot artists Ira Paine and Doc Carver.[144]

5TH CALL

In general, the great illusionists and the famous conjurers—Alexander Hermann, Harry Kellar, Howard Thurston, and Harry Houdini—were technologists of sorts, requiring a fully equipped stage, elaborate apparatus, elephants, cards, and handcuffs. Professor Seiden, an old-time professional trickster, tutored the master of the oral tradition of magic, Max Malini (né Max Katz). (Malini performed for the Baron de Rothschild, John Jacob Astor, John D. Rockefeller, and Al Capone. Jay singles him out for being "a master both of human psychology and the 'ability to think on his feet'" [87], perhaps a pedagogical concept whose tradition originated with conjurers.) His teacher, Professor Seiden, the eminent master of legerdemain and prestidigitation, entitled his acts "Séance Satanique." The professor was "Fire King and Ventriloquist." In case one believes that we are tightroping ourselves around the most aerial forms of speculation, think again. The connection to the telephone is always a matter of the tightrope, and so it must come as no surprise that the great Malini was also hosted by Alexander Graham Bell: "At a dinner given by Alexander Graham Bell, Malini asked Mr. Wu, the Chinese minister, to tear up a card and retain one little piece. The other pieces magically vanished" (87–88).

6TH CALL

The connection with AGB having been firmly established—evidence of the telephone company at table and elsewhere will be forthcoming, a matter of little else than scholarly conjuring—we now turn to the most distinguished genius of magic and telephonics, "The Greatest Novelty Act on Earth," "The Protector of Suffering Humanity," "The Idol of Scotland," "The Electric Wizard," Walford Bodie, M.D. Like AGB, he was grown in Scotland. He did magic, ventriloquy, and hypnotism. "He performed remarkable experiments with electricity, and as 'Faith Healer' cured people on the vaudeville stage." His parents wanted him to study medicine or prepare for the Presbyterian ministry. But, get this: "AN EARLY INTEREST IN ELECTRONICS, HOWEVER, LED TO EMPLOYMENT WITH THE SCOTTISH NATIONAL TELEPHONE COMPANY." The telephone, "especially in rural Scotland, was in its infancy, and this job provided Bodie with a practical education in electricity that he would later use to his advantage on the stage" (127). Born in 1869, he was about twenty years younger than AGB. Bodie's stage was set with "awesome-looking devices. Strange whirring noises were heard and sparks flew across the proscenium as a young girl stepped forward to assist him. As he touched her hand, every hair on her head stood straight up." Like Benjamin's punk messenger, she was somewhat of a crier, a receptacle of horror. For Bodie's fascination with the body electric coincides with the first court-sentenced electrocution, that of convicted murderer William Kemmler at Sing Sing Prison in 1890. Vaudeville mimed the thing to catch the conscience of the state, though it can also be maintained that the state followed upon vaudeville's magical acts of disappearing the other, since the idea itself of electrocuting a living body came from an animal show.[145]

Bodie performed mock electrocution in apparent complicity with the public outrage at what was thought to be an inhumane **death technology**. A volunteer from the audience would be brought on stage, hypnotized so he would feel no pain, and placed in a replica of the chair used at Sing Sing. (Later, in 1920, Bodie obtained and exhibited the *actual* chair used in the first electrocution. It was a gift from his friend, the American mystifier, Harry Houdini. As Jay notes, the back cover of Bodie's pamphlet *How to Become a Hypnotist* looks like a still from the cinematic images of Frankenstein, in other words, the monster reinterpreted as an effect of the electric chair. (Mary Shelley herself, as we know, began the narrative jolt by shattering little Victor F. with an electrical switch that altered the nature of the family tree. In this regard *Frankenstein* can be said to be a reading of electricity as the trauma zone of origin.) Bodie was able artificially to electrocute by his method of wiring the subject and rigging the stage. The subject was placed in a chair that was insulated where it touched the floor. The copper cap was connected by a wire to a large condenser, and the current passed through the condenser, wire, and cap to the subject. The electricity made to flow was not "current" or "dynamic" as was the case in state executions but, rather, "static" electricity, which was innocuous. Bodie's success encouraged the proliferation of imitators. But of all of his stunts none, asserts Jay, was ever more widely copied than the electric chair. Audiences found this act shocking. Displacing state sadism, theater acts functioned simultaneously to represent and to shock-absorb death sentences. The "shocking" signifier by now has transvalued into a staple of national aestheticism.[146] One wonders, therefore, what a rigorous reading of the relation in the twentieth century of Power to electric power or the very concept of the desire to shock would yield in terms of a theoretical political science.[147] The state, as we know, is wired, electrically fenced, and set up as an immense surveillance apparatus. The wire often

turns barbed,

electrically binding the

subject's body.

▬▬▬ As for Mr. Bodie, he went on to found the Bodie Electric Drug Company. The company also made Electric Life Pills, "the greatest discovery of the age, renews health and vigor," and produced Hypnotic Discs (134). In addition to making psychological and physiological claims for types of healing, Bodie advertised, under "Secrets of State Hypnotism and Stage Electricity," his discovery of "Bloodless Surgery." Thereupon, a good number of imitators sought to manipulate electricity for illusionist and healing ends, many of these calling themselves "Professors of Electricity and Bloodless Surgery." The screen supplied a mimetic version of Bodie's tenure through Charlie Chaplin, who impersonated Bodie, thus encouraging a link between slapstick and the new fact of electrically dislocating body parts. The members of Bodie's family and assistants were, to name but two, Mystic Marie and La Belle Electra.

▬▬▬ Due in the main to his "misrepresentations" concerning medical electricity, Bodie was dragged through the courts. What technology does not go to court? In view of our subject, the question of fraudulent procedure by scientific method invites critical dismantling. A partial rehearsal of the case will make the points self-evident. The presiding judge, Justice Darling, was drawn into the rhetoric of wit for which Bodie in a sense was first brought to trial. The case received a good deal of attention in the London press. Here's the lineup. In 1909 Charles Irving, a former appendage and assistant to Bodie, sued to recover £1,000 in damages for alleged misrepresentation. Irving had bought into Bodie's system and had paid to learn the sciences of hypnotism, mesmerism, bloodless surgery, and medical electricity from a man whom he believed to be a qualified doctor. ▬▬▬ On the stand, Irving explained that the "magic circle," a stunt, for instance, where men from the audience came on stage to join hands with Bodie as the current ran through him, were also paid assistants who contorted themselves on cue. Hypnotic subjects were also purported by Irving to be paid confederates. Justice Darling pointed out that Mr. Irving was to be taught hypnotism, which is a *real science,* and not "stage tricks." The space of representation is here at issue, converging in a meeting place prepared for legal, medical, scientific, and more literary-theatrical institutions. Let us tap into an excerpt from the hearings:

Counsel: Did he hypnotize you? ☛

[A member from the audience, *George*] *Dyas*: He tried to, but he didn't.

Counsel: Do you know what hypnotism is? ☛

Dyas: I don't know, exactly.

Justice Darling: Tell us what you do know. ☛

Dyas: It's when somebody has got a "fluence" over another person and tries to put him asleep.

Justice Darling: There are lots of counsel who have that influence on judges. ☛

[Bodie himself takes the stand.]

Counsel: Where did you graduate in medicine? ☛

Bodie: I have not graduated. [Earlier, Bodie's counsel had admitted that "Dr. Bodie is not a registered medical practitioner in any country" and that Bodie had previously been enjoined against using the letters "M.D." after his name.]

Counsel [reading from *The Bodie Book*]: "In the U.S. I took my degree of doctor of dental surgery." Is that a lie? ☛

Bodie: Oh, it's a showman's privilege.

Counsel [reading]: "And then I went to China, Japan, and other countries in the Far East to study these sciences which are called occult." ☛

Bodie: I have admitted that's not true. Showman's privilege.

Counsel: You have continually represented yourself as an M.D., have you not? ☛

Bodie: No, only on one occasion. It means Merry Devil. Theatrical managers call me that.

In Justice Darling's summation he raised the following points, which to a large (third) degree are capable of dashing the legal hopes of psychoanalysis itself: "It would be strange, if after attending thousands of cases Dr. Bodie has not been able to bring forward a number of persons to say they had been cured. One would like to know more definitely what had been wrong with these individuals before they saw Dr. Bodie. One would like to be certain they were not merely cases of hysteria which a strong will might cure" (146). Certainly, if it were a matter of a strong will, Dr. Bodie could have brought forward "a number of persons to say they had been cured." At any rate it seems clear that the court was interested in getting Bodie on a number of counts, including the way he conducted mock electrocutions, which he assimilated to the genre of horror. Generated as electrical spectacle, the state displayed its punitive contrivances as a freak effect of science fiction. ■ The jury awarded £1,000 in damages to Mr. Irving. A short time after the trial Bodie issued a New Year's greeting in a theatrical journal. Under his picture were the following credits: Freeman of the City of London; Doctor of Medicine and Master of Surgery, Barrett College (Diploma); Doctor of Science, Arts, Letters, and Literature, London (Diploma); Doctor of Electro Therapeutics, Chicago College of Medicine and Surgery (Diploma), and so on (146). In addition Bodie commissioned a striking full-color lithograph showing scenes of the trial accompanied by the following copy:

> *The* GREAT *and* ONLY DR. WALFORD BODIE
> A GREAT VICTORY *in the* HIGH COURTS *of* LONDON
>
> *An expert electrician appointed by Mr. Justice Darling swore on his oath in the witness box that* DR. WALFORD BODIE *who coupled himself up to a 16-inch spark induction coil had passed 30,000 volts through his body—a feat never before attempted or duplicated by any living electrician. This stupendous and daring feat was accomplished by* DR. BODIE *before a British jury of 12 Honest Men.* (146)

■ The court had been called upon to arbitrate between the scientific and the fictional, the realm of the real and the illusionist's regime of ironic doubling. In a sense, this cannot as such be arbitrated when the coherency of science's other remains so radically in place, that is, out of place as concerns prescriptive constative discourse. Like hypnosis, the entire discourse governing Bodie's reaction angles itself on performative aspects of language acts. The problem may involve a space in which speech acts fall under speech stunts—and, let's face it, Justice Darling's reading of hysteria ("which a strong will might cure") does not cut it as concerns the difference between a stunt and a doctor's willful intervention.

7TH CALL

If we connect Bodie's language to that of another stunt phenomenon we will have practically hooked up the telephone, or at least assembled the basic telephonic structures that would also endlessly be brought to trial. The other phenomenon concerns telepathic channeling. Transmitting signals from one subject to another, this was often carried out as a rival to spiritualism. Stuart Cumberland's brochure announces the sublimation to earthly person-to-person calls: "From upwards of one thousand famous Divines, Statesmen, Scientists and others who have given Mr. Cumberland their moral support in his crusade against the follies and shams of modern spiritualism." His most well known books were *A Thought Reader's Thoughts* (London, 1888) and *People I Have Read* (London, 1905). The connection to the other is a reading—not an interpretation, assimilation, or even a hermeneutic understanding, but a reading. This reading, however, like the telephone, displaces the book. Britishers James Edwyns and Alfred Capper did mind telephonics similar to those of Cumberland. Edwyns called himself "Champion of the World in Thought Reading," claiming Bishop and Cumberland allowed him "undisputed possession" of the title. "Edwyns conducted mind reading tests with contact, non-contact, and while connected to a helper holding an ivy twig" (189). A connection consisting of noncontact hearing was one of the principal aims of illusionist work, which never ceased to provoke medical and scientific interest.

Click.

ty-
#2
The Circuit
383

•
•

•
•
•

Take it from the circuit, January 19, 1955. Immense transmission problems. Restitutive tendency of the pleasure principle—the principle which brings the living being back to death—and the living apparatus of Freud. Jacques Lacan on the line: "There is an essential link which must be made right away—when you draw a rabbit out of a hat, it's because you put it there in the first place."[148]

Transmission pr.o.b.l.e.m.s. . . . .
. . . . / . . . . / . . . . a lot is happening here, a kind of frank machinery that makes you feel as if Freud had been put on call waiting. Lacan, operating the junction, puts him through. Not without a major inclusion of the telephone and Bell System. On January 19 the room is filled with communications spooks. Maurice Merleau-Ponty had given a lecture to the Société Française de Psychanalyse, entitled "Philosophy and Psychoanalysis," the evening before. He had touched off a hermeneutics of telecommunism when he wrote —*D'abord comprendre les Communistes* (77). Tonight, in the context clearly circumscribed as one of telephone and communications, Lacan raises his objection. Take it:

> . . . And this is in fact an objection which we could well have made yesterday evening to Merleau-Ponty. At some point in the symbolic system's development, not everyone can speak with everyone else. When we talked of closed subjectivity to him, he said—*If you can't talk*

with communists, the foundation of language vanishes, for the foundation of language is that it is universal. Well of course. But one still has to be introduced into the circuit of language, and know what one is talking about when one talks about communication. And you'll see that this is essential in relation to the death instinct, which seems the opposite. (83)

Lacan builds back to the telephone by first crediting Freud with having constructed a living apparatus. "The organism already conceived by Freud as a machine, has a tendency to return to its state of equilibrium—this is what the pleasure principle states" (79). Still, as technologically tuned as the master may have been: "He was missing something" (82). Lacan opens the field grandly, remarking the state of contempo . . . .

. . . . The great adventure of the research concerning communication began at some distance, at least ostensibly, from our concerns. Rather let's say, for how are we to know where it all began, that one of its significant moments is to be found in the company of telephone engineers.

The Bell Telephone Company needed to economise, that is to say, to pass the greatest possible number of communications down one single wire. In a country as vast as the United States, it is very important to save on a few wires, and to get the inanities which generally travel by this kind of transmission apparatus to pass down the smallest possible number of wires. That is where the quantification of communication started. So a start was made, as you can see, by dealing with something very far removed from what we here call speech. It had nothing to do with knowing whether what people tell each other makes any sense. Besides, what is said on the telephone, you must know from experience, never does. But one communicates, one recognises the modulation of a human voice, and as a result one has that appearance of understanding which comes with the fact that one recognises words one already knows. It is a matter of knowing what are the most economical conditions which enable one to transmit the words people recognise. No one cares about the meaning. Doesn't this underline rather well the point which I am emphasising, which one always forgets, namely that language, this language which is the instrument of speech, is something material? In this way it was realised that there was no need for everything that gets inscribed on to the small sheet of an apparatus which has been more or less perfected, and become electronic in the meantime, but which in the end is still a Marey's apparatus, which oscillates and represents the modulation of the voice. To obtain the same result all that is needed is to take a small slice from it, reducing the whole oscillation by a great deal—of the order of 1 to 10. And not only does one hear, but one recognises the voice of the dearly beloved or of dear Mrs So-and-so, at the other end. The things of the heart, the conviction passed on from one individual to another comes over in its entirety. The quantity of information then began to be codified. This doesn't mean that fundamental things happen between human beings. It concerns what goes down the wires, and what can be measured. Except, one then begins to wonder whether it does go, or whether it doesn't, when it deteriorates, when it is no longer communication. This what is called, in psychology, the jam, an American word. It is the first time that confusion as such—this tendency there is in communication to cease being a communication, that is to say, of no longer communicating anything at all—appears as a fundamental concept. That makes for one more symbol. You must get acquainted with this symbolic system, if you want to gain entrance to entire orders of reality which very much concern us. (79)

—•—•

Telephone and the jam, the step beyond a transparency of communication: these desires have established their birthright in the telephone system, which in many ways also comes down to America. In "The Circuit" Lacan rewires the subject, making it imperative to think the law of transmission according to telephonic logic. Telepathy, transference, and the discourse of the other which condemns me to reproduce, tie me to the telephone apparatus of which I am a part. I am integrated in a circuit, transmitting on automatic and speed dial:

> Think back on what we said in preceding years about those striking coincidences Freud noted in the sphere of what he calls telepathy. Very important things, in the way of transference, occur in parrallel in two patients, whether one is in analysis and the other just on its fringes, or whether both are in analysis. . . .
>
> This discourse of the other . . . is the discourse of the circuit in which I am integrated. I am one of its links. It is the discourse of my father for instance, insofar as my father made mistakes which I am absolutely condemned to reproduce—that's what we call the *super-ego*. I am condemned to reproduce them because I am obliged to pick up again the discourse he bequeathed to me, not simply because I am his son, but because one can't stop the chain of discourse, and it is precisely my duty to transmit it in its aberrant form to someone else. I have to put to someone else the problem of a situation of life or death in which the chances are that it is just as likely that he will falter, in such a way that this discourse produces a small circuit in which an entire family, an entire coterie, an entire camp, an entire nation or half of the world will be caught. (89–90)

•— •—— —— •••

• •••• —

•—— •— •• ——•—

•—•• •• •—• • —•••

Verifying The Line: BIO^2

"Bell himself": what did you mean by this? There are indications that urge us to double or triple Bell, to multiply him into a Bell system. There are exhaustive material funds enabling us calmly to assert the cryptological inflection of Bell's work. It engages a line on the complex terminal of speculative telephonics. Let us not submit every piece of what follows to interpretation but leave it to stand as a companion piece at the side of the other, in the connectedness of a receiver to a transmitter. Perhaps it all started at the piano bench. According to *Alexander Graham Bell and the Conquest of Solitude,* a good deal connected to his mother raised a fever pitch, always somehow relating to crossing the sound barrier. "His mother was also a good pianist, able to hear every note and shading by fastening her ear tube to her ear and resting the mouthpiece on the sounding board. . . . She taught [his brothers] Melly and Ted to play well, but Aleck excelled them both. He learned to read music at sight with great facility. Music could flood his mind like wine, keeping him sleepless and intoxicated through the night and leaving him with a headache in the morning. . . . His mother came to call such seizures his 'musical fever'" (*Bell,* 22). This piano, which contains so many keys, for the Bells as for Watson and the history of the deaf, provides the sound-board for telephonic virtuoso performances. The figure of Eliza Bell, AGB's mother, fixes a live telephone wire hammered into the concept of an instrument. Ever since Beethoven's deaf composing, the piano became the externalized thing corresponding to the acoustical ideas of a nonhearing inwardness. Bell's name was artificially pumped up. That is to say, he soon found his "given name" inadequate, annexing it with what Bruce refers to as an "extension": "Perhaps it prompted him to another extension. To be named Alexander Bell was no distinction in his family, so he decided to take a middle name. As he puzzled over possibilities, a young man from Canada, who had been a pupil of Melville Bell's for a couple of years, came to board with the family. Aleck probably took a fancy to the guest and certainly did to his name, which was Alexander Graham. On Aleck's eleventh birthday, March 3, 1858, wine was set on the table, and Alexander Melville Bell asked the family to fill their glasses. He then made a little speech about his second son's past and future and concluded by proposing a toast to the health of 'Alexander Graham Bell'" (*Bell,* 22). The artificial and belated link to the two poles of his name, the missing middle, the need for a self-naming or even a renaming, already participated in the structure of invention. AGB invented his signing, admitting a foreign particle to span the distance between the repetitions of the same: Alexander Bell. The profound intimacy linking AGB to his brother Melly weighs in heavily. A creature of science, representation, and magic, Aleck's brother Melly was a young showman of sorts. With Aleck he could "substitute for their mother at the piano. Melly had extraordinary gifts for mimicry and sleight of hand, both of which supported his taste for practical jokes. In exercising his Bell inheritance, Melly found his element in the comic monologue" (*Bell,* 24). In a crucial way, Melly never left AGB's side, even after he perished; it is therefore important to acknowledge their proximity to one another. For if the mother was already a telephonic instrument in her own right, Melly will have provided the mandate and contractual imperative for its invention. What we are here calling "the invention" is created in a kind of preliminary dumb show, as it were, following the commission of Melville Bell, who challenged (or commanded) the two siblings to build a speaking machine.

—•—

The project brought Aleck and Melly closer together than they had ever been before. Ted's bent was for art, but Melly shared Aleck's fascination with science and invention. And Aleck's recent stride toward maturity helped reconcile Melly to his com-

pany. Aleck and Melly began by studying De Kempelen's book, then agreed upon a division of labor: Aleck to make the tongue and mouth of the apparatus, Melly to make the lungs, throat, and larynx. No available anatomical work told them all they needed to know about the larynx, and so with heavy hearts they decided to sacrifice their pet cat to science. (*Bell*, 36)

•—•—•

Like so many things of experimental science, the apparatus, an abomination, requires the sacrifice of that which was living, and in some metonymical sense, attached to the family (a "pet cat," the family pet, the other member). It gets worse; the ritual murder performed on behalf of Melly's half of the project might have been eluded if the boys had consulted their father. Perhaps this was their way of consulting him, however. "They called upon a medical student, a friend of Melly's, to dispatch the cat painlessly. Instead, he took the cat into the Milton Cottage greenhouse and before the boys' eyes poured nitric acid down its throat [Aleck's half of the project]. Only after it had raced around in agony for some time could he be persuaded to open an artery and end its suffering. Aleck and Melly renounced such expedients thereafter, and half a century did not erase Aleck's horror at the memory" (*Bell*, 36). This dead animal, like the one that stared down Watson, acts as a partial origin of the telephone, its totem, in fact, whose guilty tab Aleck would have to pay. We cannot be sure that the narration of horror has been rendered in full; yet it seems at this point quite sufficient to know that a horror was remembered at the birth of the first speaking machine commissioned by the father, and that this horror involves sacrifice, murder, and the family pet. At bottom, a dead animal sublimated into a maternal cry. "At last the brothers united their creations. . . . The machine then cried out 'Mama!' Aleck and Melly tasted triumph when a persistent demonstration of this feat on the common stairway at 13 South Charlotte Street brought a tenant down to see 'what can be the matter with the baby'"

(*Bell,* 36–37). Melly's story continues, linking him to the vaudeville connection without which the telephone cannot be conceived. "During the winter of 1865–1866, Melly invented a machine of some sort that was tested and pronounced perfect by two interested gentlemen, though nothing seems to have come of it. By the summer of 1866 he had settled in the family's former apartment at Edinburgh as his father's tenant. His spirits ran high as ever. He advertised the coming of a celebrated Russian prestidigitator, 'the Great Loblinski,' hired the Edinburgh Music Hall, appeared with false beard and accent, and carried off a successful performance. Meanwhile he found time to teach elocution, cure stammering, and, on the evidence of testimonials, to do it well" (*Bell,* 49). The tabulations of loss form around the brothers. Aleck was first to lose his brother Ted. On May 17, 1867, Aleck wrote in his diary: "Edward died this morning at ten minutes to four o'clock. He was only 18 years and 8 months old. He literally 'fell asleep'—he died without consciousness and without pain, while he was asleep. So may I die! AGB." For "everyone but Ted," continues Bruce, "life resumed" (*Bell,* 53). If Ted was associated with painlessness and an exemplary way to die, Melly would always be linked to pain and catastrophic loss. He was the way pain was kept alive, the way by which Aleck had to live, in commemorative disjunction. Unlike Ted, Melly will not "fall asleep" in Aleck but keep waking, agonizing, and agitating. The sleepless night of Melly's death keeps vigilance in his part of the apparatus. But he has not yet died; it is still 1867, and Melly is only about to die (like everyone else). He has just announced his engagement to a woman whose name suggests the ear canal, Miss Caroline Ottoway. Aleck begins to be plagued by "nasty headaches" (*Bell,* 54). Ted's death brought about renewed intimacy, suspending a movement of separateness that AGB had initiated. Thus "Ted's death had ended Aleck's resistance to living with his father and mother, now left to themselves at Harrington Square. . . . While his parents vacationed in Scotland that July, Aleck settled himself in the house at Harrington Square and, having somehow encountered a seafaring native of Natal, set about transcribing Zulu clicks into Visible Speech. Duly credited to 'the Author's son (A.G.B.),' these made the final page of the Visible Speech book" (*Bell,* 54). (What if the click of the telephone still communicated along some frequencies with this Zulu click?) AGB's dreams of earning a university degree were dashed when he married, so to speak, his parents. Aleck's brother Melly had had a son at Edinburgh on August 8, 1868. Named after Ted, he "looked just as Melly had at that age" (*Bell,* 62). Early in 1870 the baby died. Melly himself is now on the decline, his health failing him, though he tries to hide this by writing home of his inventions in the old workroom at the top of 13 South Charlotte Street. He writes, for instance, of "his new speaking machine, with 'a very curious whispering and inflecting glottis'" (*Bell,* 63). Melly's conversion: he turns toward spiritualism during the summer and fall of '68. Melly begins sending his skeptical father material on spiritualism, urging him to "test the phenomena" (*Bell,* 63). More importantly for the fate of communications history, **Melly cuts an irreversible deal with Alexander Graham Bell.** Melly made "a solemn compact that whichever of us should die first would endeavor to communicate with the other if it were possible to do so" (*Bell,* 63). The contractual terms put the survivor of the other on the receiving end. Aleck had to be in a state of preparedness to receive the call. The invention originates with the dead. It's not the living but the first to die who has to make efforts to communicate. The contract designates Aleck as receiver.

Beyond the pact, Melly drew other kinds of contracts with his brother. Once, when he was feeling ill, he wrote in terms such as these: "My dear Aleck, I *do* wish you would give me a line now and then" (*Bell,* 66). Perhaps this does not appear as an extraordinarily articulated request, nor worded in such a way as secretly to spell out the lines which, on his behalf, were later to be connected. However, Aleck did not at the time honor the request of his living brother. He did not read between the lines of the solicited line, and continued his own work without extending a line in his direction. This frozen state of nonresponse was to be the last hiatus in their communications systems. "Aleck and his parents awoke to the truth only upon an urgent call from Edinburgh. Aleck hurried north to take charge of Melly's professional engagements and help [his wife] Carrie with household matters. He found his brother very near death from tuberculosis, though conscious and lucid" (*Bell,* 66–67). He died on May 28, 1870. "He was buried at Highgate Cemetery beside Ted and Grandfather Bell. The news of Melly's death, though no surprise to Aleck, hit him hard. Even in his old age, the look on his face would impress his grandchildren with the depth of his feeling when the tragedy was mentioned. '<u>I well remember,</u>' <u>he wrote several years later</u>, '<u>how often</u> —<u>in the stillness of the night</u>—<u>I have had little séances all by myself in the half-hope</u>, <u>half-fear of receiving some communication</u> . . . and honestly tried my best without any success whatever" (*Bell,* 66–67; italics added). Nonetheless the structures installed by the compact would inform his somnambular persistence in putting up lines between invisible, disembodied voices.

After Melly's death, Aleck's health was fragile. Following Melly's funeral his father grows anxious, demanding Aleck's survival: "His father, more worried than ever about Aleck's health . . . asked his only living son to emigrate with him,

Eliza, and Carrie to Canada. Aleck felt trapped. He remembered later having walked the London streets for a long while that night trying to see a way out. He was now his parents' only living child; he could not let them go alone . . . he felt ties of strong memory and sentiment with his native land. . . . Back at Harrington Square he found the light still burning in his father's study and entered the house thinking he would refuse or at least resist, seeing his whole future happiness at stake. His father and mother sat there silently, holding each other's hand and looking at him inquiringly. A sense of their loneliness undid his resolution, and somehow he found himself unable to keep back words of comfort, which they grasped as consent" (*Bell,* 67). Being the only one left, Alexander Graham Bell became at least three people. Enfolding his brothers within him, the last to carry the patronym, and a certain oedipal regression imposingly suggests itself, save that his parents collapsed into a *single* other, a suffering alterity which could not be left alone. To leave his parents on their own would be to devour their history, depriving them of what was in hope their own, a future of a name, a narrative to guarantee that a certain existence took place in the past. Aleck tried to have the ghost of his consent revoked. He writes a letter to his father, who, however, doesn't let him off the hook. It includes these lines:

The dream that you know I have

cherished for so long has *perished*

with poor Melly. It is gone and for *ever*. **If**

you exult at this please have the

heart not to let me know it. I do not

wish to have it referred to again. Do

not think me ungrateful because I

have been unhappy at home for the

last two years. I have *now* no other

wish than to be near you, Mama, and

Carrie, and I put myself

unreservedly into your hands to do

with me whatever you think for the

best. I am, dear Papa

Your affectionate and *only* son,

Aleck.

"He may have hoped to be let off his promise, but his father took him at his word" (*Bell,* 67–68). The only one remaining, Aleck is taken into parental custody. "A young Australian with a bad lisp had come to take lessons from Melly. In two weeks of concentrated work, Aleck managed to cure him. The young man wrote home: 'I hardly ever now speak the old way though that habit of course had been of twenty-four years standing. Hurrah!' Aleck meanwhile paid bills and disposed of Melly's piano, and conjuring apparatus" (*Bell,* 68). These do not compose indifferent objects of elimination. For inasmuch as Aleck had genuinely wished to communicate with Melly within the assigned horizon of an equipmental spiritualism, then it was to be displaced into a different genre, and the compact can never be read henceforth *à la lettre,* that is to say, according to a restricted vision of a long-distance conjuring. Both the piano and conjuring apparatus were instruments to be, in the Hegelian sense, *aufgehoben* in the telephone, at once eliminated but preserved. Henceforth, Aleck was to honor his contractual agreement according to a somewhat different, more down-to-earth or globalized apparatus of conjuring. In the chapter entitled "The Private World of Alexander Graham Bell," Bruce muses over the grand isolation of the inventor. The scenes set by AGB's gloom relink him to the figure of Melly. The chapter begins by enumerating the multiple communications with which Bell's name is to be associated: "No one word covers all his activities, but the one that covers most is the word 'communication.' It applies to his work as a young teacher of speech, as a phonetician, as an advocate and teacher of speech for the deaf, as inventor of the telephone, as an organizer and collaborator in the development of the phonograph and the airplane, as a frequent and masterful public speaker, and as backer and adviser of key journals in the fields of general science, deafness and geography" (*Bell,* 307). Still, by the testimony of his son-in-law David Fairchild, "'Mr. Bell led a peculiarly isolated life; I have never known anyone who spent so much of his time alone.' Bell's lifelong habit of working alone through most of the night and sleeping through most of the morning; . . . his nocturnal ramblings in woods or on city streets; his hours of solitary piano-playing after everyone else had gone to bed—these were the evidences Fairchild offered" (*Bell,* 308–309). There is nothing to prohibit our understanding of the piano as the continued conjuring apparatus of Melly, with whom in one way or another AGB was always to play a duet, if only carrying the somnambulist's part himself.

The degree to which Aleck's inventions followed upon the steps of a catastrophe, loss, and the event of pain, can be demonstrated along the lines of other de-

vices he was to innovate. One example of this kind may suffice, though you are asked to remember that it remains one among many. On August 15, 1881, while the Bells were summering in Massachusetts, a son was born to them prematurely. He suffered from a breathing difficulty. "He lived several hours and, being strong and healthy otherwise, might have pulled through if regular breathing could have been established" (*Bell,* 316). Since AGB had gone to Washington during that time in an effort electrically to locate the assassin's bullet that was killing President Garfield (in late July and early August 1881), he later assumed a position of culpability toward the expired child and Mabel. Mabel helped him assume this posture: "You might not have gone to Washington, but have stayed with me and all might have been well" (*Bell,* 316). According to the biographer, "Aleck repressed his feelings more sternly, but his actions showed them. He cabled . . . a notice for *The Times* of 'our little Edward's' birth and death. He also set to work on a 'vacuum jacket' machine for artificial respiration" (*Bell,* 316). In Paris, during the November after the baby's death, "having gone with Mabel and the two girls to Europe for change and distraction from grief, he had a French artist paint a small canvas from a young Rockport artist's portrait of the dead infant in its casket, a portrait Mabel did not know had been made" (*Bell,* 316). Aleck's pedagogy was modulated to suit this loss, for he started inducing his daughters to "grieve at the loss of a doll," for "we may take another little one to our arms but it can never take the place of the other. . . . If you were to lose a child through your own carelessness . . . love it and care for it—and treat it so that it should not die" (*Bell,* 316). We have here a direct hit on the uncanny, the doubling of an automaton that stands and mutilates as a sign of the irreplaceable other. Producing a doll, Bell uses a replacement to demonstrate the "irreplaceable." A child, classically lost through one's own carelessness, ought to be treated, according to the pedagogy of the uncanny, "so that it should not die." While Bell suggests a simultaneity of preservation in the language of the hypothesis ("if you were to lose a child"), his recuperative efforts always come belatedly, in the form of equipmental invention and supplement. In time, Bell's Frankensteinean pathos becomes more explicit. In a letter of 1897 he allows: "Suppose that you had been trying for a long long time to stimulate a *corpse*[!]—and had failed after many efforts to get any response—and as you sit with the lifeless hand in yours, grieving over the dear departed—just imagine what your feelings would be—if the supposed *corpse should return the pressure of your hand*!" (*Bell,* 320). Bruce adds this observation, recalling to us that more than one son had perished: "How many times since his sons died had the fantasy of the revived corpse risen in Bell's mind?" (*Bell,* 320). Reanimation governs the equipmental compulsion.

But it was one
corpse, fragmented into
other figures,

and into the figure of others, that supplied the impulse. This corpse never ceased dying serially. In other words, it was never entirely at rest but infiltrated a network of private communications. His sons, named after his brothers, came to double for the deaths that had instituted the abyssal ground of AGB's discoveries. His brothers "lived" in that ground. What remains of these departed fragments of whose galvanized corpses we speak through each day? **In** a sense, Bell was being vampirized by these figures, as his very few superstitions suggest. "In due course he would go to bed, at which juncture he yielded to his once confessed superstition: a fear of having moonlight fall on him while he slept" (*Bell,* 324). The nocturnal inflection of mind was always part of the calculation, something to be averted, like the vague light of lunacy. "He did not attempt to explain the feeling, except to point out the derivation of 'lunacy' from the Latin word for moon. Nevertheless he felt strongly enough about it not only to ward it from himself but also to check the rest of the sleeping family on nights

of full moon  to pull curtains or place screens so as to shield them also" (*Bell,* 325). **(AGB** was soon appointed chairman of an ad hoc committee, one most likely proposed by the eminent bacteriologist and epidemiologist George M. Sternberg, who commented on the spreading of disease caused by spitting on sidewalks. However, AGB was unable to get himself out of bed in order to preside over a meeting in protest against expectoration on the sidewalks of Washington. "Let them spit all they've a mind to," said Bell, with which words "he retreated under the covers and went instantly to sleep again" [*Bell,* 325]. Guided by an instinct of consistency, AGB's gesture clarifies the public exposure of disease shared by the public space of the spreading word as one of the consequences of the public telephone. The telephone has no immune system.) **Like** the figure of Kafka's "Neighbor," AGB was sensitive to telephonic walls to the point of phobia. "In his private study, Bell refused to have a telephone. Indeed, he found the one-sided conversation of someone else at a telephone so distracting that he would not have it within earshot of his work (although otherwise he loved to amuse Mabel and himself by repeating such fragments to her and trying to reconstruct the other side)" (*Bell,* 327). In his later years these facts were elaborated by newspaper reporters to have the inventor banishing his aberrant creation from his house. "This fable amused Bell, and he gave it further currency by whimsically repeating it. Sometimes also, when a telephone message disrupted his plans, he would ask jokingly, 'Why did I ever invent the telephone?'" (*Bell,* 327). After his death, however, Mabel got fed up with the "newspaper notion" that her husband had scorned his great invention. "'There are few private houses more completely equipped with telephones than ours at 1331 Connecticut Avenue,' she protested. 'Mr. Bell's one regret about the telephone was that his wife could not use it or follow his early work in sound,'" (*Bell,* 327–328) wrote his wife after Bell's death. There is something not to be forgotten, or rather, something to be retained within the parameters of this anecdote's cognitive value. The one-sidedness of the telephone in which Bell perceived a difficulty carves a far-reaching side; it includes ha

lf a conversation, ha

lf a head and headset, and not

at all his other ha

lf. In other words, while it has been offered that the telephone was principally fitted to the needs of Mabel Bell, it would appear that the occultic 1331 Connect-i-cut telephone lines were installed for the altogether other interlocution, what we have marked off as the connecting cuts of a pact with the sibling. In the early parts of his biography, Bruce calls this communications network the "tribe of elocutionary Bells" (*Bell,* 14).

AGAINST APARTHEID

If Mr. Bell was a lifelong student of the voice and its double, its filtration and reproduction, he also was a voice against oppression. Again, a theoretical politics should not be overlooked in the implications of letting the other speak. Sadly, Bell's own optimism may have been crushed by systems that monopolize the vote and the voice; yet we would be remiss in omitting mention of Bell's profound disgust with racism in America.

■ The telephonic connection was always meant to cross so-called racial lines. In the constellation mapped by our reading, it foreshadows the philosophic satellite that Derrida has launched against apartheid. Blindly connecting—blind in the sense of justice—technosophical poetics stem in part from an antiracist bent. The telephone responds to what Derrida calls "racism's obsidionality, to the obsessional terror which, above all, forbids contact."[149] Bell writes of an exchange echoed on board a ship bound for America in 1892: a young shipboard acquaintance "in the smoking room talked in rather an insulting and sneering way of the 'niggers' of the South. I replied that I thought the negroes were entitled to equal rights with himself. It looked at first as if there might be some sharp words. The other gentlemen, however, so promptly sided with me that Mr. Kean very wisely allowed the subject to drop and devoted himself to making himself agreeable" (*Bell*, 229–330).

■ Many further examples in the biography show Bell's anxiety over ethnocide in North America, suggesting the radical disavowal of "naturalized" conventional severances between human subjects, which to him were intolerable. Beyond the abolition of the untouchable in race "relations," and his abhorrence of separateness or contactlessness, the case of AGB raises another point—a point, indeed, of contact. The inscription that Bell has made on media technology as a voice-giving force suggests the private formation constituting the suffering other within. In Bell's case, it may be read from the felt predicament of his perished brother. Doubled by his sons, half repeated by his wife and mother who were deaf to sound, the figure of a lost brother (which also recuperates the idiom of black naming) offers individual and unique articulations of such suffering that for the most part denies itself but gets reinvested in an artificial substitute (a doll, a telephone). There is an opening, a wounding for holding the other, for giving voice to the other's suffering and alterity. The wound admits alterity without, however, colonizing the other. The telephone has taught us that the other calls to originate the self. The relatedness to alterity, this audacity of a "reach out and touch" within a space of contact-taboo and wounding is responsible, in the case of AGB, for an activist perspective from which oppression aligns itself with the phantom. In other words, racism cuts into the effect of an externalized phantasmata of incorporation. The other, suffocating within, begins a correspondence with the persecuted historical subject. Aimed at breaking out of carcerating structures, the telephone blasts through prison walls, racial barriers, or the desolation of home. Rescue missions are formed, the "Call for Help" instituted. ■ The politics of AGB's writing ought never be undermined, even if it has been perverted historically by the politics of inanity. ■ Still, the black population of South Africa does not have a telephone line. At the same time, when I hear you, it is only by telephone.

SILENCE

Bell's relationship to Helen Keller, an allegory of carceral isolation, in itself would merit study. For now let it suffice merely to indicate the coherency of his somnambulism, his sensitivity for the suffering locked up in the other, and his desire to make this silence speak. Bell's own daughters, it is said, experi-

enced some jealousy over his attachment to Helen Keller. "For her part, one of her early letters, written a few months after her teacher first came to her, was to 'Dear Mr. Bell,' and it said among other things, 'I do love you.' And more than thirty years later, when he was seventy-one, she wrote him: 'Even before my teacher came, you held out a warm hand to me in the dark. . . . You followed step by step my teacher's efforts. . . . When others doubted, it was you who heartened us. . . . You have always shown a father's joy in my success and a father's tenderness when things have not gone right'" (*Bell,* 404). This extends the primary gesture to isolate, "you held out a warm hand to me in the dark," not so much for its sentimental undertow but because it shows in which way AGB points, to where his being stretches, as if Helen Keller would speak from another place, almost an instrument of the beyond. Things, asserts Bruce, went wrong for Helen Keller more than once in those thirty years, "and Bell was there with a helping hand" (*Bell,* 404). AGB shows his essential hand in the following episode. A short story, "The Frost King," which she wrote in 1891 at the age of eleven for Anagnos's birthday and which Anagnos then published, "was found to echo the plot and wording of a children's fairy tale published nearly twenty years earlier, a story unknown to Annie Sullivan and not in the books available to Helen. It turned out to have been read to her at the home of a friend in Annie's absence more than three years earlier. At the Perkins Institute a solemn committee (Mark Twain in his outrage called it 'a collection of decayed human turnips') cross-questioned the bewildered and frightened child at great length" (*Bell,* 404). Annie Sullivan had been sent out of the room. Eventually the committee was to conclude that Helen had unwittingly summoned the story from her memory rather than from her imagination as she supposed. The ordeal crushed Helen's spirit. She became allergic to books for months and doubted "her own originality for years" (*Bell,* 404).
● The author of the original story, Margaret Canby, wrote that Helen's version was no plagiarism but "'a wonderful feat of memory' and an improvement on the source. 'Please give her my warm love,' added Miss Canby, 'and tell her not to feel troubled over it any more.' Mark Twain was more emphatic, recalling the time when he himself had unconsciously plagiarized a passage from Oliver Wendell Holmes. 'To think of those solemn donkeys breaking a little child's heart with their ignorant and damned rubbish about plagiarism!' he wrote. 'I couldn't sleep for blaspheming about it last night'" (*Bell,* 404). Bell, who had helped Annie Sullivan trace Helen's exposure to the story, saw things more telescopically. Like others, he pointed out that "'we all do what Helen did,' that 'our most original compositions are composed exclusively of expressions derived from others.' But he also observed that Anagnos had

'failed to grasp the importance of the Frost King incident,' and that 'a full investigation will throw light on the manner in which Helen has acquired her marvelous knowledge of language—and do much good'" (*Bell,* 404–405). ● Bell, as usual, intervened to put an end to a parting; he put his pathos of regathering and binding into an event that bears recounting.

In 1897 Arthur Gilman, headmaster of the Cambridge School at which Helen was preparing for Radcliffe College, decided that Miss Sullivan was endangering Helen's health by pressing her too hard in her studies. Having temporarily persuaded Helen's mother of this, he tried to separate Helen from her beloved teacher. Gilman did his best to win Bell's support for the move. But Bell had boundless faith in the wisdom and dedication of Annie Sullivan, and when she appealed to him for help he dispatched his assistant, the venerable John Hitz, to investigate. Afterward Bell wrote Gilman that nothing could justify parting Helen and Annie except evidence that Annie was in some way unfit for her charge; and as to that, his free conversation with Helen had revealed her to be a "living testimonial to the character of Miss Sullivan." (*Bell,* 405)

Mrs. Keller repaired to Massachusetts and, finding Helen in excellent health and determined to stay with Annie, agreed with Hitz and Bell that Gilman was wrong. That was the last time efforts were made to part Helen and Annie Sullivan. ● In January 1907 Helen wired Bell, "I need you." A command to which he was historically sensitive, "Come here, I need you" engaged him automatically. Bell left Washington at once. "She was to speak in New York at a meeting for the blind; but Annie, who usually repeated her speech for those who might have difficulty understanding it, had come down with a cold. Bell left Washington at once and lent his matchless voice to the occasion" (*Bell,* 407). ● The drama naming Helen Keller's rescue unfolds her autobiography, *The Story of My Life*. Supplemented by her letters and those of Annie Sullivan, "it both recounted and attested to one of history's most moving triumphs" (*Bell,* 408). And, tracing her existence in language, it opens on this scene of dedication:

TO

ALEXANDER GRAHAM BELL

Who has taught the deaf to speak and enabled
the listening ear to hear speech from the
Atlantic to the Rockies,
I Dedicate
this Story of My Life

But Helen Keller, too, was a member of the Melville body. The principal movement of thought and invention would continue to bear the name of Melville, however disseminated or concealed the name of the departed brother would remain. When Bell became a grandfather he was most deeply struck by the child named after his brother.

> **It was with Melville, however, that Bell came closest to playing the role his own grandfather had played with him. David Fairchild may have preempted that role with Sandy, whose strong bent for serious science gave his professional scientist father an advantage over his amateur scientist grandfather. By the time Melville Grosvenor was ten, on the other hand, he had to compete with a brother, four sisters and the *National Geographic Magazine* for his father's attention. Perhaps Melville's name, that of Bell's dead brother, touched a cord of memory in the old man. Melville's shyness might have reminded Bell of his own boyhood. And in any case, Melville had a two-year headstart over the other grandchildren. (*Bell,* 459–460).**

Whatever excuses the biographer might wish to offer, the fact remains that his somewhat irreverential prose exposes the possibility, later partially revoked by a logic of "in any case," that AGB was attracted to the name of the child for whom he became his own grandfather again. This return suggests a reappropriation of Melville as his missing own, as himself, the thing to which he became irrevocably connected. As his own grandfather and thus father to his father, Aleck could care for the father, look after him, console him over his loss but also offer himself as the other, the departed brother whose loss moved the minimal family across the Atlantic. The story of Aleck and Melville was to be eternally repeating, Aleck to Melville, Aleck as Melville, his grandfather and himself, all shareholders in the Melville corporation. ● At the risk of repetition—his risk and ours—we can say that Alexander Graham Bell could not tolerate separation. The name of the abyssal catastrophe from which the telephone was cast out, as its monument, was Melville, to whose departure Aleck launched a massively distributed sign of no. The departure of the other, his incommunicability, was a point of radical resistance. Freely translating "Lazarus, arise!" *Come here, I want you,* poses the demand that Alexander Graham Bell inspired into all telephonics. ● And he resisted the departure of the other, even if he was himself the other. Midnight passed, when it became August 2, 1922. At about two in the morning, Mabel was resting on a sofa when David Fairchild felt the dying man's pulse suddenly fade. He called Mabel to her husband's side. Aleck's breathing grew slower and more labored. She spoke his name: and he opened his eyes for the last time and smiled at her again. "Don't leave me," she begged him. His fingers clasped hers with the old sign for no. ● "Even as his pulse could no longer be felt, she could feel his fingers move in the last feeble effort to comfort and communicate." In a sense, AGB continued to communicate after his death; his word was no, written in the flesh of his wife's hand whose lines we have not yet begun to read, crossing like fate's assent. At his death, and after his death, Alexander Graham Bell was deaf; he wrote by hand. He was pointing, or what is called signing. The biographer closes his account in error, given the logic uncoiled by the will of a narrative which the telephone has been weaving. "The silence closed about him forever."

The
effect
of
the
phantom
still
holds
the
line.

Melville
Bell
Grosvenor
is
literary
executor
of
the
Alexander
Graham
Bell
Collection

deposited
with
the
National
Geographic
Society
in
Washington.

Sometimes I absolutely dance with apprehension around the telephone, the receiver at my ear, and yet can't help divulging secrets.

Kafka, "My Neighbor"

Classified

♦ **1. Jean-Luc Nancy,** *L'oubli de la philosophie* (Paris: Galilée, 1986), 56.

♦ **2. Laurence A. Rickels,** in *Aberrations of Mourning: Writing on German Crypts* (Detroit: Wayne State University Press, 1988), 395, offers a line on the yes-saying that accrues to the telephone by treating the postulation of a no: "Freud argues that there is no *no* in the unconscious: instead, things are more or less cathected—*besetzt* (occupied). According to both Freud and Kafka, there is no *no* on the phone." The yes which the telephone calls to itself should at no point be confused with Nietzschean affirmation, however, which requires a double yes threaded through the eternal return of the Same. This is why it is necessary to begin with the telephone as the pose of reactivity—a suspension, as Rickels argues, of the *no*.

♦ **3. Walter Benjamin,** "Berliner Kindheit um Neunzehnhundert: Telephon," in *Illuminationen,* Ausgewählte Schriften (Frankfurt: Suhrkamp, 1961), 299–300.

♦ **4. See the syn**copated drama of frantic telephone calls and incarceration in Janet Levine's "Out of South Africa," *New York Times Magazine,* September 20, 1987, section 6.

♦ **5. The topos of *enervation*** as critical impetus can be situated within a historical typology of mood, or *Stimmung.* The age of nerves, while no doubt beginning to stir in the corpus of Nietzsche's works, has acquired its peculiar heuristic value through Walter Benjamin, who has introduced the "rights of nerves" as a principle of reading and valuation in his essay on Karl Kraus: "He found that (the nerves) were just as worthy an object of impassioned defense as were property, house and home, party, and constitution. He became an advocate of nerves" (*Reflections,* trans. Edmund Jephcott [New York: Harcourt Brace Jovanovich, 1978], 261; *Illuminationen* [Frankfurt: Suhrkamp, 1955]). And if we were to follow a reading that creates a kind of strategic enervation?

♦ **6. *I,* 12 The trans**lation repeats the exclusion of Husserl. The relationship of rumor to a telephonic logic is by no means contingent, as Rickels, *Aberrations of Mourning,* 288, confirms: "*Gerücht* (rumor) is linked etymologically to *Ruf* (call) and even in the sixteenth century, for example, was virtually synonymous with *Geschrey* (scream). That is, *Ruf,* which means not only call but also name and reputation, is related to *Gerücht* which, as a collective noun, signifies a great many, if not too many, calls."

♦ **7. Philippe Lacoue-Labarthe** presented as supplement to his thesis an interpretation of Heidegger's politics (*La fiction du politique: Heidegger, l'art et la politique,* [Strasbourg: Association de Publications près les Universités de Strasbourg, 1987]) which further permits us to understand Heidegger's engagement in terms of the call: "Les énoncés (sur l'Allemagne, sur le travail, sur l'Université, etc.) sont purement et simplement programmatiques et s'organisent du reste en de multiples 'appels' [The statements (on Germany, on work, on the University, etc.) are purely and simply programmatic; these statements are organized, moreover, according to multiple 'calls']" (18). Before considering the question of Heidegger's calls, Lacoue-Labarthe elects to situate a reactivity of deafness: "Etre ou se dire 'heideggérien' ne signifie donc rien, pas plus qu'être ou se dire 'anti-heideggérien.' Ou plutôt cela signifie la même chose: qu'on a manqué, dans la pensée de Heidegger, l'essentiel; et qu'on se condamne à rester sourd à la question qu'à travers Heidegger pose l'époque [To be or to consider oneself a "Heideggerian" does not mean a thing, not more than being or considering oneself "anti-Heideggerian." Or rather, this means the same thing: that one has overlooked what is essential in the thinking of Heidegger, and that one is thus condemned to remain deaf to the question that made its mark through Heidegger]" (16). See also his review of Victor Farías's *Heidegger et le*

Nazisme in *Le Journal Littéraire,* no. 2 (December 1987–January 1988): 115–118, which in more general terms argues that Heidegger's political involvement with fascism is neither an accident nor an error but ought to be treated first of all as a fault in thinking. Heidegger, however, began establishing a philosophical distance to the state in *Introduction to Metaphysics* (1935) and through his *Schelling* (1936), where he very clearly disputes the confusing mergers of the official philosophy of value, the concept of world and lived experience (*Erlebnis*), as well as anti-Semitic discrimination in philosophical thought (particularly in terms of Spinoza). Lacoue-Labarthe reminds us of Mrs. Heidegger's article on girls in the Third Reich, which, if you ask me, is laced with some of Mr. H.'s rhetoric.

◆ **8. Jacques Lacan,** "The Field of the Other and Back to the Transference," *The Four Fundamental Concepts of Psycho-Analysis,* trans. Alan Sheridan (New York: Norton, 1977), 203–260; *Le séminaire de Jacques Lacan, Livre XI, 'Les quatre concepts fondamentaux de la psychanalyse'* (Paris: Seuil, 1973).

◆ **9. A number of** somewhat unmapped access roads to fascism have been discovered by way of the aestheticization of forms in the totalitarian state. An aesthetic will to power has been most recently treated in Lacoue-Labarthe's *Fiction du politique,* where the author discerns the roots of a "national aestheticism." Our decoding systems are engaged here on a more technological register of commanding utterance. We attempt to situate the peculiar idiom of nazism—as does, no doubt, Lacoue-Labarthe—historically after the death of God, when the transcendental ceiling came crashing down and every body was on the line. The telephone installs itself as directory assistance for all other technological executions, asserting a place of a nearly traceless politics of denunciation, ideological clarification (Heidegger on the phone to Jaspers praising the Führer's beautiful hands), extermination. The committee for the Wannsee Conference of 1942, where the "final solution" was passed, depended on the telephone, initiating a whole politics of telephone ordering systems. For a well-considered reading of the Third Reich and general technology, consider Jeffrey Herf, *Reactionary Modernism: Technology, Culture, and Politics in Weimar and the Third Reich* (Cambridge: Cambridge University Press, 1984). The detail of Herf's book is presupposed by our argument, of which two phrases can be provisionally isolated at this time: "Although technology exerted a fascination for fascist intellectuals all over Europe, it was only in Germany that it became part of the national identity" (10). "German anticapitalism was anti-Semitic but not anti-technological" (9). See also Gert Theunissen, "Der Mensch der Technik," in *Der Deutsche Baumeister,* no. 2 (Munich, 1942), and L. Lochner, *Goebbels Tagebücher* (Zurich, 1948), to get a sense of the "pure present" and abolition of History desired by National Socialism. In his review of Suzanne Lorme's translation of J. P. Stern, *Hitler—Le Führer et le peuple,* introduced by Pierre Aycoberry (Paris: Flammarion, 1985), Eric Michaud suggests nazism's desire for disjunctive instantaneity and the technological imperative. The Führer's rhetoric, though full of jarring contradiction (his discourse concerning "the Jews in each of us," his *speeches* against speaking and for pure action, etc.), in its perlocutionary character, tended to stress a "Führer-unmittelbarer Entscheidung," a kind of unbendable immediacy (1030). This immediacy tends to be held together by a notion of magic and the "magic vision" that the Führer attributes to himself and grafts onto technology. Michaud makes a footnote out of this link which needs a magnifying gaze to set it in relief. After citing Herman Rauschning's *Hitler m'a dit* (Paris: Coopération, 1939) on Hitler's surpassingly magic vision which allows him to overcome the Christian God, he adds: "Il est vrai que la technique a permis cette illusion de toute-puissance et surtout d'*omniprésence* divine du Führer: de l'automobile à l'avion, de l'effigie infiniment reproduite à la transmission radiophonique, la technique pouvait donner ce sentiment de l'immédiat propre à la fulgurance de l'action magique, qui dissout les barrières de l'espace et du temps sensibles. [It is true that technology allowed for this illusion of the divine omnipotence, and especially the divine *omni-*

presence of the Führer: from the automobile to the aeroplane, from the infinitely reproducible effigy to radiophonic transmission, technology could give that feeling of immediacy known in the fulguration of the magic act which could dissolve the sensible barriers of space and time]" (1029; trans. Peter T. Connor, hereafter PTC). Michaud links the irrepresentable space of a pure present to the devouring fire of an "immediate action." From this angle it might be offered that, in the Nazi state, even art is submitted to technology to the extent that it has always ever been a "tool": "C'est aussi pourquoi il n'y a pas d' 'art nazi': il n'y a qu'un usage de l'art, de la médiation de l'art et de la pensée pour contraindre les hommes à l'action immédiate, de même qu'il y a, dans les camps de la mort, usage des victimes pour leur propre anéantissement" [This is also why there is no "Nazi art." There is only a use of art, a mediation of art and thought so as to force men into immediate action, in the same way that, in the death camps, the victims were used for their own annihilation]" (Eric Michaud, "Nazisme et représentation," in *Critique: Revue générale des publications française et étrangères* 43, no. 487 [December 1987]: 1034; trans. PTC).

While nazism was phantasmatically invested in technology, a nuance should be signaled: Hitler himself apparently lagged behind the projects and projections of his scientific subordinates. To his comparative "naiveté" in the regime of potential technologies, we seem to owe the suspension in Germany of plans to build an atomic bomb and advances in aviation. The representations which Hitler understood and to which he had access were, in terms of what was projected as possible—if necessary, global destruction—relatively crude and simple. It should be clear that we are not speaking here of the effects of Hitlerian death machines, but merely pointing out his limited technovision in terms of what was asserted to be materially at hand. Laurence A. Rickels's "Final Destination," in *Aberrations of Mourning,* discovers the body counts that will help future researchers link Hitler's rapport to technology with his bunker/crypt (161–162).

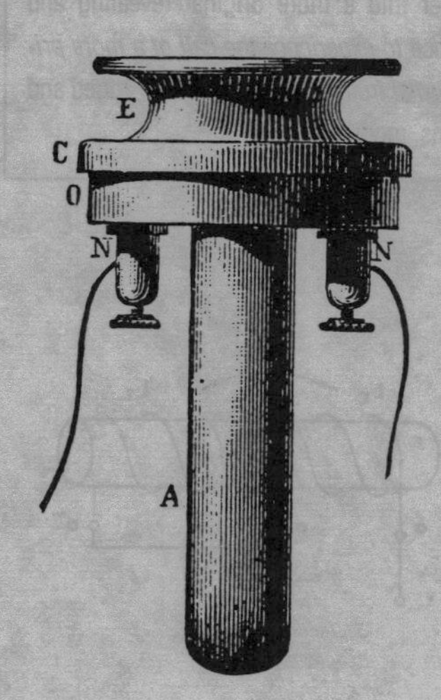

◆ **10. In the section** of his article entitled "Der Einsatz des Mediums: Schalten" in "Pronto! Telefonate und Telefonstimmen" (*Diskursanalysen 1: Medien,* ed. F. A. Kittler, M. Schneider, and S. Weber [Opladen: Westdeutscher Verlag, 1987]), Rüdiger Campe produces evidence for Husserl's telephobic strain. "Edmund Husserl hat das Telefonieren offenkundig nicht geliebt. Der Philosophieprofessor in Göttingen besass (1900–1916) keinen Anschluss, der Ordinarius in Freiburg hatte von 1916–1920 eine Nummer, dann schaffte er sie für beinahe die ganze übrige Amtszeit ab. [This information has been retrieved from state and university libraries in Karlsruhe, Hannover, and Göttingen.] Wenn die These vom impliziten Thema Telefon bei Husserl gehalten werden kann, deutet das auf eine 'hinterhältige Verwandschaft' der Phänomenologie zwar nicht zu den 'empirischen Analysen des Menschen,' aber zum medientechnischen Alltag des philosophen [It was publicly known that Edmund Husserl had no love for telephoning. This professor of philosophy in Göttingen (1900–1916) did not own a hookup; this Ordinarius in Freiburg had a number between 1916 and 1920, but then disconnected it for nearly the entire remainder of his tenure. If the thesis can be maintained that there exists an implicit telephone theme in Husserl, this points to an 'underhand relationship' of phenomenology not to the 'empirical analyses of a person' but rather to the quotidian media-technical life of the philosopher.]" ("The Engaging of the Medium: Switching on [the Line]" in "Pronto!

Telephone Calls and Telephone Voices," trans. Anna Kazumi Stahl, hereafter AKS).

◆ **11. A mode of** revealing, technology models different readings in the so-called early and later Heidegger. *Die Technik und die Kehre* did not appear until 1962 (Pfullingen: Günther Neske), while *Vorträge und Aufsätze,* containing "Die Frage nach der Technik," was published in 1954, also by Günther Neske. By the time of this essay, Heidegger asserts: "Everywhere we remain unfree and chained to technology whether we passionately affirm or deny it. But we are delivered over to it in the worst possible way when we regard it as something neutral; for this conception [*Vorstellung*] of it, to which today we particularly like to do homage, makes us utterly blind to the essence of technology" (*TQCT,* 4). Early in the essay, building his way to the place of questioning technology, Heidegger raises the issue of "being responsible and being indebted:" "Today we are too easily inclined either to understand being responsible and being indebted moralistically as a lapse, or else to construe them in terms of effecting. . . . In order to guard against such misinterpretations of being responsible and being indebted, let us clarify the four ways of being responsible in terms of that for which they are responsible" (*TQCT,* 9). Still, the chief characteristics of technology as that which Heidegger comes to call "the challenging revealing" is that "everywhere everything is ordered to stand by, to be immediately at hand, indeed to stand there just so that it may be on call for a further ordering" (*TQCT,* 17). He calls whatever is ordered about this way the "standing-reserve" (*Bestand*). Whatever "stands by in the sense of standing-reserve no longer stands over against us as object" (*TQCT,* 17). Yet "an airliner that stands on the runway is surely an object. Certainly. We can represent the machine so. But then it conceals itself as to what and how it is. Revealed, it stands on the taxi strip only as standing-reserve, inasmuch as it is ordered to ensure the possibility of transportation. For this it must be in its whole structure and in every one of its constituent parts, on call for duty, i.e., ready for takeoff. . . . (Seen in terms of the standing-reserve, the machine is completely unautonomous, for it has its standing only from the ordering of the orderable.)" (*TQCT,* 17). Near the end of the essay Heidegger evokes the essence of technology in a mood of apprehension, "holding always before our eyes the extreme danger. The coming to presence of technology threatens revealing, threatens it with the possibility that all revealing will be consumed in ordering and that everything will present itself only in the unconcealedness of standing-reserve. Human activity can never directly counter this danger. Human achievement alone can never banish it," and so forth (*TQCT,* 33). This comes on the footsteps of the hierarchical difference that Heidegger has installed to protect technology against another abyssal risk, that of parasitic contamination, or what Derrida calls an "anoppositional differance" (*Memoires for Paul de Man,* trans. Cecile Lindsay, Jonathan Culler, and Eduardo Cadava [New York: Columbia University Press, 1986], 140).

"What is dangerous is not technology, there is no demonry of technology, but rather there is the mystery of its essence. The essence of technology, as a destining of revealing, is the danger. . . . The threat to man does not come in the first instance from the potentially lethal machines and apparatus of technology. The actual threat has already affected man in his essence. The rule of Enframing threatens man with the possibility that it could be denied to him to enter into a more original revealing and hence *to experience the call of a more primordial truth*" (*TQCT,* 28; italics added and trans. modified).

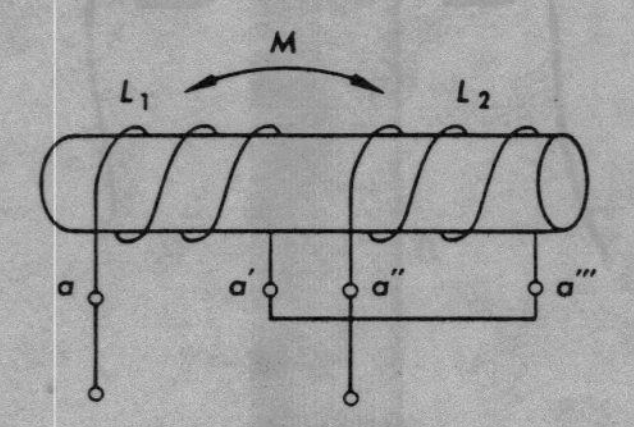

It would be compelling to trace the calls that explicitly are placed in *TQCT,* of which we engage only one instance: the moment in which Heidegger has Plato accepting the call of Ideas for which he cannot claim the right of invention, as he only responded to them. "The thinker only responded to what addressed itself to him" (*TQCT,* 18). One trait that will distinguish Heidegger's later take on technology resides in the *Ge-stell,* translated by William Lovitt and others as "Enframing," which, fundamentally, is a calling forth. It is, writes Lovitt, a "challenging claim," a "demanding summons that 'gathers' so as to reveal" (*TQCT,* 19). I feel that it becomes necessary not to bypass Heidegger's memory of *Gestell,* something that we might assign to the bodybuilding of Mary Shelley's *Frankenstein,* whose "frame" occupies scenes of nomination. Listen: "According to ordinary usage," starts Heidegger, "the word *Gestell* (frame) means some kind of apparatus, e.g., a bookrack. *Gestell* is also the name for a skeleton. And the employment of the word *Ge-stell* (Enframing) that is now required of us seems equally eerie, not to speak of the arbitrariness with which words of a mature language are thus misused. Can anything be more strange? Surely not. Yet this strangeness is an old usage of thinking" (*TQCT,* 20). Even though it is elsewhere achieved in the spirit of denial, there is no reading of technology that is not in some sense spooked, even when Heidegger displaces the focus to *Ge-stell,* at whose basis a skeleton rises. The eerie, uncanny dimension of technology is precisely what engages us, as is the rapport to grief or loss within Heidegger's technohermeneutics of mourning: In "The Turning," writing on the restorative surmounting of the essence of technology, Heidegger uncharacteristically designs a wounding (*wunden*) which is to be dressed, covered over, overcome: "the coming to presence of technology will be surmounted (*verwunden*) in a way that restores it into its yet concealed truth. This restoring surmounting is similar to what happens when, in the human realm, one gets over grief or pain" (*TQCT,* 39). The surmounting of Enframing, as a surmounting of a destining of Being, is precisely what causes us to pause and wonder. Perhaps "the essence" of Heidegger's dream of restorative overcoming might be located in this sheltered allusion to a grief or pain under promised anesthesia. What would constitute the successful mourning but another forgetting? What was this thinking trying to overcome, subdue, and carry over to a convalescent home of Being?

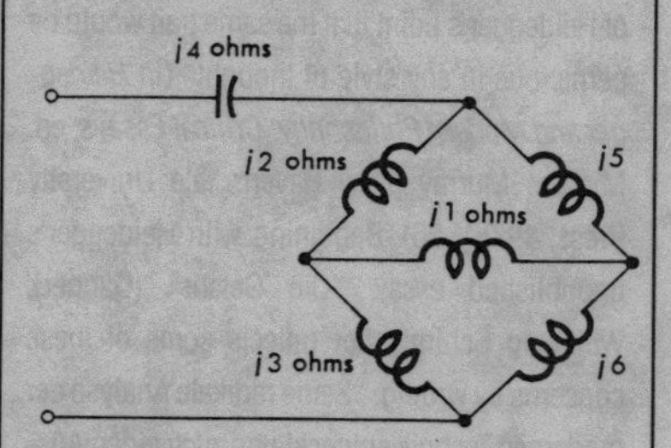

To resume, Heidegger, in *TQCT,* wants to bring to light our relationship to its essence. The essence of modern technology, he writes, shows itself in *Ge-stell,* Enframing. But simply to indicate this still fails to answer the question concerning technology, "if to answer means to respond, in the sense of correspond" (*TQCT,* 23). You see, *TQCT* is itself posed as a call to which Heidegger responds in the sense of correspond. So much is by this time on call: "It is stockpiled; that is, it is on call" (*TQCT,* 15). The split, however, is a bit too clean, for Enframing is "nothing technological, nothing on the order of a machine. It is the way in which the real reveals itself as standing-reserve. . . ." Above all, "never too late comes the question as to whether and how we actually admit ourselves into that wherein Enframing itself comes to presence" (*TQCT,* 24). As if elaborating the problematic within which we, like Kafka's landsurveyor, wander, Heidegger articulates the lesson of discernment now, as if, again, he responds to our call; this time he picks up the relay saying yes, OK, I see your point: "For man becomes truly free only insofar as he belongs to the realm of destining and so becomes one who listens and hears [*Hörender*], and not only one who is simply constrained to obey [*Höriger*]" (*TQCT,* 25). Finally, we note Harold Alderman's conclusion of his essay "Heidegger's Critique of Science and Technology," which ends on a sense of futurity that, once again, promises a beyond technology to which we raise our questions: "We are all finally technicians and if we are to be at home in our own world we must learn to accept that fate as both a gift and a burden. With this acceptance will come the chance of moving beyond technology. Thus the burden of science and technology lie not in their calculative style but rather in their insistent and aggressive spirit. It is, surely, part of Heidegger's point that the same trait would be pernicious in any style of thought" (In *Heidegger and Modern Philosophy: Critical Essays,* ed. Michael Murray [New Haven: Yale University Press, 1978], 50). Beginning with Heidegger's unpublished essay, "Die Gefahr" (Danger), Wolfgang Schirmacher reflects some of these concerns by writing: "Seine radikale Analyse der modernen Technik entdeckt uns auch einen Ausweg aus ihr [His radical analysis of modern technology also discloses for us a way out]." See his impressive reading of how metaphysics fulfills itself in modern technology in *Technik und Gelassenheit: Zeitkritik nach Heidegger* (Freiburg/München: Verlag Karl Alber, 1983), 21.

◆ **12. Albert Einstein,** *The Collected Papers of Albert Einstein,* vol. 3, *The Berlin Years: 1914–1933,* ed. John Stachel (Princeton: Princeton University Press, forthcoming). At about the same time, Norbert Wiener initiated a profound discussion of the fundamental revolution in technique in which he links telephonic theorems to cybernetics. See *Cybernetics, or Control and Communication in the Animal and the Machine* (Cambridge: Technology Press of M.I.T., 1949) and *The Human Use of Human Beings: Cybernetics and Society* (Boston: Houghton Mifflin Company, 1950).

◆ **13. Jacques Derrida,** *Ulysse gramophone: Deux mots pour Joyce* (Paris: Galilée, 1987), 108.

◆ **14. See Jacques Derrida,** "Otobiographies: The Teaching of Nietzsche and the Politics of the Proper Name," trans. A. Ronell, in *The Ear of the Other: Otobiography, Transference, Translation,* ed. Christie V. McDonald (New York: Schocken Books, 1985), 21–22; originally *L'oreille de l'autre,* ed. Claude Lévesque and Christie V. McDonald (Montreal: Vlb Editeur, 1982): "Today's teaching establishment perpetrates a crime against life understood as the living feminine. . . . There has to be a pact or alliance with the living language of the living feminine against death, against the dead. The repeated affirmation—like the contract, hymen, and alliance—always belongs to language: it comes down and comes back to the signature of the maternal, nondegenerate, noble tongue. . . . History or historical science, which puts to death or treats the dead, which deals or negotiates with the dead, is the science of the father. . . . the good master [teacher] trains for the service of the mother whose subject he is; he commands obedience by obeying the law of the mother tongue and by respecting the living integrity of its body" (21–22).

◆ **15. Friedrich Nietzsche,** "On Redemption," in *Thus Spake Zarathustra* (New York: Penguin Books, 1987), 138; *Also Sprach Zarathustra, Friedrich Nietzsche Werke III* (Berlin: Ullstein, 1969), 321.

◆ **16. Nietzsche,** "On Redemption," 138.

◆ **17. Nietzsche evokes** the telephone, a kind of transcendental SPRINT to the beyond, in *Genealogy of Morals*; but already in the stages of foreplay that figure "the seduction of the ear," Nietzsche, in *The Birth of Tragedy,* starts wiring his texts telephonically. In the competition between phenomenal image and the sonic blaze, who would be so petty as to deny the possibility that Dionysus is a telephone? "The Dionysian musician is, without any images, himself pure primordial pain and its primordial re-echoing" (*The Basic Works of Nietzsche,* trans. Walter Kaufmann [New York: Random House, 1969], 50; *Die Geburt der Tragödie, Werke in zwei Bänden* vol. 1 [Munich: Carl Hanser, 1967]).

◆ **18. James Joyce,** *Ulysses,* (New York: Random House, Vintage Books, 1961), 153. I offer thanks to my colleague, Professor John Bishop, for the discussion we had in the summer of 1987, tapping into Joycean telephonics and the absent tense. *Notes from my stenopad:* "Origin of space in the maternal body. Origination,

Genesis beginning: 'Hello Hibernia! Matt speaking. Lucas calling, hold the line.' 'Spraining their ears, listening and listening to the oceans of kissening, with their eyes glistening. *psadatelopholomy, the past and present (Johnny Mac Dougall speaking, give me trunks, miss!) and present and absent and past and present and perfect *arma virumque romano*.' (*Finnegan's Wake* [New York: Viking Press], 258) 'phone man on mogapnoised (technical term for difficulty in speaking). remarkable clairaudience. I am amp amp amplify. 77 saywhen saywhen static Babel whoishe shoishe, (499–500). Priority call clear the line. Joyce talking to son in NY—the devil was playing havoc with static. 'moisten your lips for a lightning strike and begin again. TELLAFUN BOOK.' breaks, ruptures abortive attempts for connection. supernatural access to the world. Television kills telephony in brothers' broil. 'Our eyes demand their turn. Let them be seen!' Cut to Balbec. Proust's grandmother. spectral agents like nymphs of the underworld who conduct spirits of humans into the flickering present. phone as umbilicus. conversation broken off. Premonition of her death. // killer telephones catalyst: bomb explosions. phone-booth confessional: phones within phones. Musil's man. Also *Der Schwierige*."

◆ **19. This was first** emitted in Hélène Cixous's lecture of November 15, 1982, at the "Colloque pour James Joyce" at the Centre Georges-Pompidou, and can now be read as "Joyce: The (R)use of Writing" in *Post-Structuralist Joyce: Essays from the French*, ed. Derek Attridge and Danie Ferrer (Cambridge: Cambridge University Press, 1984). Derrida's commentary runs: "pour relancer ce qu'Hélène Cixous vient de nous dire; la scène primitive, le père complet, la loi, la jouissance par l'oreille, *by the ear* plus littéralement, par le mot d' 'oreille,' selon le mode 'oreille,' par exemple en anglais, et à supposer que jouir par l'oreille soit plutôt féminin. [To bring up again what Hélène Cixous has just said to us: the primal scene, the complete father, law, coming through the ear, more literally *by the ear,* through the word 'ear,' as in English for example, and which leads one to suppose that the ear's coming is

◆ **20. Ernest Jones,** "The Madonna's Conception through the Ear," in *Essays in Applied Psycho-Analysis* (London: Hogarth Press, 1951); originally in *Jahrbuch der Psychoanalyse*, vol. 6 (1914). No attempt will be made to resume this richly connoted essay. Jones addresses the ear and its position of privilege as receptive organ (273), treating among other elements the pneuma that generates thought and semen (298), noise, Christian Logos, and "an old German picture which was very popular at the end of the fifteenth century" (reproduced by P. C. Cahier, *Caractéristiques des Saints dans l'art populaire*, 1867): "In this the Annunciation is represented in the form of a hunt. Gabriel blows the angelic greeting on a hunting horn. A unicorn flees (or is blown) to the Virgin," etc. A second example is even less ambiguous, for in it the passage of God's breath is actually imagined as proceeding through a tube; over a portal of the Marienkappelle at Würzburg is a relief-representation of the Annunciation in which the Heavenly Father is blowing along a tube that extends from his lips to the Virgin's ear, and down which the infant Jesus is descending (reproduced by Fuchs, *Illustrierte Sittengeschichte; Renaissance; Ergänzungsband* [1909, S. 289]), (331). Further along (345) we read: "We are not told whether Jesus was actually born, like Rabelais's Gargantua, through his mother's ear, as well as being conceived through it. . . . That

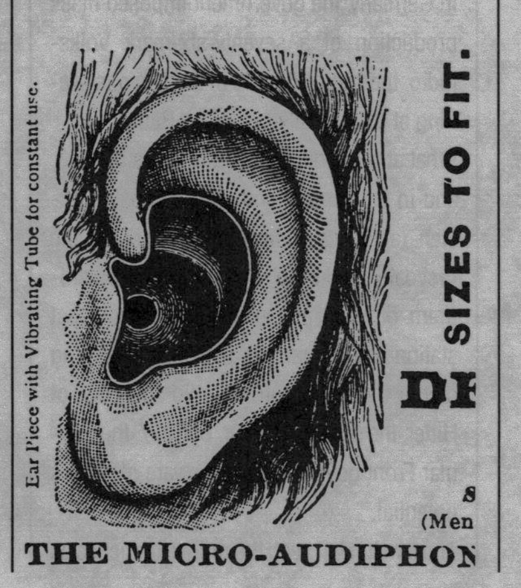

the danger of this form of conception is regarded by Catholics as not having entirely passed is shown by the custom with which all nuns still comply of protecting their chastity against assault by keeping their ears constantly covered, a custom which stands in a direct historical relation to the legend forming the subject of this essay (see Tertullian, *De Virginibus Velandis*)." We have isolated the more telephonically constructed illustration of the ear's pregnancy from which Jones extrapolates anal origins for the immaculate aural conception, the sacred ear overwhelming the repressed body of earlier anal-sadistic zoning laws.

◆ **21. Consider, for** example, Alice Yaeger Kaplan's argument in *Reproductions of Banality: Fascism, Literature, and French Intellectual Life* (Minneapolis: University of Minnesota Press, 1986), where, in a discussion of radiophony, she momentarily smuggles in the telephone. It should be noted that Kaplan assimilates a notion of "telephonocentrism" to a primary model of radiophony, leaving the telephone somewhat out of the order:

> The administrators of fascist radio stations sometimes connected their broadcasting success to real crowd-gathering. In the Italy of the 1930s, Mussolini organized a radio show called the "Workers, Ten Minutes" that interrupted all activity in factories, unions, and public squares. But there were other ways to spread the consumption of sound. In Germany, the government imposed mass production of a seventy-six-mark Volksradio, then sold 100,000 of them in one evening at a nationally organized Radio Fair.
>
> What about radio in the house? As of 1933, and in the same month that Le Poste Parisien (a French radio station) initiated the first daily "wake-up" weather and news program directed at the private listener, that station also began, as part of its morning diet, a translation of the radio speeches of Hitler, the new chancellor. By 1937, the Popular Front government was aware of radio's potential. . . .
>
> The tension between the radio experience as a private experience and as a public one is at the heart of radio ideology. Radio and telephone were the first electrical "personal appliances," the first electric machines to leave the factories and become "part of the furniture." Radio gave people a sense of intimacy with electricity, a sense of control over technology: at the same time, radio's "wirelessness," the invisibility of its method, made it subject to the greatest mystifications. . . .
>
> It is into this radio world, this ideologically vulnerable space of listening, that Rebatet, as fascist reader, receives the texts of Céline. . . . In a prophetic misreading, the American Federal Communications Commission officials who monitored and transcribed the Italian broadcasts didn't recognize the word Céline and recorded it as Stalin, thus substituting a political totalitarian label for what is now recognizable as the quite specific telephonocentric of a French fascist aesthetics. (135–137)

Kaplan points us to Pierre Sansot's *Poétique de la ville,* which describes "the revolution in perception that accompanied the appearance of radios, telephones, and refrigerators in daily life. . . . His distinction is crucial for an understanding of the fascist as someone excited by the extension of perceptual powers that comes with radio-hearing, aerial viewing, and so on" (141).

◆ **22. Maurice Blanchot,** *The Space of Literature,* trans. Ann Smock (Lincoln: University of Nebraska Press, 1982), 32; *L'espace littéraire* (Paris: Gallimard, 1955). Page numbers in parentheses refer to Blanchot's chapter, "The Essential Solitude," 19–34.

◆ **23. Juliet Flower MacCannell,** "Oedipus Wrecks: Lacan, Stendhal, and the Narrative Form of the Real," in *Lacan and Narration: The Psychoanalytic Difference in Narrative Theory,* ed. Robert Con Davis (Baltimore: Johns Hopkins University Press, 1983), 911. Philippe Lacoue-Labarthe "L'Imprésentable," in *Poétique* 1975): 53–95.

◆ **24. See Derrida,** *The Ear of the Other,* p. 10: "Forcing himself to say who he is, he goes against his natural *habitus* that prompts him to dissimulate behind masks."

◆ **25. What is the call** to which Western European thinking is subject? Essentially a call, thinking *qua* thinking names something, calls something by name. By naming, says Heidegger, we call on what is present to arrive. In a sense, *What Is Called Thinking?* presents itself as the drama of an unprecedented long distance. While in the passages we are reading it appears to in-stall something like a *maternal superego* to arrange a call surpassing the child's initiative, it essentially never lets go of the call which, indeed, organizes the very possibility of thinking: "Which is the call that claims man's thinking?" (*T,* 160). "The call as destiny is so far from being incomprehensible and alien to thinking, that on the contrary, it always is precisely what must be thought, and thus is waiting for a thinking that answers to it. We must submit, deliver ourselves specifically to the calling that calls," and so on. (*T,* 165). "What call directed this thinking to begin?" (*T,* 167). "In this address, however, the source of the call itself appears, though not in its full radiance nor under the same name. But before inquiring about the calling that encompasses all Western and modern European thinking, we must try to listen to an early saying which gives us evidence how much early thought generally responds to a call, yet without naming it, or giving it thought, as such" (*T,* 168). "In the using there is concealed a command, a calling" (*T,* 196). "We are trying to hear the call for which we ask" (*T,* 215).

Many more instances of calling might have been cited, but near the end of part 2 of this work a crucial juncture is articulated when Heidegger asks what is subject to the call, a question around which we coil our reading: "does the call which calls us into thinking issue from being, or from Being, or from both, or from neither?" (*T,* 218). Indeed, lecture 1 of part 2 is devoted to the call, to what calls on us to think, leaving us merely to indicate the network of significations (both said and unsaid) on which Heidegger assembles essential calling structures. It would be more rigorous to get you to promise to read this lecture, but I'll let you listen in for verification. "'To call,' in short, means 'to command,' provided we hear this word, too, in its native, telling sense. For 'to command' basically means, not to give commands and orders, but to commend and entrust, give into safe-keeping, keep safely. To call means: to call into arrival and presence; to address commendingly" (*T,* 118). "What calls us to think, and thus commands, that is, brings our essential nature into the keeping of thought, needs thinking because what calls us wants itself to be thought about according to its nature" (*T,* 121). "This town is called Freiburg. It is so named because that is what it has been called. This means: the town has been called to assume this name. Henceforth it is at the call of this name to which it has been commended. . . . every name is a kind of call" (*T,* 123). "In reality, the calling stems from the place to which the call goes out. The calling is informed by an original outreach toward. . . . This alone is why the call can make a demand. The mere cry dies away and collapses" (*T,* 124).

In his letter to Peter Connor, Werner Hamacher elaborates the question of the call when he responds to the literary journal's call for papers, or rather, for an "intervention," what the journal designates as the "appel à l'enseignement."

> Warum wird der Ruf als etwas gedacht, das weniger genommen, aufgenommen und vernommen wird, als vielmehr, sei's von einer bestimmten Instanz, einem Subjekt, einem Prinzip, vorzugsweise einem moralischen, sei's von einer bestimmten Situation, *gegeben* wird? Und wenn jeder Ruf, der da ergeht, einen Gerufenen in Anspruch zu nehmen bestimmt ist (aber auch das ist fraglich)—, ist es schon ausgemacht, dass ich auch höre, dass ich diesen Ruf höre und ihn höre als einen, der für mich bestimmt ist? Ist es nicht vielmehr so, dass die Minimalbedingung dafür, überhaupt etwas als etwas hören zu können, darin liegt, dass ich es weder als für mich schon bestimmtes, noch als irgendwie sonst orientiertes auffasse: denn ich bräuchte nicht

erst zu hören, wenn Herkunft und Bestimmung des Rufes, der Ruf als Ruf schon gewiss, bestimmt wäre. Nach der Logik des Anrufs, des Rufs, des *appel,* und damit der Forderung, der Verpflichtung, des Gesetzes, kann kein Ruf einfach als er selbst seinen Adressaten erreichen und jedes Hören vollzieht sich im Bereich der Möglichkeit, nicht hören zu können, als Aufhören. Hören hört auf . . . : es hört auf etwas wie ein Geräusch, einen Laut, einen Ruf; und so hörend, hört es immer auf zu hören, weil es sich anders nicht immer weiter als Hören, zum Hören bestimmen lassen könnte. Hören hört auf. Immer. Hören Sie. . . .

Why is the call thought of as something which, rather than taken, taken down, or taken in—be it from a specific agent, subject, principle, preferably a moral one—will be *given*? And if each call which issues is destined to make demands on the one who is called (but this is also questionable), is it already settled that I will hear, that I will hear this call and hear it as one destined for me? Is it not rather the case that the minimal condition to be able to hear something as something lies in my comprehending it neither as destined for me nor as somehow oriented toward someone else? Because I would not need to hear it in the first place if the source and destination of the call, of the call as call, were already certain and determined. Following the logic of calling up, of the call, of the *appel,* and along with that, the logic of demand, of obligation, of law, no call can reach its addressee simply as itself, and each hearing is consummated in the realm of the possibility not so much of hearing as of being able to listen up by ceasing to hear (*Aufhören*). Hearing ceases. It listens to a noise, a sound, a call; and so hearing always ceases hearing, because it could not let itself be determined other than *as* hearing *to* hearing any further. Hearing ceases. Always. Listen. . . .

("Interventions," *Qui Parle: Journal of Literary Studies* 1, no. 2 [Spring 1987]: 37–42, trans. Adam Bresnick). As in *What Is Called Thinking?* the question posed in Hamacher's text by these calls does not elude their technicity or technological mutation. At the heart of his calling structures, Heidegger never ceases to raise the question concerning technology; this can occur, however, without arrangements for an explicit hookup. Nonetheless, the contiguity of neighborhoods cannot be pushed aside in what concerns a cartography of the Heideggerian text. Thus lecture 2 situates the call ineluctably within a technological age. Heidegger asks where the machine as power generation belongs: "Modern technology is not constituted by, and does not consist in, the installation of electric motors and turbines and similar machinery; that sort of thing can on the contrary be erected only to the extent to which the essence of modern technology has already assumed dominion. Our age is not a technological age because it is the age of the machine; it is an age of a machine because it is the technological age" (*T,* 24).

◆ **26. Martin Heidegger,** "Letter on Humanism," in *Basic Writings,* ed. David Farrell Krell, trans. Frank A. Capuzzi and J. Glenn Bray (New York: Harper and Row, 1977), 221–222 (trans. modified); "Brief über den Humanismus," in *Wegmarken* (Frankfurt: Vittorio Klostermann, 1967), 145–194.

◆ **27. In "Street-Talk,"** I have tried to show that *après-ma-mort*—a syntax of futural writing taken from Rousseau's *Rêveries*—belongs to a particular instance of truth-reporting that represents a response to rumorological paranoia. Interviews granted to the loudspeakers of public *Gerede* are destined for disclosure after the death of the author as an apocalyptic event, the end as revelation of a truth. These texts are often intended as rumor-control devices aiming to neutralize a proliferation of fabulations around the dead author (Hamlet: "I am dead; thou liv'st; report me and my cause aright"). Rousseau, Eckermann, Heidegger, can be seen to share this kind of project. "Street-Talk" goes back to interview the man on the street who essentially stands to lose his name (*Studies in*

Twentieth Century Literature 2, no. 1 [Fall 1986]: 105–131).

◆ **28. Reliability governs the essence** of toolness in Heidegger, furnishing the grounds of all possible performances. The essence of the tool lies in its use, in other words, its essence is inextricably linked to its dissolution. In his seminar of October 13, 1987, at Johns Hopkins University, Werner Hamacher pointed to the paradoxical logic inhabiting the Heideggerian shoe, which displays a crucial inaccessibility to technical, logical, or phenomenological description. To the extent that it shows itself in and through its *usage,* the shoe, like the tool, offers us no theoretical access whatsoever. It shows itself only when it does not "show" itself but is performing (its task, its service). Hence the tool is as such no longer a tool when considered as tool. This is why Heidegger finds himself in a desperate situation when, as theoretical analyst, he has to "use" the shoe. This would require him to assume something like the place of the farmer's wife, who performs the essence when "performing" the shoe. Hamacher's lecture focuses what he calls "the opening of the tropening of the shoe" in a historical way—a finite way which therefore does not amount to its truth.

◆ **29. Philippe Lacoue-Labarthe,** *Le sujet de la philosophie: Typographies 1* (Paris: Flammarion, 1979), 112–184.

◆ **30. Martin Heidegger,** *Die Kategorien und Bedeutungslehre des Duns Scotus, in Gesamtausgabe,* vol. 1, *Frühe Schriften* (Frankfurt: Vittorio Klostermann, 1978), 195–196; cited in *SW,* 207.

◆ **31. Consider the heights** scaled by Laurence A. Rickels in "Kafka and the Aero-Trace," in *Kafka and the Contemporary Critical Performance: Centenary Readings,* ed. Alan Udoff (Bloomington: Indiana University Press, 1987), 111–127.

◆ **32. Jacques Derrida** reads Heidegger's hand in *Psyché: Inventions de l'autre* (Paris: Editions Galilée, 1987). A grammatology of the

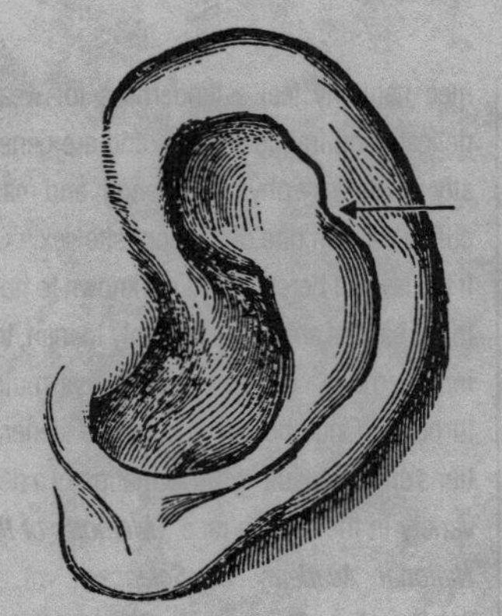

deaf would have to show the resistance posed by the hearing subject to signing and to a general writing that threatens to bypass vocality. The legal history of the deaf would provide an abundant space of reference for this sort of study, recalling, for example, the controversies surrounding citizen status, marital and property rights of the deaf evidenced in congressional records of the nineteenth century in the United States of America. It's not a pretty sight. I should like to indicate thanks to Gregg Lambert for first calling my attention to this metaphysical snag from which the telephone cut loose.

A place to start reading for a genealogy of *scientific* morals might be the introductory remarks in "Upon the Formation of a Deaf Variety of the Human Race: A Paper Presented to the National Academies of Sciences at New Haven, November 13, 1883," which begins:

> The influence of selection in modifying our breeds of domestic animals is most marked, and it is reasonable to suppose that if we could apply selection to the human race we could also produce modifications or varieties of men. . . .
>
> We can see around us everywhere evidences of the transmission by heredity of characteristics, both desirable and undesirable, but at first sight no general selective influence appears to be at work to bring about the union in marriage of persons possessing the same congenital peculiarities. On the contrary, sexual attraction often appears to operate after the manner of magnetical attraction—"unlike poles attract, like poles repel." Strong, vigorous, and robust

> men naturally feel a tenderness for weak, delicate and fragile women, and are generally repelled by physical strength and masculine traits in one of the opposite sex. . . . If the laws of heredity that are known to hold in the case of animals also apply to man, the intermarriage of congenital deaf-mutes through a number of successive generations should result in the formation of a deaf variety in the human race. (*Memoirs of the National Academy of Sciences,* vol. 1 [Washington: Government Printing Office, 1866], 179–180).

◆ **33. In the *Interpretation of Dreams*** (1900) Freud falsely credits Goethe with having written the essay which provided the first impulse toward what he was to call Psychoanalysis. See the dream in which Goethe mounts his terrorist attack (*The Interpretation of Dreams,* vol. 5 of *The Standard Edition of the Complete Psychological Works of Sigmund Freud,* ed. and trans. James Strachey [London: Hogarth Press, 1974], 662, hereafter *SE*; *Die Traumdeutung,* vol. 3 of *Gesammelte Werke* [Frankfurt: S. Fischer, 1968], hereafter *GW,* vii–xv, 1–626).

◆ **34. Mikkel Borch-Jacobsen,** *Le sujet freudien* (Paris: Flammarion, 1982).

◆ **35. Jacques Derrida will** call up the metaphysical spectrality of Heidegger's *Geist* and a humanist teleology in *De l'esprit: Heidegger et la question* (Paris: Galilée, 1987).

◆ **36. See Derrida's** discussion of Freud and Nietzsche in "Spéculer sur Freud" (*CP,* 275–437).

◆ **37. While the history** of telephony grows out of the most eerie of channels, Mr. Stowger's story in fact may be somewhat less spooky than it appears at first sight. The reason he, as undertaker, took it upon himself to invent the automatic switch is that the wife of his rival undertaker was the town operator, and she would transfer all beseeching calls to her husband. Even so, there is no moment in telephone history that is not threaded through the underworld or touched by a wave of demonry.

◆ **38. Derrida takes** apart the implied hierarchy separating off science from thinking in "Acts: The Meaning of a Given Word," in *Memoires,* 108:

> Let it quickly be said in passing that, if we wish to analyze that nebula named "deconstruction in America," it is necessary *also,* not only, but also, to take account of this problematic under all of its aspects. There is no deconstruction which does not begin by tackling this problematic or by preparing itself to tackle this problematic, and which does not begin by again calling into question the dissociation between thought and technology, especially when it has a hierarchical vocation, however secret, subtle, sublime or denied it may be. This leads . . . to our no longer being able to subscribe (for my part, I have never done so) to Heidegger's sentence and to all that it supposes: *Die Wissenschaft denkt nicht,* science does not think. . . . Heidegger marks within this phrase the rigorous necessity of an essential exteriority and of an implicit hierarchy between, on the one hand, thought as memory (*Denken, Gedächtnis, Gedanc*) and, on the other hand, science, but also technology, writing and even literature.

Reading Heidegger's sentence stating that "the essence of technology is nothing technological," Derrida affirms that the thinking of this essence "is therefore in no way 'technological' or 'technicist'; it is free of all technicity because it thinks technicity, it is not scientific because it thinks the scientificity of science. Heidegger would say the same thing of all determined sciences, for example, of linguistics, rhetoric, etc. The thinking of the rhetoricity of rhetoric (within the history of philosophy, a derived and belated technological knowledge) is in no way a rhetoric" (109).

As the title *Memoires* perhaps promises, this text treats the abyss of anamnesic fidelity whose apocalyptic force is filtered through a telephone conversation of finality. The performative death sentence is doubled in the sense that Paul de Man discloses his "tu-meurs!" when calling. The call of the dying friend is lodged somewhere between memory and hallucination, which leads Derrida to write of the inexistence of the past or of death, their *literal* nonpresence:

> Tout cela, comme je vous le disais [on the telephone several days before] me semble prodigieusement intéressant et je m'amuse beaucoup. Je l'ai toujours su, mais cela se confirme: la mort gagne beaucoup, comme on dit, à être connue de plus près—ce "peu profond ruisseau calomnié la mort." (All this, as I was saying to you, seems exceedingly interesting to me, and I am greatly intrigued by it. I always knew it, but it proves to be so: Death repays, as they say, closer acquaintance—"this shallow calumniated stream called death.") This is the final line of Mallarmé's "Tomb of Verlaine."

◆ **39. This constitutes a** major thematic in Rodolphe Gasché's *The Tain of the Mirror: Derrida and the Philosophy of Reflection* (Cambridge, Mass.: Harvard University Press, 1986). See in particular "The Infra-Structure as Arché-Trace," 187.

◆ **40. Lacan,** *Four Fundamental Concepts.*

◆ **41. Gasché,** *Tain of the Mirror,* 103.

◆ **42. Ibid.**

◆ **43. Jacques Derrida,** "Différance," in *Margins of Philosophy,* trans. Alan Bass (Chicago: University of Chicago Press, 1982), 20; "Différance," in *Marges de la philosophie* (Paris: Minuit, 1972).

◆ **44. Lacan,** *Four Fundamental Concepts,* 198.

◆ **45. Jacques Derrida,** "Coming into One's Own," trans. James Hulbert, in *Psychoanalysis and the Question of the Text,* ed. Geoffrey H. Hartman, Selected Papers from the English Institute, 1976–1977 (Baltimore: Johns Hopkins University Press, 1978), 133.

◆ **46. Lacan,** *Four Fundamental Concepts,* 105.

◆ **47. The story of Irma,** her susceptibility to infection and the displaced thematics of childbirth, initiates, in its capacity as "Specimen Dream" (*Mustertraum*), the *Interpretation of Dreams* (*SE,* 4: 106–120; *GW,* 2–3).

◆ **48. While Freud's understanding** of technology, and of the telephone in particular, suggests a stance of cautious inquiry, he at no point assumes an attitude of denial concerning its in-stallment. Far from being disseminated or morcellated into hidden holding patterns of a text, Freud first picks up the telephone as early as the *Project for a Scientific Psychology* under "The Disturbance of Thought by Affects": "For instance, it has happened to me that in the agitation caused by great anxiety I have forgotten to make use of the telephone, which had been introduced into my house a short time before. The recently established path succumbed to the state of affect. The facilitation—that is to say, what was old-established—won the day. Such forgetting involves the loss of the power of selection, of efficiency and of logic, just as happens in dreams" (*SE,* 1:414). Forgetting the telephone's existence suspends the logic of the real where anxiety produces an effect of thought disturbance. And yet, going by Lacan's account, the real is precisely that which is missed like a missed appointment, which would grant this forgetting the reality of the real—the effects on which we are working: the hyperreality of the forgotten telephone (*SE,* 1:283; "Entwurf einer Psychologie," in *Aus der Anfangen der Psycho-analyse* [London: Imago, 1950]).The telephone rings Freud's text again when he delivers rules to analysts. In "Psycho-analytic Method of Treatment," he advises:

> Just as the patient must relate all that self-observation can detect, and must restrain all the logical and affective objections which

> would urge him to select, so the physician must put himself in a position to use all that is told him for the purposes of interpretation and what is hidden in the unconscious, without substituting a censorship of his own for the selection which the patient forgoes. Expressed in a formula, he must bend his own unconscious like a receptive organ toward the emerging unconscious of the patient, be as the receiver of the telephone to the disc. As the receiver transmits the electric vibrations induced by the sound-waves back again into sound-waves, so is the physician's unconscious, which has directed his associations, from the communications derived from it. (*SE,* 1:283).

We should stress that the receiver acts as a kind of translating machine which at no point enjoys a direct line to a logos; in this way we can understand the necessary distortions involved in the physicians' reconstructions of the patients' unconscious. In other words, it would now appear that Freud inserts in the telephone its dose of the imaginary via the Babel transfer. As Cynthia Chase reminded us in her paper for the 1985 Convention of the Modern Language Association, the dream-story of the "Witty's Butcher Wife" takes off when the telephone is found to be out of order and shops are closed. Witty hysterics appear to assert the need for an unsatisfied wish as irreducible. Hence no free wish-flow, no telephone, a butcher for a husband (in French, Lacan takes up the question of *la belle bouchère* in conjunction with the mouth being stopped up—from the verb *boucher,* to stop up, a figurative mouth—which is where the telephone comes in, or this at least is where it might have been connected). Consider also the telephonic overflow into texts about or introducing Freud. One example: Ernst Kris's introduction to *The Origins of Psycho-Analysis:* "Reading these letters is rather like listening to someone speaking on the telephone" (*Letters to Wilhelm Fliess, Drafts and Notes: 1887–1902* by Sigmund Freud; ed. Marie Bonaparte, Anna Freud, Ernst Kris; trans. Eric Mosbacher, James Strachey [New York: Basic Books, 1954], 3). But beyond the telephonics inscribed along the trajectories of Freudian interpretation, one can imagine the telephone as effect of psychoanalytic insight and the eventual need, therefore, for a Psychoanalysis of the Telephone whose range of material symptomatologies would involve hang-up calls, osbcene phone calls, phobias, compulsions (including telephone "sex"), minitels, pregnaphones, car telephones, and other drives.

◆ **49. In terms of civilization,** discontent, and cross-cultural telephone wiring—no doubt setting an entirely different milieu of transmission neuroses—there exists the genre of telephone manners. For an early American example of the telephone book of manners, may I refer you to the work of Emily Post, who provides correctional facilities for the subject of marriage licenses to postal etiquette systems and other engagements:

> LONG DISTANCE CALLS
>
> Of first importance, *don't shout!* [she shouts by means of italics]. When you telephone long distance don't raise your voice. You will only distort it. . . . Speak slowly and distinctly into the transmitter with the mouthpiece about an inch from your lips. Avoid mumbling or hastily running your words together.
>
> When calling long distance, keep on the tip of your tongue what you have to say, say it promptly. Receiving the reply, say "good-by" and hang up. If you have several things to say, write them down and read them off. (Emily Post, "Courtesy on the Telephone," in *Etiquette: The Blue Book of Social Usage,* 3rd ed. [Funk and Wagnalls, 1960], 445)

◆ **50. See Friedrich A. Kittler** on the typewriter in *Gramophon, Film, Typewriter* (Berlin: Brinkmann und Bose, 1987).

◆ **51. Marshall McLuhan,** *Understanding Media* (New York: Signet, 1964), 111.

◆ **52. Ibid.,** 53.

◆ **53. Ibid.,** 53.

◆ **54. Reading "one of Hegel's other voices,"** Jean-Luc Nancy ("*Vox Clamans in Deserto,*" in *Notebooks in Cultural Analysis,* vol. 3, *A Special Issue on 'Voice,'* ed. Norman F. Cantor, [Durham, N.C.: Duke University Press, 1986]) argues that voice "precedes the subject, which means, of course, that it is intimately linked with the subject—and I will agree with you, that voice frays a path for the subject. But it is not the subject's voice" (8). At one point along the polyphonic path, Nancy ties the voice to the maternal breast, which is where we left off. Voice, he maintains, is always shared; it begins where the retrenchment of the singular, unique being begins. (Later, with speech, it will recreate his ties to the world and he will give meaning to his own retrenchment.) Crying out in pure disparity, which bears no distinct meaning, Nancy's *cri/écrit* reads:

—Each voice cries out in the wilderness, like that of a prophet. And it is in the wilderness of forsaken existence, prey to both lack and absence, that the voice first makes itself heard. Listen to what a woman says, a mother. [Making you listen to a woman, Nancy grants the voice of a woman to you, to him, who, preceding him, here follows Nancy: indetermination itself.]

(*Projected on a screen, the face of Julia Kristeva says these words:*)

. . . la voix répond au sein manquant

. . . the voice responds to the missing breast,* or is set off because of the extent to which the coming of sleep seems to fill with voids the tension and attention of waking hours. The vocal cords stretch and vibrate in order to fill the emptiness of the mouth and the digestive tract (in response to hunger) and the breakdowns in the nervous systems in the face of sleep . . . the voice will take over from the void. . . . Muscle, gastric, and sphincter contractions, reject, sometimes simultaneously, the air, food, and feces. Voice springs from this rejection of air and of nutritive or excremental matter; in order to be vocal, the first sonorous emissions not only have their origin in the glottis, but are the audible mark of a complex phenomenon of muscular and rhythmic contractions which are a rejection implicating the whole body. (6)

[*BUT: "when sucking has come to an end, the penis also becomes heir of the mother's nipple. If one is not aware of these profound connections, it is impossible to find one's way about in the phantasies of human beings, in their associations, influenced as they are by the unconscious, and in their symptomatic language" (Sigmund Freud, "Anxiety and Instinctual Life," *New Introductory Lectures on Psychoanalysis,* ed. James Strachey, *SE,* 22:78; *Neue Folge der Vorlesungen zur Einführung in die Psychoanalyse, GW,* 15:84–85).]

Listen again:

. . .—If voice says nothing, that doesn't mean that it doesn't name. It is the voice alone, which says nothing, but which calls out.

—If voice says nothing, that doesn't mean that it doesn't name. Or at least, it doesn't mean that it doesn't fray a path for naming. The voice which calls, that is to say the voice which is a call, without articulating any language, opens the name of the other, opens the other to his name, which is my own voice thrown in his direction.

—But if there are still no names, no language. There is nothing to stabilize the call.

—Yes there is, the voice calls the other only there, where as other, he can come. . . .

. . .—the voice calls the other nomad, or else calls him to become a nomad. (13)

◆ **55. Samuel Weber** offers an analysis of the crisis in phenomenality in "The Sideshow; or, Remarks on a Canny Moment" (*Modern Language Notes,* 88 [1973]: 1102–1133), where he reads by linking castration, narcissism, and the uncanny. Weber's discussion appears to disclose the field for reading the mother telephonically. Since he traces the horizon within which we insert our reading, it may be helpful to cite that moment of discovery when the subject is confronted with the desired object which shows itself to be almost nothing, "but not quite":

> For what the child "discovers"—that is, interprets—as "castration" is neither nothing nor simply something, at least in the sense in which the child expects and desires it to be: what is "discovered" is the absence of the maternal phallus, a kind of negative perception, whose object or referent—perceptum—is ultimately nothing but a difference, although no simple one, since it does not refer to anything, least of all to itself, but instead *defers itself indefinitely*. To use a language made popular by Lacan: castration inscribes the phallus in a chain of signifiers, signifying the sexual difference, but also as the difference (and prohibition) which necessarily separates desire—in the Freudian theory at least—from its "object" (cf. "La signification du phallus," in *Ecrits*, 1966 [Paris: Seuil, 1971], 103–115). . . . The determination of castration not as an event or mere fantasy but as a structure bears implications both for the articulation of the subject and for its access to reality.

◆ **56. Freud,** *New Introductory Lectures*, chap. 1; Lacan, "The Split between the Eye and the Gaze," in *Four Fundamental Concepts*: "That in which the consciousness may turn back upon itself—grasp itself, like Valéry's Young Parque, as seeing oneself seeing oneself—represents *mere sleight of hand*. An avoidance of the function of the gaze is at work here" (74; italics added).

◆ **57. Lacan,** *Four Fundemental Concepts*, 47.

◆ **58. Sigmund Freud,** "Recommendations to Physicians Practicing Psycho-Analysis," *SE*, 12:111; "Ratschläge für den Arzt bei der psy-

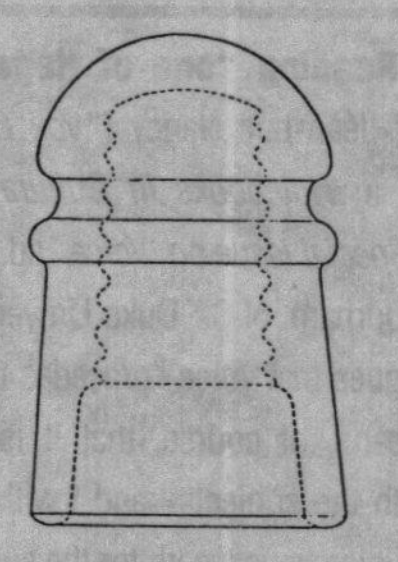

choanalytischen Behandlung," *GW*, 8:376–387.

◆ **59. Sigmund Freud,** "The Psycho-Analytic View of Psychogenic Disturbance of Vision," *SE*, 11:210–218; "Die Psychogene Sehstörung in psychoanalytischer Auffassung," *GW*, 8:94–102.

◆ **60. Ibid.**, 217.

◆ **61. Ibid.**

◆ **62. Ibid.**

◆ **63. Ibid.**, 216.

◆ **64. Also see Jean-Luc Nancy's** discussion of this split in *La remarque speculative* (Paris: Galilée, 1973).

◆ **65. Sigmund Freud,** "The Psycho-Analytic view of Psychogenic Disturbance of Vision," *SE*, 11:216.

◆ **66. Ibid.**, 218.

◆ **67. Juan Antonio Cabezas,** *Cien años de teléfono en España: Crónico de un proceso técnico* (Madrid: Espasa Calpe, 1974), 14.

◆ **68. What does it mean** to respond to a citation uttered "in the name of the law"? This question is raised in Kafka's parable "Before the Law," where a subject responds to a summons that was perhaps never materially issued but

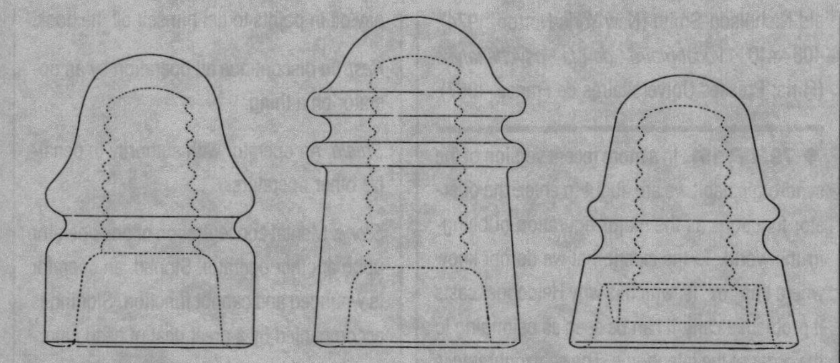

which also never ceases to call one before the law. The parable, inserted in a fold of *The Trial* but also published independently, reminds us that this trial convenes for the purpose of gathering tropological evidence for the hearing, a summons, rumorological terror and the telephone. At one point Joseph K. is summoned by telephone to appear before the law, on a Sunday. The law comes down hard on him, tightening the grip of Sunday's conventional piety and the telephone's ruthless atemporality of appointment. As for the man from the country who in "Before the Law" responds to a kind of Kantian call, he gradually goes blind. Jacques Derrida has elaborated a Kantian imperative in Kafka in "Devant la loi," trans. A. Ronell, in *Kafka and the Contemporary Critical Performance: Centenary Readings,* ed. Alan Udoff (Bloomington: Indiana University Press, 1987), 128–149. In *The Castle,* the telephone rings in another way, initiating the mock substantiality of the title "land surveyor," which K. then assumes. It responds to K.'s claims just as K. responds to the immaterial summons that called him to the Castle territory. The telephone is placed on top of his head. For other operations of Kafka's telephone see Winfried Kudzus, "Musik im *Schloss* und in *Josefine, die Sängerin,*" in *Modern Austrian Literature* 2, no. 3/4 (1978): 247, as well as his interpretation of acoustic-oral motifs at the end of the novel, "Changing Perspectives: Trial/Castle," in *The Kafka Debate: New Perspectives for Our Time,* ed. Angel Flores (New York: Gordian Press, 1977). Jeffrey M. Peck, "The Telephone: A Modern Day Hermes," *CKCL* 12 (September 1985), 3, offers a reading of "*Apparat*" in the polyvalent senses of surveyors' tools, bureaucratic apparatus, and the telephone. See also Wolf Kittler, *Der Turmbau zu Babel und das Schweigen der Sirenen* (Erlangen: Palm und Enke 1985), 7–10.

◆ **69. Peter Canning,** "Fluidentity" (in *SubStance,* no. 44/45 [1984], 40), which pertinently discusses the sado-militarist phantasm, and the drive to pollute and devastate the body of the mother.

◆ **70. Gilles Deleuze and Felix Guattari,** *Anti-Oedipus: Capitalism and Schizophrenia,* trans. Robert Hurley (Minneapolis: University of Minnesota Press, 1983), 88; *Capitalisme et schizophrénie* (Paris: Minuit, 1973).

◆ **71. Ibid.**, 67.

◆ **72. Ibid.**, 131.

◆ **73. Ibid.**, 88.

◆ **74. Ibid.**, 40.

◆ **75. Derrida,** "Devant la loi," 130.

◆ **76. Eugen Bleuler,** *Dementia Praecox oder Gruppe der Schizophrenien* (Leipzig: F. Deuticke, 1911).

◆ **77. Deleuze and Guattari,** *Anti-Oedipus,* 69.

◆ **78. J. Laplanche and J. B. Pontalis,** *The Language of Psycho-Analysis,* trans. Donald Nicholson-Smith (New York: Norton, 1974), 408–410; *Vocabulaire de la psychanalyse* (Paris: Presses Universitaires de France, 1967).

◆ **79. *DP,* 151.** In a more recent version of the syndromic habit we are about to enter, the operator functions as the major figuration of being-in-the world. To the extent that we do not know where this "in" is, which is why Heidegger casts it problematically, it can be seen as belonging to the order of the telephonic. The schizophrenic is the on location of being-in-the world. For the schizo the "operator" is typically in-the-world. Consider in this regard a few vocabulary fragments taken from *Operators and Things: The Inner Life of a Schizophrenic* (San Diego: A. S. Barnes, 1958), 168–169, by the pseudonymous Barbara O'Brien:

> *Operator.* A human being with a type of head formation which permits him to explore and influence the mentality of others.
>
> *Thing.* A human being without the mental equipment of operators.
>
> *Board.* Applied in layers to the minds of things. Serves as protection. . . .
>
> *Extend.* Ability of the operator to concentrate over distances. . . .
>
> *Dummy.* A thing with very little lattice work. Dummys are controlled almost entirely by their operators. . . .
>
> *Block.* The concentration of the operator which blocks the mind of the thing and prevents its location or influence by other operators.
>
> *Cordon.* Blocking the thing by a number of operators.
>
> *Cover.* A device used by operators to work upon a thing's mind without disturbing other operators. . . .
>
> *Horse.* A term used by operators regarding things which can be worked the most easily. . . .
>
> *Hook.* Putting an operator in a position where he must move in some direction or pay off in points to get himself off the hook.
>
> *Rest.* To discontinue all operation by an operator on a thing.
>
> *Shield.* An operator with authority to penalize other operators. . . .
>
> *Stone.* Mental concentration of one operator upon another operator. Stoned, an operator is wounded and cannot function. Stoning is accompanied by a great deal of head pain.

◆ **80. Still, compared with** a hysteric's narration, the one told by an obsessional neurotic is accompanied, says Freud, by an impressive lack of affect. Much like Schreber, Rat Man was always connected to machines of a telephonic order, beginning possibly with the enema treatments regularly administered to him at an early age. The talking nanny behind him, carving a direct line to anality, makes way for paternal insertions arranged around the key word, "rat." We are reminded here of Deleuze and Guattari's suggestion that every *mot d'ordre,* or command-judgment, constitutes a death sentence (*Mille Plateaux: Capitalisme et Schizophrénie II,* [Paris: Minuit, 1980], 135; published in English as *A Thousand Plateaus: Capitalism and Schizophrenia,* trans. Brian Massumi, [Minneapolis: University of Minnesota Press, 1987]). To the extent that "Heidegger" could at all be assimilated to such structures, which technospheric pressures impose upon him, it would be necessary first to determine how the phone call from the top command bureau arrived at him, that is, whether it did not enter itself as a death sentence/judgment/command. For a critical interpretation of these structures see Leonard Shengold, *The Halo in the Sky: Observations on Anality and Defense* (New York: Guilford Press, 1988).

◆ **81. M. Ball,** "La folie du doute," *Revue scientifique de France et de l'étranger* 3rd ser., vol. 30 of the collection (Paris, 1882), 4:43–46; cited in *DP,* 84.

◆ **82. Jung,** *Psychology of Dementia Praecox.* In a recent text on the schizophrenic subject, W. G. Kudzus ("Writing in Translation: Louis Wolfson, Paul Celan," in *Qui Parle*, Special Issue on Paranoia and Schizophrenia, ed. Peter Connor, Adam Bresnick, et al, 1988) delineates "the traces BETWEEN the tongues" which are shown to have some bearing upon AT&T. Rooted in Louis Wolfson's novelistic treatise, *Le schizo et les langues ou la phonétique chez le psychotique (Esquisses d'un étudiant schizophrénique,* (Paris: Gallimard, 1970), Kudzus's interpretation exterritorializes the propositions consisting in "How to cut out of one's mother tongue. . . . How to keep out one's mother tongue." "Labial passage is a matter of life and death. The young man, one reads, drinks a certain type of milk from a certain type of container" (3). Kudzus asserts this vital link that will flow into our dialactate: "Readers are given a glimpse of what they do when they use the channels of communication provided to them by their mother tongue and AT&T" (2). As should become evident in the text accompanying the "dismemberment" of Ma Bell into AT&T "the movement away from mother's tongue is psychotically driven." Kudzus identifies Wolfson's writing as "zero zone writing of sorts; no acknowledged language, little or no sanity, no results. In this process, the beginning and end are less important than the live zone in which writing occurs." See also Gilles Deleuze, "Schizologie," introduction to Wolfson, *Le schizo et les languages.*

◆ **83. Deleuze and Guattari,** *Anti-Oedipus*, 36.

◆ **84. Ibid.**, 85.

◆ **85. It may seem that we** have accelerated too violently against the signified or content of a particular schizo utterance. It is not as if the selection of a particular work or index can be voided of any litcrit reading of any sort. Why is she determined to read Schiller's "Bell" and not another poem, laundry note, or graffitti fragment? In his book *Reading after Freud: Essays on Goethe, Hölderlin, Habermas, Nietzsche, Brecht, Celan, and Freud,* (New York: Columbia University Press, 1987), Rainer Nägele reminds us what kind of massacres take place in Schiller's "Bell." In a context that hollows out the "status of the speaking subject and its legitimation to speak," Nägele interprets: "In Schiller's Lied von der Glocke anxiety creates surreal images of castrating, bloodthirsty women (*Weiber*) who turn into hyenas with the teeth of panthers tearing the twitching hearts of their enemies to pieces" (52).

◆ **86. The phone is dead.** But this precisely is the place of Michel Foucault's particular *écoute*; he conceived of his task as that of reconnecting disconnected telephone lines to those who were, and still are, denied the receiver, which is also a mouthpiece: Is not madness the absence of the telephone? Whereas one could argue that Nietzsche's texts are immunologically active—this is how his "pathos of distance" can be read, if violently, as originating in an immunopathological demand—that they operate within a hygenic of the obsessional neurotic, overly sensitive to stench, Foucault's work solicits exposure or rather enters zoned-off spaces where one is seduced into contamination. If reading Foucault does not produce an effect of scandal, then his discourse has been sanitized, neutralized, expulsed from the filth and aberration which it at one point wanted to let speak. The "carceral subject" could come from Berkeley, the telephone booth, *Zelle,* your *cabine,* or Foucault's *Discipline and Punish: The Birth of the Prison,* trans. Alan Sheridan (New York: Random House, Vintage Books, 1979); *Survieller et punir: Naissance de la Prison* (Paris: Gallimard, 1975).

◆ **87. From Paul Auguste Sollier's** *Le mécanisme des émotions* (Paris, 1905), 4: 208, cited in *DP,* 163.

◆ **88. Deleuze and Guattari,** *Anti-Oedipus*, 84.

◆ **89. One has by now become** so heavily anesthetized by the repetition in contemporary discourse of "always already," that it might be useful to call time out in order to review its sense and strategy. I'll put you through to Rodolphe

Gasché's thoughts on the matter. . . . .

. . . .*Always-already* is an expression that may have found its first systematic use in Heidegger's thinking, where it denotes both the temporal mode of the fore-understanding in which the meaning of Being is available to the *Dasein,* and the specific mode of anteriority in which Being claims man. *Always-already* names something prior to, and it thus seems to correspond to the formal determination of the *a priori.* To speak of *always-already* rather than of *a priori* becomes a necessary move, however, when, as in Heidegger, the temporal character of Being itself is at stake. The *a priori,* which in the ontological tradition serves to denote the determinations of Being, contains the idea of a temporal succession in a very pallid way at best. In Heidegger's thinking, therefore, the *always-already* stands for a temporal priority, which, as that of Being, has nothing to do with time as it is known according to its vulgar concept.

Always-already is put to a similar use in Derrida's philosophy, where it designates the temporal mode of a certain accidentality, contingency, and supplementarity shown to be "constitutive" of presence and essence. Presence and essence within the metaphysical tradition, as Husserl has demonstrated, presuppose the fundamental form of idealization that is the "always again" (*immer wieder*). Whereas this structure accords a privileged position to the protentional dimension of intentionality, Derrida's use of the *always-already* focuses on an anteriority that is, rather, of the order of the retentional dimension of intentionality. But if the *always-already* in Derrida stands for a past and a passivity older than presence and essence, this does not mean that Derrida simply privileges retention. In the same manner that Heidegger's *always-already* names a temporality that is radically different from the vulgar concept of time, Derrida's *always-already* points at a radical past, at an absolute past and passivity that can never be fully reactivated and awakened to presence. Yet, if the absolute past of the *always-already* effaces itself and is from the outset in retreat, it nonetheless leaves a mark, a signature that is retraced in the very thing from which it is withdrawn, that the essence or the presence that it constitutes is this past's belated reconstitution. What is *always-already* has never, and can never, be present itself. The very possibility of essence and presence hinges on such a past, according to Derrida.

The *always-already* is thus not mere wordplay or the result of linguistic infatuation. It is an expression that implies an anteriority to essence and presence, that not only would no longer be a determination *of* Being, as is the *a priori,* but that would also take priority *over* Being: if, as Derrida contends, Heidegger's radical temporality of Being is still caught in the vulgar concept of time that it was supposed to displace, the radical past to Being could no longer be altogether of the order of Being. The specific nature of the time of the quiddity of that past hinted at by Derrida understands Being itself from the past (and not only beings, as in the case of Heidegger). (Rodolphe Gasché, introduction to Andrzej Warminski, *Readings in Interpretation: Hölderlin, Hegel, Heidegger* [Minneapolis: University of Minnesota Press, 1987], x–xi).

◆ **90. Walter Benjamin's DC** in the essay "The Destructive Character," in *Reflections,* clears the way, creating the "cardiac strength" according to which Benjamin paced himself and all urgent writing. The DC is a signal that does not, however, need to be understood (understand me, love me, feed me, put me to bed: this chain of demand belongs to the creature of *ressentiment*). I have tried to handle this in "Street-Talk," see above, n. 27.

◆ **91. Philippe Lacoue-Labarthe,** *La poésie comme expérience* (Paris: Bourgois, 1986).

◆ **92. Heidegger,** *TQCT,* xv. Indeed, how scandalous is this thing? We need to bear in mind that Being is given in ways which are modified by age and the understanding-of-Being allotted to the Dasein: as ousia, entelecheia, actualitas, position, absolute Idea, Geist, and in the modern world, in alignment with Heidegger's later thinking, in the charge of Gestell. In *Die Grundprobleme der Phänomenologie* (Frankfurt: Vittorio Klostermann, 1975), Heidegger is perhaps more explicit than in *Sein und Zeit* as to the understanding of ourselves beginning with things that confront and distress us in everyday life. In a crucial passage devoted to "Dasein's factical everyday understanding of itself as reflection from the things with which it is concerned," he offers:

> We say that the Dasein does not first need to turn backward to itself as though, keeping itself behind its own back, it were at first standing in front of things and staring rigidly at them. Instead, it never finds itself otherwise than in the things itself, and in fact in those things that daily surround it. It finds *itself* primarily and constantly *in things* because, tending them, distressed by them, it always in some way or other rests in things. Each one of us is what he pursues and cares for. In everyday terms, we understand ourselves and our existence by way of the activities we pursue and the things we take care of. We understand ourselves by starting from them because the Dasein finds itself primarily in things. The Dasein does not need a special kind of observation, nor does it need to conduct a sort of espionage on the ego in order to have the self; rather, as the Dasein gives itself over immediately and passionately to the world itself, its own self is reflected to it from things. This is not mysticism and does not presuppose the assigning of soul to things. It is only a reference to an elementary phenomenological fact of existence, which must be seen prior to all talk, no matter how acute, about the subject-object relation. In the face of such talk we have to have the freedom to adapt our concepts to this fact and, conversely, not shut ourselves off from the phenomena by a framework of concepts. It is surely a remarkable fact that we encounter ourselves, primarily and daily, for the most part by way of things and are disclosed to ourselves in this manner in our own self. Ordinary understanding will rebel against this fact. As blind as it is nimble, it will say: That is simply not true and cannot be true; this can be clearly demonstrated.

Sure, this reading of the way we go through things may be on the side of the inauthentic. But things are not so simple. The inauthentic is not simply negative:

> This inauthentic self-understanding of the Dasein's by no means signifies an ungenuine self-understanding. On the contrary, this everyday having of self within our factical, existent, passionate merging into things can surely be genuine, whereas all extravagant grubbing about in one's soul can be in the highest degree counterfeit or even pathologically eccentric. The Dasein's inauthentic understanding of itself is neither ungenuine nor illusory, as though what is understood by it is not the self but something else, and the self only allegedly. Inauthentic self-understanding experiences the authentic Dasein as such precisely in its peculiar "actuality," if we may so say, and in a genuine way.

The Dasein must be *with* things. We have been exploring the radical possibilities for the dwelling-*with* that things disclose to us. I would like to thank M. A. Greco for bringing to my attention Heidegger's intentionality of comportments toward things as demonstrated in the above quotations from *The Basic Problems of Phenomenology,* trans. Albert Hofstadter (Bloomington: Indiana University Press, 1988), 159–161. For a discussion of the technical manipulation of the thing and what Heidegger calls "Zuhandenheit," see Pierre Alféri, *Guillaume D'Ockham. Le Singulier* (Paris: Les Éditions de Minuit, 1989), 139ff.

◆ **93. Of course not.** But check out the works of poet, essayist, animal trainer Vicki Hearne to be sure. See especially "How to Say Fetch" and other telephonically informative systems in *Adam's Task: Calling Animals by Name* (New York: Random House, Vintage Books, 1987).

◆ **94. Cf. the way Jacques Derrida** manages the structure of "allegory" in *Memoires for Paul de Man.*

◆ **95. Swimming. It creates** a sonic space, a trace-making pad from which so much has been launched without, as it were, making too much of a splash. The swimming pool functions as a specially telling sonic space in figuring the deaf, as for instance occurs in the film *Children of a Lesser God.* I wanted to consider both ears separately in order to deconstruct, in this place at least, the guarantees we might think we have about being entirely hearing; one of the ears plunges into deafness—a problem which would have created possibly more waves when rights were being balanced for the deaf subjects of this nation. AGB fought to have the deaf officially listed under a category held distinct, in our houses of Congress, from the space of the "feeble-minded." Swimming. I think of Johannes Peter Eckermann, Goethe's transmitter in *Conversations with Eckermann,* for whom swimming laps into writing. Also of *What Is Called Thinking?* "We shall never learn what 'is called' swimming, for example, or what it 'calls for,' by reading a treatise on swimming. Only the leap into the river tells us what is called swimming"(21). Or of Jean-François Lyotard on swimming in "Several Silences," in *Driftworks,* Semiotext(e) Series (New York: Columbia University Press, 1984), 90–110.

◆ **96. A study still remains** to be written on Frankenstein and electric circuitry. The novel goes along the lines of a felt split between art and science, sexual difference and the mother's unmournable death. (When he takes leave of the city Victor visits the graveyard—everybody's resting there, but no mention of mother.) Electricity and the phantasm of reanimation. See Peter Haining, *The Man Who Was Frankenstein* (London: Frederick Muller, 1979). Read it. It focuses the electrician who turned Mary Shelley on: Andrew Crosse. On electricity and melancholia, for instance: "To a degree, this company lifted Andrew Crosse out of the mood of melancholy brought on by his mother's death, and there are indications he began to start playing jokes again with electrical machines" (37). Moreover, the monsterized figure, often going under the name of "the frame" may be read as a frame literalized in the sense of *Ge-Stell.*

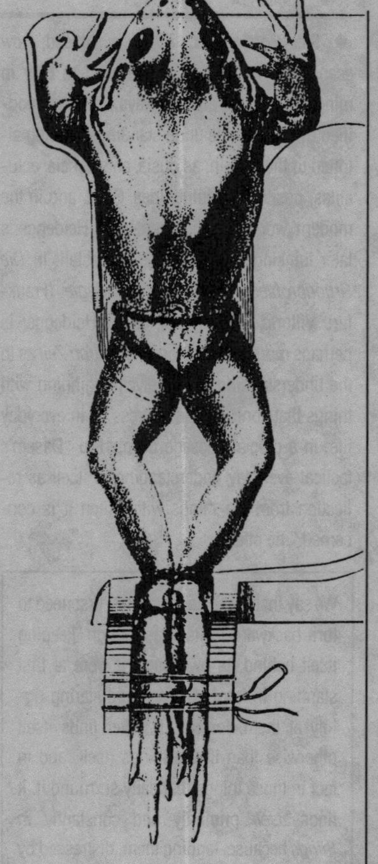

◆ **97. See Albert Hofstadter's** introduction to *Poetry, Language, Thought* on "thinking that responds and recalls" (*P,* xi). See also n. 11, which links *Gestell* to its skeletal basis.

◆ **98. Jacques Derrida,** *Truth in Painting,* trans. Geoff Bennington and Ian McLeod (Chicago: University of Chicago Press, 1987); *La verité en peinture* (Paris: Flammarion, 1978).

◆ **99. Cf. Alexander Graham Bell's** Heideggerian poetry of communication with the earth:

> Mr. Bell went on to describe instances in which airs sung or played upon a musical instrument are transmitted by a telephone, when it is not known whence they come; but the strongest proof of the extraordinary sensibility of this instrument consists in its becoming possible by its means to transmit speech through bodies which might be supposed to be non-conductors. The communication with the earth through the human body can be made in spite of the intervention of shoes and stockings; and it may even be affected if, instead of standing on the ground, the person stands on a brick wall. Only hewn stone and wood are a sufficient hindrance to communication, and if the foot touches the adjoining ground, or even a blade of grass, it is enough to produce electric manifestations. (Théodose Achille Louis Du Moncel, *The Telephone, the Microphone, and the Phonograph* [*TMP*, 55].)

◆ **100. Sarah Kofman** has interpreted this Freudian figure of the all too self-sufficient woman ingrowing the narcissistic complex in *The Enigma of Woman: Woman in Freud's Writings,* trans. Catherine Porter (Ithaca: Cornell University Press, 1985); *L'enigme de la femme: La femme dans les textes de Freud* (Paris: Galilée, 1980).

◆ **101. Heidegger,** *TQCT,* 13.

◆ **102. Ibid.**

◆ **103. In Woody Allen's film** of collapsed media (*The Purple Rose of Cairo*), the single object that traverses both asserted worlds is a white telephone which plays out its potential as that which engages inner and outer dimensions simultaneously, the real and the fictive. Cinema went for the telephone without reservation, at times assigning to it lines of an enigmatic theater of visible speech. It is a rare thing on camera, particularly in the case of television, for anyone, when hanging up the phone, to utter a "goodbye." The call interrupts narrative without granting itself closure. The telephone inevitably tends to participate in a scene metonymically to call up a death sentence; it is a commanding machine of terroristic performative competence. Alfred Hitchcock's *Dial M for Murder:* **"That has a pretty guilty ring to it."** / "It's delayed action" (Bob Cummings). Or the hanging phone culminates in having the character juridically declared to hang. See also John Auerbach's *The Phone Call,* wherein the one who picks up the phone finds herself under orders to kill. She fulfills the command. Turns out to have been a wrong number. In this light consider also *Lady in a Cage, Pennsylvania 6–5000, The Man who Envied Women,* and Kurosawa's *High and Low,* as well as the entire gamut of the *Poltergeist* series and spin-offs. For the sheerly electric conjunction, *Cell 2455: Death Row* furnishes a good example of imaging two pieces of technology together: the electric chair and the telephone. At the scheduled moment of execution, the electrocutee is intended to receive pardon, but the governor's secretary doesn't get through on time, having dialed a wrong number.

◆ **104. *P,* 112. In the** culture of philosophy, the reference to "a new value theory" signals a compelling gap that holds Heidegger at a distance from competing currencies deposited by National Socialist philosophers. In the first draft of his paper "The Meeting at Magdeburg: German Philosophy in 1933" (University of California, Berkeley, January 1988, typescript), the philosopher Hans Sluga focuses *Wertphilosophie* in order to analyze the relationship of German philosophy as a whole to that of National Socialism. Examining the principles of the Deutsche Philosophische Gesellschaft (DPG), a philosophical society that existed from 1917 until the end of the Second World War, Sluga discovers a spectrum of philosophical positions informing "1933." Heidegger was, he argues, "by no means the only German philosopher who became entangled with National Socialism. The involvement of the DPG and its leading members—all of them established academics—with Nazism was in any case more public and more official than Heidegger's. From the perspective of the DPG Heidegger was, in fact, almost something like an outsider; as a result, one of his students found reason to complain in the *Blätter* in 1942 that it had become 'fashionable to dismiss Heidegger in a disrespectful manner as a phenomenon of a past epoch' " (22).

While Sluga maintains that Heidegger was, when compared with the DPG, "after a quite different and deeper critique of the technological age," he allows: "It was then not strictly speaking the issue of technology that separated Heidegger from the DPG" (23). "Technology and the crisis of technology were themes often enough discussed in the pages of the *Blätter*. Prominent members of the DPG such as Hans Freyer and Hermann Glockner were, in fact, also leading philosophers of technology and continued to play that role in post-war Germany. The idea that the contemporary crisis, on whose reality they all agreed, was a crisis of technology and of technological thinking was indeed a common doctrine among conservative German thinkers in the first half of the twentieth century." See also "Artificial Limbs. Functionalist Cynicisms II: On the Spirit of Technology," in Peter Sloterdijk, *Critique of Cynical Reason,* trans. Michael Eldred (Minneapolis: University of Minnesota Press, 1987), 450 and passim, on the *Homo prostheticus* as a storm trooper itching for action, the Fourth Reich, Hans Freyer, the technology of the likable Nazi, and Friedrich Dessauer's *Philosophie der Technik. Das Problem der Realisierung* (Philosophy of technology: The problem of realization), which promises a "critical metaphysics" of technology. (Originally published as *Kritik der zynischen Vernunft* [Frankfurt: Suhrkamp, 1983].)

When Heidegger became disenchanted with the destinal promise of the National Socialist revolution, he began to assimilate its movement to a reading of error and technology.

In his introduction to *Poetry, Language, Thought,* Hofstadter similarly evokes the hollowness of the technological age when consulting the task of the poet. For Heidegger, he writes, citing Hölderlin, this "time of technology is a destitute time, the time of the world's night, in which man has even forgotten that he has forgotten the true nature of being. In such a dark and deprived time . . ." (xv). This is why we are traveling the path of technological light, for however nuanced and "deep" Heidegger's encounter with technology may be, its effects, as well as the context of its expression, propose peculiar acts of self-blinding which the telephone writes out for us.

◆ **105. Cf. Jacques Derrida's** discussion of the towers of Babel in *The Ear of the Other,* 152, where the subject, as in our case, is translation. Working through something like "telephone" always involves an element of spiraling transpositions, a translative vertigo. "What did you say? Are you still there?" signal the fact that translational activities govern the milieu of all telephonic utterances, doubling the translation of sound waves back into voice simulation: "the so-called original is in a position of demand with regard to the translation. The original is not a plenitude which would come to be translated by accident. The original is in the situation of demand, that is, of a lack or exile. The original is indebted a priori to the translation. Its survival is a demand and a desire for translation, somewhat like the Babelian demand: Translate me." See also "Des tours de Babel," trans. Joseph F. Graham, in *Difference in Translation,* ed. Joseph F. Graham (Ithaca: Cornell University Press, 1985), 165–209.

◆ **106. We think we know** where the mouth is, what it does, how to circumscribe this gap whose piercing watchdogs are armed to the teeth. Maybe we do "know," if knowing includes the unconscious habitat or a reading of Kant. Still, it poses problems. Neither quite inside nor entirely on the outer side of the body, a place of expulsion or incorporation, the mouth cannot be said to be locatable within a topology of the body. Lacan reminds us somewhere of Freud's decision to envisage masturbation as a mouth kissing itself, the place of a total receiver in touch with its rim. And we haven't even begun to talk of the tongue, be it native, mother, or tasting. Gregory L. Ulmer opens a discussion on the hollows of the body, its resonating chambers (ear and vagina, mouth and rectum), in *Applied Grammatology: Post(e)-Pedagogy from Jacques Derrida to Joseph Beuys* (Baltimore: Johns Hopkins University Press, 1985), 57–62:

> Part of the interest of drawing on theories of orality (as the first libidinal experience, it forever marks desire, determining the nature of our satisfaction and dissatisfaction) for the deconstruction of the philosophemes is that against the appropriation of all other senses by sight in Plato's use of *eidos,* "psychoanalysis reveals that in childhood phantasms this mode is not attached solely to oral activity but that *it may be transposed to other functions* (e.g. respiration, sight)" (Laplanche and Pontalis, 288). Moreover, in support of a methodology attempting to theorize (epithymize) repulsion, this stage includes an "oral-sadistic" phase concurrent with teething in which the activity of biting and devouring implies a destruction of the object; "as a corollary of this we find the presence of the phantasy of being eaten or destroyed by the mother" ([Laplanche and Pontalis, *The Language of Psychonalysis*] 288).

It seems necessary to engage oneself on this line if only to observe that, while the telephone may call up the spitting image of the father—this will be at issue with the Bell paradigm—the mouth is related, according to several essential filiations, to the maternal. Thus beyond, or with, the Joycean umbilicus, there is always the issue of the mouth, which throws up the activity of what we have gathered as the maternal superego. This threatens to bite, devour, destroy, but also to be bitten, devoured, and to pacify. In Watson's case you have to go further down the buccal cavity to find the father. His force erupts in the swallowing disorders documented in the autobiography.

◆ **107. In "Devant la loi,"** Jacques Derrida cites Hegel's exposition of the empty nature of the tabernacles whose "location" is the same placeless topic, an abstaining nothing: "Hegel narrates a story about Pompey, narrating it in his own way. Curious to know what was behind the doors of the tabernacle that housed the holy of holies, the triumvir approached the innermost part of the temple, the center (*Mittelpunkt*) of worship." There, says Hegel, he sought "a being, an essence offered to his meditation, something meaningful (*sinnvoll*) to command his respect; and when he thought he was entering into the secret (*Geheimnis*) before the ultimate spectacle, he felt mystified, disappointed, deceived (*getäuscht*). He found what he sought in "an empty space" and concluded from this that the genuine secret was itself entirely alien and extraneous to them, the Jews; it was unseen and unfelt (*ungesehen und ungefühlt*)" (143).

◆ **108. The assignment of** aberrations to acoustics owes its prominence in "the science of sound" of the nineteenth century to earlier works, such as Ernst Florens Friedrich Chladni's *Entdeckungen über die Theorie des Klanges* in 1787 and *Die Akustik* (1802). Thomas Young, in particular, began investigating the phenomena of interference shortly thereupon, followed by Wilhelm Ernst, and Eduard Weber who, dedicating their works to Chladni, produced *Wellenlehre auf Experimente gegründet, oder über die Wellen tropfbarer Flüssigkeiten mit Anwendung auf die Schall- und Lichtwellen* (Science of waves based on experiments, or on the wave of nonviscous fluids with application to sound and light waves; 1825). In addition, see H. Matthews, *Observations on Sound* . . . (1826); Sir Charles Wheatstone's *Experiments in Audition* . . . (1827), the numerous investigations of Jean Baptiste Joseph Fourier, Georg Simon Ohm, and Christian Johann Doppler; and Franz Melde's important *Lehre von Schwingungscurven* (Science of oscillation curves; 1864). In the foreword to *Observations on Sound,* Matthews writes:

> The author, reflecting on the nature of sound, has discovered that the kind of buildings used as churches, chapels, courts of justice or other places in which sound should be of the first consideration, are by

> no means adapted to convey it distinctly. . . . The valuable time and patience of the courts of justice need not (at present) be unprofitably exhausted in the vain endeavor to comprehend the indistinct utterances of witnesses;—the almost impossibility of which frequently turns the stream of justice out of its proper course. . . . Improvement in the science of sound is of consequence as respects a still more sacred subject than even justice itself—Divine Knowledge. . . . Echo does not politely wait until the speaker has done; but the moment he begins, and before he has finished a word, she mocks him with ten thousand tongues.

One discussion of such passages, which sounds a note of schizoanalysis, occurs in an article by Wolfgang Scheres "Im Vorwort . . . schreibt Matthews von den buchstäblichen Deterritorialisierungen, die Sound dort vornimmt, wo eigentlich Recht gesprochen gehörte (In his foreword, Matthews writes of the literal deterritorializations induced by sounds that replace the proper pronouncement of law) ["Klaviaturen, Visible Speech und Phonographie: Marginalien zur technischen Entstellung der Sinne im 19. Jahrhundert" (Keyboards, visible speech, and phonography: Marginal notes on the technical distortion of the senses in the 19th century), *Diskursanalysen* 1 (1987): 43–44]).

Of course AGB had things to say about the telephone's noise production as well, which, rather than seeming wholly "random" appears instead to mark the moment of the instrument's greatest autonomy and asserts the dimension of a kind of "transcendental noise." Compare the following statement, if you will, with Kafka's noise reception in *The Castle*:

> When a telephone is placed in a circuit with a telegraph line, the telephone is found seemingly to emit sounds on its own account. The most extraordinary noises are often produced, the causes of which are at present very obscure. One class of sounds is produced by the inductive influence of neighboring wires and by leakage from them, the signals of the Morse alphabet passing over neighboring wires being audible in the telephone, and another class can be traced to earth currents upon the wire, a curious modification of this sound revealing the presence of defective joints in the wire.
>
> Professor Blake informs me that he has been able to use the railroad track for conversational purposes . . . and Professor Pierce has observed the most curious sounds produced from a telephone in connection with a telegraph-wire during the aurora borealis. (*TMP*, 55)

In *Aufschreibsysteme* 1800/1900 (Munich: Wilhelm Fink, 1985), Friedrich A. Kittler connects Nietzsche himself to the noise machine when he allows that the philosopher has shown a special sensibility for random noise. Designating Nietzsche as somewhat of a telephonic apparatus hooked into his own writing, Kittler argues:

> Nietzsche aber schreibt vor und nach weissem Rauschen. So wörtlich erreicht ihn der Appell deutscher Aufsätze, "eigne Gedanken und Gefühle zu belauschen," dass Gedanken und Gefühle in ihr Gegenteil umschlagen: Der Lauscher hört ein "Summen und Brausen der wilden Partein," die in ihm den unschlichbaren, "Bürgerkrieg zweier Heerlager" ausfechten. Wo eine vorsprachliche, aber zu Artikulation und Bildung fähige Innerlichkeit stehen müsste, ist alles nur, "als ob ein Rauschen durch die Luft ginge." Der schauderhaft unartikulierte Ton, den Nietzsche in seinem Rücken hört, summt also in den Ohren selber . . . [p.] 189.

Nietzsche writes, however, before and after white noise. So literally does the call of German essays reach him, "overhearing one's own thoughts and feelings," that thoughts and feelings turn into their opposites: the eavesdropper hears a "buzzing and roaring

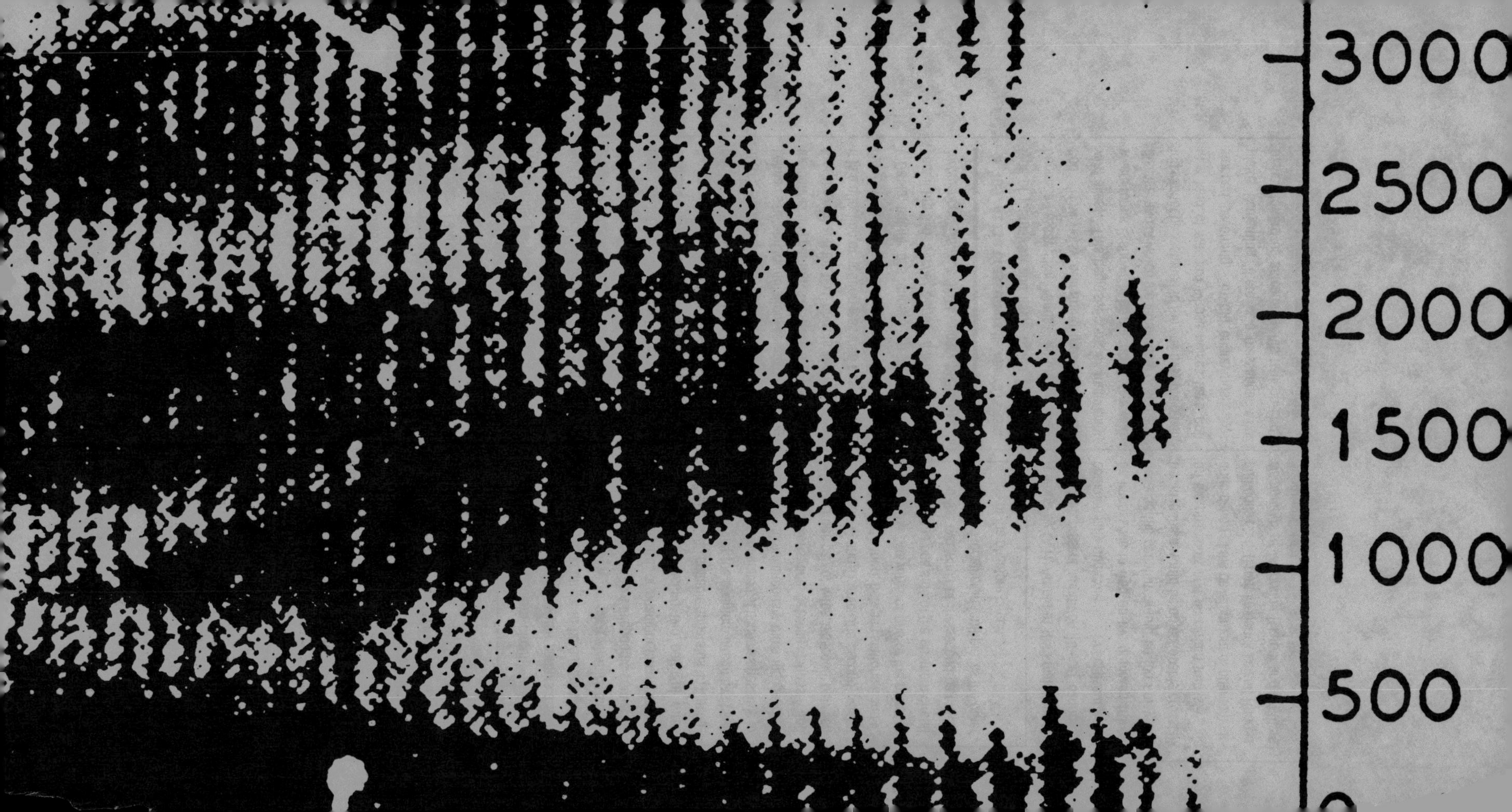
3000
2500
2000
1500
1000
500

> of the wild parts," battling out within him the invisible war of two army camps. Where an interiority which is prelingual and yet capable of articulation and education must stand, there everything is only "as if a rustling noise had gone through the air." The dreadfully unarticulated sound, which Nietzsche hears behind his back, thus is buzzing in his own ears. . . . (Trans. AKS)

For more noise, see Michel Serres, who, posing the critic as parasite, produces the insight uttered by critical activity: "I am noise" (*The Parasite,* trans. Lawrence R. Scher [Baltimore: Johns Hopkins University Press, 1982] 123; *Le Parasite* [Paris: Grasset, 1980]). In a skillful parasiting of the parasite, Bonnie Isaac reminds us that in the case of Serres, Lyotard, and Derrida, "the question is political and linguistic: can there be anything like a code or contract without 'the energy of noise,' 'the furor of coding' (Serres, *Genèse,* Grasset, 1982)" ("Parasiting, Text, Politics, or Genesis and Apocalypse," paper presented at the annual meeting of the International Association of Philosophy and Literature, New York, 1987). Serres's project, according to Shoshana Felman's helpful formulation, counts "in finding the connecting pathways between myth and history, the real and the text, objects and language; it is a question of nothing less than suspending the opposition between science and poetry" ("De la nature des choses ou de l'écart à l'équilibre" in *Michel Serres: Interférences et turbulences. Critique* 380 [January 1979]: 4).

◆ **109. At the crossroads** between a certain type of journalism and itself, Walter Benjamin begins an essay, "Karl Kraus," with this quotation: "How noisy everything grows [Wie laut wird alles]." This begins a complex materiality where rumor is shown to be co-constitutive with disease, and in which the temporality of spreading cannot be assigned to the one over the other in a kind of war text whose noises have not stopped becoming. "In old engravings," explains Benjamin, "there is a messenger who rushes toward us screaming, his hair on end, brandishing a sheet of paper in his hands, a sheet full of war and pestilence, of cries of murder and pain, announcing danger of fire and flood, spreading everywhere the 'latest news.' News in this sense, in the sense the word has in Shakespeare, is disseminated by *Die Fackel* (The Torch)" (*Reflections,* trans. Edmund Jephcott [Harcourt Brace Jovanovitch, 1978], 239).

◆ **110. The telephone has always been** inhabited by the rhetoric of the departed. While the eeriness of some of its appelations may have sunk out of sight, we might submit, in addition to the alarm known as "William's Coffin," the entry for US Patent No. 348, 512, August 31, 1886:

> The name of "phantom circuit" has been given to the scheme which permits a telephonic talking current to be superimposed on two pairs of wires, each of which simultaneously transmits a telephonic conversation. This third, or phantom circuit, is obtained by connecting two pairs of wires together, with suitable apparatus, in a peculiar way. After the phantom circuit has been properly constituted, it becomes possible to carry on simultaneously three independent conversations: one, between stations A and B, over one pair of wires; a second, between stations C and D, over the second pair of wires; and a third, between stations E and F, using the two wires of one of the pairs, in multiple as one side of the phantom circuit and the two wires of the second pair, also connected together in multiple, as the other side of the phantom circuit.

A report by C. H. Arnold in 1899 maintains that "in their present condition [these] cannot be commercially duplexed . . . . because it would be impossible to ring on the duplexed trunks, because the phantom would be too noisy, and because there would be objectionable crosstalk on the phantoms and on certain trunks. . . .In anticipation of the development of phantom circuit coils . . ." (From Frederick Leland Rhodes, *Beginnings of Telephony,* [Harper and Brothers, 1929] 189–193).

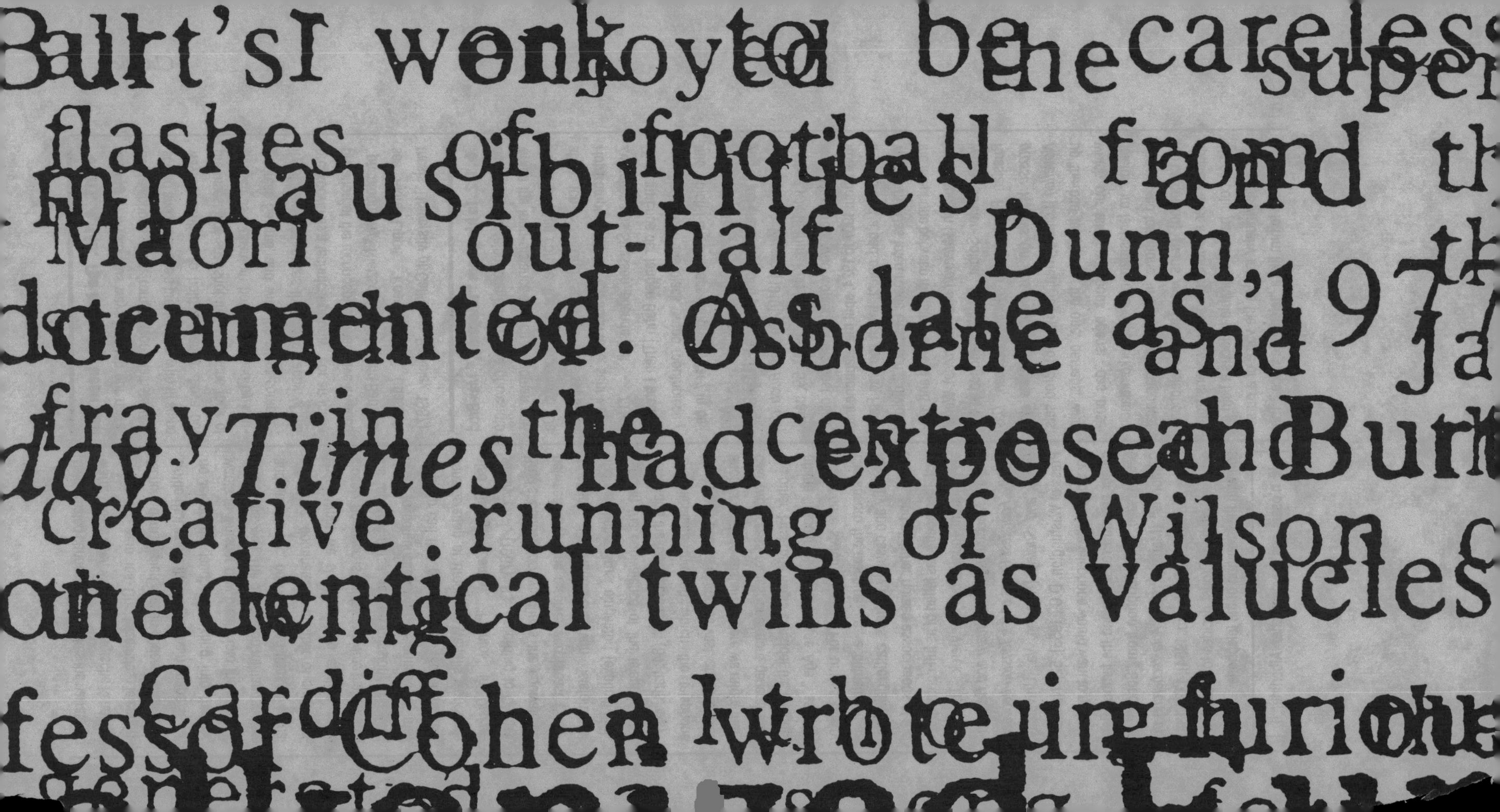

Burt's I work to be careless super

flashes of football from th

mplausibilities, and

Maori out-half Dunn, th

documented. As late as 197

documented. Osborne and Ja

fray in the centre and Burt

day Times had exposed

creative running of Wilson c

on identical twins as Valueless

Cardiff

fessor Cohen wrote in furious

◆ **111. *A*, 140. The horse has been galloping** in mysterious ways through our narrative telephone wires: from Watson's father to the schizo and Nietzsche's breakdown, who in some way all continue to hold a séance above our premises. The snapshot that Nietzsche took of himself as a phantom horse, whipped by Lou-Andréas Salomé, and with the silent complicity of Paul Rée, poses the scenography of his breakdown as a technical priority. For an interpretation of the technospirits that have invaded "phantography," Nietzsche, and Roland Barthes, see Akira Lippit, "Phantography" (master's thesis, University of California, Berkeley, 1987).

◆ **112. In his poem "Telephon,"** Max Brod describes the telephone booth as a grave into which the long-distance speech of woman animates a living corpse, the grave opening: "Da atme ich . . . Und sehe in die schwarze Holztrompete. / In die ich auch rede, sehr weit / Zwischen uns Strassen, eilende Zeit, . . . / Und Dich am Ende der langen Bahn [Then I breathe . . . And see in the black, wood mouthpiece / Into which I am also speaking, very far / In between us, streets, time that hastens, ... / And you at the end of the long passage]" (Max Brod, *Tagebuch in Versen* [1910], in *Das Buch der Liebe Lynk* [Berlin: Kurt Wolff, 1921], 59; trans. AKS.] Max Brod, who worked for the post office from about 1907 to 1924, split the telephone into a good and a bad object, much the way Franz Werfel, in "Das Interurbane Gespräch," divides the telephone between the father's word and maternal speech (*Vaterwort und Muterrede*). Werfel was a "Telefon-Soldat" in WWI stationed at the Russian Front. In his *Weltkriegsroman, Das grosse Wagnis* (in *Ausgewählte Romane und Novellen* [Leipzig/Wien, 1918], 4:16), Brod sets up the bad telephone, the one, perhaps, with which our telephone book opens: "das böse Telefon: im fantasmagorischen Oberkommando [the wicked telephone: in the phantasmagorical top command]" (trans. AKS). The good telephone appears after a wounded soldier awakens from his narcotic haze and, unable to focus a field of vision, he virtually inhales the voice of a nurse who speaks to him like a "telephone voice." The hallucinated connection provokes the narrator to warn: "Wehe aber, wenn die magische Kette riss, wenn . . . kein ins Ohr kitzelndes Telephonlachen dem Gallert neuen Odem einblassen wollte [But woe if the magic chain snaps, if . . . no telephonic laughter, tickling into the ear, wants to whisper new breath into the gelatin]" (72; Trans. AKS). The opposition military/sadism and aural/erotic, posed behind lines of sexual difference, dominates a number of such teletexts. What we shall want to explore more closely, however, is the *telefeminine* that sutures the topoi of nurse, rescue mission, and what Brod, in conjunction with Melanie Klein, may agree to call the "good breast." For a different consideration of Brod and Werfel's works see also Rüdiger Campe, "Pronto!" in *Diskursanalysen* 1, (1987): 83. According to Campe, Brod's *Balletmädchen* affirms the equivalence between telephone receiver and breast ("ausdrücklich die Äquivalenz von Telefonhörer und weiblicher Brust eingeführt [explicitly advancing the equivalence of the telephone receiver and the female breast])" (84; trans. AKS) The literature through which the telephone threads its peal is of course vast, and deserves another study to sustain it. Here we might indicate two access routes, one more general than the other. First, one might consider the insights of the "Pindar of the Machine Age," as Hart Crane once styled himself: "For unless poetry can absorb the machine, i.e., acclimatize it as naturally and casually as trees, cattle, galleons, castles and all other human associations of the past, then poetry has failed of its full contemporary function" (quoted by Peter Vierek, "The Poet and the Machine Age," in *Dream and Responsibility: Four Test Cases of the Tension between Poetry and Society* [Riverton, Va.: University Press of Washington, D.C., 1953], 52). No *literary* study of the telephone would want to make a detour around Proust. Beyond the famous Balbec passage, the description from "Sodome et Gomorrhe" (Marcel Proust, *A la recherche du temps perdu* [Paris: Gallimard, 1954], 133–134) deserves citation. Proust decides to credit Edison with the invention of the telephone:

> Je n'osais pas envoyer chez Albertine, il

était trop tard, mais dans l'espoir que, soupant peut-être avec des amies, dans un café, elle aurait l'idée de me téléphoner, je tournai le commutateur et, rétablissant la communication dans ma chambre, je la coupai entre le bureau de postes et la loge du concierge à laquelle il était relié d'habitude à cette heure-là. Avoir un récepteur dans le petit couloir où donnait la chambre de Françoise eût été plus simple, moins dérangeant, mais inutile. Les progrès de la civilisation permettent à chacun de manifester des qualités insoupconnées ou de nouveaux vices qui les rendent plus chers ou plus insupportables à leurs amis. C'est ainsi que la découverte d'Edison avait permis à Françoise d'acquérir un défaut de plus, qui était de se refuser quelque utilité, quelque urgence qu'il y eût, à se servir du téléphone. Elle trouvait le moyen de s'enfuir quand on voulait le lui apprendre, comme d'autres au moment d'être vaccinés. Aussi le téléphone était-il placé dans ma chambre, et, pour qu'il ne gênât pas mes parents, sa sonnerie était remplacé par un simple bruit de tourniquet. De peur de ne pas l'entendre, je ne bougeais pas.

I dared not send round to Albertine's house, it was too late, but in the hope that, having supper perhaps with some other girls, in a café, she might take it into her head to telephone me, I turned the switch and, restoring the connexion to my own room, cut it off between the post office and the porter's lodge to which it was generally switched at that hour. A receiver in the little passage on which Françoise's room opened would have been simpler, less inconvenient, but useless. The advance of civilisation enables each of us to display unsuspected merits or fresh defects which make him dearer or more insupportable to his friends. Thus Dr. Bell's [!] invention had enabled Françoise to acquire an additional defect, which was that of refusing, however important, however urgent the occasion might be, to make use of the telephone. She would manage to disappear whenever anybody was going to teach her how to use it, as people disappear when it is time for them to be vaccinated. And so the telephone was installed in my bedroom, and, that it might not disturb my parents, a rattle had been substituted for the bell. [Scott-Moncrieff substitued a rattle for the bell and Bell for Edison.] (*Cities of the Plain,* trans. C. K. Scott Moncrieff [New York: Random House, Modern Library, 1927], 180–181).

Proust crafts a rhetoric of anxiety in the description that follows, and which opens a horizon of "torture" and waiting until finally, the "sublime noise" of Albertine's call erupts. "And I settled down to listen, to suffer" (Proust, *Cities of the Plain,* 180). Finally, the immigration to an American literature would seem indispensable to a telecommunications satellite of literary emission. Ann Gelder has brought to my attention the exemplary case of Mark Twain's *A Connecticut Yankee in King Arthur's Court,* where the child is baptized "Hello, Central!":

"Hello, Central! Is this you Camelot?—. . . here standeth in the flesh his mightiness The Boss, and with thine own ears shall ye hear him speak!"
Now what a radical reversal of things this was; what a jumbling together of extravagant incongruities; what a fantastic conjunction of opposites and irreconcilables—the home of the bogus miracle become the home of a real one, the den of a medieval hermit turned into a telephone office!
The telephone clerk stepped into the light, and I recognized one of my young fellows. . . .
"What was that name, then?"
"The Valley of Hellishness."
That explains it. Confound a telephone, anyway. It is the very demon for conveying similarities of sound that are miracles of divergence from similarity of sense. But no matter, you know the name of the place now. Call up Camelot." (*The Works and Papers of Mark Twain* [Berkeley and Los Angeles:

University of California Press, 1979], 229–230).

◆ **113. In order to read** the great narrative of a parasitical relationship, it often becomes necessary to encounter a phantom that is agitating in one or both figures. In his autobiography, Watson makes it abundantly clear that something is remote-controlling him, calling him to the telephone and the Bell system. Due to logical constraints, it has seemed to me more sensible at this time to pursue the phantom haunting Bell, and to leave Watson's ghosts somewhat restlessly ringing their chains. Watson's transmissions, always responding to the controls of an Other, suggest, in the autobiography as elsewhere, his deep involvement in the ghostly above—which to a certain degree, however, may be due to the spirit of the times. Yet this spirit is precisely the one that permitted technology, like Lazarus, to arise. The psychoanalytic theory of the phantom and unconscious transmissions are first articulated in Nicholas Abraham and Maria Torok's *The Wolf Man's Magic Word: A Cryptonymy,* trans. Nicolas Rand (Minneapolis: University of Minnesota Press, 1986); *Le verbier de l'homme aux loups: une cryptonymie,* preface ("Fors") by Jacques Derrida (Paris: Flammarion, 1976).

The question of Watson's "headset," which we have managed to raise a number of times, is not an arbitrary one. In many ways, Watson models his body representations by telephonic regulation. The eyes are always slighted, hierarchically ordered under the aural senses. We might linger a moment longer on the base of the head before turning in the text to the palms of Watson's hands, where we read his lines. Watson's rapport to his eyeballs were, oddly, in the effeminate, as he puts it. Due to his "unmanly" anxieties, his orbs were one of the first pair to receive protection from incoming missiles. (There is of course nothing more manly than this ocular anxiety; just read Freud on Dr. Coppola and Company.) His ocular sensitivity is thematically sustained throughout the autobiography, revolving in chapter 6 around "safety-first devices and warning cards [that] were unknown then and so was industrial insurance. If we hurt ourselves we suffered the consequences" (47). Getting metal chips into the eye was "one of the worst accidents that could happen to us. We were continually taking things out of each other's eyes, generally using a looped bristle from our bench brush, an operation in which I became quite expert. An oculist would have been horrified at our methods but an accident had to be serious before a doctor was called in." No emergency calls, no house calls as far as the eye can see. Watson "had one severe experience when a hot brass chip struck my eyeball and laid me up a day or two, and after that I wore goggles when doing any work that set the metal chips flying, although my fellow workmen scorned such things as effeminate" (48).

◆ **114. John Brooks,** *Telephone: The First Hundred Years* (New York: Harper and Row, 1976), 74.

◆ ***115. A History of Engineering*** *and Science in the Bell System: The Early Years* (1895–1925), ed. M. D. Fagen (New York: Bell Telephone Laboratories, 1975), 516.

◆ **116. A remarkable text was** published to mark the dispersal of the maternal body of the telephone into AT&T. Its special quality consists in the way it gathers up a lexicon of mutilation and hallucination which does not merely "confirm" our reading but, registering the extent to which the corporate unconscious can speak, it exposes a layer of latent terrorism under the changing surface of telephonic ownership. The pamphlet, entitled *American Heritage* and subtitled *Breaking the Connection: A Short History of* AT&T (June–July 1985), shows a dangling, lopped off telephone receiver, next to which one can read:

Hello? Hello?

Read the prose of self-mutilation and essential phantasms of corporate identity and disintegration. After establishing the facts ("On January 8, 1982, the organization announced that within two years it would tear itself apart, and on January 1, 1984, it made good on its promise"), body disintegration takes over, and corporate paranoia suggests itself ready-at-hand:

> Before its dismemberment, the American Telephone and Telegraph Company, also known as "Ma Bell," had been by many standards the largest company on earth. In the range of its influence, in assets, and in its impact on the daily lives of ordinary people, it dwarfed not only other companies but also nations. . . .
> The legal term for what occurred on January 1, 1984 is divestiture, but that word seems inadequate as a description of the corporate equivalent of a many-limbed giant ripping off limb after limb, flinging the pieces in all directions, and leaving the landscape **littered with big, bleeding hunks of**
> **its**
> **former self.** (65).

One intuits who directed the hand of the writer(s) here, Bataille or Schreber. At any rate, AT&T ("also known as Ma Bell") makes no bones about having ditched Mother in the transaction. Several years prior to divestiture, chairman of AT&T Charles L. Brown, "shocked some of his own employees" when he announced the evacuation of the maternal:

> Brown suggested that the comforting image of Ma Bell might not fit this new company: "Mother," he concluded, "doesn't live here anymore."
> Brown was premature; Ma Bell did not pass away until New Year's Day, 1984. Now that she is gone, we might take a moment to remember her remarkable life. What did she mean to us? *How did she get so big and strong?* What is her legacy? How will we manage without her? (66; italics added).

So Ma Bell, as it turns out, was assassinated not because she was becoming frail and weak, edging toward something of a natural death, but, on the contrary, because she left these boys wondering how she had become such a tough mother, how did she get so big and strong? But by eliminating her, the company rips into its own image, bleeding hunks, as it says, of its former self, fragmenting into an excremental scene of litter in body parts: the violent and repressive birth of the maternal superego. The pamphlet eventually moves into a heroics of war and the space age. "The science underlying electrical communications is at the very heart of modern war," wrote Walter Gifford to AT&T's shareholders shortly after Japan's attack on Pearl Harbor. . . . "AT&T also played a major role in the postwar development of guided antiaircraft missiles and in the development of the nation's air-defense radar system. The space age opened new frontiers for the company. A communications satellite designed by Bell scientists, Telstar, was launched in 1962, and the first earth-moon telephone call was completed in July 1969, less than one century after Alexander Graham Bell spilled acid over his clothes and completed the first room-to-room telephone call" (78). AT&T, incidentally, maintains the telephone as a "tool." Ma Bell's suppression in-stalls a maternal superego around which the corporate members organize their remorse, which once again reminds us of the feminine trace deposited in the technologies. Consider in this regard Joseph W. Slade's discussion of Eugene O'Neill's "Great Mother of Eternal Life" (in "Dynamo") and the "feminization of electricity" in "American Writers and American Inventions," in *The Technological Imagination: Theories and Fictions,* ed. Teresa de Lauretis, Andrea Huyssen, and Kathleen Woodward, Theories of Contemporary Cultures Series (Madison, Wisc.: Coda Press, 1980), 40–42.

◆ **117. Rhodes,** *Beginnings of Telephony,* 31–32.

◆ **118. Ibid.**, 32.

◆ **119. Ibid.**, 187.

◆ **120. Moses' Mouthpiece is Aaron.** Moses Returns to Egypt. Moses, difficult of speech, is given the staff with which to perform the signs, as God says. First Exodus, then the Straubs' film on Schoenberg's *Moses and Aaron.*

> But Moses said, "O Lord, I have never been a man of ready speech, never in my life, not even now that Thou hast spoken to me; I am slow and hesitant of speech." The Lord said to him "Who is it that gives man speech? Who makes him dumb or deaf? Who makes him clear-sighted or blind? Is it not I, the Lord? Go now; I will help your speech and tell you what to say." But Moses still protested, "No, Lord, send whom Thou wilt." At this the Lord grew angry with Moses and said, "Have you not a brother, Aaron the Levite? He, I know, will do all the speaking. He is already on the way to meet you, and he will be glad indeed to see you. You shall speak to him and put the words in his mouth; I will help both of you to speak, and tell you both what to do. He will do all the speaking to the people for you, he will be the mouthpiece, and you will be the god he speaks for. But take this staff, for with it you are to work the signs." (Exodus 4:10–17, New English Bible)
>
> Meanwhile the Lord had ordered Aaron to go and meet Moses in the wilderness. Aaron went and met him at the mountain of God, and he kissed him. Then Moses told Aaron everything, the words the Lord had told him to say and the signs he had commanded him to perform. (Exodus 4:27–31, New English Bible)

◆ **121. Rüdiger Campe,** "Pronto!" in *Diskursanalysen* 1 (1987): 73, points up the relationship of the Bell apparatus and E. T. A. Hoffmann's *Automate* in a different way, building it by means of romantic linguistic and music theories which are based on von Kempelen's speaking machine (and deceptive chess players). In the case of these machines and of romantic literature it often becomes impossible to decide whether the machine or the woman has spoken, sung, or produced any sort of sound at all. ¿What about these invisible women who are thought to open or close the speech canals?

◆ **122. We haven't yet spoken** about lighting up on the phone, smoking and the telephone, telling time per cigarette, ashes, language incineration. Wait. Let me get a cigarette. The lighter? . . . Fire! The end passages from J. D. Salinger's *Franny and Zooey* (1961; reprinted, New York: Bantam Books, 1985), 201–202 (the dead brother impersonated on the line), present a phenomenology of hanging up:

> However, she puffed nervously at her cigarette and, rather bravely, picked up the phone.
> "Hello, Buddy?" she said.
> "Hello, sweetheart. How are you—are you alright?"
> "I'm fine. How are you? You sound as though you have a cold." . . .
> "Where am I? I'm right in my element, Flopsy. I'm in a little haunted house down the road. Never mind. Just talk to me." . . .
> For joy, apparently, it was all Franny could do to hold the phone, even with both hands. For a fullish half minute or so, there were no other words, no further speech. Then: "I can't talk anymore, Buddy." The sound of a phone being replaced in its catch followed. Franny took in her breath slightly but continued to hold the phone to her ear. A dial tone, of course, followed the formal break in the connection. She appeared to find it extraordinarily beautiful to listen to, rather as if it were the best possible substitute for the primordial silence itself. But she seemed to know, too, when to stop listening to it, as if all of what little or much wisdom there is in the world were suddenly hers. When she had replaced the phone, she seemed to know just what to do next, too. She cleared away the smoking things, then drew back the cotton bedspread from the bed she had been sitting on, took off her slippers, and

> got into the bed. For some minutes, before she fell into a deep, dreamless sleep, she lay just quiet, smiling at the ceiling.

SPEED CALLING. Beginning perhaps with Moses and Aaron, several brothers have been put on the line. Lisa A. Webster, Columbia University, reminds us of Virginia Woolf's *The Waves,* an elegiac novel commemorating her lost brother. These are some citations that she left on my answering machine:

> —"I am half in love with the typewriter and the telephone. With letters and cables and brief but courteous commands on the telephone to Paris, Berlin, New York, I have fused many lives into one. . . . I love the telephone with its lip stretched to my whisper."
>
> —"Toast and butter, coffee and bacon, the *Times* and letters—suddenly the telephone rang with urgency and I rose deliberately and went to the telephone. I took up the black mouth. I marked the ease with which my mind adjusted itself to assimilate the message—it might be (one has these fancies) to assume command of the British empire . . ."

Click. A week later Lisa calls to say I should consider the crucial telephoning in *To the Lighthouse* as well, all having to do with loss and the maternal. She hopes I'm fine. Click.

◆ **123. David Wright,** *Deafness* (New York: Stein and Day, 1969), is discussed in Oliver Sacks's review essay, "Mysteries of the Deaf," *New York Review of Books,* March 27, 1986 pp. 23–33. Reading Harlen Lane, *When the Mind Hears: A History of the Deaf* and Harlen Lane, ed., *The Deaf Experience: Classics in Education,* as well as Nora Ellen Groce, *Here Spoke Sign Language,* Sacks discusses the manual alphabet (or finger spelling) and the sacrificial maneuvers that led to the demise of sign language. This necessarily brings him to say a few things about the reformist bent of AGB, who is placed among those "who clamored for an overthrow of the 'old-fashioned' sign-language asylums, and for the introduction of 'progressive' oralist schools" (32).

> But the most important and powerful of these "oralist" figures was Alexander Graham Bell, who was at once heir to a family tradition of teaching elocution and correcting speech impediments (his father and grandfather were both eminent in this); tied into a strange family mix of deafness denied—both his mother and his wife were deaf, but never acknowledged this; and, of course, a technological genius in his own right. When Bell threw all the weight of his immense authority and prestige into the advocacy of oralism, the scales were, finally, overbalanced and tipped, and at the notorious International Congress of Educators of the Deaf held at Milan in 1880 (though deaf teachers were themselves excluded from the vote), oralism won the day, and the use of Sign in schools was "officially" proscribed. The deaf were prohibited from using their own, "natural" language, and thenceforth forced to learn, as best they might, the (for them) "unnatural" language of speech. And perhaps this was in keeping with the spirit of the age, its overweening sense of science as power, of commanding nature and never deferring to it. (32)

Sacks reminds us of one consequence of this decision: the hearing and not deaf teachers now slipped into the position of the master pedagogues. His statistics show the gradual decrease in hearing teachers who would know any sign language at all. *Children of a Lesser God* dramatizes this point by unfolding the colonizing desire of a hearing teacher whose conviction translates the usual subjugation of the woman into making her give up, if not her career, then at least her sign language. The guy practically forces her to speak and to stop cleaning toilets. At the same time it ought to be stated, however, that a judicious interpretation of Bell's position on oralism would have to go through the metaphysical demands of the day. If Bell aimed at the perfectibility of the vocal cords, it was principally for the purpose of securing human rights for deaf-mutes, whose essential humanity, as we earlier suggested, depended upon a logocentric membership card. By a simple but juridically necessary tautology, Bell was able to prove that the silent nonhearing citizen was capable of performative vocality. Hence, one statement characteristic of Bell: "It is well known that deaf mutes are dumb merely because they are deaf, and that there is no defect in their vocal organs to incapacitate them from utterance. Hence it was thought that my father's system of pictorial symbols, popularly known as visible speech, might prove a means whereby we could teach the deaf and dumb to use their vocal organs and to speak" (*TMP,* 43).

◆ **124. In *Congenital and Acquired*** *Cognitive Disorders,* ed. R. Katzman (New York: Raven Press, 1986), 189–245. In part 6 of his essay "Mysteries of the Deaf," Sacks makes a number of observations concerning the Mosaic code which should, I hope, reinforce some of the things that have been claimed here, though the critical passage to signs in the dialogue between God and Moses (Exodus 3:4) may complicate any hope for a linear itinerary.

> The subhuman status of mutes was part of the Mosaic code, and it was reinforced by the biblical exaltation of the voice and ear as the one and true way in which man and God could speak. And yet, overborne by Mosaic and Aristotelian thunderings, some profound voices intimated that this need not be so. Thus Socrates' remark in the *Cratylus* of Plato, which so impressed the youthful Abbé de l'Epée [the first literate deaf-mute in the world, along with de Fontenay, Desloges, Jean Massieu, Berthier, his students and those of the Abbé Sicard and Roche-Ambroise Bébian. De l'Epée also invented a system of "methodical" signs enabling deaf students to write down what was said to them through a signing interpreter—a method so successful that, for the first time, it enabled ordinary deaf pupils to read and write French, and thus acquire an education. His school, founded in 1775, was the first to acquire public support]: "If we had neither

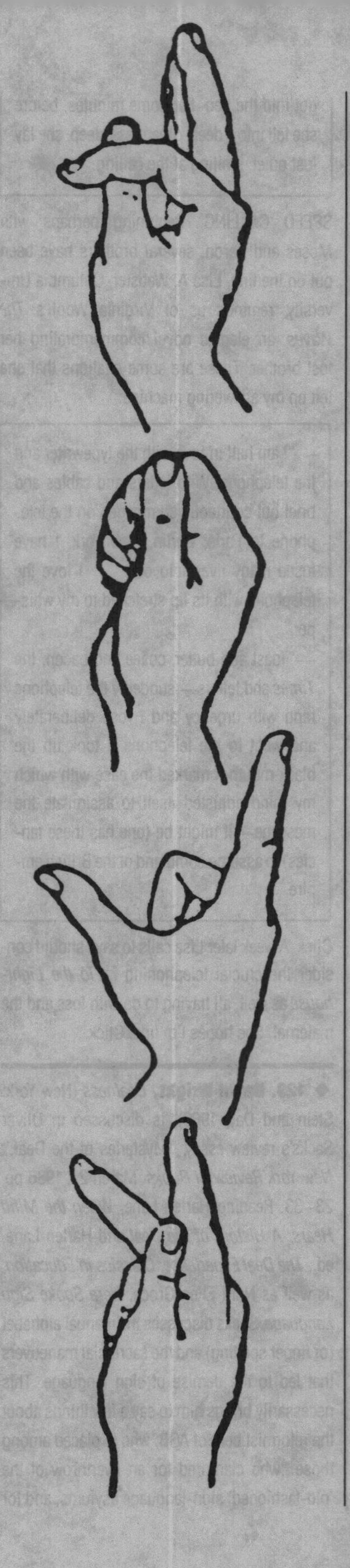

> voice nor tongue, and yet wished to manifest things to one another, should we not, like those which are at present mute, endeavor to signify our meaning by the hands, head, and other parts of the body?" (27)

◆ **125. Sacks,** "Mysteries of the Deaf," 24.

◆ **126. In Rousseau's final work,** the supplement to his *Confessions,* the author signs off by designating his happiest moment, which consists in breeding a sort of litterature. Having described a combat zone in which rumor has made repeated attempts to gun him down in the streets, he launches a counterattack when he claims responsibility for another sort of incalculable proliferation. Not unlike Bell, he transfers linguistic accounts to the controlled districts of animal breeding. Until this point, he has been shown to be pursued brutally by rumorous utterances that fly at him wherever he steps in the double hermeneutics of the promenades—double because this work is concerned with the intersecting marks of public and private discourses. Of the most pressing desires asserted in the text, one consists in putting up a stop sign before the proliferant effects of public circulation. With the aim of containing these, he establishes a space where so-called internal, formal, private structures of a literary language control external, referential, and public effects. In a scene that exemplarily underscores the structuration of a foreign species of utterance imputable to rumor, and over which he can exercise little control, Rousseau suddenly attains to a moment of balance and tranquility. "The founding of this colony was a great day," writes Rousseau, father of the French Revolution, about his newly founded rabbit colony. The rabbits, replicating the rhetoric of rumor "could multiply there in peace." But unlike rumor, they could multiply, he writes, "without harming anything." "We proceeded in great ceremony to install them on the little island where they were beginning to breed before my departure." The rabbits, like the rumor and other phobias were thus "beginning to breed before my departure," a major thematic of Rousseau's exit text. Rousseau's linguistic investments are eventually shown to be locked into his self-positioning as founding father of a rabbit colony, where questions that have been at the root of articulated anxieties—paternity, posterity, conditions for transmitting to a future, the wild proliferation of an alien species, and the hope of language containment—are generously raised (Jean-Jacques Rousseau, *The Reveries of the Solitary Walker* [New York: Penguin, 1981] chap. 5; *Les rêveries du promeneur solitaire,* in *Oeuvres complètes de Jean-Jacques Rousseau,* ed. Bernard Gagnebin and Marcel Raymond, (Paris: Gallimard, 1959). Paul de Man has treated the schism separating private and public, referential effects of language in *Allegories of Reading* (New Haven: Yale University Press, 1979) part 2: "Rousseau."

◆ **127. The link between nipple** breeding and the new eugenics movement in America was fast in coming. In the "Chain of Generation," the author writes of how "Bell set out to determine whether the extra nipples, mere vestiges in that generation, could be made functional and hereditary by selective breeding, and whether ewes thus equipped would bear and raise a significantly higher proportion of twins. . . . Bell succeeded in developing a strain of ewes with at least four milk-producing nipples" (*Bell,* 416). AGB's hobby of twenty-four years' standing brought him, by the time of his death in 1922, "a multinippled flock" (*Bell,* 417). Now, here goes:

> In 1913 Bell collaborated with his son-in-law David Fairchild, the new president of the American Breeders' Association, in drawing up articles of incorporation for the society, which soon after was renamed the American Genetic Association; and Bell contributed occasional essays on eugenics and sheep-breeding to the Association's *Journal of Heredity*.
>
> The decline of the eugenics movement was already beginning with the infiltration of racists like Madison Grant who, aside from the moral stigma they brought to it, thoroughly corrupted its scientific quality, which was already tainted by naive oversimplification of human traits and the crude forcing of

them in a Mendelian pattern. The racists used the movement's fading prestige, along with the xenophobia and political reaction of the postwar period, to help slam the door on immigration in the early twenties. But responsible scientists had already begun to dissociate themselves from the eugenics movement. Fortunately, the American people, though still susceptible to the pseudoscience of racism, were too tolerant, optimistic, and ethnically varied to stomach racism's social and political corollaries. In Germany, encouraged by perverted eugenics, racism culminated in the incomprehensible horror of Nazi genocide.
It is not easy to look back across that abyss to its sunny approach and see the early eugenics movement as the benign application of science to humanitarianism that claimed the sympathy of men like Bell, Galton, and Jordan. But justice to Bell requires the effort. It also requires a look at his position in the spectrum of eugenics thought (*Bell,* 418).

◆ **128. The condensed milk dialactate,** if you will, is the way Kathleen Woodward starts recounting the Technological Revolution in her introduction to *The Technological Imagination: Theories and Fictions*. "Dialactate" was coined to capture the flow of this argument by Matt George, University of California, Berkeley.

◆ **129. Ulmer, *Applied Grammatology,*** 61, reviews perspectives shedding light on mourning as the idealization and interiorization of the mother's image.

◆ **130. Jacques Derrida,** "Fors," *Georgia Review* 21, no. 2 (1977).

◆ **131. Jacques Derrida,** "Economimesis," in S. Agacinski, Philippe Lacoue-Labarthe, Sarah Kofman, and Jean-Luc Nancy, *Mimesis: des articulations* (Flammarion, 1975), 90.

◆ **132. De Lauretis, Huyssen, and Woodward,** *The Technological Imagination,* 3.

◆ **133. Ibid.**, 4.

◆ **134. Ibid.**

◆ **135. Pacific Bell,** San Francisco, 1987.

◆ **136. Franz Kafka,** 1922 diary entry, and the eruption of a native foreign tongue: "April 27. Yesterday a Makkabi girl in the office of *Selbstwehr* telephoning: 'Prisla jsem ti pomoct.' Clear, cordial voice and speech. Shortly thereafter the door opened to M" ([Makkabi was the name of a Zionist sports club. *Selbstwehr* was a Prague Zionist weekly. The Czech means "I came to help you"; Franz Kafka, *Diaries 1914–1923,* ed. Max Brod, trans. Joseph Kresh [New York: Schocken Books, 1965]; 128. *Tagebücher* 1910–1923, ed. Max Brod [Frankfurt: Fischer, 1980]). See also Rickels's discussion of Kafka's phone calls to Felice which, in *Aberrations of Mourning,* 279–293, opens up the telephone switchboard at the Hotel Occidental. Kafka's scene of the switchboard deserves to be recalled here:

> Over there for example were six bellboys at six telephones. The arrangement, as one immediately recognized, required that one boy only receive calls, while his neighbor transmitted by phone the orders the first had written down and passed on to him. These telephones were of the newest variety, the kind not requiring booths since the ring was not louder than a chirp, one could speak into the phone in a whisper and still the words arrived at their destination in a thunderous voice owing to special electrical amplification. That is why one scarcely heard the three speakers at their telephones and could have believed they were mumbling to themselves and observing some process unfold within the receiver, while the three others, as though benumbed by the noise penetrating to them, though inaudible to bystanders, dropped their heads onto the paper which it was their duty to write on. And here again there was next to each speaker a boy standing by to help out; these three boys did nothing but alternately lean their

heads and listen to the operators, and then quickly as though stung looked up the telephone numbers in huge yellow books—the turning masses of pages were by far louder than the sounds of the phones (*Gesammelte Schriften,* ed. Max Brod [New York: Schocken Books, 1946], 2:197).

◆ **137. Marguerite Duras,** *Le Navire Night: Césares, les mains négatives, Aurelia Steiner* (Paris: Mercure de France, 1979). All subsequent page numbers in this chapter refer to this work. This text is put into dialogue with Jacques Derrida's *Eperons: Les styles de Nietzsche* (Paris: Flammarion, 1978).

◆ **138. Friedrich Nietzsche,** *The Gay Science* (New York: Random House, Vintage Books, 1974), 60.

◆ **139. On the other, darkened** side of the scientific coin, Nietzsche, a contemporary of the telephone and horror shows, was exposing science as an illusionist's play. This, like all Nietzschean broadcast systems, including Zarathustra's special newscast, was in part to be interpreted as good news, science having shed or moulted the assimilations of truth to positive valuations. In an essential way, science couldn't care less about truth, producing thereby what Maurice Blanchot conceives as a positive trait: for the first time, writes Blanchot, "the horizon is infinitely opened to knowledge—'All is permitted.' When the authority of old values has collapsed, this new authorization means that it is permitted to know all, that there is no longer a limit to man's activity." Moreover,

> Nietzsche, we are told, had only a mediocre acquaintance with the sciences. That is possible. But, in addition to the fact that he had been professionally trained in a scientific method, he knew enough of it to have a presentiment of what science would become, to take it seriously, and even to foresee—not to deplore—that from now on all the modern world's seriousness would be confined to science, to the scientist, and to the prodigious power of technology. On the one hand, he saw with striking force that since nihilism is the possibility of all going beyond, it is the horizon for every particular science as well as for the maintenance of scientific development as such. On the other hand, he saw no less clearly that, when the world no longer had any meaning, when it only bears the pseudo-meaning of some non-sensical scheme or another, what can alone overcome the disorder of this void is the cautious movement of science, its power to give itself precise rules and to create meaning (but of a limited, and so to speak, operational kind)—a power, therefore, to extend its field of application to the furthest limit or to restrict it immediately. Agreed. And that, once more, is reassuring. The moment Nihilism outlines the world for us, its counterpart, science, creates the tools to dominate it. The era of universal mastery is opened. But there are some consequences: first, science can only be nihilistic; it is the meaning of a world deprived of meaning, a knowledge that ultimately has ignorance as its foundation. To which the response will be that this reservation is only theoretical; but we must not hasten to disregard this objection, for science is essentially productive. Knowing it need not interpret the world, science transforms it, and by this transformation science conveys its own nihilistic demands—the negative power that science has made into the most useful of tools, but which it dangerously plays. Knowledge is fundamentally dangerous. . . . present-day man . . . possesses a power in excess of himself even without his trying to surpass himself in that power ("The Limits of Experience: Nihilism," in *The New Nietzsche: Contemporary Styles of Interpretation,* ed. David B. Allison [Cambridge, Mass: MIT Press, 1985], 121–127).

◆ **140. See Freud's chapter 30,** "Dreams and Occultism" for a remarkable interpretation of thought transference, the telepathic process, and "transformations, such as occur in speaking and hearing by the telephone" (*SE,* 22:55). In the *New Introductory Lectures on Psycho-analysis,* the telephone arrives on the scene of metonymy when Freud concedes: "It may be that I too have a secret inclination towards the miraculous which thus goes half way to meet the creation of occult facts" (*SE,* 22:53). On the way to science and occultism, Freud shows himself prepared to elasticize his earlier views: "When they first came into my range of vision more than ten years ago, I too felt a dread of a threat against our scientific *Weltanschauung,* which, I feared, was bound to give place to spiritualism or mysticism if portions of occultism were proved true [cf. his posthumously published paper "Psycho-Analysis and Telepathy,"1941]. To-day I think otherwise. In my opinion it shows no great confidence in science if one does not think it capable of assimilating and working over whatever may perhaps turn out to be true in the assertion of occultists" (*SE,* 22:54–55).

◆ **141. This doubling over of the dice** suggests a moment in the structure of the eternal return of the Same as described by Gilles Deleuze in *Nietzsche and Philosophy,* trans. Hugh Tomlinson (New York: Columbia University Press, 1983); *Nietzsche et la philosophie* (Paris: Presses universitaires de France, 1983).

◆ **142. Ricky Jay,** *Learned Pigs and Fireproof Women* (New York: Random House, Villard Books, 1986), vii; unless otherwise indicated, page numbers in parentheses refer to this work. In *Mythologies,* (Paris: Seuil, 1957), 199–201, Roland Barthes offers the vaudeville section "Au Music-Hall" within which telephonic demands unfold: unlike the theater, where time is always connecting ("le temps du théâtre, quel qu'il soit, est toujours lié" [199]), the music hall is by definition, interrupted; it is an immediate time . . . the time is cut ("est par définition, interrompu; c'est un temps immédiat. . . . le temps est coupé" [199]). Vaudeville, according to Barthes is not an Anglo-Saxon fact for nothing but emerges in a world of urban density and great Quaker myths: "la promotion des objets, des métaux, et des gestes rêvés, la sublimation du travail par son effacement magique et non par sa consécration, comme dans le folklore rural, tout cela participe de l'artifice des villes" (201). The perpetual dialogue with gestures encourages objects to lose the sinister implacability of their absurdity: "artificiels et utensiles, ils cessent un instant d'*ennuyer*" (201). ("It is not without reason that the music hall is an Anglo-Saxon fact, born in the world of brusque urban densities and great Quaker myths of work: the promotion of objects, metals and fantasy gestures, the sublimation of work by its magical effacement and not by its consecration, as in rural folklore—all this goes with the artifice of cities. The city rejects the idea of a formless nature, reducing space to a continuum of solid, brilliant and *fabricated* objects, to which precisely the act of the artist grants the prestigious status of a thought that is entirely human. Work, above all when mythicized, makes matter happy because, spectacularly, it seems to envisage it: metalicized, set into motion, recaptured, manipulated, entirely luminous with motion, in perpetual dialogue with gestures, objects here lose the sinister implacability of their absurdity: artificial and utilitarian, they cease for an instant to be *boring*" [trans. Karen Sullivan]). Also see Sol Yurick, *Behold Metatron, the Recording Angel,* Foreign Agent series: (New York: Semiotext[e], 1985), 24: "Magic embodies a primitive theory of electromagnetism and telecommunication. Magic desires to achieve telepathy and teleportation. Voodoo, for instance, contains the notion of a communicating medium and the communicants who believe in it. The Catholic Church is a communicating organism with an apparatus of switches and relays and a communicating language for the input of prayers through a churchly switchboard up to Heaven, and outputs returned to the supplicant."

◆ **143. P. 58. Marie-Hélène Huet** has traced the relationship of deformity to a mother's gaze in "Living Images: Monstrosity and Representation," *Representations,* ed. Svetlana Alpers and Stephen Greenblatt (Berkely and Los Angeles: University of California Press, 1983).

◆ **144. Friedrich Kittler** expounds upon the connection Remington between the rifle and typewriter in *Aufschreibsysteme 1800/1900.*

◆ **145.The Electric Chair and** The Telephone. An isolated chamber. The first pages of Plath's *Bell Jar:* the Rosenbergs. Electrocution/telephone wires. Sinister counterparts lodged within a telephonic relation to one another; two parts of a single apparatus of state. Death sentence and reprieve, same frame. The same goes for Kafka's "Penal Colony": the expulsed interiority of the subject upon which torture executes its sentence. Hence the rise of liberal determinations in the ethicity of inflicted pain (as long as it doesn't rip into the subject, keeping out of the presumed space of interiority—save the soul, the heart, etc.). According to a 1953 Gallup poll, the American public strongly favored electrocution over lethal gas, while hanging and shooting had very few supporters (12 percent registered no opinion, or recommended "drugs" or "any of them, but let the prisoner choose") (*The Death Penalty in America: An Anthology,* ed. Hugo Adam Bedau [Hawthorne, N.Y.: Aldine, 1964], 19). Also:

> In the late 1880's, in order to challenge the growing success of the Westinghouse Company, then pressing for nationwide electrification with alternating current, the advocates of the Edison Company's direct current staged public demonstrations to show how dangerous their competitor's product really was: If it could kill animals—and awed spectators saw that, indeed, it could—it could kill human beings as well. In no time at all, this somber warning was turned completely around. In 1888, the New York legislature approved the dismantling of its gallows and the construction of an "electric chair," on the theory that in all respects, scientific and humane, executing a condemned man by electrocution was superior to executing him by hanging. On 6 August 1890, after his lawyer had unsuccessfully argued the unconstitutionality of this "cruel and unusual" method of execution, William Kemmler became the first criminal to be put to death by electricity. Although eyewitness reports allege that the execution was little short of torture for Kemmler (the apparatus was makeshift and the executioner clumsy), the fad had started. Authorities on electricity, such as Thomas Edison and Nikola Tesla, continued to debate whether electrocution was so horrible that it should never have been invented. The late Robert G. Elliott, electrocutioner of 387 men and women, assured the public that the condemned person loses consciousness immediately with the first jolt of current. The matter continued to generate scientific interest until fairly recently. Despite the record of bungled executions, the unavoidable absence of first-hand testimony, the disfiguring effects, and the odor of burning flesh that accompany every electrocution, the electric chair remains the only lawful mode of execution in most American jurisdictions.

See the *Report* of the New York Legislative Commission on Capital Punishment (1888), 52–92; R.G. Elliott, *Agent of Death: The Memoirs of an Executioner* (New York: Dutton, 1940), cited in Bedau, *Death Penalty,* and in Barrett Prettyman, Jr., *Death and the Supreme Court* (New York: Harcourt Brace, 1961), 105ff., where several bungled executions are cited by the defense in the case of Louisiana ex rel. *Francis vs. Resweber,* 329 U.S. 459 (1947).

◆ **146. Western Culture has produced** a multiplicity of shock absorbers built into electric pleasures; that is to say, the same code that was used to touch the rift of essential traumatism now becomes the guarantor of invention and jouissance. "Shocking" has asserted itself as a highly valorized category, beginning no doubt with the earthquake of Lisbon and Mary Shelley's shattered oak tree; what shock awakens, opens desire's channels, a high-tech sensor of the Kantian sublime. In other words, according to a rather classical logic, the object of terror becomes the very thing entrusted with creating the conditions for triggering a pleasure. The degree to which the socius takes pleasure in a meta-

Connecticut at a loss over execution

SOMERS, Conn. (AP) — Connecticut has a death chamber, an electric chair, and its first condemned killer in years, but there's no one left in the state prison system who remembers how to carry out an execution.

A jury last week sentenced Michael B. Ross, 27, to death for the serial murders of four teen-age girls, forcing state officials to start studying how to make the chair operable and how to carry out the instructions for an execution outlined in Connecticut law.

"A good reference is what they do in other states," Department of Correction spokeswoman Connie Wilks said Monday as she led reporters and photographers on a tour of the death chamber at Somers State Prison.

Wilks and other officials said they don't know how electricity is fed into the 5-foot-tall oak chair, how an occupant is strapped into it or how much voltage is required to execute someone.

The last person to die in the chair, which has small gouges in the arms where prisoners' hands lay, was Joseph "Mad Dog" Taborsky, who was convicted of killing seven people during a robbery and was executed in May 1960 in the now-closed Connecticut State Prison in Wethersfield.

phorics whose seat is the electric chair still needs to be measured: it's hot, a blast, it blew me away, etc.

◆ **147. The place where an encounter** might be arranged between an imaginary typology of electric currents and political science can be seen as rooted, for starters, in the writings of Benjamin Franklin. Having stolen fire from the heavens, Franklin, according to Immanuel Kant, represents for us the new Prometheus. Appropriating the fire, Franklin then directs its promotion; refusing patents, he propagandized, rather, for his inventions. In a letter to the French scientists Barebeu Dubourg and Thomas François Dalibard, he gathers up the thematics of slaughter, electricity, and a flock of sheep in Scotland. The section under the heading "Humane Slaughtering" is worth tapping into:

> My Dear Friends,
>
> My answer to your questions concerning the mode of rendering meat tender by electricity, can only be founded upon conjecture; for I have not experiments enough to warrant the facts. All that I can say at present is, that I think electricity might be employed for this purpose, and I shall state what follows as the observations or reasons which make me presume so. . . .
>
> The flesh of animals, fresh killed in the usual manner, is firm, hard, and not in a very eatable state, because the particles adhere too forcibly to each other. At a certain period, the cohesion is weakened, and, in its progress towards putrefaction, which tends to produce a total separation, the flesh becomes what we call tender, or is in that state most proper to be used as our food. It has frequently been remarked, that animals killed by lightning putrefy immediately. This cannot be invariably the case, since a quantity of lightning, sufficient to kill, may not be sufficient to tear and divide the fibres and particles of flesh, and reduce them to that tender state, which is the prelude to putrefaction. Hence it is, that some animals killed in this manner will keep longer than others. But the putrefaction sometimes proceeds with surprising celerity. A respectable person assured me that he once knew a remarkable instance of this. A whole flock of sheep in Scotland, being closely assembled under a tree, were killed by a flash of lightning . . . the putrefaction was such, and the stench so abominable . . . and the bodies were accordingly buried in their skins. It is not unreasonable to presume, that, between the period of their death and that of their putrefaction, a time intervened in which the flesh might be only tender, and only sufficiently so to be served at table. Add to this that persons, who have eaten of fowls killed by our feeble imitation of lightning (electricity), and dressed immediately, have asserted that the flesh was remarkably tender. Etc. (Benjamin Franklin, *The Autobiography and Other Writings,* ed. L. Jesse Lemisch [New York: New American Library, 1961], 236–237).

Yet another perspective on this subject emerges from *The Education of Henry Adams* in "The Dynamo and the Virgin (1900)," where the difficulty of situating electricity within the traditional parameters of a history is articulated. (Boston: Houghton Mifflin, 1974). A force whose potentiality lies in destruction ("almost as destructive as the electric tram"), it inspires "further respect for power" (380). Indeed, "before the end one began to pray to it. . . . its value lay chiefly in its occult mechanism. . . . The forces were interchangeable if not reversible, but he could see only the absolute *fiat* in electricity as faith." A comparative reading with Schreber recommends itself as Adams continues, naming himself at once in the third person:

> He wrapped himself in vibrations and rays which were new. . . . The economies [of force], like the discoveries, were absolute, supersensual, occult; incapable of expression in horse-power. . . . In these seven years man had translated himself into a new universe which had no common scale of measurement with the old. He had entered a

> supersensual world, in which he could measure nothing except by chance collisions of movements imperceptible to his senses, perhaps even imperceptible to his instruments, but perceptible to each other, and so to some known ray at the end of the scale. . . . The rays that Langley disowned, as well as those which he fathered, were occult, supersensual, irrational; they were a revelation of mysterious energy like that of the Cross; they were what, in terms of mediaeval science, were called immediate modes of the divine substance.
>
> The historian was thus reduced to his last resources. Clearly if he was bound to reduce all these forces to a common value, this common value could have no measure but that of their attraction on his own mind. . . . yet his mind was ready to feel the force of all, though the rays were unborn and the women were dead.

Check it out, 381–383: the discussion of "his own special sun" and the metaphysics of electricity en route to the paranoiac blaze, a connection made evident to me by Gary Wolf. Then follow the thin span linking Adams to Robert Gie, the altogether innovative designer of paranoiac electrical machines: "Since he was unable to free himself of these currents that were tormenting him, he gives every appearance of having finally joined forces with them, taking passionate pride in portraying them in their total victory, in their triumph" (*L'art brut,* no. 3, p. 63). Then take the transit to Victor Tausk, "On the Origin of the Influencing Machine in Schizophrenia," *Psychoanalytic Quarterly* 8 no. 2 (1933): 519–556, and return to Deleuze and Guattari's *Anti-Oedipus* on what can be considered the epochal shift cut by electric flow, for example, the short-circuiting of the oedipal machine:

> The satisfaction the handyman experiences when he plugs something into an electric socket or diverts a stream of water can scarcely be explained in terms of "playing mommy and daddy," or by the pleasure of violating a taboo. The rule of continually producing production, of grafting producing onto the product, is a characteristic of desiring-machines or of primary production. A painting by Richard Lindner, "Boy with Machine," shows a huge, pudgy, bloated boy working one of his little desiring-machines, after having hooked it up to a vast technical social machine—which, as we shall see, is what even the very young child does. (7)

Go on to 240–241: The electric flow installs the paradigm for a language opposed to a signifier that strangles and overcodes the flows and in which no flow is privileged, "which remains indifferent to its substance or support, inasmuch as the latter is an amorphous continuum." The electric flow serves to illustrate "the realization of such a flow that is indeterminate as such." In this regard, consider also Lyotard's generalized critique of the signifier in which the signifier's coded gaps are short-circuited by the "figural" (*Discours, figures* [Paris: Klinsieck, 1971]).

◆ **148. "The Circuit" in** *The Seminar of Jacques Lacan,* ed. Jacques-Alain Miller, trans. Sylvana Tomaselli (New York: Norton, 1988), 81. All page references in this chapter are to this work.

◆ **149. Jacques Derrida,** "Racism's Last Word," trans. P. Kamuf, *Critical Inquiry* 12 (Autumn 1985): 290–299; "Le dernier mot du racisme," in *Art Contre / Against Apartheid, les Artistes du Monde Contre l'Apartheid* (1983).

CRISIS HOTLINES

Including Poison Control

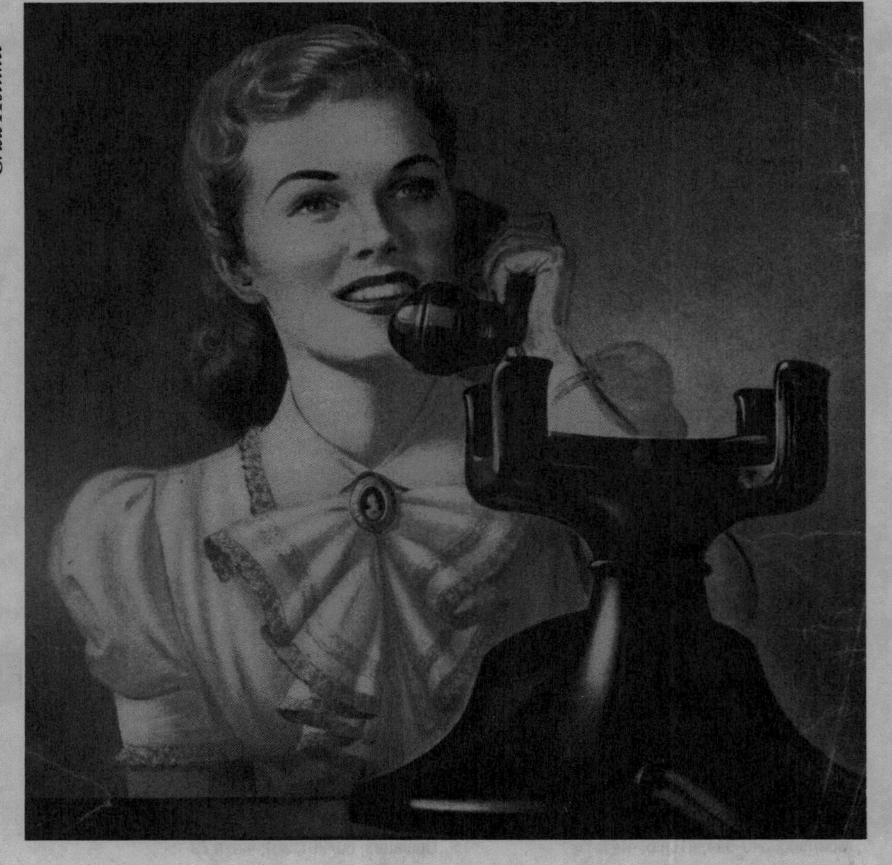

A Message of Confidence

The War has brought many changes to the Bell System. The Nation needed telephone facilities in new places. It needed more facilities in the usual places. It needed all facilities in a hurry.

Shortage of essential materials brought new problems and new achievements in research and in manufacturing. Telephone calls increased about ten million a day.

Yet all this has been done without great change in your telephone service. Millions of subscribers have felt no difference. The record as a whole has been good. That is the way it should be and the Bell System aims to keep it that way.

But when war needs delay your call, when you can't get just the service or equipment you need, let's put the blame right where it belongs — on the war.

THE BELL TELEPHONE SYSTEM

Service to the Nation in Peace and War